THE GONCOURT JOURNALS
1851–1870

Goncourt, Edmond de,

The Goncourt Journals

1851–1870

Edited and translated from the *Journal*
of EDMOND and JULES DE GONCOURT
with an Introduction, Notes and a
Biographical Repertory

by

Lewis Galantière

Doubleday, Doran & Company, Inc.

GARDEN CITY   NEW YORK

1937

Introduction

WHEN, IN DECEMBER 1849, Edmond and Jules de Goncourt settled down in a flat in the rue Saint-Georges, in Paris, Edmond was twenty-seven years old and Jules barely nineteen. They had been orphaned a year, were comfortably off without being rich, had travelled through France and seen Algeria, and passed their time as amateur etchers and painters of water colours. Edmond had been the head of the family since the death of their father fifteen years before. Jules was the baby of the family, and from being his mother's darling, with the death of Mme de Goncourt in 1848 he became Edmond's. Men had played no part in their upbringing; and out of this cause perhaps flowed the effect that there was something persistently womanish in their natures and their life. They were extravagantly neurasthenic, constantly subject to megrims, thrown into frenzies of incapacity and self-pity by noises, insomnia, indigestion. They lived in a kind of maidenly orderliness, surrounded by the delicate products of eighteenth-century craftsmanship and, later, the artful horrors of the Japanese dragon world. Jules, who is repeatedly characterized as a *joli garçon,* manifested from time to time a spirit which might generously be called lustiness. It is possible that the diaries are equivocal by design, but one has the impression that that Maria who visited the brothers over a period of years, beginning in

[v]

1858, did not find in their flat a polyandrous relationship but came for the pleasure of Jules alone. The references to mistresses of earlier years are clearly Edmond's, and there is reason to assume that this elder brother, "of soldierly bearing" as he is described by his contemporaries, exhausted his nerves and his imagination in writing, collecting (he rather than Jules was the collector), and in looking after his younger brother.

One evening in 1850, as the two sensitive and aristocratic young men sat painting water colours, they began, "urged on by I know not what inspiration," to write a farce together. A three-act play called *Abou Hassan* followed the farce into the fireplace, after which they composed a sort of novel, an extravaganza entitled *En 18—*. The novel was published, and on the day of publication they first took themselves seriously as men of letters—and started their diaries.

The profession of man of letters has not an ancient history: rhetoric, dialectic, oratory, can show more quarterings than the composition of imaginative prose. The notion of the writer as artist—and in particular the *prosateur,* for the poet always tends to write as seer—is probably the peculiar invention of the nineteenth century, born with somebody like Gautier, proceeding through Flaubert to Henry James, and already in our day vitiated by the alternative (and sometimes concurrent) preoccupations of men of letters with social ethics and the "big money" forthcoming from film rights. The Goncourts commenced authorship when this notion, and behind it the general ideal expressed as "art for art's sake", was an article of burning faith. In their day, besides, there still flourished that virulent contempt for the *bourgeoisie* which was born with the Romantics of 1830, was heightened by the vulgarity of the great railway and industrial fortunes built up in the reign of Louis Philippe, and is characteristically incarnated in the person of Théophile Gautier. Men writing seriously in the 1850's were bound to be solemnly conscious that they were practising an art.

The Goncourts were by no means little men. They possessed a considerable culture. Their sensibility was infinitely exquisite and responsive. They were excited by the shapes and colours of the external world, and this excitation was, with the years, disciplined by an intensive and deliberate training in exact observation. Since they were at the same time remarkably intuitive, it was natural that they should not merely paint a man or draw a house front, but be impelled to divine a character and imagine a household.

Two influences pulled them in contrary directions. Their aristocratic and feminine refinement drew them to the admiration of prettiness rather than beauty, and *le joli* became one of their animating passions. Of that eighteenth century about which they wrote so much, they hated its intellectual ferment and loved only what in it was material—its fans, its porcelains, its paintings. Meanwhile, rising up from a long immersion in Balzac, they saw in the streets and the people of Paris a rich vein open to exploitation by someone who would deal realistically with *le vrai* (as it was called), sparing none of its hideousness, describing item by item every rag, missing tooth, mephitic smell, squalid shame. Even when they took the past for their subject, a like concern with the *menu fait* prompted their choice of materials. They were the first, it seems, to find in an eighteenth-century bill of fare, an invitation to a ball, a shopkeeper's advertisement, contributions to social history.

If we except such hors d'oeuvres as their few plays and occasional journalism, the thirty volumes, more or less, which the Goncourts produced up to the death of Jules on the twentieth of June 1870 fall into two categories. On the one side we may place books about the things they loved—personages and society in the century preceding their own, and its painters and engravers. On the other side stand the novels they wrote about a world they loathed, a world that sickened them—the world of the impoverished, the defeated, the hysterical.

Their books on painting continue to enjoy some reputation, which will doubtless be greater when their subjects come again into fashion. I confess to a weakness for their writings on the eighteenth century. Michelet praised their industry; and though the books are not history, but are rather a series of picture albums, they give off, nevertheless, a certain atmosphere. One can feel the moral texture of the century in the three volumes on the mistresses of Louis XV, in the anecdotes, witticisms and gestures collected in *La Femme au XVIIIᵉ siècle,* and in the bits which they strung together to make their books on society in the Revolution and under the Directory.

But the novels are another matter. Dismal, airless, written only for the sake of the "scientific, clinical observation" with which the authors fancied they were scrutinizing human beings who were to them so many monstrosities; shapeless, lopsided, filled with whole chunks of décor minutely described and scenes recounted in detail, all of no significance to the march of their story or the personality of their characters; written partly in a gibberish of which the poor dears were actually proud, perhaps because it cost them more effort than to write French; concentrated with nerve-racked anguish upon *the thing seen*—their novels are something of a trial. They elected these subjects, not because of a concern for social reform, not because they had themselves known these horrors and were bitterly moved to expose them, but because, first, these lovers of *le joli* were also men of a morbid inquisitiveness who were fascinated by the repellent; and second, it had not been done before and they felt themselves born to innovate.

And they were innovators. They were the progenitors of a whole brood of writers, among them Zola, Alphonse Daudet, the proletarian novelist Jules Vallès, the whole of the Académie Goncourt, who claimed them for ancestors. Charity nuns, domestic servants, prostitutes, artists' models, had indeed appeared in literature before; but they had never been the cause of literature, had never been the heroines of fiction, until the Goncourts wrote *Sœur Philomène, Germinie Lacerteux, Manette Salomon.* This was of itself enough to establish a school; and, bearing in mind the generosity and rebelliousness of youth, when we remember the novelty of the Goncourts' language, and that their books were almost uniformly received with critical vilification ("sculptured slime," "literature of putrescence"), it is easy to understand that younger writers followed them with enthusiasm. It is this which explains why Edmond de Goncourt, who outlived his brother twenty-six years, wrote a dozen books of his own, received the world of letters on Sundays in his celebrated *Grenier* at Auteuil, and founded the Académie Goncourt for the encouragement of young realists, had a grand old age. When in 1895 a banquet of three hundred covers was organized in his honour, telegrams poured in from every quarter of the globe, Georg Brandes, for example, sending this message from Copenhagen: "All the Scandinavian writers will be with me to-day when I exclaim, 'Glory to the Master Initiator!'"

The judgment has more than once been pronounced that the *Journal des Goncourt* was their best book. Reasons for this judgment are not far to seek. Despite the loyalty, the scrupulous severity, with which they practised their profession, despite the fifty titles which, between them, they published in forty-five years of writing, it is not too extravagant to say that their passion was not literary composition. Except under the readily comprehensible impulsion of vanity, they could have been happy, probably, without publishing a single book. What they loved was collecting objects and documents and recording their own feelings and observations. I say "their own", and I mean not the observations and feelings of creatures of their imagination. There is a difference. The filling of their diaries, not the writing of their books, consoled them for their inability to accept life in a world they detested; and their collection of bric-a-brac, paintings and precious books, which became celebrated, was the other solace of their existence. In the circumstances, that they did plan, write and finish novel after novel of the kind they produced must seem to anyone who has known the torment of literary composition—the terror of the blank page, as Mallarmé put it—a kind of moral heroism, a triumph of will. In this struggle lies the direct explanation of their many bouts of lassitude and enervation.

Only a part of the diaries has been released for publication; and though the nine small volumes now available in French include entries made over the whole period of record, from 1851 to 1896, it would appear that material of high and perhaps scandalous interest is still withheld. The volume in the reader's hands was designed to contain a translation of the most informing and agreeable pages of the best years of the diaries—that score of years ended with the death of Jules, when both brothers were alive to compare notes and discuss their hates and loves before recording them; those years when the world of letters still stirred them to admiration or fulmination; when they still attended first nights, supped in public, and sat fortnightly in the company of Gautier, Sainte-Beuve, Flaubert, Renan, Taine, and occasionally Turgenieff or another foreign visitor, at the famous Magny dinners. Freed from the tormenting thought of construction, of placing a scene, a person or a document deftly and tellingly within the framework of a larger composition, the Goncourts could indulge in the diaries their special taste for the instantaneous and exercise their particular genius for the anecdote or the portrait in miniature. Except in so far as was needful to display what manner of men they were and how they lived, the reader of this translation has been spared most of the pages in which they bemoaned their lot and recorded their ills. Omitted also are a good many epigrams which failed to come off. Nearly everybody they spoke of at all is here, and the great of their day are almost never absent. The presence of these great, incidentally, has been too much stressed. It is worth remarking that quite apart from recording painstakingly their not invariably precious words, the Goncourts painted a whole world in their diaries. Town and country, café and theatre, drawing room and street scene, out front and backstage, *femme entretenue* and imperial princess, academician and bohemian—it is society under the Second Empire that is in this book, not merely a literary circle.

Certain footnotes, it will be observed, are signed "E. de G."— they are Edmond de Goncourt's. For the notes unsigned, the responsibility is mine.

LEWIS GALANTIÈRE

[x]

Foreword

THIS JOURNAL is our nightly confession, the confession of two lives never parted in pleasure, in work or in toil, the confession of two twin spirits, two minds engaged in receiving, from contact with men and things, impressions so like, so identic, so homogeneous, that this confession may be deemed the elaboration of a single ego, of a single *I*.

In this day-to-day autobiography appear those people whom the accidents of life threw into the path of our existence. We have portrayed these men and women exactly as they appeared on a given day and at a given hour, reverting to them in the course of our journal, displaying them later under different aspects, accordingly as they showed themselves altered and modified. Least of all have we been concerned to emulate those compilers of memoirs who paint their historic figures all of a piece, in a single unrelieved light; or paint them in colours grown chill and damp with the recession in time of their meeting. In a word, our ambition has been to show meandering humanity in its *momentary reality*.

If the reader wonders now and then whether the changes we note in people who were intimate with us, or dear to us, were not really due to changes that took place in ourselves, it will not dismay us. Certainly, that is possible. We are quite aware that we have been emotional, nervous, unhealthily impressionable creatures, and therefore at times unjust. Nevertheless, we are perfectly sure that, although we may occasionally have expressed ourselves with the injustice of prejudice or the blindness of unreasoning antipathy, we have never consciously misrepresented those of whom we speak.

I say, therefore, that what we have tried to do is to bring our contemporaries to life, for posterity, to paint them in their living, animated resemblances. We have employed to this end the vivid stenography of conversation, the physiological surprise that springs from gesture, the record of those swiftly passing moments of emotion in which a personality reveals itself, those *imponderabilia* which lend intensity to a human being, and, finally, a little of that feverishness which is characteristic of the heady life of Paris.

And in our insistence that each still-warm remembrance shall be instinct with life in this work hastily set down on paper and sometimes not reread, the reader will find our syntax of the moment and our occasional *passportless* word, just as they came to us. We have invariably preferred those phrases and expressions which least blunted and *academised* the vividness of our sensations and the independence of our ideas.

This journal was begun on the second of December 1851, the day on which our first book was put on sale and the day of the stroke by which Louis Bonaparte made himself dictator of France, preparatory to making himself emperor of the French. The whole of the manuscript may be said to have been written by my brother at the dictation of us both. This was the method we employed in writing these memoirs. When my brother died I considered that our literary work was ended and I determined to seal the journal as of the twentieth of January 1870, where his hand had written its last lines. But then I was seized by the bitter desire to recount to myself the final months and the death of my beloved brother, and almost immediately thereafter the tragic occurrences of the Siege of Paris and the Commune impelled me to continue this journal. It is still, from time to time, the confidant of my thoughts.

EDMOND DE GONCOURT

Schliersee, August 1872.

[xii]

THIS JOURNAL was to have been published for the first time, twenty years after my death. Such was my firm resolution when, staying last year in the country with Alphonse Daudet, I read to him one of the notebooks composing the journal, which he had asked me to bring with me. Daudet enjoyed the reading, waxed enthusiastic about the degree of interest attaching to things told while the impression was still warm, begged me to publish fragments of what I had read, grew affectionately insistent upon having his way with my will, and spoke of all this to our common friend, Francis Magnard, who was good enough to suggest publication in the *Figaro*.

Here, then, is the journal—or at least that part of it which it is possible to make public during my lifetime and during the lives of those whom I observed and painted *ad vivum*. No part of these memoirs has been published before, although here and there, in the journal, will be found bits of a novel or a biography which had already been published in that novel or that biography.

I beg the reader's indulgence for the first few years. We were then not yet the masters of our instrument, were still somewhat imperfect writers of *notes from nature*. The reader will recall, also, that in the beginning our acquaintance was very small, and consequently our field of observation was bound to be limited.

E. DE G.

1851

December 2.—On the Day of the Last Judgment, when men's souls will be led before the Seat by towering angels who, while the long day of question and answer goes on, will stand dozing like court attendants, their chins resting on their issue gloves, and when God the Father, in His august white beard, looking the way the academicians paint him in the cupolas of our churches, shall interrogate me about my thoughts, my acts, the events to which I lent the complicity of my eyes, on that day I shall say to Him, "Alas, Lord, I witnessed a coup d'état."[1]

But what is a stroke of state policy, what is a violent and unconstitutional change in government, for people who on that very day are to publish their first novel? By the irony of misfortune, this is the case with us. This very morning, while we were still dreaming lazily of edition after edition, of a sale that would sat-

[1]On the second of December 1851 Charles Louis Napoleon Bonaparte, nephew of Napoleon I and son of Louis Bonaparte, king of Holland, who had been elected president of the second French Republic on the tenth of December 1848, on the urging of his half brother, the Duke de Morny, bastard of the queen of Holland and the Count de Flahaut, ordered the arrest of the leaders of both the Republican and Royalist parties in France, dissolved the National Assembly, suppressed by force the protest of the people of Paris, and made himself dictator of France. His dictatorship was ratified by a plebiscite; and in the following year the Second Empire was established on ratification by a second plebiscite, citizen Bonaparte becoming emperor of the French and taking the style of Napoleon III. Vide Arnaud, René: *Le Coup d'état du deux décembre,* Paris, 1928.

[1]

isfy the elder Dumas himself, there was a banging of doors and with a great deal of noise in swept our cousin Blamont, an ex-guardsman now turned a grizzly conservative, full of asthma and peevishness.

"By God," he panted; "it's done!"

"What? What's done?"

"The coup d'état!"

"The devil you say! And they are bringing out our novel to-day!"

"Your novel? A novel! Do you think the country's got time for novels today?"

With which, in a gesture that was habitual, he pulled his frock coat tight across his abdomen as if it were a sword belt, took his leave, and was off to carry the triumphant news across the town, from Notre-Dame-de-Lorette to the Faubourg Saint-Germain, to all the still drowsy households of his acquaintance.

We sprang hastily out of bed and in a moment were in the street, in our old rue Saint-Georges, where already the newspaper offices of the *National* were occupied by troops. Once in the street our eyes—we confess our egocentricity—went instantly to the hoardings. Among all the bills, freshly pasted up, announcing the new troupe, its repertory, its drill, its leading men, and the removal of the manager from the Élysées Palace to the Palace of the Tuileries, what we were looking for was the placard that was to announce to Paris the publication of *In the Year 18—* and to introduce to France the names of two more men of letters, Edmond and Jules de Goncourt.

That placard was missing from the hoardings. And this was the reason. Gerdes, who by a singular stroke of chance was the printer of both the *Revue des Deux Mondes* and our novel, Gerdes, obsessed by the notion that a political chapter in our book could be interpreted as an allusion to the event of the day, and meanwhile, also, at bottom suspicious of our strange, incomprehensible, cabalistic title, which seemed to him to hide a secret reference to the eighteenth of Brumaire (ninth of November 1799)—that day when another Napoleon had made himself master of France—Gerdes, being a man lacking in heroism, had on his own responsibility flung our announcements into the fire.

December 15.—"Jules, Jules, an article by Janin in the *Débats!*" It was Edmond, in bed, calling out the welcome and unexpected news. There it was, the Monday *feuilleton*, talking about us apropos of everything and about everything apropos of us, twelve columns of it, stirring and scrambling up a review of our book with reviews of *La Dinde truffée*, by Varin and *Les Crapauds immortels* by Clairville and Dumanoir: an article in which Janin belabours us ironically and forgives us with esteem and with serious criticism; an article presenting our immaturity to the public in friendly fashion and with a benevolent word of forgiveness for its daring.

We sat without reading a word, hypnotised by the ugly type of the newspaper in which our names seemed to be printed in something that enchanted our glance as no work of art will ever be able to enchant it. Our breasts were suffused with joy, with the joy of our first literary communion, one of those joys that, like the joy of first love, can never be experienced twice. We never walked this day, we ran. We went off to thank Janin, who received us roundly, with a great jovial smile, scrutinized us, shook hands with us, and said, "Well I'm damned! You look just as I thought you would."

Dreams, castles in Spain, and the temptation to think ourselves almost great men, knighted by the critic of the *Débats*, fondling the illusory expectancy of an avalanche of articles in all the newspapers.

December 21.—Janin, when we called on him, had said to us, "Look here, the theatre is the only way to get on." On the way home it occurred to us to write, for the Théâtre-Français, a review of the year in the form of a dialogue between a man and a woman sitting beside the fire during the last hour of the old year. We wrote the little thing and christened it *New Year's Eve*.

Janin had given us a note to Mme Allan and here we were, on the fifth story of a house in the rue Mogador, in the flat of the actress who brought Alfred de Musset back from Russia.[2] A Byzantine virgin, with a halo of gilded copper, was in the room to remind us of the woman's long residence in Russia. She sat putting the last touches on her toilette before a three-panelled psyche glass that almost closed her in and formed a screen of mirrors round her. The celebrated actress was agreeably cordial in a harsh, raucous voice—a voice we did not recognize and which she is able to transform into music in the theatre.

She said we might come back the next day. I was touched. From the beginning Mme Allan had a way of encouraging me as I read the play to her, a way of sending forth little flattering murmurs for which one would kiss an actress's slippers. In short, she agreed to play the part and undertook to learn it and play it on the thirty-first—today being the twenty-first.

It was two o'clock when we tumbled down her stairs and rushed off to Janin. But it was his *feuilleton* day and there was no seeing him. He sent word that he would talk to Houssaye about us the next day.

From him we bounded in one leap to the office of the manager of the Théâtre-Français, to whom we were utterly unknown. "Gentlemen," said he to begin with, "we shall not be putting on any new plays this winter. That decision is final. I can do nothing about it." Then, touched by the sight of our long faces he added: "Let Lireux read your play and report on it. If the reading is favourable, I'll see that you are performed."

It was then four o'clock. A cab disgorged us at Lireux's.

"But, gentlemen," the woman who opened the door said to us harshly; "you know very well that Monsieur Lireux cannot be disturbed. He is doing his *feuilleton*."

"Come in, gentlemen!" a good-natured voice called from within.

We walked into a proper writer's hole, the sort Balzac might have lived in, smelling of bad ink and the warm odour of an un-

---

[2]It was not Musset in person that Mme Allan brought back but, as Legouvé says, "A thing she had unearthed, a Russian translation of a little comedy never before acted"— *Un caprice,* by Musset, which she had performed with success in St. Petersburg. That was in 1847; till then nobody in France had believed that Musset's enchanting comedies, most of which he had written fifteen years before, were playable.

made bed. The critic very kindly promised to read our play that evening and submit his report the next day.

From Lireux's we rushed to see Brindeau, who would be playing opposite Mme Allan. Brindeau was not at home, but he had promised to return by five o'clock and his mother insisted that we wait. The house was filled with nice chattering little girls. Six o'clock came and still no Brindeau. Eventually, we decided to run him down at the Théâtre-Français at half-past seven. "Good Lord!" he shouted, running back and forth in his dressing room, naked beneath a white robe; "really, no chance of hearing your play read." And he galloped off after a comb or a tooth brush. "Tonight, after the play?" we suggested. "No, I'm taking supper with friends. Wait a bit. I'm off stage about a quarter of an hour in this play. I'll read your script then. Wait for me in the theatre." When the play was over we grabbed him and he agreed to do the part.

From the Théâtre-Français we took the manuscript to Lireux, and the next day at nine o'clock we were back to Mme Allan's, where we found her surrounded by her family—schoolboys—and told her what we had been up to.

December 23.—Sitting on a bench on the theatre landing, palpitating and quaking at the slightest sound, we heard, through a door that shut behind her, Mme Allan send forth in that ugly voice of hers, "That's not nice at all."

"Sunk!" one of us said to the other with that spiritual and physical collapse which Gavarni has painted so well in the picture of the crumpling of a young man in a cell in the Clichy Prison.

1852

End of January.—On the twelfth of January there appeared the first number of *L'Éclair,* described as "A Weekly Review of Literature, the Theatre, and the Arts." Since then we have been playing at publishing, with Villedeuil.[1] Our review has an office on the ground floor in a new street, the rue d'Aumale. It has a responsible manager who is paid five francs per binder's signature set up in type. It has a policy, which is the assassination of classicism. It carries free advertisements and promises prizes to its readers. We spend two or three hours a week in the office, and whenever we hear a footstep in the street we wait in the expectation of subscribers, inquirers or contributors. Nobody comes in. Not even a contributor, which is incredible. Not even a poet, which is even more miraculous. A red-haired girl named Sabine, who is our only visitor, asked one day, "Who is that man, sitting there so sadly?" We answered in chorus, "That is the cashier."

With the faith of apostles and the illusions of shareholders, we continue bravely to bring out our review in a vacuum. First Villedeuil was forced to sell his collection of *Decrees of the Kings of France* to eke out the paper's existence. Then he turned up a moneylender out of whom he got five or six thousand francs.

[1]Pierre Charles, Count de Villedeuil, a young cousin of the Goncourts, who had, in December 1851, proposed that they found the review together.

Managers, at the rate of five francs a signature, follow one after the other. The first one, a Latin Quarter painter named Pouthier, was succeeded by one Cahu, a fellow as fantastic as his name, who has a philological bookshop near the Sorbonne and is a member of the Academy of the little town of Avranches. Cahu made way for an old army man with a tic which makes him stare constantly at the place where his epaulettes should be and spit over both his shoulders.[2]

In the six thousand francs which Villedeuil was supposed to have been lent by his usurer there was included a sizeable sum represented by two hundred bottles of champagne. The wine began to go bad, and the founder of *L'Éclair* had the notion of advertising the review by giving a champagne ball by way of prize to his subscribers. All of *L'Éclair's* acquaintance was invited, including Pouthier, an architect out of a job, a picture dealer, a number of people scraped up in chance meetings, and a few nondescript women. Nadar, who had just begun a series of caricatures for our review, took it upon himself to open the shutters of the shop during the ball and invite all the passers-by off the street in order to liven up our family party.

Undated.—"Tragedy! Lord, how dull those old tragedies are! Who could be a flatter actress than Rachel?"[3] It was Janin holding forth with all the skipping about from topic to topic of one of his own weekly articles. "Actors are always playing the same part. I write about actresses, but never about actors. When actresses are very ugly, like Lagier, for example, they seem to have some talent. But if they are not ugly I never mention them. A play ought to be as simple as two and two makes four, and there should be women in it. Then it's a success. . . . Do you know that Mademoiselle B—— asked me to let her have five hundred francs the other day? Why? said I. To make up a thousand, so that F—— would become her lover." Janin burst out laughing.

[2]Cp. old Giroudeau, nicknamed "Coloquinte", in Balzac's *Un Grand Homme de province à Paris.*

[3]Janin forgets, in 1852, that in 1838 he adored Rachel and called her "a golden blade in a sheath of clay."

"Novelty? The public want something new? Come, come! If the *Revue des Deux Mondes* changed the colour of its covers it would lose two thousand subscribers. . . . By the way, that was a good job you did, your article on that decorator, Possot. Have you any of his work? . . . Oh, attacks on me don't bother me. What can they say about me? That I am stupid? That I am old? That I am ugly? Well, what of it? That Roqueplan, a man covered over with *aes alienum,* as Sallust says! Look here, there is a young man, author of a book called *Sappho,* who hit the nail on the head, the rascal! In his preface he speaks of . . . writers who go into lending libraries to praise their own books. . . . What I wanted was, right there before the judges, to tell them how I had lived, show them my whole life. . . . But when anybody tells me I don't know the French language, me who know nothing else—for I know no history, no geography, nothing . . . But French! That bowls me over! All the same they won't stop me from having all Paris at my funeral."

And as he accompanied us to the door of his study he said, "You see, young men, you mustn't have too, too much conscience."

Undated.—When Gavarni went to Bourg with Balzac in order to try to save Peytel,[4] he had to repeat to him again and again, "Now look here, this thing is serious, Balzac. You will have to

[4]The story must be told, if only as an example of the vagaries to which that bewildered genius was so frequently subject. In 1839 a solicitor named Peytel, living in the small town of Belley, some sixty kilometres from Bourg, was accused of having murdered his wife. Balzac, who had known Peytel, believed him "incapable" of the crime and sought to rouse the press in his favour. Meanwhile, he went down to Belley, forced his way into the bedroom of the magistrate (whom he found in a dressing gown, winding up his watch, for it was nine in the evening and bedtime in the provinces) and pleaded vehemently the cause of his friend, insisting that Mme Peytel had been an adulteress. At that moment a head was thrust forth between the curtains of the magistrate's bed, and a voice exclaimed, "You lie, sir!" Balzac turned to the magistrate: "What is this woman doing here?" The magistrate: "She is doing, sir, what every respectable woman is doing at this hour of the night. She is lying in her husband's bed." Balzac became the butt of every wit and *chansonnier* in France; the upshot of his intervention was that he witnessed the beheading of Peytel at Belley.

Voltaire defended Calas and became the hero of Europe. Balzac—though this was his aim—could not do as much with Peytel, nor, it might be added, Anatole France with the Socialist party.

behave during the few days we spend here"; and he stuck as close as possible to the great writer. One day he had to leave him for two hours, and when he got back he found Balzac on the town square. He had button-holed the subprefect of the district and was telling him how little girls amuse themselves in boarding schools.

During the whole time Gavarni had to see that Balzac kept himself clean. One day, unable to contain himself any longer, he said to him, "Ah, Balzac, why haven't you a friend—one of those simple-minded, affectionate, middle-class people—they exist, you know—who would wash your hands for you, keep your tie straight, look after you in the way you haven't time to look after yourself." Balzac cut him off: "Oh!" he exclaimed. "If I had a friend like that I'd pass him along to posterity."

August.—I found Janin lighthearted and cheerful, despite his gout. "When they came to fetch my grandfather to the guillotine," he said, "he had the gout in both feet. As a matter of fact, I am not complaining. They tell me it ensures you ten more years of life. I have never been ill, and," he added with a smile, "I still have what it takes to be a man."

A little actress from the Théâtre-Français, whose name I do not know, having asked him if he had seen a certain play, "What!" he shouted, jerking up in his chair. "Do you mean to say that you haven't read my review?" With which he threatened her and terrified her by swearing that she would never get anywhere if she did not read him regularly, if she did not keep abreast of literature, if she did not do as Talma and Mlle Mars did—read every important review.

October 22.—The first number of *Le Paris* appeared today. It is, we believe, the first daily paper devoted to literature since the creation of the world. We wrote the leading article.

We are supping out a good deal this year. Idiotic suppers where they serve peaches *à la Condé,* early peaches that cost eight francs each; where the meat course is priced at eighty francs and you drink mulled wine made of Léoville 1836; where the company is made up of trollops picked up at Mabille[5] and shopworn sluts who devour these feasts with shreds of the saveloy they had for dinner still in their teeth. One of them exclaimed innocently, "Look, it's four o'clock. Ma's just peeling her carrots."

[5]Mabille was a notorious public dance hall, established in 1840. It was there that Chicard invented the cancan.

1853

January.—The editorial offices of *Le Paris* were moved after a few months from the house at 1, rue Laffite, where the Maison d'Or restaurant is, to the rue Bergère, above the editorial offices of the *Assemblée Nationale.*

The curiosity of the place is Villedeuil's office which he had decorated with the hangings and the silver-fringed, black velvet curtains of his drawing room in the rue de Tournon where, at one time, he gave gruesome punch parties with all the candles snuffed out. Next to his office is the cashier's cage, a real cage with a real grille behind which has been put Lebarbier, the grandson of the eighteenth-century vignettist, whom, with Pouthier, we had fished up from the depths of the life of Bohemian Paris. A survivor of that anti-Bonapartist sheet, *Le Corsaire,* has a little room in which he makes up the paper. He is yellow haired, popeyed, and undersized, with a stare like the Italian *jettatore,* and is one of the few writers who escaped the dragnet in which the government rounded up the anti-Bonapartist pressmen on the night of the Second of December. He is the father of a family and also a kind of church, preaching good morals and crossing himself from time to time like a saint strayed into a band of malefactors; despite all of which he goes farther than any of us in freedom of expression. In his spare time he writes a column for the paper entitled "The Memoirs of Madame Saqui."

Every day there would come into the editorial rooms Murger with an air of humility, a moist eye, and the pretty epigrams of a dramshop Chamfort; Aurélien Scholl with his monocle screwed in tight, his witty cholers, and his ambition to begin earning 50,-000 francs next week by writing novels in twenty-five volumes; Banville with his hairless face, his high-pitched voice, his clever paradoxes, and his humorous caricatures of people in words; and Alphonse Karr with his inseparable companion, Gatayes. Others who wandered in were: a skinny chap with long greasy hair named Eggis who was the personal enemy of the French Academy; Delaage, who was Ubiquity made man and Banality made a handclasp, a clammy, doughy, viscous fellow who was like a benevolent white-of-egg; and friend Forgues, a refrigerated Southerner with something about him that was like Chinese fried ice and who was always turning in, with a diplomatic air, an artistically sharpened article; and Louis Énault, dressed up in cuffs and in the excessively shapely and la-di-da getup of a drawing-room ballad singer; and Beauvoir would often turn up and bubble over like champagne foam, sparkling and overflowing, talking about murdering his wife's lawyers and flinging into the air vague invitations to chimaerical dinners. Gaïffe would come round to plant himself on a divan where he spent whole afternoons together, stretched out and dozing, and coming to only in order to throw disquieting interjections into old Vernet's virtuous phraseology.

In the midst of all these people would be Villedeuil, giving orders, making speeches, going and coming, writing letters, innovating, with every week a discovery of a fresh system of advertising or of awarding prizes to readers, a fresh scheme, or a new name that was going to bring the paper ten thousand subscribers in two weeks.

The paper is getting on: it makes no money, but it does make a lot of noise. It is young and independent and is the inheritor of the literary convictions of the romantics of 1830. In its columns there is all the ardour and fine zest of a cloud of sharpshooters marching along in ragged order and without discipline, but all of them filled with a handsome contempt for subscriptions and subscribers. Yes, yes, there is mettle here, and audacity, and reck-lessness, and there is devotion to a certain ideal mixed up with a little madness, a little ridiculousness—a paper, in short, whose uniqueness, whose honour, consists in not being a business.

February 20.—One day towards the end of last December Ville-deuil came in from the Ministry and said in a fifth-act voice:

"The paper is being prosecuted. Two articles were found offensive. One of them is by Karr. The other is an article with verses in it. Who put verses into an article this month?"

"We did," said we.

"Then it's you who are being prosecuted along with Karr."

We had apparently written something that was going to seat us on the criminals' bench in the police court absolutely as if we had been two gentlemen arrested in a *pissotière*. The article, which had appeared in the issue of the fifteenth of December 1852, was entitled "Journey from number 43, rue Saint-Georges to number 1, rue Laffite": a journey from where we then lived to the then offices of the paper, in which we passed in review, in rather whimsical fashion, the industries, the shops where curious things were made, the dealers and women dealers in pictures and bric-a-brac that lay along our route, and, amongst others, the shop of a woman once a well-known painters' model. Fol-lowing is the part of the article on the score of which we were hailed into court.

"In this shop lies the most beautiful body in Paris. Once a model, she has now become a picture dealer. Over a stack of china cups hangs a Diaz, and I know one more beautiful. It is a picture of a young man and a young woman. The adolescent's hair is mingled with the loosened hair of the lady, and Venus, as Tahureau says:

"Croisant ses beaux membres nus
Sur son Adonis qu'elle baise;
Et lui pressant le doux flanc;
Son cou douillettement blanc,
Mordille de trop grande aise.

[13]

"That Diaz, my friends, has travelled wide; but Heaven be praised, it has returned to the fold. I met someone who knew the story of all its travels and who told me the last one. Mlle X having sent the picture to Mlle Y, Mlle Y sent it back with this letter:[1]

" 'My dear fellow-actress,

" 'This Diaz is really too little veiled to adorn my small house. I love the dishabille of a charming wit, but I cannot agree to that nakedness which Molière's Arsinoë liked so well. Do not think me a prude. But why should I deprive you of a picture which, for my part, I should feel obliged to hide?

" 'Thank you a thousand times, nevertheless.

" 'Y.'

"And Mlle X took back her Diaz, tra-la, with a hey-nonny-no she took back her Diaz. Having hung it again on a wall in sad mourning for its absence, she wrote Mlle Y:

" 'Dear Y,

" 'I am a madwoman and it was almost blasphemy to have thought my little picture worthy of your house. But my idiocy has at least rewarded me with a rare bit of information about the sincerity of your modesty. Allow me, despite this, to say a word in defense of the repertory of comedy which you invoke, I am afraid, under a misapprehension, since it is precisely in pictures that Arsinoë dislikes nakedness:

" 'Elle fait des tableaux couvrir les nudités.
Mais elle a de l'amour pour les réalités.

" 'I take back my little Diaz, slightly embarrassed by its bold excursion, and I shall hide its embarrassment in my alcove, where only Monsieur A—— will be able to see it.

" 'X.' "

As for those verses by Tahureau, we did not find them in

[1]In his engaging little book, *Rachel,* M. J. Lucas-Dubreton relates that a certain Mlle Nathalie, of the Théâtre-Français, lured away from Rachel her lover of the moment, Émile Augier (author *inter alia* of the play you read in French class, *Le Gendre de Monsieur Poirier),* and thought it amusing to compensate her *chère camarade* by sending Rachel the Diaz "Venus and Adonis." Hence these letters, and hence *"Monsieur A——."*

Tahureau's works, the first editions of which are of the greatest rarity; we took them out of the *Tableau historique et critique de la poésie française et du théâtre français au XVIᵉ siècle,* by Sainte-Beuve—a work awarded honourable mention by the French Academy. It sounds incredible, doesn't it? and yet it is absolutely true. But as a matter of fact, the commissioner of police who had ordered our prosecution was the same who, for twenty-four hours, had played with the idea of prosecuting I don't remember what author of a line of asterisks which appeared in a number of *Le Paris* and which had seemed obscene to this same M. Latour-Dumoulin.

It must be said, however, that this prosecution was scarcely a literary affair. *Le Paris* was deemed by the government to be a successor to *Le Corsaire.* And the commissioner of police, M. Latour-Dumoulin, was personally wounded by Villedeuil's airs, for when Villedeuil, having sent in his card one day, was not immediately received, he had got back into his carriage and driven off. Rightly or wrongly, he was accused of speculating on the short side. They went so far as to complain that he did not solicit for his review invitations to the emperor's palace when Nieuwerkerke lectured there. As for ourselves, we were presumed to be enthusiastic supporters of the Orleanist party, because the Passy family were connections of ours.

The next day, which was a Saturday, Villedeuil drove us to the Palace of Justice in his yellow barouche, a barouche that was part ceremonial chariot of Louis XIV and part operating table. Never had so triumphal a vehicle borne men to the police court. And the master of the carriage, for whom this trial was a great matter of exhibition, had had made by his tailor, for this ceremony, a prodigious ribbed box coat with five Scotch capes, the kind of travelling coat in which exiled noblemen step down from a coach in the melodramas at the Ambigu Theatre. Our arrival at the iron gates of the palace was like something in a fairy tale—this young man, bearded to the eyes, wearing that coat, and stepping out of a golden coach. The tipstaff at the courtroom door tried to prevent his entering. "But," exclaimed Villedeuil, "I am much more guilty than they are. I am the proprietor of the review!"

At that moment he would have given carriage, horses and coachman to be prosecuted himself.

We were eventually saved by the postponement of the case, for in the intervening week there was a change of prosecutor. De Royer was succeeded by Rouland, who had Orleanist relations. He was a connection of Janin's wife, and she was able to interest him in us. Also, relations were still maintained between Rouland and the Passy family, who spoke warmly in our favour. Thus, on Saturday, the nineteenth of February, the presiding judge of the Sixth Chamber pronounced a judgment in which we were acquitted, but admonished.

1854

End of February.—Hard at work all this winter on our history of social life during the Revolution of 1789. Mornings we bring home a bundle of four or five hundred pamphlets from M. Perrot's, who lives near by in the rue des Martyrs. (This M. Perrot is a poor, a very poor, man who collects rare pamphlets which he picks up at a couple of sous apiece along the quays, sometimes having to pawn his watch—a silver watch—in order to be able to buy them.) All day long we go through these revolutionary papers, and at night we write our book. No women, no social life, no pleasures, no amusements. We have given away our old evening clothes and have had no new clothes made, expressly in order not to be able to accept invitations. Intensive, unceasing, continuous brainwork. For the sake of a little exercise, and so that we may not fall ill, we allow ourselves a brief stroll after dinner through the darkness of the outer boulevards, where nothing will so draw our eyes as to distract us from our work and haul us up out of the spiritual depths of our labours.

Undated.—Célestin Nanteuil, the painter, told us that when Gérard de Nerval came back from Italy he was absolutely penniless, but he brought back with him four thousand francs' worth of marble chimney pieces; and also that in the extreme poverty of the end of his life he still retained such a taste for luxury that he would make himself tiepins out of gold paper.

Undated.—Prayer of an old man of our acquaintance:

"O Lord, let the water I pass be less cloudy, let the little flies not sting me, let me live long enough to pile up another hundred thousand francs, let the Emperor not be overthrown so that my government securities may rise, and let the rise in Anzin Coal shares be maintained."

His housekeeper had orders to read this aloud to him every night, he repeating it with hands palm to palm.

Grotesque! Sinister! Wouldn't anybody say? And at bottom, what is it but prayer, naked and unashamed?

May.—Chabouillet, the architect, who is not easily nonplussed, was still a little overcome when he told me, today, of an interview he had a few days ago with the manager of one of the smaller boulevard theatres who had consulted him about certain changes to be made in the house.

"Your theatre was intelligently designed," Chabouillet said to him.

"This, a theatre? This is not a theatre. This is a brothel."

"Come, now!"

"Exactly as I have the honour of telling you. Sir, this is not a theatre, and what I mean is very simple. I pay my actresses fifty or sixty francs a month. Why? Because my rent is 30,000 francs a year. My actors get not much more, and you can imagine what a job they all do. Often one or other of the women lectures me, protesting that she cannot live on my fifty francs and that she will have to do the men in the audience in order to eat. What can I do about it? My rent is 30,000 francs. Therefore, I say my theatre is not a theatre, it is a brothel."

End of August.—We came up here to Sainte-Adresse to spend a month sea bathing and someone introduced to us a stock speculator named Turcas, a grandson of the composer, Cherubini. This

Turcas is cordiality incarnate. His mania is hospitality. Two days after we met him we were practically forced to take all our meals with him, and here we are, members of his household, leading an easy, lazy existence. His little house is hidden in a bower of climbing roses and stands in a small garden in the middle of which is a divan of grassy lawn. He has a mistress named Brassine, a big, beautiful girl out of the Palais-Royal Theatre, two or three rowboats of which we make good use, and, out on the beach, a wooden bathing house where we spend our time in delightful idleness, smoking our pipes and drinking grogs—endless pipes and grogs.

Brassine brought with her a friend named D—— who is in the troupe at the Folies-Dramatiques. D—— is what is called in a certain argot a *gripper*: she nibbles at one like a kitten and is constantly jollying one like a street arab. A pretty and exasperating little beast. She and I had goaded each other on in verbal battle and were carrying on a teasing war when one evening, as I was on my way home from Turcas'—it was eleven o'clock, and her hotel was shut—she appeared through the window on her balcony in a white dressing gown. I was with A——, who had been paying very strenuous court to her. Laughing, he and I began to climb the trellis to her balcony. A—— quit very soon; the trellis did not seem to him safe. But I, once I had started up, went most seriously on with it. In a flash, I had suddenly been overcome by a passion for that woman on the balcony. She stood, meanwhile, half laughing and half scolding me. This went on for several seconds during which someone who was inside my skin loved that woman, desired her, and aspired to her as if he meant to pluck forth a star from the heavens.

I climbed up avidly and feverishly, like a madman. I had been drawn into the orbit of that white robe and its white radiance. Finally I reached the top and jumped the balcony. For the length of fifteen feet I had been in love. I verily believe I shall never be in love in all my life except in such gusts. I spent the night with that woman, and she said, seeing the way in which I looked at her, "You certainly are strange! You look like a kid staring at a jam sandwich." But I was already sober, and I was worrying lest, the next morning, she ask me to give her a little marmoset I had bought during the day at Le Havre.

That night was like the stripping of a soul. She told me the story of her life—a thousand sad and sinister things that she would interrupt with a *zut!* which seemed to drink tears. In the skin of this urchin I saw a melancholy little person, dreaming, musing, a sort of drawing on the back of a theatre placard. After each embrace her heart would knock like a cuckoo in a village tavern clock. It was a ghastly sound. It was pleasure ringing the death knell. "Oh, I know well enough," she said. "If I dissipated for six months I should be dead. I'd die with lungs like this. . . . If I started going out to supper every night, it wouldn't take long."

Undated.—I have a chaste young friend whose family—both men and women—are in despair over the fact that he has not a mistress. They see in this chastity the degeneration of the race, and they scold and lecture him constantly in order to persuade him to go with prostitutes. The most worried of all the family are two uncles who are saddened by the bad conduct of their nephew. Both are ladies' men. The first is the sentimental and languorous sort who, having been surprised by his sister-in-law in the bed of a lady who had just left her country house, said plaintively, "I couldn't get anything from her, and I wanted at least to have the warmth of her body." The other uncle makes a practice of trying to seduce everything feminine that chance sends his way. My young friend assured me that he would be made the sole heir of the first uncle, the sleeper in empty beds, if he would but take a mistress and choose this uncle as confidant and as intermediary for the wangling of money out of his father and mother for the purpose of keeping the said mistress.

1855

January.—I ran onto a mistress I had had during my last year in school. I remember having desired her very much and loved her a little, and I can still see her in that tiny flat in the rue d'Isly at noon, with the sun streaming in and settling itself down like a bird. I would open the door, mornings, when the water carrier arrived. She would go down the street in a little bonnet to buy two cutlets for us and would put on her petticoat before she cooked them; and we would lunch off one end of the table out of the electro-plate utensil and drink out of the same glass. There were still girls like her in those days, girls with a little of the *grisette* left under their cashmere shawls.

I met her again. She was still the same girl, with the eyes I had loved, her little nose, her lips flat as if crushed by kisses, her supple figure. And yet she was not the same. The pretty girl was not on the town any more; she was living respectably, conjugally, with a photographer. Housewifery had left its mark on her. The shadow of the savings bank lay on her forehead. She mends linen now, looks after her kitchen, scolds her servant like a legitimate spouse, and is studying English and the piano. She frequents only married women and is ambitious to be married herself. She has buried her Bohemian existence in the cooking pot. Her lover, an American named Peterson, whose blood was bothering him and who took a mistress only because it was doctor's orders, drags her to a café every evening and there, by way of amusement, he plays dominoes with her, surrounded night after night by the same faces of his compatriots.

This man, who is stolidity and ponderation incarnate, emerges from his imperturbability only over dominoes, and then not in a café but in bed. They go to bed. Just as she is dozing off she feels her American stirring and rumbling indistinctly; soon he flies into a passion over the mistakes she made, her lack of concentration, her flighty French brain. She succeeds in dropping off to sleep, nevertheless, but after a half-hour or an hour of furious silence during which he is eating himself up, the American shakes her awake in order to say to her, "If you had put down the five-three instead of the two-three we would have won." And with that he goes back over the whole game.

She has started colouring stereoptic portraits, and this, Peterson thinks, she does very well. The other day he gave her all the portraits of the Moutard's Club to do, indicating which member was blond, which dark, which red haired, and so on. Her whole past lay there before her eyes. She knew by heart the colour of hair of every member. But her specialty is the colouring of photographs of dead children. She added *gouache* wings to one of them, one day, and the child's mother, seeing it already in heaven, paid her handsomely. Since then my erstwhile mistress lends them all wings.

Monday, March 26.—Our *History of French Society under the Directory* was brought out on Saturday. We went today to see old Barrière, who had written so paternally about our book on the Revolution. He came in, holding two or three sheets of paper in his hand, and said, "You've come after a review. Well, here it is, half done." With that he began to talk about the revolutions of 1789 and 1848, telling us that on the fifteenth of May 1848 Mme Barrière, who was giving examinations to school teachers in the Town Hall, had just written on the blackboard a problem in the use of the participle when there was a loud noise and someone shouted to her to run. The names of the members of the

Provisional Government were written up on that blackboard just below the problem in the use of the participle.

Undated.—Gavarni told us that the first time he saw Balzac was in Girardin's editorial office at *La Mode*. He saw a plump little man with fine dark eyes and a slightly broken, turned-up nose, who was talking volubly in a loud voice. Gavarni took him for a bookseller's clerk. Gavarni said that Balzac's back, in profile, presented a straight line from his head down to his heels, with the exception of a single curve at the calves. As for what the novelist looked like in front, his outline was the absolute contour of the ace of spades. And Gavarni even started to cut out a card to show us the exact silhouette of the man's body.

Then Gavarni began to talk to us about the Duchess d'Abrantès and her salon, where for a time he went frequently. All sorts of people met in that salon. One day he saw Admiral Sydney Smith go down on one knee to kiss the duchess's hand. The duchess was a very stout woman with a little of a fishwife's voice, but she carried herself wonderfully and was beautifully bred. There was always present a battalion of old ladies who had preserved that certain something which belongs to women who were once beauties. One day Gavarni saw there a small woman who seemed in a common way very well off and, as he put it, "stank of the lower middle class." He asked who she was, and the answer came back, "Madame Récamier."

August.—Nobody has yet expressed in literature the contemporary French melancholia, not a *suiciding* melancholia, not blasphemous, not despairing, but a good-humoured melancholia, a sadness which is not without sweetness and in which there is a slight smile of irony. The melancholias of Hamlet, of Lara, of Werther, even of Chateaubriand's René, are characteristic of more northerly peoples than the French.

From the heights of pleasure we have dropped straight into boredom. We are badly organized and quick to be sated. One week of love disgusts us for three months. Indeed, we emerge from passion with dejected souls and sickened hearts, dead to desire and possessed by a vague, shapeless, endless gloom. Our body and our mind have mornings-after so grey that they cannot be described, when life seems as stale as flat wine. After a few impulses and ardours we become the prey of a spiritual repugnance which makes us feel that we could vomit up the orgy of the night before. Replete and surfeited with material things, we come away from those lace beds as if they were so many anatomical museums. Nobody can know what disconsolate surgical memories we retain of those lovely, pleasing bodies.

Undated.—Every four or five hundred years savagery becomes necessary to revivify the world. The world would die of uninterrupted civilisation. There was a time in Europe when, an old population of a pleasant land being reduced to a decent state of anaemia, there would come down from the North, on its back, a horde of six-foot barbarians to remanufacture its race. Now that there are no longer any savages in Europe, the workers will be doing this job in another fifty years. And the job will be called the social revolution.

September 26.—I am at Gisors, and like a radiant shade all my childhood rises up before me. My faded little memories are reborn in my mind and in my heart, and every corner of the garden and the house is a reminder, a thing refound, though it is also a tomb of the pleasures I am never to know again. Seeing again these beloved places, I remember this person and that, my childhood companions and the little girls with whom we played: the two Bocquenets, the elder of whom could run so fast but knew nothing of the art of dodging; Antonin, who seemed to us a young lion; Bazin, who complained constantly and never stopped being angry when he lost; Eugène Petit, Louis's foster brother, who used to play the flute for us in the dormitory in which we all slept. And I cannot forget the very benign Jupiter of our band, the constitutional king of our games, "old Pourrat," Louis's tutor, who had the wit to teach us to play and the good sense to enjoy our games with us as much as we did—and whose only defect was that he would read us his famous tragedy entitled, *The Celts.*

And the little girls: Jenny, who had already the pretty little mug of a *soubrette;* and Berthe, who used to kiss the lining of my caps and collect in a box the pits of the peaches I ate. And Marie, who had the most beautiful hair and eyes in the world.

And the suppers of two dozen apple pies we were given to eat after we had put on our plays and Mme Passy had laid away the costumes in the great room where we now sleep! And M. Hippolyte Passy, a bald old man with a few white hairs at the temples and a lively, darting, brilliant little eye! He loved to chatter and would talk continuously about anything at all in a lisping voice, the words pouring out and the thought crystal clear. He was universal knowledge. He had read everything, seen everything, and would as soon tell you how to make a cabinet of ministers as how to make a bootlace. Along with this he was very proud of his disdain of received opinion and accepted theories, and professed to see in the governmental structure of the different countries merely so many various forms of corruption and venality. His admirable memory furnished him an arsenal for the demolition of illusions and alleged loyalties, and was well seconded by an easy-tempered irony and the smile of an old man who has seen it all before. Approving and appreciating only that which was *useful,* he was contemptuous of art and all that went with it, and at an industrial exposition he would have a good word only for a thripenny pocketknife. He scoffed relentlessly at religion, and, like all his generation, which had been brought up on Voltaire's *Maid of Orleans,* his Voltairianism was inexhaustible, as were his sly digs against the government of God, His charter (the Bible), and His responsible ministers. He was a drawing-room orator, and sitting by the fire he could talk with infinite charm, loving paradoxes and the theses of scepticism, sending caustic retorts to left and right, controverting principles, belittling mankind with anecdotes never heard before and great events with small details, more concerned, at bottom, not to seem ignorant than really to know, more anxious to charm the listener than to subjugate him, to shine than to convince, and speaking ill of God, of man, and of things to the greater glory of conversation. His love of conversation was so great that one evening, bedtime having not yet brought to an end a discussion he was having with his nephew at Cauterets about the Merovingians, he insisted that the younger man share his room, which happened to contain two beds, so that all night long M. Passy's daughter, who had the next room, wondered if her father had not gone mad and marvelled to hear him talk to himself from midnight until five in the morning.

October 18.—One evening at Gavarni's, Balzac said, "I should like one of these days to be so well known, so popular, so celebrated, so famous, that it would permit me . . ." Try to imagine the most enormous ambition that has entered the mind of man since time began; the most impossible, the most unattainable, the most monstrous, the most Olympian, ambition; an ambition that neither Louis XIV nor Napoleon had; an ambition Alexander the Great would not have been able to satisfy in Babylon; an ambition forbidden to a dictator, to a nation's saviour, to a pope, to a master of the world. He, Balzac, said simply, ". . . so celebrated, so famous, that it would permit me to break wind in society and society would think it a most natural thing."

1856

May 6.—Home from Italy with a head that feels as if a museum of canvases and statuary were being installed in it. I go out to take the pulse of literature in the offices of the little reviews and find it beating faster again. Where? I cannot say. Neither a school nor a party left; not an idea and not a flag. Attacks delivered as if they were so many chores; insults hurled without a grain of indignation. The farce writers become the wits of the town, and backstage squabbles about nothing at all. Michel Lévy and Jacottet, those publishers, become the Maecenases of all who blacken paper for a living. Not a single young man, not a single young pen, not a single raging protest. No reading public, but only a certain number of people who enjoy spending their hour of digestion over easy newspaper prose, who like to be told stories, while travelling, by a book with many stories in it, who read not a book but twenty sous' worth. The publisher Véron, an Augustus Caesar secretly sprinkled with incense by the Society of Men of Letters. The banker Millaud, giving royal blowouts by way of alms to all the trumpeters of Renown and the middle article. Fiorentino decorated. Mirès, thanks to his banking house, praised in verse.

Undated.—These past days a vague melancholy, discouragement, indolence, lethargy of mind and body. Feeling more than ever this despondency of my return, which is like some great disappointment. We come back to find our life stagnating just where it was. When one is away one imagines that any sort of unexpected thing might happen the moment one got out of a cab again before one's door. But nothing happens. Your life hasn't taken one step forward. It is like swimming in the sea with the feeling that one is constantly swimming in the same place. Reacquiring old habits, getting back one's taste for the dull routine of dreary life at home, is a nuisance. Things round me that I know, that I have seen and seen again a hundred times, fill me with an unbearable sensation of insipidity. I am bored by the few monotonous and repeatedly scrutinized ideas that trot back and forth through my head.

And other people, to whom I looked forward in the expectancy of entertainment, bore me as much as myself. They are exactly as I left them. Nothing has happened to them, either: they have simply gone on existing. They use the words I have always heard them use. What they tell me I knew before. The handshake they give me is the same as it was in the past. Nothing about them is changed—neither their waistcoat nor their mind, neither their mistress nor their place in society. They have done nothing extraordinary. There is no more anything new in them than in me. No one has even died amongst the people I know. I am not actually unhappy: it is something worse than that.

Undated.—When Murger wrote *La Vie de Bohème* he had no notion that he was writing the history of a social world which was to become a power within five or six years, and yet that is the fact today. This world, this freemasonry of publicity, reigns and governs and bars the way to every well-born man. Such a man is called an *amateur,* and with that word he is killed. He may have behind him the folio volumes of a learned Benedictine monk or may possess a little of the phantasy of a Heine—no matter: he is called an amateur by all those in the pay of the daily rags. Nobody realizes it, but this advent of Bohemia means the domination of socialism in literature.

May.—I met today the model of mistresses, the mistress of a young Englishman with phthisis, an Italian woman so concerned for her lover's disease that she will not let him go out evenings but shuts herself up with him, chats, smokes cigarettes, rests, and lies eternally in a chaise longue in an attitude that shows off a bit of her white petticoat and the red bows on her slippers. Three or four Englishmen and Germans come to call, bring with them their pipes, a half-dozen Hegelian ideas, and a great contempt for French policy which they characterize as *sentimental.* The lady of the house goes out almost as little during the day as in the evening. She has retained in Paris her Italian habits of seclusion, and fills her time, when she finds a novel in *Le Constitutionnel* that looks as if it will not run to twenty-four volumes, by translating it into pure Tuscan. A charming atmosphere, but too many pictures of friends and relatives. The little sitting room is like a Temple of Friendship. Of all these portraits there is only one that is interesting from the psychological point of view: it is a portrait of the mistress by the lover's mother.

May 31.—Gavarni talked to us about his disgust with, and lack of interest in, things once accomplished. "Whatever I do, I do because of its difficulties and because the thing is not easy to do. My garden, for instance: once it is finished I should gladly give it away. There are men who paint landscapes: I enjoy creating landscapes in relief. Well, what do you expect me to do with a drawing when I have finished it? There is nothing to do but give it away."

Then he talked about the theatre and argued against scenic illusion and in favour of the unadorned boards, saying that he admired only two plays—Molière's *Précieuses ridicules* and his *Bourgeois gentilhomme,* because they were lessons in philosophy given in the most tangible form possible, in the form of action . . . He interrupted himself to ask, "Have you ever looked carefully, not at the stage but at the audience? Have you ever examined those faces? How anybody, after having seen an audience, can talk to it, I don't know. A book, at any rate, is something with which a man becomes acquainted while he is alone with it; but a play is something presented to a mass of human beings brought together, an agglomeration of stupidity—— "

He broke off, left the theatre, and after a silence during which he was lost in thought, he exclaimed, "Ah, research! There's a real monomania for you! Whether I do one lithograph more or less makes very little difference to my reputation, but if there were a Gavarni Theorem, now . . . That would be something, wouldn't it?"

June 9.—Rue du Bac, beyond two or three courtyards, a vast house, withdrawn, tranquil, placid, with greenery here and there and a great patch of sky. A door through which steps are heard for several seconds before it is opened by a lackey wearing no livery. A drawing room furnished in rosewood and red velvet and looking as if inhabited by a rich and respectable commoner, but over the piano a copy of Perugino's "Marriage of the Blessed Virgin" and, facing it, a Gothic "Baptism of Our Lord" from Bruges.

"Will you come into my study, gentlemen?"

Books everywhere. Little pictures hung either side the fireplace and, on the gilded frame of the mirror, a miniature portrait of a nun.

"Oh," said the master of the house; "that is a costume for a play. Yes, a member of my family, who took the part of a nun in a play, decided to have her portrait painted in costume. Manners, gentlemen, of the kind that interest you—the manners of the eighteenth century. My family adored the theatre. Look here." And from a shelf he took down a book: *Plays* by the Count de Montalembert, below which was printed, "performed in the theatre at Montalembert." . . . "Your depiction of Paris interested me extremely: it is very curious. . . . I wrote to you. . . . Yes. . . . It was the vivacity of your style that was against you. The Academy is a lady whom these things do not amuse. You are aware that I am of your mind, and not of hers. . . . All these town houses; it was very interesting to read about them in your book. . . . I remember that when we returned from exile, there was a horse turning a grain mill in our theatre. . . . If only you had been able to collect the oral traditions in the provinces. Unfortunately, that is something which is dying out. . . . In the opening chapters of his *Paysans,* Monsieur de Balzac drew a portrait of the peasantry as the Revolution had changed it. Not flattering, indeed, but so true. I come from the Morvan, and I said to myself, he must have come down here."

Then he added: "I want *Le Correspondant* to publish a review of your book. I have no one to do it at the moment; young Andral is so lazy. Have you a friend who would do it for us? It will have to be someone able to write for the parish houses and the châteaux."

M. de Montalembert has long lank grey hair, a full face, the features of an old child, a sleepy smile, deep but listless eyes, a nasal voice lacking incisiveness, a gentle and relaxed cordiality, a feminine softness in manner and in handclasp, and a clerical dressing gown.

June 16.—Lunched with Chennevières at Versailles. Chennevières very happy, rejoicing. He has just bought, in the Perche,[1] a tumble-down estate called Saint-Santin which seduced him by the date 1555 cut in an old stone. At last he has found lodgment and asylum for the books and portraits done by his friends, which he had been wearily carting about from place to place for years. Much as he loves the exhumation of insignificant personalities, of little mediocrities of provincial art—a love which condemns this distinguished and original mind to works that are far beneath it—Chennevières still sees on the horizon of his thought some little Norman or Breton tale. One of them would be the story of a young man springing to arms in the uprising of 1832[2], captured, imprisoned in Mont-Saint-Michel, and there elaborating the policy which would have made the Legitimist Party prevail if it had been adopted, the policy of decentralisation, which was the Duchess de Berry's policy.

[1] An ancient Norman earldom whence come the famous *percheron* horses.

[2] In 1832 the Duchess de Berry, daughter-in-law of Charles X, who had been deposed in 1830, sought to lead an insurrection against his successor, Louis Philippe, in the Vendée. The uprising failed and she was for a time imprisoned.

Others at lunch were—Paul Mantz, a short dark-haired man with an intelligent twinkle in his eye and a monosyllabic utterance; Dussieux, a professor in the military school at Saint-Cyr, who looked like a professor though he spoke like a military man and threw one the scrutinizing glance of a police officer from behind his blue glasses; Eudore Soulié, whose face, ageless and plump, gave him the look of a gibbon, his hair astounding, tousled, and almost wiglike, but who had an urchin's gaiety and mischievousness and laughed in a falsetto voice.

After lunch Chennevières took us off to see the Fossé d'Arcosse collection of manuscripts. A study, the walls of which are hidden behind high cupboards, glass cases, pictures, sculptures, knick-knacks, and miscellaneous relics of history. Here, for example, is Louis XVI's hammer, forged by the royal hands; the hourglass that told time for Henri III; Louis XV's shoe buckle; Charles VIII's hunting knife; and an order to pay Lajouski, the Septembrist,[3] 1500 livres, signed Philippe Égalité. Here, again, is a proof before the letter of Debucourt's "Promenade in the Palais-Royal Gardens," bought in 1810 on the Pont-Neuf for fifteen sous; there Boucher's drawing, "Vulcan's Forge," for which forty sous was paid.

Someone having pronounced a name, M. Fossé d'Arcosse, a tall bony old man, said, as he was going through a sheaf of historical papers, "Yes, yes. I'll get round to them. I know. The family has two branches, and I'll tell you something interesting about them. Under Louis XIV each branch had a fortune of 100,000 livres. One invested its money in land and is now worth 400,000 francs; the other bought government securities, and what with declining markets and bankruptcies, its capital has been reduced to 500 francs."

Sitting under the trees at the Café de la Comédie we were joined by Théophile Lavallée, with his gypsy face and red shapeless lips, the lips of a Venetian mask in a painting by Longhi. He

[3]Two things one may be sure of in any French publication. First, some relation to reality, however remote; secondly, an absence of editorial conscience and of all concern with proofreading. "Lajouski" may have existed: I doubt it: the Goncourts must have written *Lazovski, q.v.* in the notes appended. A "Septembrist" was an instigator of the massacres of September 2–4, 1792.

talked very interestingly of the religious beliefs left by Robespierre to his friends and in particular about one Henri Clemance, a juror on the revolutionary tribunal who later became a schoolteacher under the Restoration of 1815 and who, when taken with wine, would confess his worship of the Incorruptible and avow frankly his belief in the guillotine. And Lavallée told us how violently he would argue with the man about his glorification of the guillotine—very liberal though Lavallée himself was—saying with truth that his generation has not yet been tamed to approval of Robespierre by such attempts to explain him as Thiers had made, or by *poetisations* like Lamartine's.

Lavallée told us that Feuillet de Conches had privately shown the emperor and empress, the other day, certain letters written by Marie Antoinette and had been astonished by Napoleon III's comment. Substantially, this was what he said: "When a man is kind he seems to others a coward. One has to be cruel in order to be thought courageous."[4]

Spent the evening with the same people at Soulié's. Delécluze, of the *Débats,* came in. Anti-Catholic conversation. It is really curious to see how fresh, ardent and militant Voltairianism still remains in this older generation. Then he talked about the paintings in the Sainte-Chapelle which he had been to see with his nephew, Viollet-le-Duc, who had exclaimed, "What we need now is a parrot for this café!" And with that he launched into an attack on polychromy in architecture and sculpture, insisting that nowhere does Pausanias say the Greeks painted their statues, and that the presence of painted sculpture at Pompeii proves nothing, since the art was by then decadent. . . . Finally, dropping art, old Delécluze talked at great length about how hard fervent Christians find it to accept death.

July 1.—Back from a day in the country, we dined this evening at the Restaurant de la Terrasse, a pothouse covered with cracked

---

[4]The emperor's character is illuminated by this bit of dialogue between him and Persigny, his straightforward minister of the interior: "Persigny, what makes you so wrathful?" "Sire, what makes you so little wrathful?" (Quoted in *La Deuxième république et le second empire,* by René Arnaud.)

gilt latticework to which cling a dozen dried-up climbing vines and across the way from which the sinking sun lit up with its dying rays the shrieking colours of the placards stuck up over the Panorama Arcade. It seems to me that never were my eye and heart more rejoiced than by the sight of this ugly plaster assailed by immense letters and scrawled over, dirtied, and smeared with the advertisements of Paris. Here everything is by man and belongs to man, except for an occasional sickly tree growing out of a crack in the asphalt; and these leprous house fronts appeal to me as nature never has done. The generations of our time are too civilised, too old, too deeply enamoured of the factitious and the artificial, to be amused by the green of the earth and the blue of the sky. At this point I shall make a strange confession: looking at a canvas by a good landscape painter, I feel myself more in the country than when I stand in the middle of a field or a wood.

July.—Out beyond the École Militaire, ground-floor quarters done up to look like white-curtained shop windows and surmounted by a single story with a large number over the door. The Big 9. A large room lighted from overhead by the wan daylight. A counter with bottles of liquor on it; unpainted deal tables; cane chairs. Seated round are infantrymen, Zouaves, workmen in tunics and grey hats, all with prostitutes sitting on their knees. The girls wear white or coloured shirts and dark skirts. They are all young, some are almost pretty; their hands look cared for and their hair is coquettishly dressed and piled up off the nape of the neck with little ornaments in it. They walk two by two between the tables, smoking cigarettes and playfully jostling one another. From time to time a singer recites some filthy verse or other in a bass voice. The waiters have long moustaches. The girls refer to the owner of the establishment as "the old marquis."

Upstairs there is a long corridor with rooms on either side, tiny cells with dismounted small shutters serving for doors, and containing by way of furniture a bed, a chest of drawers, a chair, and, on the floor, a pitcher of water and a basin. On the walls, one or two of those little framed pictures you win at country fairs, showing summer, or spring, and in almost every room, hanging from a little lead mirror, a toy Zouave like a child's doll. These things are specially manufactured for houses of prostitution in garrison towns and quarters.

These twenty-sou women are not in the least like the terrible creatures drawn by Constantin Guys: they are poor, miserable little prostitutes trying laboriously to ape the elegance of the tarts of the Saint-Georges Quarter.

July 16.—Reading Edgar Allan Poe is a revelation of something that criticism does not seem to suspect the existence of. Poe, a new literature, the literature of the twentieth century: the scientific miracle, the creation of fable by *a+b;* a literature at once monomaniacal and mathematical. Imagination the product of analysis; Zadig become an examining magistrate;[5] Cyrano de Bergerac become a pupil of the astronomer, Arago.[6] Things here play a greater part than beings. And love, love which Balzac had already reduced to second place after money—love makes way for other sources of interest. In a word, the novel of the future, bound to concern itself more with the story of what happens in the brain of humanity than in its heart.

July 22.—At Gavarni's, who showed us some marvellous water colours scarred with clarity, with sunlight, with life—pinks, yellows and blues of an inimitable wash, and figures prodigiously blotted in their skilful construction—drawings to which he has lent a Chinese tone by exposing his paper in a room full of tobacco smoke.

[5]Perhaps not an examining magistrate, but certainly a great detective, a Dupin and a Sherlock Holmes *avant la lettre.* You remember how Voltaire's Zadig learned that it was sometimes dangerous to know too much. Walking disconsolately in the environs of Babylon he was asked by the empress's eunuch if he had seen a little lost dog. " 'It is not a dog but a bitch,' said Zadig modestly; 'it is a very small spaniel, has only recently had puppies, is lame in one leg, and its ears are very long.' " In a moment the emperor's huntsman came along to ask if any one had seen a runaway horse. The horse, also, Zadig described in detail. Necessarily, Zadig was apprehended and charged with the theft of both the favourite animals, although in reality he knew no more about them than Holmes, on the evidence of Dr Watson's brother's watch, knew about Watson's brother. But what he knew, he had learned exactly as Holmes had got his knowledge.

[6]Cyrano having written imaginary journeys to the sun and moon, the connection is plain.

He told us that he was doing a series to be called "What Men Deserve", and thereupon he commended to us the love of stupid women. He once knew a woman who wrote him seven pages of nonsense every day. Towards the end he would read only half she wrote, but that half was enough to set him laughing. "Yes," he went on, "I shall have to burn those reams of letters from our citizens' wives. This one in particular, though she belonged to the highest rank of middle-class women, once gave me a rendezvous for five months and eight days thence. I was to slip through the vegetable-garden gate. Five months and eight days later I was at Versailles, in a large park in the middle of which stood a Louis XIII château. I looked up at the windows. Not a light, except just under the roof. Probably a bloody servant reading a novel by Madame Cottin. There was a wide stretch of lawn to be crossed in bright moonlight. And by the way, a fine drizzle was coming down. I threw pebbles against my beloved's window. Nothing doing. I went back into the park and ripped away two long branches. But how to tie them together? Impossible to tear off the leather strap on my pouch. Finally I wore it down with the cock of my pistol. Having lashed my branches at both ends, I beat on the window with them. Madame comes down to the ground floor and tries to open a window. The house is barricaded: impossible to open it. And there we stand making gestures at each other, I on the ground and she above me at the window. After a bit she tries another window and it gives way. She opens it. And I, standing in my socks, hand up to her my hunting boots with a pound of mud clinging to each boot. You can imagine what a face she made, my lady-citizeness. A frightful night of love. It seems I was an hour late."

Undated—It occurs to me that, in a play or another form, I could rehabilitate a witty parasite by making him cry out, at the end of a dinner given by his host, "What! you miserable fellow! I amuse you; I succeed in persuading laughter to penetrate that stupid, empty skull of yours; and you reproach me for accepting in exchange this horrible dinner?"

Undated.—Asselineau, lying asleep.

The wife of a bookseller, opening the shutters at his windows and sitting on the edge of his bed, says: "Ah, what a day! What a beautiful day to go to the country."

Asselineau, stretching himself while the sun's rays tickle his face, replies: "The country? The country! I haven't a sou."

The bookseller's wife answers: "Not a sou? Come, come! What about all these little books here? Aren't they money? Money you can have whenever you please? How much do you want for this?" And she reaches up above her head and pulls down, with both her hands, a whole row of books.

"The devil!" shouts Asselineau. "My books! My darling books! Will you get out of here, you pest!"

"Tell me," the woman says with a confident smile, "how much? You shall have whatever you ask."

Looking out at the azure sky, Asselineau hazards a figure without thinking. The woman bends very close to him, murmurs, "You are not very reasonable," and persuades him so tenderly that finally he accepts the price she offers him.

And she carries the books off to her husband and comes straight back with the money—which she and Asselineau spent on a day in the country.

Undated.—When M. Pasquier got his title of duke from Louis Philippe he went to call on Royer-Collard, out of whom he was able to get no more than, "It has not demeaned you."

October 16.—Grey days. Black days. Refusal, rejection by everybody, great and small. Little treasures of new historical writing refused by *L'Assemblée Nationale* because they contain shocking expressions, by the *Gazette de Paris* because they are too long. All our efforts, even our small successes, lead to nothing. Our publisher still not reassured after our two volumes of history. Our book on the Directory, which we wrote with every nerve in our bodies, has sold five hundred copies. . . .

After the sweet life of Gisors we lead a life of turmoil, of useless and disappointing bustle, filled with discouragement. Bored, we stroll aimlessly about and look at things; and by way of curing our state we buy two old Saint-Cloud teapots, embossed with silver gilt in a box with a fleur-de-lys lock. In these dark hours our remedy for *de-blackening* our souls is to gaze with enchantment at the gay brightness of something old and beautiful, at an example of bright porcelain gilded with dull gold, a pretty relic of the great industrial art of the eighteenth century.

This despair, this doubt not of ourselves or our ambitions but of our Age and the means at our disposal, instead of degrading us so that we make concessions, serves to fortify and make more whole, more intractable, more bristling, our literary conscience. For a moment we hesitate, and wonder whether we should not think and write absolutely for ourselves, leaving to others the clamor, the public, the publisher. But, as Gavarni says, nobody is perfect.

October 24.—What a charming conversationalist and amusing wit this Banville is, with his stories about the theatre of a kind no one ever writes, his philosophically jesting observations, and his deeply bitten etchings of actors and actresses; and what a delightful comedian and perfect actor he is himself when he portrays this world of the boards; and how singular the art he has, with his gentle yet piercing irony, of unveiling whatever is infamous or ironical in backstage life. And the charming, outrageous, stupefying paradoxes, the paradoxes of a truly cultivated man, in whose hyperbolic exaggeration there always lies an infinitesimal grain of truth and good sense, that drop constantly from his lips.

December 25.—Sold to the publisher, Dentu, our *Intimate Portraits of the XVIIIth Century* (two volumes), for the writing of which we spent between two and three thousand francs on manuscript letters.

1857

January 3.—Editorial offices of *L'Artiste*. Théophile Gautier, heavy of face, features sagging into deep creases, the countenance full of lassitude, a dozing physiognomy woken by, as it were, the intermittent comprehensions of a deaf man, with hallucinations of hearing which make him listen over his shoulder when he is spoken to face to face.

He was repeating and reiterating lovingly this phrase, *The idea is born of the form,* a phrase which Flaubert had pronounced to him this morning and which he thought the supreme formula of their school and wished to see written upon every wall. Beside him sat a great serious dark-haired fellow, mad about Egypt, who had under his arm a plaster cast of some Cheops or other and was explaining in solemn phrases his working schedule: he goes to bed at eight in the evening, gets up at three in the morning, drinks two cups of black coffee, and works until eleven o'clock.

Gautier, emerging like a ruminant from its digestion, and interrupting Feydeau, said:

"It would drive me mad. What wakes me up in the morning is that I dream I am hungry. I see red meats, tables groaning with food, banquets like Camacho's wedding feast.[1] The meat

[1] See *Don Quixote,* chs. XX–XXI. Extraordinary, what, out of the "classics", sticks in the mind in the different countries. Despite the Doré illustrations, *Don Quixote* is not better known, more widely read, in France than in England; yet *"festin de Gamache"* comes straight out of Cervantes and is a common French locution while remaining an allusion that few Englishmen would recognize. Incidentally, a more curious example is the "Lovelace" out of *Clarissa Harlowe,* pronounced by the Russians "Love-a-lass" and used commonly in pre-Soviet Russia to signify that which an Englishman means when he refers to "a Don Juan."

gets me out of bed. When I've had breakfast, I smoke. I get up
at half-past seven, and all this takes me to eleven o'clock. Then I
drag forward an armchair, I put paper, pen and ink on the desk
—my wheel of torture, for I hate to write, I have always hated to
write; besides, it's so useless! . . . Well, when I settle down I
write as unconcernedly as a public scribe.[2] I don't write quickly
—he's seen me write—but I go straight on, because, you see, I
don't try to do any better than what comes of itself. An article
or a page is something spontaneous; it's like a child: either it
exists or it doesn't. I never think of what I am about to write: I
take up my pen and write. I am a man of letters and am presumed
to know my job. I and my paper are much the same as a clown
and his tanbark. And besides, I have in my head a syntax in
perfect order. I throw my sentences into the air and I can be
sure that they will come down on their feet, like cats. It's very
simple: all one needs is to have a good syntax. I will undertake to
teach anybody how to write. I could start a course in *feuilleton*
writing in twenty lessons. Look here: here's my script: not a word
blotted. . . . Hello, Gaïffe! What, no copy?

"My dear chap, it's strange, but I have lost my talent. I know it
by the fact that idotic things are now able to amuse me. It's
idiotic, I know; but I don't mind: it makes me laugh. For me,
literature is a violent state in which I can maintain myself only by
extravagant means."[3]

"And yet you were *talentous*."

"All I care about now is to wallow in women."

"There is still drink left to you."

"No, thanks. If I drank I should have blue fibrils in my nose,
and the wild courtezans would love me no longer. I should be
obliged to take twenty-sou girls. And in that case I should become abject and repugnant."

[2]Certainly in Gautier's youth, and very likely still in 1857, public scribes were established at street corners and in the sheltering nooks of many public monuments in
Paris. Their signs invariably read *"Au Tombeau des Secrets."* They wrote not only letters (at ten sous for civilians and five for soldiers and maidservants out of work), but
verses, acrostics, epitaphs, epithalamiums, petitions and anything else that circumstance
might demand.

[3]A slightly altered version of this declaration was put by the Goncourts into the
mouth of the hero of their novel, *Charles Demailly*.

Undated.—Never has a century been more full of humbug than this one, even in the domain of science. For years the giddy-pated scientists have been promising us every morning a new miracle, a new element, a new metal, solemnly engaging themselves to warm us with copper pipes stuck into water, to kill or cure us with trifles, to make us all live a hundred years, and so on. And all this grandiose humbugging leads to membership in the Institute, to decorations, to salaries, to the respect of serious people. Meanwhile, the cost of living rises, doubles, trebles, decuples; there is a shortage of raw foodstuffs, or they deteriorate; even death in warfare makes no progress—as we saw at Sebastopol— and the cheapest goods are still the worst goods in the world.

January 20.—As we were talking in the offices of *L'Artiste* of Flaubert who, like ourselves, had been dragged into the police courts, and I was explaining that the government desired the death of romanticism, which had become high treason, Théophile Gautier broke in:

"Truly, I blush for my profession! For the very small sums which I am obliged to earn because otherwise I should starve to death, I allow myself to say the half of a quarter of what I think —and even then I risk being haled into court with each sentence I write."

Undated.—Louis said to me today, "By the way, I shall probably be able to get you some documents on Boucher, you know."

"How?"

"Through his granddaughter."

"You know her, then?"

"No, but I've met a doctor who is curing her of a disease, a disease that . . . Anyway, she gave him two pastels which came from Boucher's country house at Château-Thierry. She is a woman of the town."

The granddaughter of Boucher a woman of the town! But after all, there was a little of this in the blood of the painter of the Impure Graces.

The other Sunday there were so many carriages in the Bois de

Boulogne that coming back to town they were routed in over the by-roads instead of the avenue de L'Impératrice.[4] Who does not keep a carriage these days? What a society! Everybody is determined to bankrupt himself. Never have *appearances* been so despotic, so imperious, and so demoralizing. The Field of the Cloth of Gold, so to speak, is outdone by the luxury in which women live, wearing whole estates on their backs. The thing has come to such a point that many shops now open credits in favour of their clientele, who pay only the interest on their debts. There is talk of the wife of a high official, whose name I was given, who wangled 30,000 francs out of her son-in-law's dowry with which to pay her dressmaker's bill. One of these days—perhaps tomorrow—a great ledger will be opened for the accounting of the public debt in matters of the toilette.

March 5.—At *L'Artiste,* Charles Blanc reproaching Théophile Gautier (and laying it on thick) with the fact that he never wrote anything dull in his articles, never gave the reader a breathing spell from the sparkle of his writing.

"See what a bad pass I am in," said Gautier. "Everything seems to me dull. My most colourful articles are to me grey, foggy. I smear them with red, with yellow, with gold; I paint like a madman, and the thing never seems to me to glow. And at the same time I am upset, because for all my striving for colour, I still adore Ingres and the pure line. My opinion of Molière? You want my opinion of Molière and *Le Misanthrope?* Well, I think it smells to high heaven. I say frankly that it is vile writing."

"How can you blaspheme like that!" Charles Blanc exclaimed.

"Sorry. I don't get anything out of Molière at all. There is a crude, foursquare sound sense in his plays that strikes me as common. I know Molière well, mind you; I've studied him. I took a big dose of a characteristic play of his, *Le Cocu imaginaire,* and then, to see if I had really swallowed the dose, I tried it out, I wrote a little play called *Le Tricorne enchanté.* We don't need to bother about the plot, do we? That's of no importance in any case. But the language, the verse: I want to tell you that mine is

[4]Later the avenue du Bois de Boulogne and now avenue Maréchal Foch.

much better than Molière's. To me Molière is an alderman writing plays."

"He dares, he dares talk like that about Molière!" Charles Blanc cried with his face in his hands.

Gautier went unconcernedly on. *"Le Misanthrope?* Slops! Perhaps I ought to explain that from one point of view I am very badly constituted. I am totally indifferent to mankind. In a play, when a father rubs his refound daughter against the buttons of his waistcoat, I remain absolutely cold: all I see is the folds of his daughter's dress. I am a *subjective* person. That is the truth: I am talking about what I feel. Of course. . . . The devil! . . . I couldn't say this in print. We mustn't belittle our consecrated classics, must we? But, *Le Misanthrope!* . . ."

March 16.—Publication of the first volume of our *Intimate Portraits of the XVIIIth Century.* Barrière, writing in the *Débats,* scolds us for devoting our talent to excessively small subjects. What the public wants is solid, compact books in which it is shown again people it has seen before and is told again things it already knew. It shies away from anecdotes that are new, and virgin documents scare it off. History viewed as we view the eighteenth century, written and elaborated with the aid of a long series of manuscript letters and unpublished documents which serve to display every side of the Age; history that is new and original, that departs from the conventional forms of historiography, will never earn us one twentieth of what we could gain by a fat, messy compilation of the known and the oft-repeated. So says old Barrière, and he is perhaps right.

March 19.—Journalists very often have the strangest illusions about the public, imagining that it can guess, when it reads their prose, whom they are angry with and are tearing to bits. The most credulous example of this is perhaps Janin. Week by week all the characters of history and fable, from the Atrides to the world of Restif de la Bretonne, are set up as so many straw men to take the beatings which Janin intends for his contemporaries; and he, with inconceivable innocence, imagines that all

Paris, all France, all Europe, knows exactly what he is up to and whose faces the masks cover. Not long ago, writing about a play on the subject of Benvenuto Cellini, he slashed the poor Italian goldsmith into ribbons. "What have you against that poor devil, Benvenuto Cellini?" someone asked him. "Don't try to be clever with me," Janin came back. "You know very well it was Bacciochi."

Undated.—Why did we not write, day by day, at the beginning of our career, the chronicle of our harsh and horrible struggle against anonymity, those stations of indifference and abuse, an audience sought and ever slipping through our fingers, a future towards which we marched resigned but often in despair, the fight of our impatient and feverish will against time and our elders, one of the great privileges of literature. No friends; no connections; everything shut against us. That silence so well organised against those who want to eat of the cake of publicity; the sadness and chagrin that would overcome us during the slow years in which we fought against the public echo without being able to teach it our name. That mute internal agony with no other witness than our own bleeding self-esteem and our own fainting hearts. That monotonous and eventless agony, written on the quick of our sufferings—what a marvellous subject! Yet no one will write it, because a grain of success, a publisher found, a few hundred francs earned, a few articles printed at one or two sous a word, one's name known to a thousand people one has never heard of and two or three acquaintances, a little publicity —as little as this can cure one of the past and pour into one's glass the potion of forgetfulness. Then these tears and these miseries seem as far away as one's childhood, old wounds remembered only when they open again.

Undated.—We saw in the porter's lodge the toilette that our neighbour, Deslions, sends by her maid to the house of the man to whom she has given a night. It seems that she has a different outfit for each of her lovers in the colour that he prefers. It consists of a dressing gown of padded and ticked satin, with gold-embroidered slippers of the same colour; a nightgown of batiste trimmed with Valenciennes lace and embroidered insertions which come to five or six hundred francs; and a petticoat trimmed with three flounces of lace each of which costs three or four hundred francs. In sum, the accessories of gallantry come to 2,500 to 3,000 francs a set and are sent off to any house whose master can afford the lady.

April 11.—At five o'clock we met, at *L'Artiste,* Gautier, Feydeau and Flaubert. Feydeau so infatuated with himself, so self-satisfied, swollen with a vainglory so genuine and so artlessly childish, that he is disarming. He asked Gautier, speaking of the first of his own *Seasons,* one of which is to appear with each solstice, "Don't you think it is a gem, really? For I wouldn't want to dedicate anything but a gem to you."

Immediately a great noisy argument began about metaphors. That fellow Massillon's phrase, "His opinions had no need to blush for his conduct," was acquitted by both Flaubert and Gautier; but Lamartine's, "He practised equitation . . . that pedestal of princes," was condemned without appeal.

From metaphors we went on to assonance, and Flaubert opined that assonance was to be avoided though one spent a week striving to eliminate it. Then Flaubert and Feydeau gave each other little recipes of their profession, shouting and waving their arms. Seriously and emphatically they defined various processes in the mechanics of the literary talent and gave vent most gravely and solemnly to ridiculously childish theories on the ways of writing, the ways of manufacturing good prose, lending so much importance to the clothing of an idea, to its colour and woof, that the idea itself became a mere peg on which to hang sonorities of language.

May 1.—Théophile Gautier, a somnolent ear, a kind and gentle twinkle in the eye, his speech dropping slowly from his lips, issuing forth in a voice too small for his body, unmusical yet after a bit agreeable and even harmonious. A quiet monologue, simple, peaceful, good tempered, moving forward without haste but never deviating from a straight line and stripped of metaphor, the words and ideas flawlessly linked together with here and there the flash of an astounding memory and scenes recalled with the clarity of a photographic plate.

"The French language is positively going out. Good Lord, they tell me that people don't understand even *my* writing in my novel, *The Mummy,* and yet I consider myself the most dully limpid writer in the world. I suppose it is because I use words like *pschent.*[5] What do they expect? I can't interrupt the story to say, a *pschent* looks thus and so. It is the reader's business to know what the words mean. . . . Not that it matters to me. Criticism and praise, reviews unfavourable and favourable—both are written without the slightest understanding of my talent. Nobody has ever remarked that all my value lies in the fact that *I am a man for whom the visible world exists."*

May 12.—Théophile Gautier, that stylist in a red waistcoat, as the public see him, brings to things literary the most amazing good sense, the sanest judgment, and a most dazzling lucidity that spurts forth in very simple little sentences spoken in a voice as gentle as a caress. On first meeting, the man seems to be withdrawn into himself, or rather buried deep in himself. Actually, he has great charm and becomes in the highest degree likable, the more one knows him. Today he told us that when he wanted to do something really well, he always began in verse, because he felt a certain hesitancy about prose, about his complete success with it; whereas a line of verse, when it is the real thing, is as sound as a soundly struck medal. He added that the exigencies of life had turned into prose many tales which he had begun in verse.

Monday, May 18.—The Brasserie des Martyrs, a tavern and a cavern containing all the great anonymities, all the bohemian writers of the little reviews; a circle of impotent and impudent fellows each trying to cadge a five-franc coin or worn idea from the other. In connection with a duel born in this dive the police

[5]Meaning the headdress of Egyptian gods and Pharoahs.

sergeant of the Quarter said to Busquet, "What! You, sir, do you intend to fight with this man? But when you are insulted in a place like that, you pick up a knife and kill the person who insults you. The police will not interfere."

Wednesday, May 20.—At the Moulin-Rouge, chilled pitchers brimming with pink champagne; women sitting on cane chairs in the midst of the puffed-out fan of their skirts; grimy young men arriving from the races; bits of paper saying "Reserved" on empty tables; M. Bardoux, with the face of a chef on a Mediterranean liner and a napkin under his arm, murmuring suggestions for dinner. At the bottom of the garden, in every window on every floor, lit up from behind as if they sat in stage boxes, women's heads bobbing greetings to left and right, hailing, some of them, their nights of old, or perhaps hailing their coin of gold.

Undated.—The painful elaborateness, the torture, of beauty, as told to us by a lady in society. Out of bed at six-thirty in the morning. At the window until eight o'clock in order that her complexion may have an hour and a half's bath of fresh air. Then, an hour in the tub. After breakfast, a period of rest taken in a pose such that nothing comes into contact with the skin of the face.

Undated.—Men like ourselves require a woman with little breeding, small education, gay and natural in spirit, to charm and please us as would an agreeable animal to which we might become attached. But if a mistress had a veneer of breeding, or of art, or of literature, and wanted to talk on an equal footing with us about our thoughts and our feeling for beauty; if she were ambitious to become the companion of our taste or of the book gestating within us, she would become for us as unbearable as a piano out of tune—and very soon antipathetic.

May 22.—I have been reading a book published in 1830, *Tales* by one Samuel Bach. How young it is! How much its scepticism is the scepticism of a man twenty years old! How thinly its irony veils its illusions! How much it is made of imagination about life instead of life itself! Set beside it the remarkable books written by young men since the revolution of 1848. How different their scepticism! How mature and sound and healthy it is! The scalpel has replaced blasphemy. If this goes on, our children will be born forty years old.

May 23.—What an insipid thing the country is and how little company it affords a militant thought! This calm, this silence, this immobility; these great trees with their leaves lank in the heat like the webbed feet of the palmiped! Women, children, and solicitors' clerks are made happy by it. But does not a thinking man feel uneasy in the country as if in the presence of the enemy, the work of God that will eat him up in the end and make of his brain a fertilizer for all this vegetation? You escape from these ideas amongst the stones of the city.

May 28.—Our play, called *Men of Letters,* is finished. Castles in Spain. We tell one another that if it makes money for us we shall have fun pulling money's leg, kicking it round, laughing at it until it weeps with rage, throwing it about and showing it how absurd it is. Since we do not believe that money can buy either happiness or sense more than a man has, we shall use it experimentally, spend it wildly in order to test privately our eccentricities, test the specific gravity of a fat sum, and see what sort of slap in the face of those who adore the mob and the plebeian rich can be delivered with money.

A pretty title for memoirs published during one's lifetime: *Memoirs of My Dead Life.*[6]

June 1.—In this world the same thing never happens twice and man ought never *redesire* that which he once thought good. Today, at Maire's, the *écrevisses bordelaises* were not a success. Ah, Maire's restaurant towards 1850! when he was nothing but a publican and when, behind his zinc bar, there was no more than

[6]Everybody knows that in Edmond de Goncourt's old age George Moore used to turn up at the celebrated Goncourt *grenier* in Auteuil.

a tiny room into which six people could scarcely squeeze. Old Maire himself would wait on you if he thought you had culinary taste, and serve you off real plate a *haricot de mouton* with morels, or an indescribable *macaroni aux truffes,* to be washed down with several bottles of those pretty little burgundies that came from the cellars of Louis-Philippe, which he had bought almost entire.

June 4.—First auction sale of photographs at the Hôtel Drouot. Everything is turning black in this century, and is not photography the black vestment of the visible world?

June 7.—Dinner at Asseline's with Anna Deslions, Adèle Courtois, Juliette and her sister. Anna Deslions, magnificent thick black hair, velvety eyes with a glance that is like a warm caress, the nose a little fleshy, lips slightly parted, the superb head of an Italian adolescent glowing with the golden colouring of one of Rembrandt's Jewish heads. Adèle Courtois, an old celebrity of the world of gallantry. Juliette, a flouncy, frizzled little blonde, her forehead entirely eaten up by hair, a little blonde with something of the Rosalba pastel in the Louvre, "Woman with Monkey," partaking of both the woman and the monkey.

Beside Juliette sat her sister, skinny and *enceinte,* looking like a big-bellied spider. All four women in evening dress with a triangle down the back, the dresses white and foaming with a thousand flounces.

The accompanist of the feast is Quidant, the pianist, a thoroughly Parisian turn of mind with a ferocious irony who christened Marchal "the painter of useful knowledge."

Conversation on the emperor's mistresses, on La Castiglione, on the empress's jealousy, interrupted suddenly by Juliette who threw out: "You know that witty thing Constance said about the emperor? 'If I had resisted, I should have been empress.'"

Juliette bouncing up and down on her chair, beating the measure with her knife on her plate, chattering in the intervals of bursts of nervous laughter and the professional gaieties of an actress.

[49]

A man's name having been pronounced, Deslions flung at Juliette:

"You know, that man you were so madly in love with and for whom you committed suicide."

"Oh, I committed suicide three times."

"But you know whom I mean. Thingumabob! . . . What's-his-name! . . ."

Juliette put her hand up to her forehead like a person looking into the distance and half shut her eyes to see if she could not discern the gentleman along the highway of her memories.

Then she burst out laughing and said:

"It makes me think of Milan, of the Scala. There was a party there who bowed to me and bowed to me; and I kept saying to myself, 'But I know that mouth, I know that mouth.' All I could remember was the mouth; that's absolutely all I could remember."

"Do you remember," Deslions asked suddenly, "when we went out in that dirty weather to see where it was Gérard de Nerval hanged himself? Yes, I even believe it was you paid for the cab. I touched the bar. It really brought me luck. You know . . . Adèle, listen: it was the very next week . . ."

After dinner Quidant imitated the trill of a cuckoo on the piano and missed a note.

Then Anna Deslions and Juliette began to waltz, and that waltz of the blonde and the dark courtezan, both white and both flying through the drawing room lined in red rep and still unfurnished, was a charming spectacle. Suddenly they whirled, and in a most casual manner Juliette caught Anna Deslions' necklace in her teeth and bit a great black pearl that hung from it. But the pearl was real and did not break under the grinding fangs.

July 6.—Exposition of painting. No painting left, nor any painters. An army of seekers after ingenious ideas. Something intriguing, not something composed, is what they are after. Wit, no touch—and that only in the choice of subject. Two ideals that fascinate everybody. The Anacreontic ideal: anagrammatic word puzzles with Eros as the subject, stuck to canvas with dust off a moth's wing; mythology rendered in a vague grey tone seen through a sentimental and silly ingenuity totally unknown to antiquity: call them cockchafers which childish men have found it amusing to hang by one leg against the marble walls of the Parthenon. Secondly, the anecdotic ideal: history in the form of farce whose sublimest reach is to compose a picture after the fashion of Molière reading *Le Misanthrope* at Ninon de Lenclos'. Not one gifted hand, not one rascally fist covering a bit of canvas with coloured cream. Nothing but adroit people, sharp lads snatching success by Paul Delaroche's short-cut; by drama, by comedy, by apologue, by everything except what belongs to painting—so that on this evidence I should not be surprised that the successful picture of one of our future salons turn out to show, against a strip of sky, either a badly painted wall or a placard with something exceedingly witty written across it.

July 11.—Off to Neufchâteau on the news that our uncle, its representative in Parliament, is dying. Funeral on the thirteenth.

We saw once more the house in which our grandfather died, that pretty specimen of the eighteenth-century middle-class town house. Here, in the winter dining room, Edmond last saw our grandfather, who had served as member for Bassigny-en-Barrois at the Constituent Assembly in 1789. He was a little old man mumbling oaths in his toothless mouth and perpetually smoking a dead pipe which he would light again and again with embers picked out of the fire with the aid of a pair of silver tongs, a cane on the chair beside him. A violent man, whose cane was not always on his chair and who, in his château, Sommeré-court, had fashioned and trained a household of servants whose devotion he had been able to win in this manner. Old Marie-Jeanne still recalls in a spirit of tender and affectionate reminiscence how that cane used to come down on them all. She herself bears the old man no malice for the times when, on grandfather's orders, she was immersed in the pool in order to cool her blood each time she let it be known that she was tempted to marry. After all, in those days a caning was considered a mark of familiarity between master and servant and became a bond between them. Indeed, grandfather was not an easygoing head of the family: our father, who was a cavalry major at the age of twenty-five and who was thought a really wild lad by his fellow-officers in Napoleon's *Grande Armée,* used to tell us that he would sometimes keep a letter from his father in his pocket for a week or ten days before daring to open it.

Ah, that old Marie-Jeanne, you should hear her, sitting at the back of her son's mercery shop, telling in her uncertain voice stories of the family's good old days, and repeating this phrase: "We left Sommerécourt. Lapierre was driving. We arrived at Neufchâteau. We discovered the crimes. We nailed them and drove back."[7]

August 23.—Murger told us the funeral oration pronounced over Planche by Buloz, editor of the *Revue des Deux Mondes:* "I had as lief have lost 20,000 francs." The truth is that old Buloz wept real tears over his friend, who, though he might have had a horror of drinking water, was nevertheless a noble and disinterested character. This evening Édouard Lefebvre told us this fact, a fact rare in our time. When Louis Napoleon was at Ham, writing books in the guise of an amateur, he would send his manuscript to Mme Cornu for review. The wife of the painter, who was in contact with the *Revue des Deux Mondes,* would send it along to Planche, and he would go over it with scrupulous care. Louis Napoleon was informed of this, and when he was elected president of France, he instructed the government to offer Planche the post of director of fine arts, without any strings to the offer. Planche refused.

September.—Reread Balzac's *Les Paysans.* Nobody has mentioned Balzac as statesman, yet he was perhaps the greatest statesman of our time, the only one who got to the bottom of our ills, the only one who saw in perspective the disequilibrium of France from 1789—saw the manners that lay beneath the laws, the facts underlying the words, the unbridled interests beneath the seem-

---

[7]The old gentleman was a criminal judge.

ing order, the abuses replaced by influences, the equality before the law annihilated by the inequality before the bench: in a word, the deceit in the program of the Revolution of 1789 which has substituted five-franc coins for honourable names and put bankers in the place of noblemen—and has done nothing else.

October.—The Café Riche seems to be in a way to become the camp of those men of letters who wear gloves. It is strange how places make their frequenters. Beneath this white and gold, on this ruddy plush, the commoners of literature dare not venture. For that matter, their great man, Murger, is busy rejecting Bohemia and passing bag and baggage over to the people of culture and of fashion. His old pals cry out against the defection, the treason, of this new Mirabeau. Deep at the far end of the Café Riche, at the rue Le Peletier end, after the theatre, between eleven o'clock and midnight, are to be found Saint-Victor, About, Mario Uchard, Fiorentino, Villemot, Lévy (the publisher), and fidgety Aubryet, drawing with his finger in the foot bath of spilled drinks spread over the tables, or abusing everybody from the waiters to M. Scribe.

Baudelaire took supper tonight at the next table to ours. He was without a cravat, his shirt open at the throat, his head shaved, absolutely the toilette of a man ready for the guillotine. At bottom, however, the whole appearance carefully staged: his little hands washed, their nails cleaned, as tended as the hands of a woman; and with this the face of a maniac, a voice that cuts like steel, and an elocution aiming at the ornate precision of a Saint-Just, and hitting it. He protests obstinately, and with a kind of harsh anger, that he has not offended good taste in his verse.

Wednesday, October 21.—Read our play, *Men of Letters,* to Paul de Saint-Victor, Mario Uchard, and Xavier Aubryet. The fifth act seemed a little rhetorical, and Saint-Victor thought the death of our man of letters was too much like the death of a sensitive plant.[8] We decided to cut it.

[8] Yet it was of this death that my brother was later to die.—E. de G.

Monday, October 26.—Our play is beginning to be talked about. It is announced in various newspapers and this evening *La Presse* reports that it has been accepted. This publicity begins to look to us like a bad omen.

In the evening, at the café in the rue Helder, Saint-Victor told me that he had submitted the manuscript to Goudchaux, who would let him have an answer by Wednesday.

Tuesday, October 27.—Went to the offices of *L'Artiste*. The notice given our play—accepted only by the press thus far—has put *L'Artiste* at my feet. Aubryet greeted me as if I were a success, spoke to me as to a great man; and I for my part found myself talking down to him from a pedestal. Various offers to write for the press, biographies, etc., etc.

December 4.—Beaufort, the new manager of the Vaudeville Theatre, told Saint-Victor that our play was neither accepted nor rejected; the fact was, he dared not produce it at this time; it seems to him dangerous and he wants to put it off.

Monday, December 7.—Dined last night at Mario Uchard's. The company consisted of Saint-Victor, the Marquis de Belloy, a big sanguine fellow who looks like a horsy, hunting nobleman; Paul d'Yvoy, a Belgian who tells Parisians, in a daily column, what is going on in Paris—white haired, a pleasant face, the look of a fifty-year-old hussar; Augier, a pipe-smoking member of the Academy, as lusty and substantial as the prose of Rabelais, a high liver with a jolly laugh, and, skirting his somewhat bald skull, a fringe of curly locks round which have been rolled a number of love affairs with ladies of the theatre;[9] and, finally, Murger, in a tail coat.

A dinner and an evening in which the conversation, rising above the level of gossip about the *bidets* of courtezans and the night tables of well-known men, was poised upon the high peaks

[9]A remark of Augier's which is too good to be hidden in the biographical appendix is his reply to the Empress Eugénie when she asked him what she could do for literature: "Vous voulez protéger les lettres, Madame; il vous suffirait de les aimer."

of thought and the great epics of literature, with all sorts of illuminating remarks from one or other of the guests, and with violent outbursts from Saint-Victor, declaring himself Latin in mind
and heart, loving nothing but Latin art and the Latin languages
and literatures, and recognizing his homeland only when in Italy.
This profession of faith he followed by a storm of execration
heaped upon the Northern countries, saying that the Frenchman
at home would probably be indifferent to an Italian or Spanish
invasion, but that he would prefer death to a German or Russian
invasion. Murger told stories of real starvation in the artists' Paris
and spoke of their camps and tepees on the banks of the Bièvre.
. . . Then the government's suspension of *La Presse* led us, who
were all men of the pen, to regrets over the passing of the reign
of Louis-Philippe, each pronouncing a *mea culpa* and confessing
his malfeasance, his impertinences, his verses *à la Barthélemy*
against the "Tyrant." The Marquis de Belloy reminded us of the
omnibus drivers who, when they met the modest carriage of the
king in the avenue de Neuilly, would raise their hats in seeming
respectful salute and then, leaning out, would shout into the old
gentleman's ear, *"Merde pour le roi!"*

Towards the end of the evening Saint-Victor, buried in a deep
chair before the fireplace like a Caesar replete and surrendered
to digestion, came suddenly to life as he heard us talk about the
Revolution and the ridiculous prices at which the beautiful
creations of the eighteenth century were then sold, and
cried out, picked up straight by the thought that had occurred
to him:

"What! Eh! If we could live those days again: only three
days!"

"Oh yes!" said we; "to be able to see it all."

"Not a bit! To be able to buy things; buy everything there
was; and pack it up. What a stroke!"

Talking at the café about a well-known journalist, someone, I
don't know who, said that as soon as anybody became slightly
intimate with him, the journalist entered him in his books, in a
real sort of banker's ledger, with receipts on one side and expenditures on the other; and the first time that he rendered a service

to the man, that went down under expenditures, and if the man did as much for him, it was balanced by an entry under receipts; and at the end of every month he drew off a balance, being careful to see that his friendship showed constantly a considerable profit.

1858

March 5.—Strange beings, our scatterbrains, our dissipators, our extravagant young men! The only money they scatter to the winds is what they worm out of usurers. Let them but come into a fortune and instantly they are sobered up, well behaved, economical, cutting expenses and piling up coppers. We know one, for example, the last descendant of a family without ascendance, who is this type of prodigal son. At the moment he positively has money of his own. He opened his secretary yesterday before friends, took out fifteen hundred real hundred-franc notes, thumbed them through several times, and said with a sigh, "I know that I owe you all money, but—it's a funny thing—it upsets me to pay it back to you. Shall we be quits for a supper party?"

Undated.—Raphael created the classic type of Blessed Virgin by painting the perfection of vulgar beauty, the absolute contrary of true beauty, which Da Vinci, on the other hand, sought in exquisiteness of type and rarity of expression. Raphael attributed to the Blessed Virgin human serenity of nature, a kind of round beauty, an almost Junoesque health. His Virgins are mature, healthy mothers, wives of St Joseph. What Raphael achieved is the ideal that the generality of the faithful imagine the Mother of God to look like. For this reason his Madonnas will remain eternally popular; they will ever remain the Catholic Madonnas, the clearest, most widely accepted, most understandable, most commonplacely hieratic Madonnas—those most closely approximating the artistic tastes of piety.

The "Madonna della Chiesa" will forever be the Academy portrait of the divinity of woman.

March 7.—. . . A strange person with whom Gavarni took pleasure in dining recently. He is an Italian, origin unknown, who once lived in London where he made acquaintances from whom, almost every day, he would cadge a few shillings with which he would gamble in the low gaming houses of the town. He frequented a stew where one was not allowed to sleep and where there was not so much as a chair to sit upon. There his nickname was The Fly, because of his habit of dropping off to sleep leaning against a wall. One evening play became very lively and a sovereign rolled off the table and over to his feet. He put forth a foot naked beneath a shoe with almost no sole, and, seizing the coin with his big toe, he stood still until dawn, not daring to pick the coin up for fear of being accused of theft. That morning, rich for the first time in his life, the first thought of this man who never went to bed was to go to bed. He knocked on the door of a lodginghouse and was admitted. At ten o'clock he was woken by the servant who asked if he would like to take breakfast with her mistresses, two ex-governesses. They liked him; in a few days he became the lover of one of them; married her; inculcated in them both a taste for gambling; and ruined them. Having ruined them, he persuaded first his wife and then his sister-in-law to become Roman Catholics; and with money received from English Catholics he went off to Hamburg to try his luck at the table, won 200,000 francs, lost them again, and now . . . Imagine what he does: he goes from pub to pub, in the Étoile Quarter, organizing a gambling syndicate among journeyman masons, he to go off to gamble in Germany for them under the surveillance of a committee of ten masons in evening clothes who, themselves, will have nothing to do but eat, drink, and stroll about while he works for them.

March 12.—This evening the talk was of 1830, and the Marquis de Belloy, to give us a notion of the fraternal spirit of the times, the generous and eccentric madness, the things great and absurd to which that spirit led, told us this story. Some time before the production of *Marion Delorme* he wrote to a friend who was studying medicine at a provincial university. The friend thought De Belloy's letter despondent, thought he must be in the need of money, collected all he could lay his hands on, and brought it to him in Paris. De Belloy had no need of it, thanked his friend, would not let him go back, and took him off that evening to see his mistress.

For several days the three were inseparable, day and night. Suddenly the friend disappeared. De Belloy went to look for him one morning and found in bed . . . a monster. The man had shaved off all his hair—eyebrows, beard and moustaches; and he confessed to De Belloy that, having fallen in love with his mistress, he had now made it impossible for himself to see her. That same night *Marion Delorme* had its first performance, and the model friend, taken to the theatre, almost caused the play to fail. Every time that he turned round to silence the *claque* of anti-romantics his monstrous face, enthusiastic and hairless, sent the house into a gale of laughter.

March 31.—"You will never be decorated!" With these words a friend began the following story:

"In the imperial villa at Biarritz there is a library of twenty-five volumes. One of those books is your *History of French Society under the Directory*. Damas-Hinard said to the empress, 'Read this; a new book that will interest you.' The empress took the book, began to read, and suddenly burst out laughing. The emperor came over and asked her why she had laughed. The empress pointed out to him the word *tetonnières*—your word for the bare-bosomed women of the time. The emperor stared at the word, reread it, made certain of the epithet—and severely shut the book."

April 11.—Reread *Le Neveu de Rameau*. What a man, this Diderot! What a river! as Mercier calls him. To think that Voltaire is immortal and Diderot merely famous. Why? Voltaire marked the death of the epic poem, the tale, the epigrammatic verse, and the tragedy. Diderot inaugurated the modern novel, the drama, and the criticism of art. The one was the last wit of the old France; the other was the first genius of the new France.

April 23.—Came away from Gavarni's with Guys, the artist of the *Illustrated London News*. A short man with an energetic countenance, grey moustaches, and the look of a grouser of the Old Guard. He walked with a slight limp and kept striking his bony forearms curt blows with the palm of his hands to adjust the sleeves, meanwhile pouring out a ceaseless, diffuse overflow of parentheses, zigzagging from idea to idea, running off the rails of his thoughts, losing them, finding them again, and calling your attention to them by a coarse metaphor, a word out of the vocabulary of the German philosophers, or a technical term from the language of art or industry, and holding you concentrated upon his words which were as if painted and visible to the eye. In that little stroll a thousand memories came back to him, and he would throw out from time to time handfuls of irony, of sketches, of landscapes, of troops devastated by cannon shot, bleeding, disembowelled, ambulances in which lay the wounded, busy fighting off rats.

And then, on the back of all this, exactly as in an album or on the back of a drawing by Decamps you might find a quotation from Balzac, there came out of the mouth of this devil of a man social observations, remarks about French-ness, or English-ness, all of them novel and not grown mouldy in books, satires that lasted only a couple of minutes, polemics summed up in a single word, a comparative philosophy of the national genius of the peoples.

One word picture is of the capture of Janina, a stream of blood with dogs splashing in it, flowing between the legs of the then young Guys. Another showed Dembinski in a blue shirt, his last shirt, flinging a gold coin, his last gold coin, on a green table, and running it up to 40,000 francs without batting an eye. And still another—the English country house; a wood of tall trees; the hunt; three changes of clothing a day and a ball every evening; a royal life led and paid for by somebody whose name might be Simpson or Thompson and whose twenty-year-old son is off in the Mediterranean inspecting his father's fleet of eighteen vessels none of which is smaller than 2,000 tons—"such a fleet as Egypt never had," Guys remarks. After which he compared us with the English, exclaiming, "A Frenchman perfectly idle, in London quietly spending his money—has anybody ever heard of such a Frenchman? The French travel to get over a love affair, or a loss at cards, or to sell cotton prints; but a Frenchman in a carriage; a Frenchman not an actor, nor an ambassador, and beside him his mother or his sister, a woman neither an actress nor yet a dressmaker—that, nobody has ever seen abroad."

April 24.—Between the chocolate soufflé and the chartreuse Maria loosened her corsets and began the story of her life.

She was born on the banks of the Marne in one of those moist and shady places beloved of the landscape painter, Huet. Her father was a poor boatbuilder. She was blonde and white skinned, and she remained white skinned under the *blackening* sun of the Brie country. She was past thirteen years old when a young man she thought an architect began to make love to her. As in the storybooks, the young man was a count, the owner of one of the neighbouring châteaux, a young man who lived very high and was constantly on the edge of ruin. She let him take her away and found herself presently installed in the château, where the young count was greatly amused by her *villagery,* her ignorance. Now and then he would lock her up in her room and bring down girls from Paris whom he would chase through the park of the château, naked beneath gauze robes that two little dogs would tear to rags with their teeth.

After less than a year the count was completely ruined, and all this ended with him escaping from the bailiffs to the roof of his château, where, like a noble lord of olden time, he blew out his brains. Our Maria was thrown out with all her worldly goods, which consisted of a watch set in pearls and two diamond earrings. Also, she was big with child. She went off to a midwife to bear her child. The midwife sold her to a brick contractor whom she hated; and in order to earn a living she went back and served an apprenticeship to the midwife who had delivered her child.

May 27.—A burst of laughter is the arrival of Maria, a joyous holiday is her face. When she comes into the room a healthy gaiety comes in with her, and her kisses are the embraces of the fields. A plump woman; blonde frizzled hair worn back from the forehead; extraordinarily kind eyes; a full-fleshed gentle face—the opulence and dignity of a Rubens. After so many skinny graces, so many sad little faces, careworn and with the clouds of eviction on their foreheads, forever scheming to gouge something out of you, wrapped up in the parturition of cadging; after all these shopworn gabbling creatures, these squawking parokeets with their miserable, unhealthy slang picked up in workshops and in the clattering cafés; after those touchy and peevish women, what a satisfaction lies in Maria's peasant health and good humour; in her peasant speech, her strength, her cordiality, her sound and expansive exuberance and contentment, the heart that is evident in her with its lack of breeding and rough tenderness. Everything about this woman delights me, as if I found myself eating simple and solid food in a farmhouse after a vile dinner in a filthy pothouse.

And to carry this Flemish body she has the slender legs of an Allegrain *Diana,* and feet with the long toes of a statue, and knees beautifully moulded.

Besides, there are times when a man needs to employ a certain coarseness of speech, above all a man of letters does, who spends his time in the clouds and in whom matter, oppressed by the brain, sometimes avenges itself. It is his way of coming down from the basket in which Socrates is hauled up in Aristophanes' *Clouds.*

August 2.—As literature goes these days, Saint-Victor is really a noble and exemplary man of letters—a writer whose thought lives constantly amidst the titillations of art or in the high-perched aeries of great ideas or vast problems, brooding with tender love and in the course of fireside travels, first upon Greece and next upon India, which he will depict for you, although he has never seen it, like a man just emerged from an orgy of haschisch, carried away by the warm, colourful, profound words in which he talks about the origin of religions as one of the grandiose and primitive puzzles of humanity; curious on the subject of the cradles of mankind, the constitutions of societies; pious and respectful, hat in hand, before the Antonines, who are to him the moral summit of humanity, his bible being the *Meditations* of Marcus Aurelius, that sage and reasonable master of the world.

And when Saint-Victor comes down from those heights to speak of our time and its men, he talks with a sort of Michaelangelesque irony, comparing, for example, Janin and his work to Rabelais's chimeara, "bombinating in the void," *chimera bombycinans in vagum.*

All this talk flowing, overflowing, on a summer night, from this eloquent man obsessed by antiquity and the past, in the shadow of a carriage moving slowly through the Bois de Boulogne with a coachman asleep on his elbow, of whom Saint-Victor says, "Wouldn't one say he was leaning on a *triclinium?*"

August 15.—The table was set out of doors, surrounded by trelliswork covered over with green climbing plants. In the entrance to the courtyard stood two handsome grey asses, saddled and harnessed in red, adorned with pompons and tufted crests in the Spanish fashion. There are nineteen of us seated round in garden chairs. Villemessant, teasing this one about his appetite and that other about his fiascos in the theatre, and crying out to his wife, "Drink some Bordeaux; it will make you live two weeks longer!" calling his daughter by a nickname and treating her as if she were a real urchin, and saying to us, "I was asked at Blois who you were and I explained that you were the brothers Lionnet, two cabaret singers, and would sing for us later on."

Among the guests was a tough old party of seventy-six who looked forty and wore white trousers, a frock coat made of *lasting* with silk hose and thin pumps. He had spent years in Napoleon I's commissariat, had later gone over to the Bourbons and participated in various important events, was intimate with many great people, and was full of those anecdotes which lend relief to the facts of history. This was Baron Penguilly, father of Penguilly, the painter.

When the French army entered Moscow he took possession of one of the palaces. Making a tour of the place he heard, in one of the bedrooms, the rustle of a skirt. He saw a foot sticking out from under a bed, pulled towards him a black-stockinged leg with a pretty woman at the end of it, and then another silk stocking and another pretty woman. One after the other, he made them his mistresses. A couple of days later one of his friends turned up who said, "You're in luck. You are the only one who has women." "But you have some madeira," Penguilly retorted. "I'll tell you what I'll do: I'll swap one of my women for ten casks of your madeira." The exchange was made.

Moscow evacuated, Penguilly was ordered by I don't remember which marshal to find room in his coach for two actresses of the French troupe that had come out with the army. First one horse died, then two, then a third, after which they had to give up the coach. The two women were perched upon a horse which, by some lucky chance, Penguilly had been able to buy. One of the two women was taken with dysentery and had to be strapped to the horse. Finally she died, and before her death she said to him, "Penguilly, when a person is dying anybody can give that person absolution"; and she forced him to hear her confession. She was the daughter of a shopkeeper in the Faubourg Saint-Antoine who had run away from home at thirteen and had lived her light-o'-love's life all over Europe. When she finished confessing, she gave him what money she had, so that prayers might be said for her at the next village. In Poland, eventually, Penguilly was able to have a mass said for her soul. He still had a letter every year from the surviving actress.

October.—Nobody has remarked (and yet the thing is self-evident to eye and ear) that the very language of Napoleon I, that language of brief sentences of command, the language preserved by Las Cases in the *Memorial of St Helena* and even better in Roederer's conversations with the emperor, was taken over by Balzac and put into the mouths of his military types and his governmental and humanitarian characters, from the monologues of his statesmen to those of his arch-criminal, Vautrin.

Undated.—A curious revelation of the luxury and misery of Paris: every winter three thousand women's riding habits are pledged with the governmental pawnshops.

Undated.—In antiquity the countryside was neither a mother nor a sister, neither a consolation nor a loving friend. It was not, as with us, Nature's elegy, the romantic fact, the homeland of reverie tinted with the pantheism of a middle-class Sunday. It represented repose, rest from the affairs of the world, an excuse for illness, a place where conversation escaped from the routine of life and the town, where thought found its recreation.

The countryside was the summerhouse of Horace's soul.

October 28.—A M. de Vailly, who does not know us any more than we know him, in an essay on our books published lately in *L'Illustration,* made a prediction about us which might perhaps come true. He said that if we fell in love we should fall in love with the same person, and that law and custom ought to make an exception in favor of our dual personality.

Sunday, November.—Gavarni, Flaubert, Saint-Victor and Mario Uchard dined with us. Flaubert's intelligence haunted by the Marquis de Sade, to whom he returns as to a mystery and a depravity that fascinate him. Being a glutton for depravity and a collector of it, being happy, as he puts it, to see a garbage man eating what he transports, he exclaimed, still on the subject of de Sade, "It is the most entertaining nonsense I have ever run across."

Leaving de Sade he launched into the most enormous and Pantagruelian ironies against the *attackers* of God, telling this story of a man who is taken fishing by an atheist friend. The

atheist casts in the net and draws up a stone on which is carved:
"I do not exist. *Signed:* God." And the atheist exclaims, "What did I tell you!"

For the scene of his novel of antiquity Flaubert has chosen Carthage, as the site of the rottenest civilization on the globe. In six months, he said, he had been able to write thus far only two chapters: a meal eaten by mercenaries and a lupanar of young boys.[1]

Thereupon Saint-Victor began to proclaim himself a Catholic as artist and man of letters, saying that he read with immense pleasure the *verbatim* reports of the Mortara case[2] because he was intensely interested in everything touching the subject of mythology. "Ah!" exclaimed this eccentric Catholic, "I know nothing more beautiful than a great ceremony in St Peter's, the cardinals all reading their breviaries in those insolently idle poses, hanging half out of their stalls—have you seen them? Have you seen them? . . . Yes, at bottom the Catholic religion is a wonderful mythology."

One of the guests compared Aubryet to a cat in an electric current. Another, enumerating the newspapers owned by Jews—*La Presse, Le Constitutionnel, Les Débats, Le Courier de Paris*—declared that they had already *domesticated* literature.[3]

November 13.—In Italian painting the space between the eyes marks the period of the picture. Between Cimabue and the Renaissance, from master to master, the eyes are set successively farther away from the nose, leaving off their Byzantine characteristic and moving towards the temples, until finally, in Cor-

---

[1] This scene was subsequently omitted from the novel.—E. de G.

[2] "In Bologna a little Jew named Mortara had been baptised, during a grave illness, by a Roman Catholic servant. Three years later the servant revealed the story to a priest. Rome had no wish to allow a Christian soul to grow up in heathen surroundings: the Jewish child was kidnapped and immured in a monastery. . . . The [French] press, hostile to the Pope, went so far as to organise a League of Parents against the abuses of theocracy." Arnaud, op. cit.

[3] *La Presse* and *Le Constitutionnel* were owned respectively by Millaud and Mirès, both Jewish bankers; *Les Débats* was owned by the heirs of the Bertins, who took it over from Baudoin, the founder, in 1799. Of the ownership of *Le Courier* no trace is to be found.

reggio and Andrea del Sarto, they are back where they were placed by the art and beauty of antiquity.

December.—In Lucian there is an astonishing and delightful modernity. This Greek, who lived when Greece was ended and Olympus was seeing its twilight, is our contemporary in mind and soul. His Athenian salt is the beginning of Parisian ironic banter. His dialogue between courtezans is like manners in our time. His dilettantism in art and his scepticism are to be found in the thought of our day. The Thessaly of Smara, the new home of the fantastic, lies spread before his donkey. His very style has the accent of our own. Our boulevards might have heard the voices he makes speak under the Lesche. An echo of his laughter is still to be heard from our boards, rising against the gods in their sky. Reading Lucian, it seems to me I am reading the grandfather of Heine: words of Greek come back to me in the German, and both men had visions of women with violet eyes.

1859

January 27.—This morning Scholl said to me something amusing about Barrière: "Yes, yes, he has talent; but he doesn't know how to make people forgive him for having it."

Undated.—Our novel, *Men of Letters,* is finished and ready to be copied. It is strange, in literature, that once a thing is done it is no longer part of oneself. The work that one is not carrying, that one is not nursing, becomes, so to say, something foreign to one. One feels indifferent to it, bored with it, almost repelled by it. This is how we have felt for several days past.

Friday, January 28.—Gavarni dropped in as we were finishing dinner. He was not hungry; he had just lunched; it was seven o'clock. Exactly like him: a mind that takes no pleasure from trumpery material things, his pleasure, his recreation from the terrible amount of work he does, consisting only in the conversation of those he calls rich people, people *full of facts,* like Guys, Aussandon and others; those complicated eccentrics who are, in themselves, a summing up and an assemblage of a heap of things; those men who speak a concrete language, whose life, as Gavarni says, "is spent in being an object of study and pleasure for the intelligence of those who drink with them, none of this ever passing over into a written or painted creation." Gavarni is dining these days at the Poissonnerie Anglaise only for the reason that the owner of this restaurant is revealing to him the various dodges by which sharpers fleece people in cafés.

He said to us that geometry should be the form of things in space. He spoke to us of things which, like fever and music, having only two attributes—intensity and time, marked by an indicator rising and falling on a fixed surface—ought to describe their own form.

He was tired, having spent days recently running from banker to banker—Rothschild, Solar and others—to raise a loan of 50,000 francs on his house at Point-du-Jour. The bankers he found to be . . . bankers. Not a grain of bitterness: merely regret at losing the time taken from his work.

April 27.—Despondency, the blackest, deepest, most intense despondency—and we sink into it with a certain bitter, raging satisfaction. Constantly in our minds is the thought of surrendering our French nationality and going to live abroad, to recreate the *free-speaking* Holland of the seventeenth and eighteenth centuries;[1] to found a review directed against everything that exists; to unlock our hearts, unseal our lips, pour forth our repugnance in a cry of anger. For a whole month troubles have been pouring down upon us. Everything misses fire; everything goes wrong; everything fails us. Our play, which the press said was accepted, is in the basket. Our half-finished novel has been handed back to us. And with all this, difficulties about re-leasing our farms, and ill health.

May 11.—A ring at the door. It was Flaubert, who had been told that we had seen somewhere a death-dealing mace, more or less Carthaginian, and had come to ask the address of the collector. He talked about the difficulties he was having with his Carthaginian novel: nothing on the subject of Carthage was to be found.

[1]The allusion is to a time when writers who were censored in their own country, e.g., Voltaire, arranged to publish their books—most often under pseudonyms or anonymously—in Protestant, republican Holland, whence the book would be smuggled.

He had to invent what might seem likely. And therewith, like an exuberantly tickled child in a toyshop, he spent a good hour going through our folios and books and collections.

Flaubert looks extraordinarily like portraits of the actor Frédérick Lemaître as a young man. He is very big, very broad shouldered, full of face, with fine large protuberant eyes under slightly swollen lids, heavy drooping moustaches, and a glowing complexion with red splotches. He spends four or five months of the year in Paris, going nowhere, seeing only a few friends, leading the cloistered life we all lead—Saint-Victor as well as he, and we as well as Saint-Victor.

This *bearishness* of the nineteenth-century man of letters is strange compared to the social life of the eighteenth-century writers, from Diderot to Marmontel. The middle classes of our time do not seek out the man of letters unless he is willing to play the part of a strange beast, a buffoon, or a guide to foreign cultures.

May 14.—Charles Edmond, who has lived everywhere and known everybody, and who now and then draws forth from his recollections a curious figure or a characteristic reminiscence, told us this story apropos of the susceptibility of Italians.

Seven years ago he was in Nice. Orsini was there at the same time, and they became intimate friends. One morning Orsini invited him to lunch; he declined, saying jokingly that he was a serious eater who liked his cut of beef, whereas Italians fed on such things as *polenta* and macaroni. He went off the same day to lunch at the house of a Russian countess to whom Orsini happened to be paying court. While he was there a certain Count Pepoli, the common friend of Orsini and Charles Edmond, called him into the anteroom. There he told him that Orsini had devoted his whole life to Italy, that he knew no more mortal insult than an offence to the Italian flag . . . and, one thing leading to another, Charles Edmond discovered that Pepoli had come as Orsini's second in the matter of the *polenta* and the macaroni.

The countess arrived at that moment. She made so much fun

of the challenge that Orsini, a little ashamed of his foolish susceptibility, made it up with Charles Edmond.[2]

May 22.—We met About at Charles Edmond's. Strolling in the woods at Bellevue he chatted, opened up, expanded. He has exactly the intelligence of a very intelligent man about town to which has been added a shade of the school usher and a little of the volubility of a fraud. He talked about his person, his greying hair, his mother, his sister, his family, his château at Saverne, the five domestics, the eighteen they always sit down at table, his shoot, his friend Sarcey de Suttières, whose novel on the "salons of the provinces" is like *Balzac in good French;* of the disappointment with which he read *Notre-Dame de Paris* this past week, of the qualities of Ponson du Terrail, and of his opinion of Mérimée. He is the "me" of success, but not too heavy-handed, not too unbearable, and preserved by witty monkeyshines, by little literary caresses for the literary men who are present and to whom he serves out quotations from their books. But in his conversation there is not an atom that is not of this world, Parisian, and out of the gossip sheets.

He talked to us about his book on the Roman Question, which had just been banned by the authorities. He maintained—and we believed him—that the emperor himself had gone over the proofs, that Fould had worked on the book, and that Morny had supplied the last chapter, "The Metropolitan See in Paris," which had been an idea taken from the St Helena *Memorial* of that

---

[2]The mention of Orsini for the first time at this late date, and as an example of Italian susceptibility, is a sort of lesson in the art of diary-keeping. The Goncourts recorded, it will be seen from what follows, only that which was strictly of interest to them. Count Felice Orsini (1819–58) was the leader of a band of Italian patriots who threw a bomb at the carriage of the emperor and empress as it drew up before the Opéra on the evening of the fourteenth of January 1858. Patriots are notoriously bad shot-putters: the imperial couple escaped unhurt. After due trial, at the close of which Orsini was allowed to deliver an oration in which he begged the emperor to "restore to Italy that independence [of Austria] which her children lost in 1849 through the fault of the French", he was beheaded on March 13. All three events—attempted assassination, trial and execution, are ignored by our diarists. "Four months later," writes Arnaud (op. cit.), "Napoleon sent secret word to Cavour, the Piedmontese minister, to meet him at Plombières and made ready for war upon Austria." Given the nature of that singular Bonaparte, it is not impossible that there is here a relationship of cause and effect.

other Napoleon, him of whose empire the present one is a counterfeit. About added that Fould had told him confidentially that apartments were being prepared for the Pope in the Palace of Fontainebleau—Fontainebleau!—to be used in the event he made any difficulties, or if Antonelli played any tricks.

August.—1. A troupe of actors.
2. A corps of dancers.
3. Puppeteers (at least three or four).
4. About one hundred Frenchwomen.
5. Physicians, surgeons, pharmacists.
6. About fifty gardeners.
7. Liquorists, distillers.
8. 200,000 pints of spirits.
9. 30,000 ells of blue and scarlet cloth.

And with this Napoleon undertook to found a civilized society in Egypt.

August 12.—Yesterday I sat at one end of the table in the château. Edmond, at the other end, was chatting with Thérèse. I could not hear what he was saying, but when he smiled I smiled despite myself, my head in the same attitude as his. Never were souls so like placed in two bodies.

Undated.—I have measured it off: in the country you want one guest to the acre.

November 15.—As my dentist was bending over me, cleaning my teeth, he said to me suddenly: "Do you ever go to listen to the priests? They are so stupid! They never tell you what God is." And my dentist's voice became apostolic: "God cannot be a man; he is essence. Only one philosopher knew it—Bacon. As for the Blessed Virgin, she is universal procreation, the reverberation of God. This is something the priests have never made clear, and yet Apollonius of Tyana saw it centuries before she was born, for she has existed in all eternity.

"How hot it is today! What strange weather! Earthquakes!

You knew there was another one at Erzerum, didn't you? Mysterious heat waves. Last year's comet. All that is the sign of something. There is going to be a great deal of housecleaning round the Pope. There will be almost no priests left. The Reign of Jesus Christ is coming. No mistake about it: it's all in the Apocalypse. The priests know it well enough. The archbishop of Paris talked about it, about the Reign of Jesus Christ, in his pastoral charge. There is a church, you know, of the Reign of Jesus Christ, that used to be over by the railway tracks, near the avenue du Maine, and is now near the Panthéon. I know a doctor who is a member. It is Swedenborgian, but that has no foundation. . . ."

Restless minds, troubled souls, religious preoccupations stirring in the shadows, rumours and murmurs of the supreme battle being fought by Catholicism, a whole mine of mysticism hatching beneath the scepticism of the nineteenth century—all this explains my dentist's speech and is explained by the Italian adventure,[3] the pastoral letters of the bishops, the offensive taken by the Church in the matter of temporal power; and in this man's words there is an echo of the fever and delirium of people's consciences. I see here, germinating already in the enlightened lower middle classes, anarchical beliefs and the social chaos which will blossom in the very near future.

Tuesday, November 13.—For the first time in our life a woman has separated us for thirty hours. That woman is Mme de Châteauroux, who has persuaded one of us to go to Rouen to copy

---

[3]"The Italian adventure" of Napoleon III (who had himself fought for Italian freedom in 1831) is too long and too messy a story for a footnote; but it may be said, at least, that it began as a "Roman adventure" when, in 1849, President Louis Bonaparte sought to put the Pope back on the throne from which a Roman revolution of 1848 had driven him, and sought at the same time to protect His Holiness's temporal subjects from the inevitable anti-liberal reaction that must follow the restoration. Chaos resulted from these inherently conflicting aims. In July 1858 the emperor plotted with Cavour, the Piedmontese minister, to free northern Italy from the Austrian dominion—and left Cavour in the lurch after two months of war in the following year. Meanwhile, French troops had invested Rome and the French *tricolore* flew over the Castle of St Angelo—but whether to protect the Papacy against Garibaldi and the Italian patriots, no one could discover. The French general elections of 1863 ultimately decided Napoleon to favour the Vatican against the Italian parties of the *Risorgimento*.

out a bundle of intimate letters written by her to Richelieu, now part of the Leber collection.[4]

Coming away from the train I ran into Flaubert, who was meeting his mother and his niece, they coming to spend the winter in Paris. His Carthaginian novel is half done.

December 9.—Two days ago, as we were on our way to the Louvre to ask permission to reproduce Watteau's drawing of the musicians at Crozat's, Chennevières told us that the museum was in a state because it had been offered another celebrated drawing, "La Revue du Roi," and could not find the wherewithal to buy it. Evidently, if it had been a drawing of the Italian or Flemish school, the money would somehow have been found—even several thousand francs would have been found. Chennevières gave us the address at which the drawing was to be seen, and we rushed off to 13, rue des Bourdonnais.

Here we are in a very small room heated by an iron stove. A large table, with an infant several months old lying on it, fills the room. A woman is sitting in the room, sewing a coarse shirt by the light of a lamp. We ask to see the drawing. From beneath the table she draws forth something wrapped in a portfolio and out of it comes the famous drawing of the Exposition of 1781.

"How much are you asking for this, madame?"

"A thousand francs."

And as we offer her 300 francs, the price to which we know her husband has about come down, after having had the drawing shown for sale to all the rich collectors in Paris, she says to a little girl who is in the room, in a curt voice, "Show these gentlemen out," thus reducing us to despair and sending us down the miserable staircase with dry throats and palpitating hearts.

[4]There were five Demoiselles de Nesle, four of whom form the heroines of the Goncourts' *Duchesse de Châteauroux et ses sœurs,* for only four out of the five successively, and at times conjointly, monopolised the amativeness of Louis XV over a period of about ten years. This is one of the most enduring of the Goncourts' books; the part played here by Mme de Châteauroux is comparable in vileness and audacity to that of La Merteuil in *Les Liaisons dangereuses.* . . . The Richelieu here mentioned is of course not Mr George Arliss' cardinal but the uncle of the ladies De Nesle, the Marshal Duke de Richelieu, an able administrator, a first-rate soldier, an epicene lecher, whom the *Petit Larousse* generously describes as *"spirituel, mais d'une moralité très douteuse."*

The next day we sent off a letter offering 400 francs—all the money we were able to lay our hands on at the moment—by way of appeasing our conscience and without the slightest hope, when, in the evening, husband and wife and even the baby at its mother's breast arrived, bringing us the drawing which we had no longer dreamt of possessing.

We spent the whole evening looking at Louis XV, memorandum book in hand, passing his troops in review, and at the microscopic soldiers and the crowd of onlookers held back by the stocks of the guards' muskets, and the chambermaids perched on tops of coaches, their skirts flying in the breeze—our pleasure mixed with a little remorse at having been able to give so little money for so beautiful a drawing to such poor people.

Undated.—Nothing is more charming, more exquisite, than the French wit of certain foreigners—the wit of Galiani, of the Prince de Ligne, of Heine.

December 15.—We have come upon some fragments of oratory by that emulator of Marat, upon the self-intoxicated eloquence of Chalier, whose phrases ring now and then like a verse of Victor Hugo. No one has really expressed the passion, the intensity, the fury, the great *delirium tremens* of that epoch. The historians of the Revolution—what meagre intelligences! We have been plunged lately into the *Memoirs* of Mme de La Roche-jaquelein. What a book! What an epic! What a novel! A mixture of the *Iliad* and the *Last of the Mohicans*. What pictures! The crossing of the Loire at Florent-le-Vieux[5] is as good as Napoleon's crossing of the Nile. And, as in antiquity, crammed with three-dimensional characters, warfare being still, then, battle between men and not between multitudes. The last of the heroes are to be found in this book. And the comedy intertwined with its tragedy, as when the remains of the ragged army togged itself out in turbans stolen from the theatre at La Flèche and stood up

[5]An incident in the Catholic-Royalist uprising of nobles and peasants, in 1793, against the Revolutionary regime. These memoirs were translated by Sir Walter Scott and published in *Constable's Miscellany* in 1827.

to be shot against the wall in old skirts. It makes one think of the discarded costume of Roman comic actors worn by Theban legionnaires. And what do you suppose happened to paintings in this Retreat of the Ten Thousand? A parish priest stood guard over them.

December.—We are at the Porte-Saint-Martin Theatre in Saint-Victor's box. It is the opening night of *The Fortune-Teller,* by Séjour and Mocquard. Saint-Victor's mouth is drawn, and in his face is that hard, stubborn look characteristic of him when he is embarrassed, or moved, or annoyed.

The house is filled with actresses' mothers, farce writers, critics, anonymous people who have a name only in the theatre, or have a hold over the manager, are creditors of the cast, relatives of the prompter or the ushers—and actresses out of work, provincial actors on holiday, writers' mistresses accompanied by their little sweethearts—not the gentlemen who keep them.

In a lower stage box, lording it over the dimly lit house, sits Jeanne de Tourbet, admirable in her pose of royal nonchalance and surrounded by a court of white ties in the shadow behind her. Here is Fiorentino, with his face and pose of a wax figure; Bischoffsheim, the friend of all the critics, flitting from box to box; little Dinah with her pretty serpentine head sitting in the balcony beside old Mother Félix and wearing a white muff. There, radiant and wrapped in gauze like a bride of Abydos, is Gisette, seated beside Mme Grangé, wife of the famous playwright; behind her, Dennery with his little fish-eyes. The patriarch of the *feuilleton,* podagral old Janin, shows the cuffs of his knitted red vest at his wrists. Doche is there with her gentle childlike eyes and attractive, irregular features crushed a little by the thrust of her blue hat. Théophile Gautier, torpid in the manner of a sphinx or a fat bonze, seems resigned in advance to anything that may come.

It is a gala night. There is a police officer outside our box, and near by is a flashing guardsman. Seated beside the box-opener is Alessandri, his eye on the corridor and his hand on an Italian dagger. The emperor and empress have arrived to applaud this play by Mocquard, the one-time compiler of *Celebrated Crimes* and now secretary to the emperor.

The play began, a play like all the others that this sort of writer always has in his desk drawer. It is not even imitation Hugo. Nevertheless, one can hear women murmur in a sort of swoon, "Oh, how well written!" But the play is not on stage; it is in the house. The plot and the drama reside in the fact that this is the night of the official announcement of the affair between Saint-Victor and the star of the play. All the lorgnettes in the house are focussed on the critic's marble face and on, exactly opposite us in the second balcony, the former mistress, the deserted Ariadne[6] Ozy in person, sitting with Virginia Duclay and staring at the ingrate over her noisily fluttering giant black fan in the midst of ironic titters.

During the interval people trampled on each other's feet in the passages where Janin sat breathing heavily on a bench and Villemessant was telling the story of the Gallifet duel[7] while Claudin floated about, Villemot displayed his white waistcoat from the Belle Jardinière stores, and Crémieux complained of pains in the chest in the voice of Grassot reciting Millevoye's verse, with Marchal standing by and hailing everybody that went past.

Saint-Victor's emotion was betrayed by his silence, by the fixity of his opera glass on the actress, and by his timid, child-like and candid cry at the fall of the curtain on the last act: "Lia alone! Lia alone!" while the audience were recalling the whole troupe and shouting, "All of them! All of them!"

The play ended. The ushers unrolled their cloths over the plush

[6]Even a sports writer in Paris will turn up a pair of soulful eyes and murmur, out of Racine's *Phèdre,*

Ariane, ma sœur, de quel amour blessée
Vous mourûtes au bord où vous fûtes laissée;

but not necessarily with more comprehension than a London bookmaker to whom might come the astounding impulse to babble suddenly, "To be or not to be . . ."

[7]Captain the Marquis de Gallifet, in a box at the Opéra with his wife and several friends on the evening of December 5, 1859, protested to the Count de Lauriston that he was "staring at the Marquise de Gallifet with singular persistence and bad taste." In the duel that followed, Gallifet was wounded. A second encounter took place a few days later. Gallifet being wounded a second time, the adversaries were reconciled— and probably breakfasted together at the Jockey Club, honour satisfied.

of the balconies. The curtain rose again showing the lamp tend-
ers carrying off the gas lamps from the walls of the décor. On the
dim stage we knocked against Fournier, who was moving about
like a black-clothed ghost in a white tie, asking people nervously
if the show was a success and saying he had seen none of it. All
this in the tone of a man asking if he was bankrupt.

Then firemen showed us down a small staircase and, at the
end of a dark passage, we saw a dressing room jammed with
people while at the door was a queue in which we stood for quite
a time. Effusions like those poured out in a sacristy after a wedding. Men stood aside to make way for avalanches of women
who flung themselves upon Lia and kissed her. Very soon, under
the influence of the general emotion of the evening and the re-
laxation of everybody's nerves, everybody was kissing everybody
else in, for the moment, perfect good faith. In the midst of this
chaos of powder puffs, pots of cold cream, boxes of false hair, in
the smoky, evil-smelling light furnished by the two copper
globes serving as gas lamps, seated on a piano stool covered
with pearl-grey morocco, Lia, looking like a little Gothic seraphim painted by a primitive master, her frail body lost in the
great folds of a brown dressing-gown, her head rising above all
the collapse of her body, responded to all the compliments
offered her on the talent she had displayed, and to the reproaches
that she had taken her scenes at too fast a pace—responded in a
voice at once tender and utterly weary, "Ah, my dears, my
dears!"

1860

Thursday, January 12.—We are in our dining room, that pretty box lined, enclosed and canopied in tapestry, against which we have hung Moreau the elder's triumphant "Revue du Roi," lighted up and enlivened by the soft glow of a bohemian glass sconce.

At our table sit Flaubert, Saint-Victor, Aurélien Scholl, Charles Edmond, Julie, and Mme Doche, whose slightly powdered hair is gathered attractively into a red net. The talk is of Mme Colet's novel,[1] *Elle et lui,* in which Flaubert is ferociously portrayed under the name of Léonce. At dessert Mme Doche went off to the dress rehearsal of the dramatization of Karr's novel, *La Pénélope normande,* which opens tomorrow night, and Saint-Victor, lacking copy for his *feuilleton,* went along with her and Scholl.

The rest stayed and talked about the theatre, Flaubert making fun of it rather rudely, as is his wont. "The theatre is not an art," he said; "it is a secret; and I got hold of that secret from one of the people who possess it. This is the secret. First, you have a few glasses of absinthe at the Café du Cirque. Then you say of

[1]Mme Colet's book was called *Lui: roman contemporain.* It was George Sand who wrote *Elle et lui,* about herself and Alfred de Musset (a subject more attractively treated in Charles Maurras's *Les Amants de Venise*).

whatever play is being discussed: 'It's not bad, but it wants cutting.' Or you say: 'Not bad, but there's no play there.' And you must be careful always to sketch plans but never to write a play yourself. After all, once you write a play, you're lost. I got the secret from an imbecile, but he got it from La Rounat. It was he who said that marvellous thing: 'Beaumarchais is a prejudice!' 'Beaumarchais?' he said: 'Phosphorus!' The swine that write plays nowadays! Let them first create a character like Cherubin!"[2]

The conversation passed on to this person and that among those in our circle, with a great deal about how hard it is to find people one can get along with, people who are not vicious, nor unbearable, nor middle class, nor ill bred. And everybody began to regret that Saint-Victor lacked certain qualities: he would make such a charming friend if only he possessed some warmth of heart, at least more than he had ever displayed towards any of us—this chap who after three years of intimacy was still capable of abruptly receiving his friends in the most chilling manner, still apt to hold out a frigid casual hand, as if a friend had suddenly become a stranger to him. Flaubert explained the man by his upbringing, saying that his triple education, the three institutions that had shaped him—the Church, the Army, and the École Normale[3]—always marked their man with an indelible seal.

We were left alone with Flaubert in the sitting room all foggy with cigar smoke, he striding back and forth across the carpet, knocking his bald head against the pendant of the chandelier, pouring out words, overflowing, delivering himself up to us as to his brothers in the spirit. He talked to us once again of his retired existence, solitary even in Paris, shut in and barred against

[2]Cherubin (a character in Beaumarchais' *Mariage de Figaro*) means to the French roughly what Peter Pan means to the English—very roughly, of course. An adolescent in love with a married woman and rather like an adorable puppy about it. Not quite so insistent, perhaps.

[3]No man—not even Flaubert—should be allowed to speak against the École Normale Supérieure de Paris. It is the last bastion of intellectual method and intellectual probity, a school that turns out a Jaurès as readily as a Bergson, a Romains even more readily than a Giraudoux. It was Philippe Le Bas, a *Normalien,* who said: "L'histoire c'est ma femme, le grec c'est ma maîtresse."

the world. His only recreation is his Sunday dinner at Mme Sabatier's, *La Présidente,* as Théophile Gautier and his friends call her. Flaubert has a horror of the country. He works ten hours a day but is a great waster of time, forgetting himself in things he picks up to read, and constantly running away from the book he is writing. He hardly ever warms to his work before five in the evening, although he sits down invariably at noon. He cannot write straightaway on a clean sheet of paper, having first to scrawl ideas over it the way a painter, beginning a canvas, experimentally smears his first colours on it before he tackles his subject.

Suddenly, counting up the few people who are interested in the choice of an epithet, the rhythm of a sentence, the *well-done* of a thing, Flaubert exclaimed, "Can you imagine the imbecility of struggling to eliminate the assonances from a sentence or the repetitions from a page? For whom? And to think that even when the book succeeds, the success you win is never the success you were after. Wasn't it the farcical side of *Madame Bovary* that made it a success? No doubt of it: success is always of a kind that misses fire. Form! Well, form. Who that reads a book is rejoiced and satisfied by the fact of form? And remark that form is the very element that makes the prosecutors suspicious of us—the tribunals being all for the classics. The classics! Another farce. Who has read the classics? You won't find eight professional writers who have read Voltaire. Read, I say; actually read him. And are there five members of the Society of Dramatic Authors who could tell you the names of the plays of Thomas Corneille? They talk about imagery: but the classics are full of imagery; there is nothing else in our tragic writers. Pétrus Borel himself would never have dared set down an image as senseless as

'Brûle de plus de feux que je n'en allumai'![4]

[4]"Ablaze with more flames than ever I lighted" is a sufficiently awkward translation. This line of verse, in Racine's *Andromaque,* I, v, is addressed to Andromache, Trojan Hector's widow, by Pyrrhus, son of Achilles and one of the victorious incendiaries of the great Asiatic city. This is Pyrrhus' way of letting Andromache know that by not requiting his love she is causing him more suffering than even the Trojans endured at his hands. As for Pétrus Borel, he is the archetype of romantic nineteenth century Gongorists.

There has never been a period in which art for art's sake was sanctified as it was in the address to the Academy delivered by a classicist, by Buffon, when he said: 'The manner in which a truth is enunciated is even more useful to humanity than that truth itself.' If that isn't art for art's sake, what is? Or La Bruyère, saying: 'The art of writing is the art of defining and portraying.' "

Thereupon Flaubert revealed that his three breviaries of style were La Bruyère, certain pages of Montesquieu, and certain chapters of Chateaubriand. And in a moment, eyes popping out of his head, face flushed, arms upraised in the breadth of reach of an Antaeus, he poured forth from his chest and his throat fragments of the *Dialogue between Sylla and Eucrates,*[5] flinging the sounds into our faces with a rumble that was like the roaring of a lion.

He went back to his Carthaginian novel, telling us of his research, his reading up of the subject, the volumes of notes he had taken, and saying, "Do you want to know my whole ambition? Give me a respectable, intelligent man, ready to lock himself up for four hours with my novel, and I guarantee to give him a cranial *bump of historical haschisch.* That is all I ask." Then he added, in a melancholy voice, "After all, work is still the best means of getting the better of life."

January 24.—We are out today (*Men of Letters*). That fever is in us which drives you out of your house and into the street. At the end of the day we found ourselves on the boulevard du Temple, in Flaubert's study, with a Buddha on the mantelshelf. His desk was covered with the pages of his novel, and the pages were nothing but scratched-out lines. About our book he was warm in his compliments, which did our hearts much good and made us happy in this frank, loyal and healthily demonstrative friendship.

During the evening we wandered through the boulevards, weighing our chances of a duel, of success, looking at the displays

[5]By Montesquieu, dated 1722. In this dialogue Sylla explains to the author's fictitious philosopher, Eucrates, why he surrendered his dictatorship, saying, "I believed that I had fulfilled my destiny when I saw that there were no great actions left for me to perform."

in the bookshops with a certain nervous excitation which we were unable to master.

Sunday, January 29.—Spent the evening at Flaubert's with Bouilhet talking about de Sade to whom Flaubert, as if fascinated, constantly reverts. "He is the last word in Catholicism," said Flaubert. "Let me explain: he is the spirit of the Inquisition, the spirit of torture, the spirit of the mediæval Church, the horror of nature. Do you know that there is not an animal, not a tree, in de Sade?" Then he talked about romanticism, saying that when he was a schoolboy he slept with a dagger under his pillow, and that, driving out, he would stop before Casimir Delavigne's country place and get up on the seat to shout vulgar abuse at the man.

Monday, January 30.—We were told at Dentu's publishing office that Janin had reviewed our *Men of Letters* in this morning's *Débats.* We bought the *Débats* and found in it eighteen columns of unmerciful slating in which Janin accuses us of having written a polemic against our craft, drawn a picture in contempt of letters. Thus do the critics speak of a book which is the best and most courageous act of our lives, a book in which what is low in letters is so displayed only in order that what is high may be raised by contrast to greater heights and be shown as yet more worthy of respect.

Tuesday, February 7.—. . . From Janin's house at Passy we went to Gavarni's at the Point-du-Jour. We found him troubled by the sort of apoplectic stroke he had on Saturday, saying, "I don't like things I do not understand." We talked of the women he had watched dance at the Opera Ball and asked if he had made any sketches of them. "No, no; but I carried them away in my mind. In six months they will be clearly present to me. The whole thing is to sum up the picture in a very simple idea. What is it, after all? A shirt without a waistline: the rest is adjustment to the caprices and fantasies of the particular woman."

Therewith he spread on our knees an album of his early litho-

graphs, which he had recently dug up, and we saw what profound, serious, patient, scrupulous studies of nature he had made
before he achieved his facility in drawing without a model,
before he reached his *imagination of the true*. The thing is visible everywhere in the album—in Feydeau's mother, Feydeau's
father; in d'Abrantès; even in Henri Berthoud's back, the drawing of that stranger's back. He stopped us at a little picture of a
dance that was like an insect ball, making fun of its meagreness,
the consciousness of the dance floor that was in the drawing, its
finish and preciosity, but where there was, nevertheless, the animation of a dance and a rather satisfying contrast of blacks and
whites, of tail coats and frocks—though he said that in those days
he had still been unable to render either black or the velvety
greys.

Sunday, February 20.—Sitting beside his fire, Flaubert told us the
story of his first love. He was on his way to Corsica. Up to that
time he had done no more than lose his innocence with one of
his mother's maids. He stopped at a little hotel in Marseilles
where a family of women from Peru had arrived with ebony
furniture inlaid with mother-of-pearl at which all the hotel
marvelled. Three women in silk dressing gowns falling in a
straight line from the back to the heels, flanked by a little Negro
dressed in nankeens and wearing Turkish slippers: in the eyes
of a young Norman who had hitherto travelled only from Normandy to the Champagne and from the Champagne to Normandy, their exoticism was very tempting. In his mind's eye he
could see them in a patio filled with tropical flowers and foun-
tains. And one morning, coming back from diving in the Mediterranean, he found himself face to face with one of these women
at the door of her room, a woman thirty-five years old, a magnificent creature; and he kissed her, one of those kisses in which one
delivers up one's soul. The result was a fountain of delight, then
tears, then letters, and finally silence.

Since then Flaubert has been back to Marseilles several times,
has inquired, and has been unable to discover what became of
those three women. The last time he went through was on his

way to Tunis, a journey necessitated by his Carthaginian novel. The house, which he had been at pains to visit on each previous voyage, was gone. He looked for it, he sought it—and he saw finally that the ground floor was given over to a toyshop and the first story to a hairdresser. He went up, had himself shaved, and recognized the wallpaper of the bedroom.

March 4.—We talked with Flaubert about Hugo's *Légendes des siècles.* What strikes him most of all in Hugo, who is ambitious to be thought a thinker, is the absence of thought. Hugo is not a thinker: he is, as Flaubert calls him, a naturalist. There is the sap of trees in his blood. Then Flaubert spoke with contemptuous anger of Feuillet, of the base court he pays to women in his novels, saying, "That proves he does not love women. Men who love women write books in which they tell what they have suffered through women, for we love only that which has made us suffer." And we said, "Yes, that explains maternity."

At that moment three fat quarto volumes were brought in from the Imperial Printing Works, on the mines of Algeria, in which he hopes to find a word he needs for his book on Carthage.

Suddenly he began to recite to us fantastically comic fragments out of a tragedy which he and Bouilhet had drafted on the discovery of vaccine, written on the purest principles of Marmontel, wherein everything, including "pockmarked as a sieve," was in metaphors eight lines long. He had worked three years at this tragedy—a witness to the oxlike persistence of his mind, even in comic imaginings worth no more than a quarter hour of joking.

When he left school he wrote a great deal but published none of it, with the exception of two short articles in a newspaper in Rouen. He regretted a volume of about one hundred fifty pages written in his first year out of school and telling of the visit of a splenetic young man to a harlot, a psychological novel too full, said he, of his personality. In *Madame Bovary,* he affirmed, there was only one character taken from life, and that at a considerable distance—the character of a paymaster in Napoleon's armies, a debauched swaggerer and blackguard who would threaten his mother with his sabre to get money out of her, went about dressed in leather breeches, with a police cap on his head and high boots on his feet, a pillar of the Lalanne Circus whose bareback riders would come to drink hot wine warmed in basins by him, while their women would give birth to children under his roof.

Undated.—Molière is a great event in the history of the middle classes, a solemn declaration of the soul of the Third Estate. I see in him the inauguration of the reign of common sense and practical reasoning, the end of high chivalry and high poetry in all things. Woman, love, all gallantry and noble follies are here reduced to the mean yardstick of the home and the dowry. Everything that implies spirit and spontaneity is here averted and checked.

Corneille was the last herald of nobility; Molière is the first poet of the middle classes.

March 10.—On *Men of Letters* I have received from Mme George Sand a letter as heartening as the handclasp of a friend. The truth is that our book is having a *succès d'estime:* it is not selling. The first day we believed in a large sale. Two weeks have passed and the book has sold five hundred copies, with no certainty of a second printing. After all, we are proud of our book and believe that despite the acrimony of the journalists it will not be forgotten; and to those who might ask us, "Do you, then, esteem yourselves so highly?" we would answer, with the pride of the abbé Maury, "Very little when we look at ourselves; very much when we look at others."

It is fortunate that there are two of us, each able to sustain the other against such indifference and such denial of success; it is good to be two, not one, when we promise ourselves that we shall violate Fortune, whom we see coquetting with so many impotent men.

Perhaps these lines, now written so calmly and without the least despair, will one day serve to teach the virtue of courage to workers in another century. Let them learn, then, that after ten years of work and the publication of fifteen volumes, after so much done in the watches of the night, after such conscientious perseverance, after success, even, and an historical work which has already taken its place in Europe, after this very novel, *Men of Letters,* in which our enemies themselves concede us "masterly power", there is not a gazette, not a review great or small, that has approached us, so that we wonder if our next novel will not have to be published at our own expense; and all this while the little rummagers of erudition and the more jejune quill drivers of the short story are published, remunerated and reprinted.

Sunday, March 11.—We get up from table. A woman with a delicate profile, a straight, pretty little nose and a wittily cut mouth, the hairdress of a bacchante lending today to her face something excited and sprightly, a woman with strange eyes which seem to be laughing at the moment when her words are most serious. All women are enigmas, but this is the most indecipherable of them all. She is like her glance, which never rests for any time on anything, and across which there pass, clouded in a single second, all the various glances that can come from a woman's eyes. Everything about this creature is incomprehensible, and I dare say she hardly understands herself. Observation cannot find a foothold here; it slides about as if on the surface of capriciousness. Her soul, her mood, the beat of her heart, are things precipitate and fleeting as the pulse of Folly. She is like a *Violante,* one of those courtezans of the sixteenth century, those instinctive and immoderate beings who wore a kind of mask of enchantment, the night smile of the Gioconda. Often, while she is jesting, there is almost the fall of a tear in the middle of her words, and almost always her tenderest phrases end with a strident *rr-r-r* that is like the rattle of irony. It is hard to be certain what this woman wants most as between the alternatives of being yours and of making fun of you.

April 10.—Flaubert, who is off to Croisset to give away his niece in marriage, came round to say good-bye. He entertained us with a description of an imaginary character who had filled his youth and that of his friends, above all his intimate school friend, Poitevin, whom he spoke of as a powerful metaphysician, a rather arid nature but of extraordinarily elevated ideas.

They had invented this character, and they would take turns slipping into its skin and expressing through its mind, so to speak, their own high spirits. The character was rather difficult to explain. He was referred to by the collective and generic name of *Le Garçon*. To them he represented the senseless rubble of romanticism, of materialism, of everything in the world. They attributed to him a complete personality with all the manias of a real person complicated by every sort of middle-class limitation of mind and sensibility. This fabrication was a slow, stubborn, heavy, and continual hoax, like the practical jokes of a provincial town or like a German joke.

Le Garçon had gestures that were peculiar to himself and were the gestures of an automaton. His laughter was jerky and strident, like that of a fantastical character, and his physical strength was enormous. Nothing can better express this strange creature, who literally obsessed Flaubert and his friends, maddened them, than the customary burlesque they went through every time they passed before the cathedral at Rouen.

One of them would say: "Gothic architecture is beautiful; it elevates the soul." Instantly he who was *Le Garçon* of the moment would exclaim in a loud voice, so as to be overheard by the passers-by: "Yes, it's beautiful; so was St Bartholomew's Eve; and the Dragonnades; and the Edict of Nantes. They were beautiful too!"[6] *Le Garçon's* eloquence would shine brightest of all in the parodies of the celebrated trials of history which they would bring off in Flaubert's father's billiard room in the hospital at

[6]*La Saint-Barthélemy* is the name given to the massacre of the Protestants in Paris during the night of the twenty-third of August 1572. Charles IX is thought to have ordered it against his will on the repeated insistence of his mother, Catherine de' Medici, widow of Henri II and mother of three kings of France. . . . *Les Dragonnades* were organized by Louvois, one of the ministers of Louis XIV, and consisted in persecutions of Protestants in Southern France, by the Dragoons, in 1681–85. . . . The Edict of Nantes was Henri IV's grant of free worship to the Calvinists in 1598. Given the sort of anti-Catholic sport in which Flaubert and his friends were engaged, it was more likely that the shouting was about the revocation of the Edict (which led to the expatriation of many Protestants from France) by Louis XIV in 1685, the year he married La Maintenon.

Rouen. They would pronounce the most fantastically comical orations in defence of the accused; there would be lusty pleadings three hours long, and funeral orations in honour of living people.

A whole history of *Le Garçon* existed, to which each of the boys contributed his part. He wrote poetry, for example, and eventually became keeper of the *Hôtel de la Farce* where a Sewage Feast was held. Homais seems to me the portrait of *Le Garçon* reduced to novel size.

June 7.—Bar-sur-Seine. Something very characteristic of our make-up is that we see nothing in nature which does not remind us of art. Here is a horse in a stable, and instantly a drawing by Géricault takes shape in our minds; and the cooper hammering a barrel in the neighbouring courtyard makes us think of a wash drawing done in China ink by Boissieu.

June.—A stupendous notion of education left by fathers to their sons under Napoleon I! The father of one of my relatives said to him: "You must learn Latin, because you can make yourself understood everywhere if you speak Latin. You must learn to play the violin, because if you are a prisoner of war in a village you will be able to play for the peasants, who will want to dance and will pay you for playing; whereas in a town, if you play the violin people will think you are a gentlemanly young man, of good family, and will receive you into their homes, and you will make useful acquaintances. And also, you must be prepared to sleep as comfortably on a gun carriage as in your own bed, and by way of practice I want you to spend eight nights sleeping on a blanket which we shall tack down on the floor."

August 24.—Aubryet gave a dinner this evening for Charles Edmond, Saint-Victor, Flaubert, Ludovic Halévy, Claudin, Théophile Gautier, and ourselves. Fifth story, rue Taitbout, an apartment with which a decorator for kept women has had his way. A drawing room lined with padded pigeon-blood silk and a ceiling by Faustin Besson. A dining room furnished with those odds and ends of porcelain and glass which Arsène Houssaye has made fashionable. We sat down to table, and immediately conversation flared up on the subject of Ponsard, who was said to be "groping Titania" in a play written in imitation of Shakespeare.

Saint-Victor said: "Have you never seen Ponsard? Imagine a comic copper writing his own farces. You were good, Théo; you gave him a fearful slating."

"Oh, me," said Gautier; "I am the fellow they always use to beat up the people I admire. I am the ass's cheekbone they use to lay out Hugo."

"Well," said Flaubert emphatically; "there's one fellow I abominate even more than Ponsard, and that is that lad Feuillet. I have read his *Jeune homme pauvre*—who has 10,000 francs a year—three times. Do you know how you can recognize that his young man is a gentleman? He can ride a horse. And what's more, in all Feuillet's books there are young men who have albums and sketch landscapes."

One of the guests sighed. "Do you chaps know what it took to make a man rich twenty years ago? Read Paul de Kock; it's there: Charles was rich, for he had 6,000 francs a year, ate truffled partridge every night, and kept an Opéra dancer—and what is more, it could have been done on that!"

Twenty-two-year-old champagne was served, and the talk was of those who had died during the Revolution, of a sort of exhumation of the Madeleine Cemetery and La du Barry's scaffold, out of which came, heaven knows how, a discussion of ancient art between Saint-Victor and Gautier, who declared that Phidias was decadent.

When we came away from table Saint-Victor said, stirring his coffee, that today was the anniversary of the Massacre of St Bartholomew's Eve and that Voltaire would have been in a fever about it. "Perfectly right!" said Flaubert in a theatrical voice. And both Saint-Victor and Flaubert were off, proclaiming Voltaire the most sincere and guileless of apostles, while we protested with all the strength of our conviction. The room was filled with shouts, outbursts and vociferations. "A martyr" . . . "In exile

part of his life" . . . "Yes, but what of his popularity?" . . . "A
sensitive nature" . . . "The Calas Case"[7] . . . "On a par with
Balzac's Peytel Affair" . . . Flaubert roared: "I say the man was
a saint!" Somebody else: "You, who are a physiologist: have you
never looked at his mouth?" Gautier: "As for me, I can't bear
the man. To me he is *priestish,* a sky pilot, the Alderman of
Deism; yes, that's what he is, the Alderman of Deism."

The dispute died down for a moment and arose again with
Horace for subject, some opining that he was a kind of Béranger
while Saint-Victor extolled the purity of his language, which
Gautier thought decidedly inferior to the admirable Latin of
Catullus. And with that we reached the question of the immortality of the soul, a subject inescapable by superior minds who
have just risen from an excellent dinner.

"It won't do," said Gautier. "Can you imagine my soul retain-
ing consciousness of my being, remembering that I wrote for *Le
Moniteur,* number 13, Quai Voltaire, and that the owners of my
paper were Turgan and Dalloz. . . ."

Saint-Victor cut in: "Or can you imagine the soul of our friend
the alderman turning up before God in gold spectacles and beginning a speech, 'Architect of the universe' . . ."

Gautier went calmly on: "We all accept the notion of oblivion
before life; why should it be hard to conceive of it after life. The
fable of the ancients, the lethal cup—that is the way it should be.
The only thing I am afraid of is that particular moment when

[7]The Calas Affair was the Dreyfus Case of the eighteenth century, and the part
played in it by Voltaire won him the admiration of all Europe. Jean Calas, a Protestant,
was a well-to-do merchant in the city of Toulouse. One of his sons desiring to follow
the law, and being, as a Protestant, ineligible for the Bar, became a Catholic. Another
son had the same ambition but was repelled by the notion of apostasy. That second son
"fell into a sadness, then into a fast . . . and by this declension" hanged himself.
Foolishly, the family thought to avert scandal by concealing the whole business; but
the town got wind of it, the good burghers of Toulouse, like a Tennessee mob, took
fire, and the father was accused of murdering his son for reasons of religion. On the
tenth of March 1762 Jean Calas was broken on the wheel and his body burned at the
stake. His property was confiscated and his family were scattered, some members
banished and others locked up in convents. Voltaire heard of this quite by chance,
acted with a vigour and a courage for which he was not ordinarily conspicuous, and
singlehanded obtained the declaration of Jean Calas's innocence on the ninth of March
1765, the rehabilitation of his name, and the restoration of his property to his family.
David de Beaudrigue, one of the overzealous municipal officers responsible for the
prosecution, went mad and killed himself.

my ego is about to enter into the night, when I shall lose the consciousness of having lived."

"There is, nevertheless, a great Clockmaker," Claudin stammered timidly.

"Oh, if we are to go into clockmaking! . . . Do you know, Claudin, that matter also is infinite? It is a recent discovery."

"Yes, yes," Saint-Victor threw in; "Heine said it first: we ask what the stars are, what God is, what life means; and our mouths are stopped with a bit of clay. But is that an answer?"

"Listen, Claudin," Gautier went on placidly and imperturbably. "Assume the sun was inhabited. A man five feet tall on earth would be seven hundred and fifty leagues high on the sun. That is to say, that the soles of your shoes, assuming you wore heels, would be two leagues long, a length equal to the depth of the ocean at its deepest. Now listen to me, Claudin: and along with your two leagues of boot soles you would possess seventy-five leagues of masculinity in the natural state."

"All that is very fine, but still . . ." Claudin was saying stiffly when Saint-Victor broke in brutally:

"Catholicism and Markowski! That is your motto, Claudin."

"You see," Gautier said, coming over to us; "the immortality of the soul, free will—it is very pleasant to be concerned with these things before one is twenty-two years old; but afterwards such subjects are no longer seemly. One ought then to be concerned to have a mistress who does not get on one's nerves; to have a decent place to live; to have a few passable pictures on the wall. And most of all, to be writing well. There is what is important: sentences that hang together . . . and a few metaphors. Yes, a few metaphors. They embellish life."

"Markowski? Markowski? What's that?" Flaubert was repeating in a corner of the room with the ignorance of a true provincial.

"My dear chap"—it was Claudin answering him—"Markowski was a bootmaker. He began to teach himself to play the violin, and also to dance by himself. Pretty soon he was organizing balls, with the aid of a number of tarts. The good Lord blessed his efforts. He escaped with his life from the several drubbings that Adèle Courtois arranged to have administered to him, and now he is the proprietor of the house he lives in."

Going down Aubryet's stairs with Gautier I asked if it did not disturb him to be no longer living in Paris.

"Oh," he said; "it makes no difference to me. This is no longer the Paris I knew. It is Philadelphia, St Petersburg, anything you like."

November 18.—My Paris, the Paris in which I was born, the Paris of the manners of 1830 to 1848, is vanishing, both materially and morally. Social life is in the way of a great evolution. I see women, children, men and their wives, families, in the cafés. The home is dying. Life threatens to become public. The club for the upper classes, the café for the lower—to this, society and the people are coming. Because of this, I feel like a man merely passing through Paris, a traveller. I am foreign to that which is to come, to that which is, and a stranger to these new boulevards that go straight on, without meandering, without the adventures of perspective, implacably a straight line, without any of the atmosphere of Balzac's world, making one think of some American Babylon of the future. It is stupid to live in a time of growth; the soul is as uncomfortable as a body in a damp new house.

Undated.—Perhaps true liberty exists for the individual only when he is not yet regimented in a flawlessly civilized society in which he loses complete possession of himself, of his family, of his goods. Particularly since 1789 the state has become dashed absorbing and has cut jolly deep into everybody's rights on pretext of the general good; and I wonder if, in the name of that absolute called The State, and given the despotism of French bureaucracy, we are not in for a tyranny far beyond anything known under Louis XIV.

November 21.—Working hard at our novel, *Sister Philomène*.

December 18.—We have decided to present the letter which, thanks to Flaubert, Dr Follin gave us to M. Edmond Simon, an interne in Velpeau's ward at the Charity Hospital. Our novel requires that we take notes in the hospital from life, from the quick, from the gaping wound itself.

Sunday, December 23.—We spent part of the night at the Charity Hospital. . . .

Far, far in the distance, through an arched glass door, I saw the movement of a little glow which brightened and became a light. Something white was coming towards me with this light and was lighted up by it. That something opened the glass door and proved to be two women, one holding a candle in her hand. When they came into the ward I saw that one was the sister, making her rounds, and the other a hospital servant. The sister must have been a novice, for she was not wearing the black veil. She was all in white, in a kind of white quilted stuff, with a white headband across her forehead. The servant wore a camisole and petticoat, a black kerchief, and on her head a nightcap.

They went over to a bed, the sister standing at the head with candle uplifted, and the servant at the foot. In a moment I heard a voice so mild and gentle that I took it to be the voice of the patient. I was wrong: it was the sister, speaking soothingly to an old woman, speaking in a firmly tranquillizing voice, the voice we use to persuade our children to do what they don't want to do. "Does your seat pain you?" The old woman muttered something in an unintelligible and irritated voice. The sister put back the blanket, took up the helpless and noisome woman in her arms and turned her over so that I saw a back covered with welts, like the back of an infant bruised by swaddling bands too tightly wrapped. Skilfully she withdrew from beneath the displaced body the soiled drawsheet and, still talking ceaselessly in a soothing voice, assured the old woman that they would lay a poultice to her, give her a drink. . . . And all this ended with the basin.

Such a scene fills one's heart with admiration; its grandeur is so simple, that in comparison the much-vaunted *thy-neighbour-lovers,* the lovers of the people, seem petty indeed. It is truly a triumph for a religion to have brought womankind, that vessel of frailty, that delicate nervous apparatus, to this victory over disgust with nature, to have placed the affectivity of a sensitive creature so entirely in the service of the sufferings of the abject, the sordid, and the impoverished. The religions of the future will be hard put to it to inspire a like devotion.

Seeing this young woman leaning tenderly over the horrible and squalid hag who was abusing her, suddenly, as one might think of a leering blackguard, there came into my mind Béranger, who thought it *screaming,* in one of his poems, to bring a Sister of Mercy and an Opéra dancer into heaven, each with the record of her services, and those services of equal value in his eyes. The enemies of Catholicism have always been lacking in respect for woman as woman, a lack which is the sign and characteristic of low-bred people; and the great patron of this fraternity, M. de Voltaire, desiring to write a trashy poem, necessarily chose as heroine Jeanne d'Arc, the nation's saint.

Undated.—About every painting that gives rise to a moral impression we may say, as a general truth, that it is a bad painting.

December 26.—We hear the tocsin ring in the chapel, and through the window giving out on the courtyard we see the corner of a pauper's hearse waiting for the corpse. . . .

We went back at four o'clock to hear prayers, and at the sound of the frail, virginal voice of the kneeling novice, offering up to God the thanks of all the suffering and the agony that rises from the hospital cots towards the altar, tears came twice into our eyes and we felt that we had not the strength to go on with our inquiry, that for the time being we had had all we could bear.

We left, and only then did we perceive that our nervous system, of whose experience we had been unconscious so long as we were using all our faculties of observation, had been stirred and shattered, without our realizing it, by everything we had been through. A dark melancholy floated round us. In the evening we were so jumpy that the sound of a dropped fork sent a shudder through all our body and filled us with an almost angry impatience.

December 27.—It is horrible, how that hospital odour follows one. I do not know if it is real or imaginary, but we are constantly washing our hands to get rid of it. The very scent we put into the water takes on—so we imagine—the insipid and nauseating smell of salve.

Undated.—It is truly remarkable that the four writers who have been haled into the police courts should be precisely those four men who are the most purely devoted to their craft and the freest from commercialism, the most wholly consecrated to art— Baudelaire, Flaubert and ourselves.

1861

January.—One of the particular characteristics of our novels is that they will be the most *historical* novels of this epoch, the novels which will contribute more facts and true verities than any others to the moral history of our time.

January 18.—Murger is dying of a disease which decomposes the living tissue. The other day, when he was trimming his moustaches, the lip came away with the hair. When I last saw Murger, about a month ago, at the Café Riche, he was gay and happy and looked in perfect health. A one-act play of his had just been produced with success at the Palais-Royal. Reviewing this trifle, the newspapers had written more about him than on the score of any of his novels; and he had said to us that it was too silly to work oneself to death over books no one appreciated, and which brought you no money; that thenceforward he would write only for the theatre and make money painlessly.

When you think of it, his death is like a death in Holy Writ, a divine chastisement of *La Bohème,* chastisement of that form of revolt against the hygiene of body and mind which results in Murger's life ending at the age of forty-two for want of vitality with which to withstand suffering, ending in complaint of the odour of rotting flesh in his chamber without realization of the fact that that flesh is his own.

Thursday, January.—There are fifteen hundred of us in the court-yard of the Dubois nursing home, breathing in an icy fog and stamping in the mud. The chapel is too small to hold all the people who have turned up from the Latin Quarter and come down from Montmartre. Looking at this mob, I thought what a singular thing is the justice rendered by this initial posterity that outlives a scarcely cold talent. Behind Heine's hearse there were scarcely six or seven people; behind Musset's, forty at the most. The coffin of a man of letters has a career parallel to that of his books.

Meanwhile, there was not the slightest sorrow in the heart of anyone in this crowd. I have never known a funeral procession to follow a dead man[1] in which there was so little talk of him. Théophile Gautier talked of a discovery he had just made about the taste of oil that had so long intrigued him in beefsteaks, saying that it came from the fact that steers are fattened nowadays on vegetable-oil cakes. Saint-Victor's subject was the bibliography of *erotica,* the cataloguing of obscene books, and he was asking the bibliophiles present to lend him Andrea de Nerciat's *Diable au corps.*

February.—One does not write the books one wants to write. There is a fatality in the first hazard that dictates the idea of the book. And there is an unknown force, a superior will, a sort of compulsion to write, which commands the work and guides the pen; so much so that at times the book which comes forth from your hands seems not to have been born of yourself at all; it amazes you like a thing that was in you unknown to yourself. This is what I feel about *Sister Philomène.*

Sunday, March 17.—Flaubert said to us today: "The story or plot of a novel is of no interest to me. When I write a novel I have in mind rendering a colour, a shade. For example, in my Carthaginian novel I want to do something *purple.* In *Madame Bovary* all I was after was to render a special tone, that colour of the mouldiness of a wood louse's existence. The plot of the novel

---

[1]Murger, of course.

was so little a subject of concern to me that, a few days before beginning to write, I had still in mind a different character to the one I created. My first 'Madame Bovary' was to have been set in the surroundings and painted in the tone I actually used, but she was to have been a chaste and devout old maid. And then I saw that this would be an impossible character."

Coming back to the house we found that Lévy had returned the manuscript of *Sister Philomène* with a note of regret, excusing himself on the score of the horror and lugubriousness of the subject. And it occurs to us that if our novel was anybody's novel, a flat, pedestrian job, the novel anyone might write, and which the public has already read a score of times, it would be accepted out of hand. Oh, one pays for the luxury of wanting to create something new!

Decidedly, men and things, publishers and public, everything conspires to give us a literary career more strewn with repulses, defeats, bitterness and hardships than any other; and after ten years of work, of struggle, of battle, of multiple attacks and few eulogies by the press, we are still reduced to publishing a novel at our own expense. And this in a time when, it is said, Hector Crémieux is paid 2,800 francs for the words of a song in a show.

Sunday, March 31.—Lunched at Flaubert's with Sari and Lagier, the conversation running wholly on the theatre. It was only in this century that actors began to seek to create the effects of *pictures* in their presence on stage. Thus Paulin Menier, standing with his back to the audience in postures copied from Gavarni's drawings; Rouvère, contributing to the stage the tortuous poses and epileptic hands out of Delacroix's lithographs for *Faust*.

Sari talked interestingly about his supernumeraries at twenty sous each, his chorus at thirty sous apiece; and of the incurable disease of the theatre which, once caught, always brings people back to it—a disease, he said, like prostitution or mendicancy. He went on: these workers, most of them very intelligent in what they do, will leave jobs paying them ten francs a day in order to earn just enough to eat a four-sous plate of onion soup in some dirty pub in the rue Basse—lured, driven out of their wits, by the accidented life of the theatre, by the free comradeship of its men and women, by the gossip and chatter backstage, and by their feverish interest in the success or the failure of plays and the *electrification* of applause.

Lagier, for her part, tried to define the *sui generis* odour of the theatre, that general odour composed of the particular smell of the illuminating gas mixed with the smell of the warm wood of the scenery, the smell of the *peppery* dust of the wings, the smell of the gluey paint of the scenery—all these combined smells of this factitious world creating a giddy atmosphere which, as she put it, makes an actress neigh with trumpeting nostrils as soon as she comes on stage.

And from the odour of the theatre she went on to the perfumes worn by particular actors and actresses, saying that Frédérick Lemaître always went on with pods of vanilla sewn into the collars of his clothes.

April 7.—Attended the dress rehearsal of a play in a small boulevard theatre, a play filled with women. It was like a prize contest in a bawdyhouse. This sort of theatre is absolutely nothing but an excitation of all the low appetites of the audience. And the highest invention that their fancy could reach was to dress their women in military costume, to graft jingoism on eroticism. A woman with a well-shaped bottom and legs not too knock-kneed, saving the French flag—irresistible, one must admit.

April 11.—We feel ourselves lucky to have been able to sell our *Sister Philomène* to the Librairie Nouvelle at four sous a copy; but we are somewhat consoled for this miserable success, after which we had to run, by the fact that on coming home we found a letter from a Russian publisher asking the right to bring out a translation of all our historical works.

Sunday, April 18.—Flaubert told us today that before taking *Madame Bovary* to Lévy, he had offered it to Jacottet, of the Librairie Nouvelle. "Your book is very good," Jacottet said; "it is *chiselled;* but of course you cannot aspire to the success of

Amédée Achard, who has two books with me now; and I cannot contract to publish you this year." Flaubert was raging: "It's *chiselled!* What a piece of insolence on the part of a publisher! I don't mind a publisher exploiting an author; but he has no right to express a literary judgment. I have always been grateful to Lévy for the fact that he has never said a word to me about my book."

Monday, May 6.—At four o'clock we were at Flaubert's, having been invited with Gleyre, the painter, to hear a reading of *Salammbô.* From four until seven Flaubert read aloud in his moving, sonorous voice that cradles you in a sound like a bronze murmur. At seven we dined, and directly after dinner, with time out for a single pipe, the reading was resumed; and between readings and summary accounts of certain sections of the book (some of them not completely finished), it was two in the morning before he got through the last chapter.

I shall write in this place what I sincerely think of the work of a man I love and whose first book I admired unreservedly. *Salammbô* is less than what I expected from Flaubert. The personality of the author, which was so well dissembled in *Madame Bovary,* comes through this book enlarged, declamatory, melodramatic, and in love with coarse colours and illumination. Flaubert sees the Orient, the Orient of antiquity, under the aspect of the Algerian bazaars. The effort is undoubtedly immense, the patience infinite, and—despite my criticism of it—the talent rare; but in this book there are none of those brilliant flashes, none of those revelations by analogy, which bring to light a bit of the soul of a nation that has passed into oblivion. As for moral restoration, our good Flaubert suffers from illusions: the sentiments of his characters are the commonplace and general sentiments of all mankind and not the sentiments of a particularly Carthaginian mankind. His Mathô is at bottom no more than an opera tenor in a barbaric poem.

It cannot be denied that by strength of will, by hard work, by the strangeness of the colour borrowed from all the colours of the Orient, there are moments when Flaubert is able to transport your brain, your eye, into the world of his invention; but he creates bewilderment rather than vision because of the lack of perspective in the drawing, the unrelieved brilliance of the tints, the interminable length of the descriptions.

And then, the syntax is too beautiful, is a syntax for old phlegmatic university professors, a syntax of the funeral oration, without a single one of those daring turns of phrase, those clean, elegant lines, those terse wheelings of the sentence, in which vibrates the modernity of contemporary style. And there are comparisons that are not fused with the sentence but are hooked on by an *as*, a *like*, so that I am reminded of those artificially forced camellias, each bud of which is fastened to the stem by a pin. And still and always those declamatory phrases; never any muted harmonies suited to the sweetness of the things that are happening or the characters who are speaking, and so on.

To my mind there is only one modern writer who was able to discover a tongue with which to make the ancients speak: it is Maurice de Guérin in *Le Centaure*.

Undated.—A pretty example of the wit of a Parisian debtor. Vachette arrived at the studio of a young painter just at the moment when the bailiff had turned up to seize his effects. The debt was settled by Vachette. "Tell me," he said; "have you many debts like this in Paris?" "Twenty thousand francs or so." "Twenty thousand francs! You'll never be free of debt." "Oh, only about fifteen or sixteen hundred of it is serious. The rest is owed to friends like you."

June 19.—Dined the other day at the Grosse-Tête, in the passage de l'Opéra, surrounded by the world of letters and the theatre. There is not a world in the world from which one comes away more despondent, with a greater sense of something unsatisfied. One has not been elbowed by men in such a place, but by reviews, by paradoxes, by witticisms. Not a word, not a handshake, in which there is any warmth, any communication of friendliness. One leaves such a place exhausted, chilled, disappointed. And yet those people live in that aridity as in their native element.

They have, more than any other group of men, a way of asking how one is, with nothing but their lips, that is more cruelly indifferent than silence.

Ponson du Terrail frequents that restaurant, his gig visible through the windows on the horizon of the boulevard—the only carriage in all Paris belonging to a man of letters. His turn-out costs the poor chap enough, both in work and in the humility of his literary position. It was he who said to the editors of a newspaper in which he was publishing a long novel serially: "Let me know three installments in advance if the thing is boring your readers, and I will wind it up in one." Really, one sells vegetables with more pride.

July 11.—Spent the day delivering copies of *Sister Philomène* to the critics and then dined with Charles Edmond, back from a few days with Victor Hugo, at Brussels. The poet had just written the last words of *Les Misérables* when Edmond arrived. "Dante," said Hugo, "made an Inferno out of poetry; I have tried to make one out of reality."

Hugo is entirely untouched by the fact of living in exile. He refuses to acknowledge that a man's fatherland is a bounded piece of earth, and repeats constantly: *"La Patrie?* What is it? An idea! Paris? I have no need of Paris. Paris is the rue de Rivoli, and I detest the rue de Rivoli."

Tuesday, September 3.—We are off with Saint-Victor on a little tour of the Rhine country and Holland.

Why is it that France, so radiant, so intellectually diffuse, so *invading* in its ideas, a nation from which so much of the world takes colour—why does frontier France, on all its borders, bow before the language and the manners of our neighbours? Why is the German frontier German? the Italian frontier Italian? the Spanish frontier Spanish?

September 18.—Gavarni was saying: "Do you want me to tell you the secret of every society, of every agglomeration of men? Each is a collection of digits without value in search of a zero, a zero which will multiply their power by ten."

Monday, October 18.—Sainte-Beuve, who wrote asking to make our intellectual acquaintance, came to call at two o'clock. He is a short, round, little man with a peasant's neck and shoulders, dressed like a country person, a sort of Béranger in appearance. He has a high forehead, a bald, shining skull, large protuberant eyes, the nose of a greedy, sensual, snooping fellow, a wide coarse mouth whose rudimentary shape is disguised by a friendly smile, and remarkable cheekbones, high knobby cheekbones, like a pair of wens. To see him with his white forehead and rosy cheeks, the pink and babyish colouring of the lower half of his face, one might take him for a provincial librarian living in the shadow of a cloister of books over a cellarful of ripe burgundy wines.

His conversation is a sort of chatter filled with tiny touches of detail, never a broad sweep of the brush; it is like the palette of a *paintress* in water color, covered with timid, pretty, delicate shades.

We spoke of his portrait of Louis Philippe, and he told us that in August 1848 General Count Dumas (as the senior general, his commission dating from the Revolution) had transmitted to M. de Montalivet a letter addressed by the king to the National Assembly, asking that he be allowed to retain his personal estate. M. de Montalivet had thrown the letter into the fire. "I shall publish that," he added.[2] And he went on: "I only saw King Louis Philippe once, when I was presented as a member of the Academy. My sponsors were Hugo and Villemain. The king took both Hugo's hands effusively and thanked him very warmly for having mentioned, in his reply to my address to the Academy, what Napoleon I had said about him."[3]

[2] A curious story, considering that Montalivet's loyalty to Louis Philippe and his concern for principle were vigorously and openly manifested over a period of years—first by his seeking to prevent the expropriation of the Orleans family's estates by the Second Republic in 1848, and again by the attempts he made, in 1851, to secure the restoration of their private fortunes.

[3] On that occasion Hugo quoted Napoleon I as saying of Louis Philippe that he had "always remained national", i.e., was not one of the princes who urged foreign powers to make war upon the French people, in order that those princes might be reinstated by the foreigner. This prince had fought valiantly against the foreigner in 1792; and in an earlier allocution Hugo had already complimented the French upon their choice of "a one-time lieutenant of Dumouriez and of Kellermann" to be constitutional monarch of France.

Then, on the subject of the French Academy, which is generally thought to be the oldest of all academies extant, Louis Philippe said that this honour belonged to the *Accademia della Crusca,*[4] and gave the date when it was founded. A king would not be expected to possess such information; but his governess, Mme de Genlis, had long ago seen to it that he got this sort of thing by heart.

He talked about *Sister Philomène,* saying that only those works possessed value which were the product of the study of nature, that his own taste for phantasy was small, that he liked Hamilton's pretty tales; for the rest, idealism, of which people talk so much, did not seem to him to be among the chief concerns of the ancients; quite the contrary, he believed that their works were realistic, although it might be that their reality afforded them more beautiful models than ours furnish us.

From *Sister Philomène* he moved to the subject of women, old ladies like Mme de Boigne, in whose company he felt something of the atmosphere of the eighteenth century; and he congratulated us on living as we did, partly in the past, living a dual existence. . . .

Then Sainte-Beuve jumped to Flaubert, saying: "One shouldn't be so long writing a book, else one finishes it too late for one's own time. Works like Virgil, of course, are different. And anyway, after *Madame Bovary* he should have written living things for us; works in which we could feel that the author was per-

[4]Richelieu, learning in 1634 that a group of men of letters had been meeting privately since 1629, and having no particular affection for private meetings of any sort, gave instructions that statutes be drafted for the transformation of the group into an academy, with the principal object of purifying the language. Letters patent were signed in January 1635; but it was not until 1637 that parliamentary suspicion of Richelieu in this regard was overcome and the letters ratified, and not until 1639 did the new academy include its full complement of forty members, nearly all now forgotten. The first history of the academy was written by that Pellisson of whom Mme de Sévigné said that he "abused the permission men had to be ugly"—which recalls Gibbon's characterization of bards and priests as "two orders of men who abuse the privilege of fiction." . . . The Accademia della Crusca was founded at Florence in 1582. Its object was the purification of the Italian language and its great work was the *Vocabolario della Crusca,* first published at Venice in 1612 and still the highest authority on the language. At the time of its foundation there were over six hundred "academies" in Italy, a record only to be matched by the women's clubs of the United States.

sonally concerned; whereas what he did was to rewrite Chateaubriand's *Martyres*."

Sainte-Beuve spoke next of the boredom of leaping from subject to subject, from century to century. "A man has no time to love. . . . We must not become attached. . . . It wears a man out: it's like ruining a horse's mouth by constant wheeling and turning to left and right. . . ." He made the gesture of a man pulling on a check rein. . . . "I have work ahead of me that will take three years—unless some accident intervenes. Well, after three years I shall have earned about what a single play would bring in if it was not a success." Then, after a silence: "Ah, the theatre! The comedy in verse seems to me finished. Either you write verse which is not comedy verse, or you write prose. . . . Yes, everything will go into the novel. The field is so vast; and it is a form that lends itself to everything. There is a lot of talent in the novel these days."

He left, giving us a cold plump hand, and saying, in the doorway: "Come to see me early in the week. . . . Later on I shall have my head in a sack."

November 3.—Dinner at Peters' with Saint-Victor and Claudin. After dinner Claudin took me off to the Délassements-Classiques. I had worked all week and needed, I don't know why, to breathe the air of a cheap theatre. From time to time one needs a little degradation of the mind. . . . In the passage I ran against Sari, who told me that Lagier had gone to Rouen to see Flaubert and had come back fearful lest solitude and work drive him out of his mind. He had talked to her about a seraglio of birds and other incomprehensible things. Concerning his immense and brain-fagging work, I don't remember who told me the other day—it might have been Mlle Bosquet, the governess of Flaubert's niece —that he had ordered his servant to speak to him only on Sundays, and then only in order to say, "Sir, it is Sunday."

Undated.—In France one is allowed to say shocking things about history. One may write that Nero was a philanthropist, or that Dubois was a saintly man. But in art and literature, conventional opinions are sacred opinions; and it may be that in this nine-teenth century it is less dangerous to tread on the crucifix than on the beauties of tragedy.

November.—I sometimes think the day will come when all the modern nations will adore a sort of American god, a god who will have been a man that lived on earth and about whom much will have been written in the popular press; and images of this god will be set up in the churches, not as the imagination of each individual painter may fancy him, not floating on a Veronica kerchief, but established, fixed once and for all by photography. Yes, I foresee a photographed god, wearing spectacles.

On that day civilization will have reached its peak and there will be steam-propelled gondolas in Venice.

1862

January 1.—New Year's Day is All Souls' Day to us. Our hearts grow chill and turn towards those who are gone.

We climbed five flights to the modest rooms of our cousin Cornélie. She was soon obliged to send us away, so filled was her room with ladies, schoolboys, men young and old, all relatives or connections. She had not chairs enough to seat them nor space in which to house them for any length of time. It is one of the admirable things about noble families, that they do not shun poverty. In the middle-class families there is no blood relationship that survives below a certain minimum of wealth or above the fourth story of a house.

Undated.—The following occurred at the Imperial Library in my presence. It suffices to judge M. Thiers, his books, and the universality of his fame.

An individual approached a librarian. "I should like a novel."

"We do not circulate novels."

"Well, then, give me a book by Monsieur Thiers."

"Which one?"

"The history of France."

"He has not written a history of France."

"A history of England, then."

"He wrote no history of England."

Whereupon the individual went off with great disappointment written all over his face.

February 15.—I was on the Quai Voltaire, in France's bookshop. A man came in, bargained for a book at great length, went out, came back, and bargained again. He was a big man with a square face and the slouching gait of a horse trader. He gave his address so that the book might be sent to him—M. So-and-so, at Rambouillet.

"Ah!" exclaimed the bookseller, writing it down; "I was there in 1830 with Charles X."

"So was I," said the big fellow. "The last time he signed his name was for me. That was twenty minutes before the deputation from the Provisional Government arrived.[1] I was there in my gig. He certainly needed money! He was selling his plate and selling it damned cheap. If only I had got there sooner! He sold 200,000 francs' worth of it. I had fifteen hundred men to feed—his Guard. I was an army contractor."

"In that case," the librarian said, "you fed us very ill. I remember that we had to slaughter a poor calf in a field."

Chance had brought together Charles X's old guardsman and the contractor who had got his hooks into the royal misfortune and bought the plate of a king at bay. The soldier was now a poor bookseller; the contractor was a fat and bloated burgher, smug in his comfortable opulence.

I wanted to see what book he had bought. It was a *History of the Crimes of the Popes.*[2]

February 19.—I believe that since the beginning of time there have never been men so absorbed, so swallowed up, in a concern

[1]Charles X, grandson of Louis XV, succeeded his brother, Louis XVIII, in 1824. A coward and a reactionary, his Ordinances of July 25, 1830, dissolving the Chamber of Deputies and suppressing the freedom of the press, provoked the Revolution of 1830 which called to the throne Louis Philippe.

[2]Edmond de Goncourt (though not his younger brother) lived long enough to realise that this chance mention of the father of Anatole France contains more to startle a twentieth-century reader than resides in the encounter of the soldier-librarian and the contractor.

for art and letters as we are. Where these are lacking, the very oxygen of our life is lacking. Books, drawings and engravings form the horizon on which we look. We spend our life thumbing pages and turning over drawings: hic sunt tabernacula nostra. Nothing can draw us, nothing can tear us away from these. We have none of those passions which lure men out of the library or the museum, which take them from contemplation, meditation, the joy found in an idea or a line or a colour. We are devoid of political ambition; and love is for us merely what Chamfort called it—"the contact of two skins."[3]

Friday, February 21.—We dined with Flaubert at the Charles Edmonds'. Conversation turned upon his love affair with Mme Colet, and her novel about Flaubert and herself, *Elle et lui.* There was no bitterness, no remains of resentment in him, as he spoke of her. Apparently she had intoxicated him with her insane and furious love. There is a truculence of nature in Flaubert that takes pleasure in passionate, high-strung women and probably wears love out by its gross emotions, its harsh transports, and its violent frenzies.

One day she pursued him to his mother's house and demanded an explanation in the presence of his mother. It appears that his mother had always felt that her son's harshness towards his mistress was in some way an injury done to all womankind. "It was the only cloud between my mother and me," Flaubert said. He confessed, nevertheless, that he had loved Mme Colet madly, to the point, one day, of wanting to kill her; and as he rushed upon her there came into his mind an hallucinating vision of himself prosecuted. "I could hear the creaking of the chair in the dock in which I sat." He went on to say that one of his grandfathers had married a primitive Canadian woman, and indeed there are times when we see something of the redskin in Flaubert's violence.

---

[3]Chamfort? The other day, at a public session of the Académie Française, Professor Louis Madelin attributed a certain maxim to "a German philosopher." Sitting between two erudites, M. André Thérive, of the *Temps,* overheard one of them murmur "Hobbes" while the other moaned into his beard "Plautus!"

Undated.—C— found himself at supper with R— at the Maison d'Or. The whim took them suddenly not to sup by themselves. One of them, after having rung in vain, went out and leant over the staircase to send the doorman to look for some of their friends. He found the man deep in a book and was sufficiently curious to ask what he was reading.

"I am reading what His Grace told me to read," the big blond fellow said with a simple air.

"Whose Grace?"

"His Grace the Bishop of Nancy, from where I come. He said to me: 'You are going to Paris. It is a place of perdition. Read Tertullian.' And I am reading Tertullian."

It was true: the man was reading a Father of the Church in the staircase of the Maison d'Or, between errands to the house of that beautiful lady, La Farcy. The imagination of man can never match the incredible and antithetical strangeness of life.

March 1.—Opening night of *Rothomago*. I went out during the interval and Gautier hooked his arm through mine, leant on me, and we stood smoking and chatting.

"This is how I enjoy the theatre," he said. "There are three women in my box who tell me what is happening on stage. Fournier is a genius. He never writes a new play. Every two or three years he rewrites *Le Pied de mouton*. He has a red décor repainted blue, or a blue décor red; he shoves in a novelty—English dancers, say—and there you are! They should all do that in the theatre. It ought to consist of one fundamental farce, with little changes introduced here and there. The theatre is so gross an art, so abject! Don't you find these times a dreadful bore? And after all, we can't abstract ourselves from our time, can we? There is a sort of ethic imposed upon us by the citizenry, to which we are forced to bow. It is essential that we be on good terms with our police sergeant. What do I ask of life? That I be left quietly alone by myself."

"Yes, you want the government to ensure your material welfare."

"That's it. I got on very well with the Orleanist government; but

the Revolution of 1848 took place and the Republic put me on
the shelf for a bit. Finally, I came to terms with the Republic.
Here I am, writing for *Le Moniteur,* and . . . these things happen—this man (Napoleon III) who veers to right and left and
back again, so that one can never guess what he is after. Meanwhile, one is not allowed to say anything at all. They won't have
sex in novels. There is a sculptural and plastic side to me which
I am obliged to repress, in writing. Now I am reduced to describing conscientiously a wall; and even so, I am not allowed to
say what is sometimes written on it.

"And then, women are on the way out. Today, as we stand
here, a woman is no more than a bit of venereal gymnastics,
dished up with a touch of sentimentality. And that's all. No
salons, no meeting place, no polite society. Look here: I went to
Walewski's the other evening. You'll admit that I am not exactly
a nobody. Believe it or not, I knew two hundred men there and
not three women. And it isn't as if I were the only one."

Monday, March 3.—A very light snowfall. We took a cab to
Théophile Gautier's, 32, rue de Longchamps, at Neuilly, to let
him see the published fascicles of our book on eighteenth-
century art.

He lives in a street of shabby, rustic houses built round courtyards filled with poultry, and fruitshops with little black feather
dusters hanging before their doors; such a suburban street as
Hervier depicts with his artistically grimy brush. We knocked
on the door of a plastered house and found ourselves in the home
of the sultan of the epithet. A sitting room with furniture in red
damask and heavy, Venetianlike, gilt woodwork; old pictures of
the Italian school with lovely spots of yellow flesh; over the fireplace a mirror lacking quicksilver and bordered with coloured
arabesques and Persian characters like something in a Turkish
café; the kind of indigent and hit-and-miss sumptuousness in
which you would expect to find an old retired actress who had
got the pictures as the result of the bankruptcy of an Italian
manager.

We asked if we were disturbing him, to which he answered,

"Not at all. I never work at home. I can only work at *Le Moniteur,* in the printing shop. They print as I write. The only thing that sets me going is the smell of printer's ink. And then, there is the law of pressure. That is inescapable. I am bound to deliver my copy. Yes, that's the only place where I can work. If I were to write a novel now, I could only write it there, where they would set it up ten lines at a go while I wrote. Looking at a proof sheet, one can judge one's work. What one has written becomes impersonal. A manuscript, now, is yourself, it's your hand, it clings to you by certain filaments, it is not detached from you. All my life I have had places arranged for me to work in, and I have never been able to work in them. I need action round me. I work well when there is an orgy going on about me; whereas if I shut myself up to write, the solitude depresses me. One might be able to work pretty well in a servant's garret, at a deal table, with cheap white paper and a pot so that one wouldn't have to go down into the courtyard from time to time."

Then he began to criticize Gounod's *Reine de Saba,* and as we confessed ourselves completely deaf to music, unless it be perhaps a military band, he exclaimed: "I am glad to hear you say that. I am the same way. I prefer silence to music. Having lived part of my life with a singer, I finally learnt to tell good music from bad; but I don't really care which is which. It's interesting, you know, that all the writers of my time are like that. Balzac execrated music, and Hugo cannot bear it. Lamartine himself, who is a human piano for sale or for hire, had a horror of it. Nobody cares for it but a few painters. Composers nowadays have reached a deadly stage of Gluckism, writing things that are broad, slow, slow. . . . They're going back to plain chant. That Gounod is a complete ass.[4] In the second act there are two choruses of

[4] My brother and I sought to depict our contemporaries essentially as human beings and tried to report their conversation in the picturesqueness of its verity. The characteristic quality, I may say the beauty, of Gautier's conversation resided in his fantastic paradoxes. To take this absolute negation of music, this grossly abusive banter, for the true feeling of the illustrious writer about M. Gounod would be to prove oneself either unintelligent or very hostile to the stenographer of this antimusical outburst.—E. de G.

Yet, as regards the Parisian world of letters, there is a good deal of general truth in the conversation here reported. Mme Arman de Caillavet and M. France, for example, were enchanted with the songs of Reynaldo Hahn, but they never listened to other music.—L. G.

Israelites and Sabaeans chattering beside a pool before washing their bottoms. A very nice chorus, I grant you; but that's all. And the whole house sighs, and there is a general *ah-h-h!* of relief, so dull is the rest of the opera. Verdi: ask me what Verdi is. Verdi is a Dennery, a Guilbert de Pixerécourt. Do you want to know what his musical ideas are? When the words are sad, he goes *troo, troo, troo;* when they are gay he sings *tra, tra, tra.* He would never have a piccolo in a funeral march. Now, Rossini would. He's the fellow who, in *Semiramide,* brings on the shade of Ninus to the air of a ravishing waltz. And there you have the whole of Verdi's musical genius."

With which Gautier began to complain of our times. "It may be because I am beginning to be an old man; but there's no air in our times. It isn't enough to have wings: you have to have air. I do not feel contemporary. In 1830, yes, it was superb; but I was two or three years too young. I was not borne along in mid-stream. I wasn't ripe. I should have written other things."

Finally we talked about Flaubert, about his methods, his patience, his seven years spent on a single book of four hundred pages. "Imagine!" exclaimed Gautier. "The other day Flaubert said to me: 'It's finished. I have only ten more pages to write. But I have already got the ends of the sentences.' You see? He already had the music of the ends of the sentences which he hadn't yet begun. He had his ends. Isn't that funny? Eh! What? Now, for my part, I believe that what you need most of all in a sentence is *ocular rhythm.* For example, a sentence that is very long in getting started should not end thinly, abruptly—except for deliberate effect. And then, often Flaubert's rhythms are audible to him alone; they escape the rest of us. A book is not written to be read aloud, but he bawls his aloud to himself. There are bawlings in his sentences which seem to him harmonious, but that you have to be able to read the way he does if you are to get that bawling effect. We both have pages, you in your *Venice* and I in a lot of things everybody knows, that are as rhythmical as anything he has written, and they have cost us much less effort.

"You know, the poor fellow has one remorse that is poisoning his life. It is going to put him in the grave. You don't know what that remorse is. It's that, in *Madame Bovary*, he stuck two genitives one right on top of the other: *Une couronne de fleurs d'oranger*. It made him miserable; but there was not a thing he could do about it, try as he did. Do you want to see the house?"

And he led us into the dining room, where his daughters sat at lunch; then upstairs into a little study from which one could see a garden of scrawny shrubs laid out in vegetable plots. There he showed us the gifts he had received from painters whose shows he had written about—tawdry little girls bearing witness to the stinginess and niggardliness of this world of art towards a man who in his criticism has built pedestals upon which so many unknown artists had been hoisted into fame by the patronage of his beautiful writing and his colourful descriptions.

March 11.—The shrewdest critic of the eighteenth century was perhaps Trublet, that sorry abbé who defined the genius of Voltaire as "the perfection of mediocrity" and had the audacity to put La Bruyère higher than Molière.

Sunday, March 16.—Went to the avenue des Champs-Élysées, near the Arc de Triomphe, to see the objects to be sold at auction by Anna Deslions, the tart who for so long lived across the court from us and who, from the fourth story of our house, launched herself into this wealth, this luxury, this reverberating, scandalous existence. After all, these women do not offend me: they constitute a break with the monotony of life, its formalism, its social rigour. They lend a little madness to the world, slap the banknote in the face, represent caprice released, free, naked and victorious in a world of solicitors with their cautious and economical pleasures.

Everything in Deslions' house is of a gross and impure luxury and of a low species of impurity. Her drawing room is white and gold; her bedroom is in pink satin with gilt in every direction; and there is a dressing room with basins and water pitchers in yellow Bohemian crystal glass, all of it enormous, gigantic, wanting the biceps of Hercules to pick it up. There are paintings whose very choice seems an irony. In the middle of a bright silken panel hangs a dark Boudin showing a man at table in a tavern and looking as if it might be a kind of family portrait, a souvenir of her base origin, the father of the tart sticking his head out in the surroundings of her wealth. On another wall are workers in the field, haymakers or gleaners, by Breton, bent and sweating under the burden of their work and bringing into this place of prostitution a vision of the tanned farm labourer tearing his daily bread from the niggardly earth.

In the library—for she has a library—I saw next to the breviaries of her trade (*Manon Lescaut, Mémoires de Mogador,*[5] and so on) a copy of Émile de Girardin's *Questions de mon temps.* Imagine the author elucidating his theory of the "triangulation of powers" to the Venus Pandemos!

As for the jewels filling a glass case, they were the casket of a Faustine, three hundred thousand francs' worth of brilliants which only yesterday had gleamed on her tawny pink skin. Looking at them, bending over them, I could see again by their light and as in the gleam of the past, La Deslions asking our servant, when we were having people to dine, asking, before we had come home, if she might not walk round our table in order to sate her eyes with the sight of a little luxury.

Thursday, March 27.—Mid-Lent. We dined at the house of Mme Desgranges. Gautier and his daughters were there; Peyrat, with his wife and daughter; and one of those interloping nobodies who always seem to make the fourteenth at a party.

Gautier's daughters have a singular charm, a kind of oriental langour. They gaze at one with slow, deep glances veiled by fine, heavy eyelids, and they walk and raise their arms in an indolent rhythm which they inherit from their father, though adding to it a womanly grace and elegance. Their charm is not altogether French but is mingled with all sorts of things French—with

---

[5]*Adieu au monde, Mémoires de Céleste Mogador,* was the title of a book published in 1854 and suppressed, in which La Mogador, born Céleste Venard in 1824, revealed the intimate details of her life as prostitute and queen of a public dance hall (Le Prado). She was a bareback rider, an actress of sorts, and, following her marriage to the Count de Chabrillan (member of an ancient family of the Dauphiné), she turned out a number of novels and farces.

almost boyish high spirits, with the vocabulary of young men rather than of girls, with little grimaces and poutings and shruggings of the shoulders, little ironies manifested in the expressive gestures of childhood—all these making of them quite different beings to well-reared young ladies, making of them pretty little individual creatures whose likes and dislikes are frankly and almost transparently clear. These girls bring into the drawing room the freedom of speech and the daring of a woman at a masked ball; and yet at bottom one perceives in them a simplicity, an innocence, an affectionate expansiveness, that is not to be found in other girls.

One of them, while aloud she showed a lack of respect for her mother, who tried to forbid her to drink champagne, told me in a low voice of her first convent infatuation, her first love. She was in love with a lizard which used to look at her with its gentle, *friend-of-man* eye; a lizard which was always on her and in her, and which would constantly peer out from her bodice, gaze at her, and disappear again.[6] The poor lizard was crushed by a wicked and jealous schoolmate, and came dragging its insides behind it to die at the feet of Gautier's daughter. She told me ingenuously that she dug a grave for it and set a cross over it, and that thereafter she refused to pray, would nevermore go to Mass, that, in short, religion died in her, so revolted was she by the injustice of this death.

March 29.—Flaubert, sitting Turkish fashion on his divan, talking of his plans, his ambitions, his dreams, confiding in us his great and continued desire to write a novel about the modern Orient, the Orient that now dresses in black. He grew animated with the thought of all the antitheses which his talent would find in the subject. Scenes taking place in Paris, scenes in Constantinople, scenes along the Nile; scenes of European hypocrisy, scenes of secret savagery in the East—drownings and decapitations in satisfaction of a mere suspicion, a mere moment of irritability: a work which would, in his own words, be rather like a ship with a Turk dressed by Dussautoy on the bridge,

[6]Compare *A High Wind in Jamaica*, by Richard Hughes, ch. IX.

forward; and aft, on the lower deck, the same Turk's harem with its eunuchs and all the ferocity of manners of the old East. Flaubert grew more and more rejoiced and delighted at the thought of painting all the diverse rabbles of Europe—the Greek, the Italian, the Jewish, mobs that would gravitate round his hero. He went on at length about the strange contrasts he would draw here and there between the Oriental becoming civilized and the European reverting to a state of savagery, like that French chemist who settled on the confines of Libya and from whom there fell away all the manners and habits of his homeland.

From this book, sketched out in his mind, Flaubert passed to another with the thought of which he said he had been playing for a long time: an immense novel, a great picture of life, to be strung on the thread of a plot in the course of which his characters would murder one another in an association like Balzac's Thirteen, and where the reader would see the penultimate survivor, a politician, sent to the guillotine by the last of the lot as ironic recompense for a worthy deed, the ultimate survivor to be a magistrate. He had also in mind to write two or three little novels, entirely simple and without subordinate action, which would deal with the husband, the wife, and the lover.

In the evening, after dinner, we went to see Gautier at Neuilly and found him still at table, though it was nine o'clock, celebrating a little Pouilly wine which he declared very pleasant, and with him his guest, Prince Radziwill. Gautier's gaiety is like the gaiety of a child: it is one of the great graces of his intelligence.

We all moved into the sitting room, and there Flaubert was asked to dance "The Drawing-room Idiot." He borrowed a tail coat from Gautier, raised his collar, and of his hair, his face, his whole physiognomy he made something, I hardly know what, which transformed him suddenly into a fantastic caricature of a cretin. Seized with a spirit of emulation, Gautier took off his frock coat and, running with sweat, his great bottom crushing down on his calves, began to dance "The Creditor's Dance", and the evening ended with gypsy songs, Prince Radziwill carrying the wild melodies in a marvellously strident voice.

March 30.—Fourth story, number 2, rue Racine. A little gentleman, quite commonplace in appearance, opened the door, said with a smile, "Messieurs de Goncourt," pushed in another door, and we were in a very large room, a sort of studio. Seated with its back to a window at the far end, through which entered the five o'clock twilight, was a grey shade in the pale glow. That shade did not rise; it offered no response to the greeting expressed in our bow and our words. This seated shade, with its slumbrous air, was Mme George Sand, and the man who had ushered us in was Manceau, the engraver. Mme Sand looks like an automaton. She talks in a mechanical and monotonous voice which neither falls nor rises and is never animated. In her attitude there is a gravity, a placidity, a something like the semi-slumber of a ruminant. Her gestures are slow, slow, the gestures of a somnambulist; and they always end—always with the same methodical movements—in the scratching of a wax match from which spurts a little flame, and the lighting of a cigarette in the woman's lips.

Mme Sand was extremely nice to us, extremely complimentary, but with ideas so childish, expressions so flat, and an amiability so doleful that it was as chilling as a bare bedroom wall. Manceau tried to introduce a trifle of animation into our dialogue. We talked about her theatre at Nohant, where plays are put on for the solitary pleasure of Mme Sand and her servant, and go on until four in the morning. Then we mentioned her prodigious faculty for work; to which she replied that her application was not *meritorious,* since it had always been easy for her. She works every night from one o'clock until four in the morning, and then works for two hours again during the day; and, Manceau added, as if he were a side-show barker displaying the points of a freak, "It doesn't matter at all if she is disturbed. It is as if you had a faucet in the house you could turn on and off. Mme Sand is like that." And Mme Sand agreed: "Yes, I don't in the least mind being interrupted by people I like, by the peasants who come to talk to me. . . ." A little humanitarian note crept in at this point.

When we said good-bye she rose, shook hands, and took us to

the door. Thus we were able to catch a glimpse of her face which is kind, gentle, serene, colourless, but its features still delicately firm in the pallid and pacified complexion, a complexion the colour of pale amber. There is in her a tenuousness and a fine chiselling of feature which her portraits, that coarsen and thicken her face, do not reveal.

April 22.—This evening we sat in Saint-Victor's box at the opening night of *Les Volontaires,* a play that was expected to alarm all Europe, a play which Paris expected to be followed by an uprising, a play on leaving which the Parisian populace would shout for a repetition of the abdication of Napoleon I. The expected did not come off. Tedium disarmed the political passions. The play would have put a revolution to sleep. Canova once made a lion out of butter;[7] Séjour has made a Napoleon out of marshmallow.

In the next box, with Gramont-Caderousse and Marguerite Bellanger, sitting at my elbow was Anna Deslions, as beautiful as ever, as placid and superb as an Io. She was in heavy mourning for her mother. An epidemic has raged this year amongst the mothers of her kind. She told me how sorry she was that we had not known each other when we were neighbours; we should have seen—we, who are writers—such extraordinary things in her flat. Then, speaking of her auction sale and of the lack of *style* of her dressing room, after having said that she wanted a private house, a house that would contain a marble swimming bath in which she would receive, she interrupted herself, was pensive a moment, and then avowed with a pretty smile that one of her dreams had come true—a garret! She was going to have this garret in Neuilly, where she planned to spend all her time doing tapestry work under the willows.

"You know," she said; "I never went out for anything I got. It all came of itself. I didn't try to make myself rich. When money came to me, I took it, that's all."

And she was telling the truth. This woman possesses the ver-

[7] The story goes that Senator Falieri saw by chance a lion modelled in butter by the stonemason's son and became his patron.

itable and intimate characteristic of the whore, which is passivity. She is the heedless and unknowing subject of the fatality of her existence. She let fortune accost her as she would let a man accost her—someone who comes upstairs, whom one accepts, who goes off, and whom one forgets.

Sunday, June 8.—Off to the country with Saint-Victor, like so many shop assistants, and on the way to the railway station we said to ourselves that Humanity was at bottom—and to its honour—one vast Don Quixote. It is true that it has its Sancho Panza, its Reason, its Common Sense; but it marches far ahead of that. The most exhausting efforts, the most enormous sacrifices of humanity have been made in honour of ideals. . . .

Nature is for me an enemy. The country is to me a mortuary. This green earth seems to me a great expectant cemetery. This grass grazes on man. This vegetation grows and flourishes on that which dies. This sun that gleams and shines so brightly is the great putrefier. Trees, sky, water—all of it is to me no more than a momentary concession. No, nothing in nature speaks to me, says anything to my soul. No, it does not touch me as I was touched a while ago by that woman seen at table, the upper part of her head looking like Andrea del Sarto's "Caritas" and below it the mouth of a ghoul in the Arabian Nights.

The face of woman and the speech of man; in these only lies my pleasure, my concern.

July 13.—The travail, the torment, the torture, of the literary life is in the birth pangs. Conceive; create: there lives in these two words, for the writer, a world of painful and anguishing effort. Out of that oblivion, out of that rudimentary embryon which is the initial idea, to bring forth the *punctum saliens,* to draw one by one out of one's head the incidents that go to the composition of a narrative, the lines that make up the characters, the development of the plot, the climax, the life of all this little world animated by you, spurting forth from your entrails, and becoming a novel—what work! It is as if you had a sheet of blank paper in your head, and your still-amorphous thought were scribbling on it in a vague and illegible hand. . . . And the dismal weariness, the infinite despair, the shame, with which you feel your powerlessness in the very moment of your ambition to create. You turn your mind over and over and it rings hollow. You grope within, and your hand touches something dead, which is your imagination. You tell yourself that you are incapable of doing anything, that you will never be able to do anything, that you are *void*.

Yet the idea is there, alluring and out of reach, like a wicked fairy in a cloud. You whip your thought along the trail; you long for insomnia in the hope of success in the fever of night; you stretch the cords of your brain to the breaking point over a single concentration. Something appears before you a moment, and then vanishes; and you fall back more exhausted than if you had been broken in a physical onset. To grope like this, in the night of the imagination, for the soul of a book and to find nothing; to gnaw one's hours away in fruitless seeking; to go down into the depths of oneself and bring nothing up; to find oneself between the last book one brought into the world, its cord cut so that one is now indifferent to it, and the next book to which one cannot give flesh and blood; to be in gestation of nothing—these are the horrors that beset the man of thought and imagination.

For many days we have been in this state of anxiety. Finally the first contours, the vague *fizzing* of our novel (*Renée Mauperin*) made its appearance this evening. It happened while we were walking behind the house in the narrow path caught between the high garden walls. A breeze was stirring like a murmur through the tips of the tall poplars. The setting sun was freezing, with heaven knows what hot vapor, the distant vegetation. On my left the thick grove of chestnut trees at the Vieille-Halle stood out black against the sky, its extremest *digited* leaves outlined against the whitening gold of the evening like the design of an arborised agate. The little gleams of light in the dark of the trees were like stars. I was reminded of the strange effect in La Berge's landscape, "Soir," that hangs in the Louvre, the night of the trees standing sharply out, their ebony leaves glued against a sky of infinite light, of a dying magnificence. Books have their cradles.

July 22.—Little by little disease is accomplishing its ruinous work in our poor servant, Rose.

July 31.—Dr Simon will be telling me shortly whether our old Rose is to live or die. I am waiting for his ring, which will be, to me, the verdict of an assizes jury coming into the courtroom. . . . "It's all over. No hope. A question of time. The disease has worked quickly. One lung gone and the other about as bad."

August 11.—Rose refuses to go to Dubois's nursing home, where we offered to send her. Twenty-five years ago, when she came to us, she went there once to see Edmond's nurse. The nurse died there, and that nursing home represents to Rose the house of death. I am waiting for Simon, who is to bring Rose a card that will pass her into the Lariboisière Hospital. She spent a good night, almost. She is all ready, even gay. We have hidden the truth from her as best we could. She breathes freer at the idea of going. She is impatient. It seems to her that she will recover, there. Simon arrived at two o'clock. "All arranged." In the cab she sat with her hand on the window ledge. I held her up against the pillow we had put behind her. Eyes blank and wide open, she looked vaguely at the houses as we passed. She stopped speaking.

When we reached the gate she insisted upon getting down without being carried. "Can you walk that far?" the porter asked. She nodded affirmatively and went on. I have no notion where she gathered the strength to walk. Finally we came into a large, high-ceilinged, cold, rigid, clean room with a stretcher in the middle of it. I sat her down in a cane-bottomed chair near a glazed window. A clerk opened the window, asked me her name, her age, and spent a good quarter hour writing on a dozen sheets of paper, all of which had a religious symbol at the top. Finally that was over. I kissed her. A man took one arm, a charwoman the other. That was the last I saw of her.

Saturday, August 16.—At ten o'clock this morning there was a ring at the door. I heard a colloquy between the maid and the porter. The door opened. The porter came in with a letter. I took the letter. It bore the stamp of Lariboisière. Rose died this morning at seven o'clock.

What a void! What a gap in our life! A habit, an affection, twenty-five years old. A servant who knew our whole life, opened our letters when we were away; to whom we told everything about ourselves. When I was very small I rolled a hoop with her, and when we went out she would buy apple pies for me out of her own money. She would wait up for Edmond until daylight to open the door for him when he went to the Opera Ball unknown to mother. It was this woman, this admirable nurse, whose hands our dying mother put into our hands. She had the keys to everything; she decided and did everything in our home. For twenty-five years she had tucked us into our beds, and every evening we made the same joking remarks about her ugliness and her ungainly body. She shared our joys and our sorrows. Hers was one of those devotions one hopes will be present to shut one's eyes for the last time, when that time comes. Our bodies, in our distress or illness, were accustomed to her tending. She shared all our manias. She had known all our mistresses. She was a chunk of our life, a piece with which our apartment was furnished, a survival of our youth; something tender and grumbling and *watchmanlike,* a kind of watchdog, that we were accustomed to have beside us, round us, and that we somehow expected to end only with the end of us.

The irony of things! This very evening, exactly twelve hours after the last breath of the poor woman, we must be off to Saint-Gratien, the Princess Mathilde having had the curiosity to make our acquaintance and expressed the desire to have us to dinner.

Thursday, August 21.—In the course of a dinner saddened by a conversation that went back again and again to the subject of our dead Rose, Maria, who was dining with us this evening, after two or three nervous pattings of her tightly curled puffed-out hair, exclaimed abruptly, "Look here! So long as the poor woman was alive I kept my mouth shut because . . . well, call it professional ethics. But now that she is dead and buried, I think you two ought to know the truth about her."

And with that we heard things about our unfortunate Rose that took away our appetite, that filled our mouths with the acid bitterness of fruit cut with a steel knife. Maria revealed to our ignorance a whole odious, repugnant and lamentable life. Those bills Rose signed, those debts she left with every kind of shop-keeper, were due to an absolutely inconceivable, a most astounding, a most incredible circumstance. Rose kept men. One of them was the son of our creamery woman, for whom she had taken and furnished a room. Another was given our wine, our chickens, our food. A secret existence of nocturnal orgies, nights out, uterine frenzies that actually prompted one of her lovers to say, "It's going to croak one of us—me or her." A passion, a sum of passions, that took in all of her—her head, her heart, her senses, with which went the ailments of the wretched woman, her con-sumption lending a sort of fury to her sensuality, a kind of hysteria, a beginning of madness. By the creamery woman's son she had two children, one of which lived six months. When, a few years back, she told us she was going home for a bit, it was to be delivered of a child. And her ardour for these men was so excessive, so unhealthy and demented even, that she, who was ordinarily the soul of honesty, robbed us, stole twenty-franc pieces which she would give to her lovers to persuade them not to de-sert her.

Following these involuntary spurts of dishonesty, these little crimes offensive to her natural uprightness, she would sink into such self-reproach, such remorse, such despondency and black fits of despair, that in this inferno, going desperately and unsated from transgression to transgression, she began to drink in order to escape from herself, to flee the present, to sink and drown for a few hours in one of those slumbers, those lethargic torpors in which she would lie all day long on a bed onto which she had collapsed while making it up.

Poor woman! What predispositions and motives and reasons she found in herself to devour herself and bleed inwardly as she did! First, there was the intermittent recoil of religious ideas, with terror of hell-fire and brimstone; and then jealousy, that quite particular jealousy that raged in her with regard to everything and everybody; and finally the disgust which, after a time, men would brutally betray for her ugliness, and which drove her more and more urgently to drink and led to a miscarriage one day as she fell dead drunk on the floor. This horrifying tearing of the veil before our eyes was like the autopsy of a pocket bursting with disgusting things in a suddenly opened corpse.

From what we were told I could see all at once all that she had been through these past ten years: the fear that we might receive anonymous letters about her; the fear that she would be denounced by some shopkeeper; the constant trepidation over the demands for money made upon her and that she could never pay back; and the shame felt by this proud creature, perverted by the abominable Saint-Georges quarter in which we live, by the company of low people whom she despised, and the painful consciousness of premature senility brought on by sodden drinking, and the inhuman exigencies and meannesses of the gutter-rats she frequented, and the temptation to suicide (so that one day I pulled her back from a window out of which she was all but falling); and all those tears that we used to think had no cause— all this mixed up with a very deep-seated affection she felt for us and an almost feverish devotion when one or the other of us fell ill.

And there was in this woman an energy, a strength of will, an art of concealment, that was incomparable. There was absolute success in keeping these frightful secrets hidden and locked up within her, without a single betrayal to our eyes or our ears or our general sense of observation, even when she had an attack of nerves (at which times nothing but moaning would come forth from her), a mystery that continued to her very death and which she must have thought buried with her.

And what did she die of? Of having stood all night in the rain in Montmartre, some eight months ago, spying on the creamery woman's son, who had driven her out, to find out who the woman was that had taken her place: a whole night spent staring at the window of a ground-floor room, from which she had come away with her clothes soaking, chilled to the bone, and mortally ill of pleurisy.

Poor creature! We have forgiven her, and we even feel deep commiseration on learning of all that she went through. But for the rest of our lives we shall be suspicious of all womankind, from the lowest to the highest. We are seized with horror at the thought of the duplicity of woman's nature, the powerful faculty, the science, the consummate genius, for lying that informs all a woman's being.

August 23.—Gautier began once more to express his judgment of *Le Misanthrope*—a Jesuit-school comedy written to be performed at the beginning of the new term. "Oh! the swine. What language! What foul writing! But of course I couldn't say so in print. After all, I have to go on earning my living. I am still getting letters abusing me for having dared compare *Timon of Athens* with *Le Misanthrope*."

From Molière he went on to the whole of the seventeenth century, that age so dull, so antipathetic, speaking a language so far beneath the opulent French of the sixteenth century and the clear speech of the eighteenth century. And off he went on the subject of the Sun King himself, Louis XIV, knocking him about, flinging turds at him in a spate of animated speech as if he were a fusion of Michelet and *Le Père Duchène:*[8]

"A skinny little beast no bigger than that! He wasn't five feet tall, your Louis the Great. Spent all his time at table and at stool. The whole age was full of stool. Read the Princess Palatine's letter. And narrow-minded, withal. Giving people pensions so that they sing his praises! A fistula in the anus and another in his nose that ran along the roof of his mouth, so that he was forever squirting out all the stews and soupstocks of his court. And what I say is true," Gautier exclaimed sharply to Claudin, who stood there, scandalized.

[8]*Le Père Duchesne* was a violent, vituperative, coarse and calculatedly angry political journal, edited by J. R. Hébert (vide notes appended) during the Reign of Terror. Specimen of the language employed: "Il faut donc, foutre! que tous les bougres qui ont du sang dans les veines et qui savent aussi que la raison est la botte secrète pour tuer la tyrannie, ne cessent de prêcher la raison. . . . Le plus grand malheur de l'homme, c'est l'ignorance, foutre!"

August 31.—We received the other day a printed card reading as follows: "The honour of your company is requested at a small family celebration which will take place at 32, rue de Longchamps, Neuilly, on the 31st August, 1862." And here we are, this evening, in the rue de Longchamps, with twenty-five or thirty other guests. The bedroom of Gautier's daughters has been turned into a theatre, with curtain, footlights, and all the chairs and armchairs in the house. The mantelshelf furnishes balcony seats. Over the door is a drawing of a naked woman, stretching herself in an amatory pose, and on the door is stuck this placard:

Neuilly Theatre

PIERROT POSTHUMUS

The curtain rises on a scene rather humorously painted by Puvis de Chavannes. The stage is just big enough for a smack in the face and a kick in the bottom. The farce begins—a farce that is like an improvisation written on a carnival night in an inn at Bergamo, full of charming verses that rise and wrap themselves in a garland round Harlequin's wooden sword. Back and forth across the stage go the whole Gautier family: Judith, the elder daughter, costumed like Esmeralda in the Italian improvised comedy, developing her soft graces; young Estelle, slim in her Harlequin suit, with her little dark snout and pretty childish grimaces; Gautier's son as Pierrot, a little stiff, a little too much in the part, too posthumus; and Gautier himself as the doctor, extraordinary as Pantaloon, flushed, made up, daubed all over with paint enough to frighten away every one of the ailments enumerated by Molière's Diafoirus; fawning, making wooden gestures, his voice transposed and altered and coming God knows whence, from the lobes of his ears, from his epigastrium, from the *calcaneum* of his heels, a rusty, extravagant voice, the voice of a clucking Rabelais.

October 19.—A story that tells everything about the Jews, that explains their wealth, their power, their swift ascension in this age of money. Mirès told Saint-Victor that at the Jewish school to which he was sent in Bordeaux they gave no arithmetic prize because everybody would have won it. This story beats even the profound remark of old Rothschild, who once said: "On 'Change there is a moment when, in order to make money, you have to be able to speak Hebrew."

Saturday, November 8.—Dined at Gavarni's with Chennevières, Dr Veyne, the former physician to the Latin Quarter, and Sainte-Beuve. The author of *Volupté* came dressed like a little provincial draper in his holiday finery. He pulled out of his pocket a skull-cap of black silk, a skull-cap at once clerical and academic, and put it on to ward off draughts. I spoke to him of his articles in the *Constitutionnel.* "Yes," he said; "I shall go on with them another twenty months, with two months of leave. I have to: I have contracted to. I have a certain gift for jumping from one subject to the next, although that is what is most tiring about the job. I lectured at the University of Liége three times a week. I gave a course at the École Normale for four years. I delivered twenty-two lectures on Bossuet. And I am giving the paper all I have, the last of my notes. I am emptying my sack. I am down to my last cartridges and am firing everything I have. Frankly, at bottom I am bored, or rather disgusted, weary. All those insults, all that calumny, for a meagre distinction that is really nothing at all, however highly people esteem it." I felt that he had been deeply wounded by an attack in a morning newspaper this very day which, while announcing that he had been invited to a rout at Compiègne, accused him of having had his friend Barbey d'Aurevilly dismissed from the staff of *Le Pays.* "If I had ten thousand francs a year of income I know what I would do; or rather what I would not do." And he confided in us that he was not going to Compiègne, where the newspapers were sending him; his health would not permit it, his ailments, his bladder. . . . He would not be able to stick it out. It was too great a chore at his age.[9]

[9]"In 1865 began the receptions [by the emperor and empress] at Compiègne. People were asked in batches for a week. All the details were arranged in advance. . . . One hundred covers at dinner, to the sound of a military band and a lackey behind each guest's chair, after which, 'to kill the evening,' there was dancing. To bed at midnight. Mornings free. At two o'clock, shooting, or a jaunt in a charabanc to the ruins at Pierrefonds. And back in time for dinner."—Arnaud, op. cit.

The talk was of modern history, of its superiority over ancient history, which never saw either the framework or the background against which events transpired. Sainte-Beuve declared that Villemain knew absolutely nothing of events beyond what was to be read in books, and that up to now no historian had known anything about the art of any epoch. The conversation moved round to the eighteenth century. "That is the age I love best," Sainte-Beuve exclaimed. "I know no more wonderful years than the first fifteen years of the reign of Louis XVI.[10] And what men! even the second-rate men, like Rivarol or Chamfort. Remember Rivarol's remark: 'Impiety is an indiscretion.' Charming. Hm! hm!"

Sainte-Beuve has a little stammer that leads him from one thought to the next, links his words together. "Hm! hm!" he went on.

"And all those people had a philosophy that we would do well to have ourselves. They didn't fret about things like the immortality of the soul. They lived like human beings, turned out the best work they could do, and were not contemptuous of material things. Nowadays we take too much religion; we take too much of it, we overdo it. And then, in those days there was a social life, which is, after all, the best of man's inventions."

With that he began to speak of Michelet with a sort of animosity, a kind of choleric rancour. "Today he writes a *vertical* style. He omits all verbs. But he has become a church; he has his believers. The first volumes of his history; the first volumes . . . good Lord, they're no better than the rest. The latest make the first seem better."

Then, one after the other, About, Lamartine and the Duke de Broglie were on the carpet. "About is a lad who made a book out

[10]It was not until 1869 that Sainte-Beuve got round to publishing his several papers against, rather than on, Talleyrand (who died in 1839); but he might very readily, meanwhile, have appropriated the most celebrated of Talleyrand's remarks: "He who has not lived in the years just preceding 1789 cannot know the pleasure of living." That the Goncourts did not instantly bring together Sainte-Beuve's appreciation and Talleyrand's is interesting only as illustrating how different may be the knowledge which two epochs separately possess of an earlier age. The 1980's will doubtless cite freely remarks of A. J. Balfour or Mr. Justice Holmes (say) which we shall not live to see in print.

of what was worth a page. His novel about the nose, now: that's one of Voltaire's epigrams: you remember. . . . But I assure you that Lamartine has wit. He has it in passing, in flowing, without stopping at it."

During the dinner we were exasperated to hear this shrewd conversationalist, this shrewd connoisseur of letters, talk arrant nonsense about art; praise Eugène Delacroix as a philosophical painter; spread himself about the expression in Hamlet's face in the picture, "Hamlet in the Graveyard"—until Gavarni cut in almost brutally with, "Expression! But you could swap Hamlet's head for the gravedigger's and not know the difference."

After dinner, seeing us smoke, Sainte-Beuve said, "Not to smoke leaves a great blank in one's life. Tobacco has to be replaced by more natural distractions . . . which do not accompany one throughout the whole of one's life." This last said with a smile of regret and of libertine sadness.

Coming back over the Versailles road, the night being fine and cold, Sainte-Beuve, in his unbuttoned grey overcoat and chamois waistcoat—he affects bright, youthful, springlike colours —Sainte-Beuve, walking with a nervous, almost raging step, talked to us about the Academy, saying that it was not what people thought it. He is on good terms with it, despite the little tricks he admits having played upon it. Political passions have had time to die down these twelve years; but, nevertheless, they crop up again from time to time, though they never come to anything. Falloux almost used force to get Sainte-Beuve's hands out of his pockets the day Sainte-Beuve refused to shake hands. "There is left only the Duke de Broglie. We never greet each other. All this, of course, goes on at the Academy only, in the family. There have been only eight of us in attendance for about six months. There are sessions, when Villemain is not present, that begin at half-past three and end at a quarter to four. If there were not an inventive fellow there, a Villemain, it would not go at all. He asks questions. He draws up pretty minutes. He is like Patin and the dictionary—he doesn't do it well, but he does it; and without him nothing would get done. It isn't for want of good will on the part of the Academy; it's simply out of ignorance. The other day, apropos of a certain word, Monsieur de Noailles said it was unknown, that he had never heard of it. He had never read Theocritus, that was all. And so it goes about everything. About books, about the prizes to be given, they come to me. They ask me what it is all about. Well, why shouldn't they inform themselves? They haven't learnt a single new name in ten years. And, moreover, there is one thing that scares the Academy stiff—that is our Bohemia. If they haven't seen a man in their drawing rooms they don't want to hear of him. They fear him. He is not a man of their circle. Because of this, I think Autran has a chance. He is a good candidate: he goes to the right watering places. They've met him there. And he is rich. What's more, he is from Marseilles, so that he has voting for him Thiers, Mignet and Lebrun, the three Provençal brethren, who urge one another on in his favor."

The little touch—there you have the charm and the pettiness of Sainte-Beuve's conversation. Never any lofty ideas; never any magnificent expressions; none of those images that detach a figure in the round. It's sharp, fine, pointed, a rain of little phrases that end by painting a character, after they have been superposed and piled up, one atop the last. An ingenious and witty conversation; but thin. A conversation in which there is grace, incisiveness, a gentle murmur, a claw, a velvet paw. In sum, not the conversation of a superior virile being.

Saturday, November 22.—Gavarni and Sainte-Beuve have organized a dinner to take place twice a month. The first one was held this evening at Magny's restaurant, where Sainte-Beuve habitually dines. There were present only Gavarni, Sainte-Beuve, Veyne, Chennevières, and ourselves; but the dinner is to be enlarged and will include other guests.

November 27.—In this age it is not enough to write a book: one must be the servant of that book and deliver it to critics, become the lackey of its success. Therefore I have had to carry my books to this one and that, to those who cut half the pages, to those who will write about it without reading it, and to still others who will get enough out of a secondhand bookseller for the book to dine off it.

One could write a very curious physiology, so to say, of men of letters, beginning with the physiognomy of their house porters, their staircases, their doorbells, and their lodgings. I have observed a sort of logic, an intimate correlation between the inhabitant and his shell, the man and his surroundings, in all of them. The man of letters usually lives at the top of a building, on the fifth story. Paris, like man himself, carries its brain at the top; its legs, that which does its running, the shop, is at the bottom; and between is its digestion, the *bourgeois* quarters.

Three homes, on three rungs of the ladder, struck me today.

Crossing a courtyard in the rue Jacob, you climb five flights and walk along a passage lined with the doors of servants' rooms, a sort of labyrinth of outoffices. There is a key in the door. After knocking in vain, you decide to turn the key, go in, and find yourself in a kind of storeroom with books strewn over the floor, and among them a pair of unpolished men's boots. From the next room, as out of a deep dream, a voice calls out, "Who is there?" You go into what looks like a shopgirl's room, a seamstress's room, and see a bedside table weighed down with new books, and in a bed a skinny, unhealthy little man. It is two in the afternoon and you have awakened him. You are in the garret of a critic, a man of great talent: M. Montégut, of the *Revue des Deux Mondes*.

Rue d'Argenteuil, almost across from the Gagne-Petit, that sooty shop where white goods are sold, in a street in which Restif de la Bretonne might have had his miserable lodgings under the tiles, you go up a dark stairway, past landings that smell of drains, four steep storeys. One of those general maids, losing her head because there is a caller and almost bowling over a little girl who runs off at the sight of you. A living room with furniture of an old-fashioned elegance; in the fireplace a damp and dreary fire going; on the walls many commonplace pictures, only some of which are framed; on a table a large illustrated New Year's issue of a review; in a corner a piano which speaks of a wife and family—a room like those dreary and solemn reception rooms in which bookbinders receive their clients. Here lives another skinny little man with long sparse hair, a pasteboard face and ferret's eyes. His name is Édouard Fournier and he is the erudite critic of *La Patrie*.

Across from La Muette, on the grounds of what was once Ranelagh[11]—I recognized the house without knowing it—was something that resembled the fumblings of children with their building blocks when they marry crenellated towers to Chinese pavilions. We went in. Flowers everywhere; Chinese ceramics in the ceiling; Watteaus painted by Ballue; glass cases filled with bric-a-brac; pasteboard architectural decoration; walls lined with imitation Chinese silks; painted blinds; carpets like moss; over-gilded bindings; doors covered from top to bottom with drawings, lithographs, two-sou photographs; a playroom with Polish billiards and Dutch tops; and stairs up and stairs down, entrances and exits as many as in a farce, with, everywhere, art objects of a kind to delight a young girl—a triumphant house with gardens, stables, coach houses, all shown off to you by an embarrassed, lugubrious, and sadly amiable man called Jules Lecomte.

December 1.—We called on Sainte-Beuve in order to thank him for this morning's review in the *Constitutionnel* of our *Woman in the XVIIIth Century*. He lives in the rue Montparnasse. The door, a very narrow door, was opened by his housekeeper, a woman of forty years who looks like a governess in a good family. We were led into a sitting room with garnet-coloured wallpaper, the furniture upholstered in red velvet and looking as if made by a Latin-Quarter upholsterer on Louis XV models. A ceremoniously cold, middle-class room rather reminiscent of the drawing rooms of the gentlemen of the Bench. Through the twisted branches of a thin black climbing vine, daylight enters wan and sad from a little garden surrounded by a high wall. We go up a complicated little staircase to Sainte-Beuve's bedroom,

---

[11]"Ranelagh" was the name given to a series of grassplots of some twenty-five acres, near Auteuil, which served as a fashionable promenade in the eighteenth century and on which were eventually built a theatre and a dance hall. In 1854 it was cut up and sold for private villas and gardens. The name was borrowed from the like establishment laid out by the Earl of Ranelagh (1636–1712) near London.

which is just over his sitting room, a bedroom in which we see, on going in, a bed covered with an eider down, opposite it two windows without draperies, on the left a mahogany bookcase filled with bindings of the Restoration period, backed with gold tooling in the Gothic taste of Clotilde de Surville.[12] In the middle of the room is a table heaped with books, and in the corners, against the bookcases, are piles of newspapers and pamphlets, stacks, litters, a chaos as if he were about to move out, the whole looking like a Benedictine monk's room in a small hotel.

We found Sainte-Beuve—I don't know why—annoyed with *Salammbô,* furious and foaming in little sentences. "To begin with, it is unreadable. And it's tragedy. At bottom it is purely classical. The battle, the plague, the famine—all bits to put into a school anthology. It's Marmontel. It's Florian." And for a whole hour, despite all we said in favour of the book (one must defend one's own kind against the critics), he spat forth, vomited up, his reading of the novel, the prey of an almost comical and childish anger.

Today Sainte-Beuve struck me by his resemblance to Hippolyte Passy[13]—the same sly look, same eye, same shape of skull, and above all the same sound of the slightly lisping voice. I have observed that all very loquacious people lisp.

Saturday, December 13.—I received, with a very nice letter of compliments upon our book, an invitation to dine this evening, from the Princess Mathilde.

We were taken up to the first floor and shown into a round drawing room pannelled in purple silk and hung with mirrors in handsome chiselled frames. Gavarni, Chennevières and Nieuwerkerke were already there, and the princess came in soon after, followed by her reader, Mme de Fly. We were seven at table. Had it not been for the plate marked with the arms of the Empire, and the gravity and impassive mien of the lackeys—true lackeys of a princely house—one would not have imagined one-

---

[12]A fifteenth-century figure, presumptive author of the *Poésies de Clotilde* which were first published in 1803 from a manuscript in the possession of Jean François Marie, Marquis de Surville.

[13]Cp. p. 25.

self at the table of a Highness, so untrammelled in spirit and speech is the atmosphere that reigns over this friendly house.

Here is the true salon of the nineteenth century, for its mistress is the perfect type of modern woman. She is as amiable as her smile—that broad smile of a pretty Italian mouth which is the sweetest smile in the world—and she possesses the charm of entire naturalness, putting you at your ease with familiar speech and with the vivacity of everything that comes into her mind. An adorable goodness of nature. Today, feeling herself amongst men, she allowed herself to say what she pleased, and it was truly charming. She complained to us prettily and wittily about the extraordinary level to which woman has sunk as compared with the age depicted in our book, and about the difficulty she experienced in finding women who were interested in art, in new literature, or possessing, if not the curiosity of men, at least some concern with rare and elevated subjects. But most of the women that one sees, that one receives, said she, simply cannot be talked to. "For example, if a woman came into the room at this moment, I should immediately be obliged to change the subject of conversation. You will see a little later. For my part, I am perfectly willing to receive any intelligent woman of our day. I should have received Mademoiselle Rachel, even her, without demur. I will ask Madame Sand any time you like."

1863

January 1.—We are sad, and even more humilated than sad, at the thought of having to dine in a restaurant today. There are certain days of the year when it is seemly to have a family at precisely six o'clock.

January 3.—The Magny dinner. Our books and our method of work have, I feel, made a great impression upon Sainte-Beuve. Our intimate preoccupation with art worries him, bothers him, and tempts him. Being sufficiently intelligent to recognise what this new element, still unavailed of by others, adds in richness and colour to history, he is making an effort to catch up with it. He fumbles, interrogates, strives to make us talk. He doesn't know, you see; and he would like to know.

The talk being of the poverty of the people and the promiscuity of their quarters, Sainte-Beuve exclaimed with an accent of 1788 humanitarianism that he could not understand how any man on a throne could be other than a St Vincent de Paul or a Joseph II. "To rehabilitate all that would be something, would be a great beginning," he said over and over again. And from these humanitarian heights he descended quickly to the subject of the little girls of the common people, a subject, said he, which he had studied closely. He remarked with much truth that after puberty they have two or three years of folly—a furious love of dancing, a man's freedom of existence; and having thus sown their wild oats and had their fling, they become settled, sedate little housekeepers and mothers.

Undated.—Flaubert told us that when he was a child he would so lose himself in books, nibbling his tongue and twisting his hair with his fingers, that he would occasionally fall out of his chair on to the floor. One day he cut his nose, falling against a bookcase.

We met at his house a young medical student (Pouchet) who is interested in tattooing and who told us some of the things he had seen: *Liberty, Equality, Fraternity,* across a prostitute's belly; and on a convict's forehead, *No Luck.*

January 26.—Lately Flaubert told me that his maternal grandfather, a good old country doctor, having wept in an inn on reading of the execution of Louis XVI and been sent off to the Revolutionary Tribunal to be tried, was saved by Flaubert's father, then seven years old, whose mother had taught him a pathetic speech which he recited with great success to the local revolutionary society at Nogent-sur-Marne, where they then lived.

January 28.—Dined this evening at the Princess Mathilde's with Nieuwerkerke, a scientist named Pasteur, Sainte-Beuve and Chesneau, the art critic of the *Opinion Nationale.* A strange face, the princess's face, with all sorts of impressions crossing it in succession, and indefinable eyes that dart sudden and piercing looks at you. Her mind is like her glance; sullen sallies, snatches of wit, words that paint a thing or a man as clearly as Saint-Simon. I don't remember of whom it was she said, "A man with the dew of a painting on his eyes."

January 31.—Magny dinner. Sainte-Beuve very cheerful, overflowing with gaiety over a family outing the night before. Véron had invited him, his housekeeper, and his servants to dinner and had taken them to the Opéra in the evening. It was a true party out of old Paul de Kock's novels.

Then he began to talk with some agitation about Planche, whom he had introduced to the Victor Hugos apropos of a translation of the *Ronde du Sabbat* which an English engraver had wanted. Planche, it appears, settled down at the Hugos' and wouldn't leave. In those days he had not begun to write; he was a blond, rather good-looking chap who talked well, but he would go on talking so far into the night that once Hugo asked Sainte-Beuve, "When does your friend sleep?" And Sainte-Beuve, amazed at the blind supporters Planche gathered round him, most of them women, declared that he had no nape to his neck, no organ of passion, and that in the distress of his impotence with Mme Dorval he had rolled over and over again on the floor so desperately that the porter had heard him in the lodge below.

From Gustave Planche he turned to the subject of Michelet, saying that his only talent consisted in magnifying tiny things and in taking the view diametrically opposed to that which common sense would dictate, granting him merely a laborious originality which, he maintained, came chiefly from Michelet's conversations with Quinet. The whole table protesting violently, and Flaubert bravely asserting his admiration for the great historian's work, Sainte-Beuve went off in a fit of real anger, pounding the table despite the painful swelling in his joints, swearing, and vociferating that all the *hystericism* of Michelet's books came from the fact that he had known only one woman and was inhabited by the desires of a priest.

Dropping Michelet, he began a picture of what Marie Antoinette must have suffered with Louis XVI, that crude and brutal oaf who dropped a paving stone on a sleeping peasant, who broke wind in answer to a courtier's request to be made first gentleman of the king's chamber, who slapped M. de Cubières in the face and, by way of purchasing forgiveness, gave him a horse which had arrived the same day from Constantinople, so that he who got slapped was able to say, "The king gave me the horse in a touching manner."

And Sainte-Beuve interrupted himself to say: "Tell me, Veyne, what is this I have here? An abscess?" And he put forth his wrist.

"No," said Veyne; "a swelling of the joints which is not even gout."

"I wasn't going to do anything about it. I just wanted to know."

"An ugly machine, this human body," one of us said.

"Not at all: it is very well put together," Sainte-Beuve retorted.

"Well put together you say. Yet in your youth your health was pretty bad."

"Oh, in my youth! In the first place, my life was not like anybody else's. I fed badly. Not enough. There was a romantic sentimentality which forbade me to eat my fill. And I would get remorseful over cheating my mistress. Yes, I didn't eat enough. Remorse, you know, is nothing but a physical weakness. Afterwards I changed. I introduced gaiety and a hedonistic philosophy into my life."

Thereupon Flaubert—yes, Flaubert—and Saint-Victor undertook to defend the thesis that there was nothing to be done with modern life; whereat everybody screamed like peacocks and flung at them, "Art is transposed on another plane, that is all the difference."

February 14.—Our Saturday dinners are delightful. The conversation touches upon every subject, and each man opens up, confesses himself a little. We talked about women. "For my part," said Sainte-Beuve; "my ideal is hair, teeth, shoulders, and the rest. Filth makes no difference." And as someone spoke of the elegant nightcaps that ladies wear in bed, he said: "My women never wear nightcaps. I've never seen anything more than a net. So far as that goes, I have never in my life spent a whole night with a woman, because of my work." Following an allusion to oriental women, he flew into a passion against their depilation. Saint-Victor came to his aid by saying, "It must look like a parish priest's chin." And the incident ended with a violent diatribe by Sainte-Beuve against the Orient, charging that it mutilated everything.

Sainte-Beuve has just written a medallion on Royer-Collard.

Still filled with his article, he quoted to us the better-known witticisms of the great man as well as one not yet repeated, which Veyne, who attended him in his last illness, had overheard. His servant having difficulty in getting him to pass water, the old man had grumbled, "The animal won't go any more." And Sainte-Beuve swooned with delight over the lofty philosophy of these words. We spoke our minds about the remarkable things that are said in conversation and are never repeated because those who said them were not people of high social or political station, instancing Grassot's superb remark to his *animal* in a urinal: "What a fool you are! Come along: all I want you to do is——." With this remark of the great comedian we were able to kill the witticism of the great *poseur*.

At bottom our absolute independence of everything official, consecrated, and academically recognized overwhelms the habits of mind, the religions, and the superstitions of respect stored up in Sainte-Beuve, and we seem to him a strange pair of blokes, two contemners who terrify him a little. Despite his literary independence of mind, he has always made sacrifices—and often with servility—to the esteem he enjoys as writer, as historian, as orator, and even as conversationalist. He has no judgment free of genuflexion before politics as we have, such as allows us to measure the inanity of a Pasquier, the superficiality of a Thiers, and the profound vacuity of a Guizot.

Nogent-Saint-Laurens, who dined with us this evening and is a member of the Committee on Copyright, declared that he favoured perpetuity of rights. Sainte-Beuve protested in lively fashion, exclaiming that writers were "paid by smoke, by noise." He went on: "A writer ought to say, then, 'Take everything I've got. Take it all and make me happy.'" Flaubert, who habitually takes the negative in every argument, exclaimed: "If I had invented the railways I shouldn't want anybody to ride on them without my permission." To which Sainte-Beuve retorted angrily, "No more literary property than any other property. There should be no property. Perpetual renovation is what is wanted. Let every man take his turn at the job."

In these few words, spurting up from what is most secret and most sincere in his soul, Sainte-Beuve revealed himself the revolutionary celibate; and he seemed to us almost one of the levellers of the Convention of 1792, a man betraying his hatred à la Rousseau against nineteenth-century society, and indeed looking physically somewhat like Jean Jacques.

Therewith somebody—I know not who—flung Hugo's name into the conversation. At the sound of that name Sainte-Beuve jumped as if bitten by a snake under the table, declaring that Hugo was a charlatan, that he was the first of the literary speculators. Whereupon Flaubert cried out that he had rather be Hugo than any man in the world. "No," Sainte-Beuve countered with great sense; "no; in literature one would not wish to be anybody but oneself. One would like to appropriate some of another writer's qualities; but still to remain oneself."

And then suddenly a great gentleness came into his voice, and he agreed that Hugo had a marvellous gift of initiation. "Yes," he said; "it was he who taught me to write verse. And one day, also, at the Louvre, he taught me to look at pictures. All of which I have since forgotten. A prodigious constitution, that Hugo. His hairdresser told me that his beard was three times as stiff as normal and notched his razors. He had the teeth of a tiger and could crack peach pits with them. And his eyes! When he was writing his *Feuilles d'automne* we would go up to the top of the towers of Notre-Dame every evening to see the sunsets—which, incidentally, did not amuse me very much. Well, he could tell from there what colour gown Mademoiselle Nodier was wearing when she sat on the balcony of the Arsénal."[1]

This was certainly the health of a healthy genius; but just the same, I wondered, if a writer is to render the delicacies, the exquisite melancholies, the rare and delicious phantasies, of the vibrant cord of the heart and the soul, is it not necessary that he be, as Heine was, somewhat crucified, physically?

[1] The Arsenal stands about a thousand yards from Notre-Dame. Mlle Nodier was the young woman to whom Félix d'Arvers addressed his otherwise unavowed love in the well-known *"sonnet d'Arvers"* beginning, "Mon âme a son secret, ma vie a son mystère. . . ." Her father, Charles Nodier, Librarian of the Bibliothèque de l'Arsénal, was better appreciated as sympathetic and cultivated counsel and host to the romantics (his soirées were famous) than as story writer.

February 23.—Magny dinner. Charles Edmond brought with him Turgenieff, that exquisitely gifted foreign writer, author of *A Nest of Noblemen* and *A Russian Hamlet.*[2] He is an attractive colossus, a gentle, white-haired giant who looks like the benevolent genie of a mountain or a forest. He is handsome, most handsome, greatly handsome, with the blue of the skies in his eyes and the charm of the Russian chant in his accent, that singsong in which there is a spot of the child and of the Negro. Touched and put at ease by the warmth of the reception accorded him, he spoke to us interestingly of Russian literature, saying that it was in the full tide of realism, both in the novel and the theatre. He said that Russians were great readers of periodical literature and blushed to confess that he and a dozen others were paid as much as 600 francs a page. On the other hand, books brought them nothing in Russia—a maximum of 4,000 francs.

Turgenieff having pronounced the name of Heine, and we having affirmed our great admiration for the German poet, Sainte-Beuve said that he had known him well, that the man was a miserable rascal; and the whole table raining protest down upon him, he shut up, covering his face with his hands while the rest of us praised Heine. Baudry told us this pretty remark made by Heine on his deathbed. His wife praying beside the bed that God forgive him, he interrupted the prayer to say, "Have no fear, my darling. He will forgive me: that's His trade."

March 1.—Flaubert's last Sunday before going off to bury himself in work at Croisset.

A man arrived, thin, gaunt, with a sparse beard and a rather harsh look about him. When he spoke, however, his rather vacant face became animated, and when he listened to you it took on a certain charm. He spoke amenable words which fell from a mouth filled with long teeth, like an old Englishwoman's. This was Taine, the incarnation in flesh and blood of modern criticism, a criticism at once very learned, very ingenious, and very often erroneous beyond imagining. There persists in him a survival of the professor lecturing to his class. This, one cannot

[2] The reference is to *A Lear of the Steppes,* presumably.

rid oneself of; but his university side is mitigated by a great simplicity, a remarkable gentleness in his relations with people, the attentiveness of a well-bred man, and great courtesy to others.

We spoke of what Turgenieff had said the night before—that Dickens was the only popular writer in Russia and that since 1830 our literature was without influence there, having been superseded by English and American novelists. Taine said that in his view their influence would increase as time went on, while the influence of French literature would continue to diminish;[3] that since the eighteenth century we had in France remarkable men in every branch of knowledge, a wonderful front rank of our intellectual army, but there was nothing behind them, they had no troops; that this was now the case and had always been the case as between Paris and the provinces. "Hachette," he added, "has just refused to publish a translation of Mommsen's Roman history. He is perfectly right. At the moment they are bringing out in Germany a new edition of the works of Johann Sebastian Bach: out of fifteen hundred subscriptions, ten came from France."

Saturday, March 14.—Magny dinner. Taine dined with us this evening, Taine with his fleeting glance, his almost affectionate consideration of others, his smooth and picturesque language enriched with historical and scientific notions, his slightly ailing distinction, and that simulacrum of the gentleman which young professors acquire who have been tutors in great families. He talked of the absence of intellectual interest in the French provinces, comparing it with all the literary societies in the English counties and German towns. He spoke about the *plethora* of this Paris which attracts and absorbs everything, fabricates everything; of the future of France which, in these circumstances, will end up with a cerebral hemorrhage. "The Paris of today," he said, "makes me think of the valley of Alexandria. Below Alexandria *dangled* the valley of the Nile, but it was a dead valley."

[3]Never was prognostication more erroneous, for at no time have French books, in particular the novel, had such a sale in Europe as in the few years following Taine's remarks. For that matter, philosophers, as will appear again and again in these journals, seem to possess a particular gift for prophecy that does not come true.—E. de G.

Apropos of a fresh eulogy of England by Taine, I heard Sainte-Beuve confide in him his disgust over being a Frenchman: "I know that people say that to be a Parisian is not to be a Frenchman; but one is, nevertheless, a Frenchman, which is to say that one is nothing, that one counts for nothing. A country full of policemen. I should like to be an Englishman: at least an Englishman is somebody. As a matter of fact, I have some English blood. I was born in Boulogne, you know. My grandmother was English."

The talk fell on About, whom Taine defended as an old classmate at the École Normale. "A lad," Sainte-Beuve put in, "who has tried to carry three great capitals on his back—Athens, Rome and Paris. You saw what happened to his *Gaëtana*.[4] Awkward, to say the least."

"You have never written about him, I believe," someone said.

"No," said Sainte-Beuve. "In the first place, he is very well known as it is. And then, he is alive; too much alive. I give the impression of being brave, but at bottom I am really very cowardly."

Thereafter we embarked upon an enormous discussion about God and religion, a discussion born of the fermentation of a good warm digestion in superior brains. Taine explained the advantages and conveniences for superior minds of the elastic Protestant dogma, which permits each to feed his faith according to his own nature and spirit. "At bottom," he said by way of conclusion, "it is all a matter of sentiment, and I believe that musical natures are instinctively Protestant, while plastic natures are instinctively Catholic."

March 28.—Magny dinner. The new member being Renan, quite naturally the subject of conversation was religion. Sainte-Beuve opined that paganism had begun as a very jolly thing and had thereafter putrefied, become a sort of pox; that Christianity was the mercury applied to this pox, but too much of the remedy

[4]What happened to About's *Gaëtana* was to happen in December 1865 to the Goncourts' *Henriette Maréchal*. About's rather ridiculous melodrama was hissed off the stage by a cabal of students because the author had "sold himself" to the authoritarian government of Napoleon III.

had been applied, and we had now to be cured of the remedy it-self. Then, dropping his lofty theories, he spoke to me in an aside of the ambitions of his childhood, of all that the passage of the troops had woken in him when he was a lad in Boulogne—his desire to become a soldier. "Military fame is the only fame," he said. "The only people I esteem are great geometricians and great captains." I could readily see that his dream might have been to be a colonel of hussars and have all the women he wanted. His true ambition might have been to be handsome; and I must say that I have rarely met a man who had missed his ambition as completely as he has done.

A battle raged round Voltaire. Both of us, speaking of the writer, and without regard to his social or political influence, con-tested his literary value, daring to repeat the abbé Trublet's opinion that Voltaire was "the perfection of mediocrity." We recognized that he had a certain merit as popularizer, as journal-ist; but nothing more. He was witty, if you like; but his wit was not of a higher order than the wit of many witty old ladies of his time. His plays? Who dares defend them? His history? Full of lies and the most pompous and stupid conventions of solemn, old-fashioned historiography. His science and his hypotheses are plainly ridiculous in the eyes of contemporary scientists. The only thing he wrote which justifies keeping his name alive, that famous *Candide,* is, after all, mere La Fontaine in prose, Rabelais *castrato*. What are his eighty volumes worth beside a *Neveu de Rameau,* or a *Ceci n'est pas un conte,* those marvels that Diderot wrote; a novel and a tale that bore in them the seeds of all the novels and tales written in the nineteenth century?

Everybody fell upon us at once, Sainte-Beuve ending by de-claring that France would not be a free country until the day when a monument to Voltaire was set up on the place Louis XV.[5] Voltaire led Sainte-Beuve into a eulogy of Jean Jacques Rous-seau, of whom he spoke as one of his household gods, a man of his own race, which eulogy someone broke brutally into with these words: "Jean Jacques was a masturbating lackey."

In the face of all this violence of thought and language Renan

[5]Now place de la Concorde.

sat mute and startled, but curious nevertheless, attentive, interested, drinking in the cynicism of the words like a respectable woman at a harlot's supper party.

Eventually they came back to God.

"It is extraordinary," said I, "how one always talks about the immortality of the soul with dessert."

"Yes," Sainte-Beuve said, "when one no longer knows what one is talking about."

Undated.—A very fine remark of old Rothschild's pronounced the other day at Walewski's. Calvet-Rogniat having asked him why Consols had gone down the day before, he answered: "Do I know why stocks go up or down? If I knew that I should be a rich man."

April 11.—Magny dinner. The Imperial Court is very interested at the moment in Marie Antoinette. Recently the Tuileries Palace asked the Imperial Library to send along all the documents on the necklace. Another time the little heir to the throne, taken to a studio, asked the painter to tell him all about the death of Louis XVII in the Temple.[6]

Sainte-Beuve betrays a very hostile sentiment against the Queen, a sort of personal hatred. He displayed some anger towards us because we defended her purity, and he set about with amusing animation to make us change our minds. Then, out of memories collected from various families, he sketched for us the "true" Louis XVI, sending to his courtiers, on waking in the morning, little pellets of dirt from between his toes. Thereupon Renan raised his mild little voice to say that one should not be too hard upon "those people"—meaning kings! They had not chosen to be kings; "and one ought to forgive them their mediocrity."

In my ear Sainte-Beuve confessed that he thought of writing about Marie Antoinette one of these days, by way of being disagreeable to the empress, who admired her.

[6]See, in the notes appended, "Marie Antoinette" for the story of the necklace and "Louis XVII" for the mystery of the young dauphin.

April 29.—M. de Montalembert wrote asking us to come and talk with him about our *Woman in the XVIIIth Century*. After complimenting us, he asked why we had not written about the provincial virtues, about social life in the provinces, that quite particular, well-marked, and characteristic existence observable in such provincial capitals as Dijon, for example, and which had now completely vanished. "Yes," he went on; "the provinces no longer send to Paris for books. They have ceased to read. When my country neighbours call on me, I lend them books and they never open them." Then he spoke of Sainte-Beuve's article on our book, and said that exactly where we were sitting Sainte-Beuve used to come in 1848 to talk to him, acknowledging that he came in order to study him, asking how he went about preparing his speeches, taking notes and rubbing his hands in glee. "I have known Sainte-Beuve in many phases of his existence. First as the idolator of Hugo and writing the best verse he ever wrote—the poems to Hugo's wife; then as a Saint-Simonian;[7] then mystically inclined, to the point of believing he was about to become a Christian; and now *very bad*. Do you know that the other day, at a session of the Academy, apropos of the dictionary, he tapped his forehead and had the audacity to say: 'After all, do you really think that what we have here is anything but a secretion of the brain?' One would not have believed that, except for a few physicians, anybody could be so materialistic. We have had rationalism and scepticism; but pure materialism was nonexistent up to a few years ago. And lately, when we were discussing the twenty-thousand-franc prize for the novel, and the name of Madame Sand came up, did not Sainte-Beuve main-

[7]Count Claude Henri de Saint-Simon (1760–1825) was the leader of a political and social school which taught a doctrine of state ownership of the means of production combined with the abolition of the inheritance of property, out of which was to come the reign of justice and the universal brotherhood of man. After his death the movement split into a political wing, headed by one Bazard, and a mystical wing, under the leadership of one Enfantin, the first being republican in theory and the second communistic as regards property and the status of woman. Bazard and Enfantin mutually excommunicated each other. The latter called himself the male Messiah and gave balls and receptions in his search for a female messiah, whom he never found. (See that masterpiece of ironic humour, Kinglake's *Eothen,* on Enfantin and Lady Hester Stanhope.) Eventually, the police intervened, and in 1832 the society was dissolved and Enfantin was imprisoned.

tain that marriage as an institution was doomed, that it would soon cease to be? . . .

"Oh, Littré . . . well . . . While I agree that the Bishop of Orleans did his duty, and was entirely within his rights, I should not have been so far from voting for him as my friends were.[8] He is an austere and honourable man who has done remarkable work. And he has this to his credit—for which I am grateful and which I esteem highly in him—that whenever he has said anything about the Middle Ages, he has rendered justice to the Germanic element which indisputably exists in our race. Apart from the question of dogma and faith, Catholicism is certainly the best heritage we have; but for the sake of equilibrium we need, in addition to that Catholicism, the mixture of the Germanic element with the Latin element. Just look at the collapse of the races of the South. Littré realises this, whereas Thierry and Guizot are still against the barbarians. Littré, on the contrary, is for them, and his point of view is very just.

"By the way, do you know that we have in the Academy another convert to Bonapartism? It is Cousin; yes, Cousin. He came to me the other day and said that we ought to elect a few harmless Bonapartists. But, said I, *reptiles* are always dangerous. He believes we ought to be content to possess our civil liberties. But it doesn't matter to me one way or the other that I may be free to make my will. What France needs is political life. But people retire from the field; they capitulate for the sake of private life."

May 11.—Magny dinner with everybody present and two new members—Gautier and Nefftzer.

The conversation came round to Balzac and stopped there. Sainte-Beuve attacked the great man: "Balzac is not realistic. A genius, if you like; but a monstrosity."

"We are all monstrosities," countered Gautier. "But who painted our age? Where can we find the society of our time? In what book if not in Balzac?"

[8]Upon Littré's election to the Academy, Mgr Dupanloup, the (liberal) Bishop of Orleans, resigned from the Academy and wrote his famous pamphlet, *A Warning to Fathers of Families* against the "materialism" of Renan, Taine and Littré. (For Littré, see biographical appendix.)

"It's all imagination, invention!" Sainte-Beuve cried harshly. "I knew that rue Langlade of his: it didn't look at all like that."

"Then in what novels do you find reality? In Madame Sand's?"

Renan, sitting beside me, spoke up. "I must say, I think Madame Sand more realistic than Balzac."

"Not really!"

"Yes indeed. The passions in her books are generalized . . ."

Sainte-Beuve broke in. "And that style of Balzac's! All twisted: a *corded* style."

"Gentlemen," Renan went on; "in three hundred years people will still be reading Madame Sand."

"In your hat! Madame Sand has no more chance of immortality than Madame de Genlis."

"Balzac is already old fashioned," Saint-Victor ventured. "And how complicated!"

"But look at a character like Hulot, in *Cousine Bette!*" Nefftzer exclaimed. "How human, how wonderful!"

"Beauty is always simple," Saint-Victor said. "There is nothing more beautiful than the feelings of Homer's characters. They are eternally fresh. You talk about *Cousine Bette:* how much more interesting Andromache is than Madame Marneffe."

"Not to me," Edmond threw in.

"What! Do you mean that?"

"Your Homer paints nothing but physical anguish. It is quite another thing to depict moral and mental suffering. And if you want the truth, any little psychological novel moves me more deeply than the whole of your Homer. I get more pleasure out of Benjamin Constant's *Adolphe* than out of the *Iliad.*"

"It's enough to drive a man mad, to hear things like that!" Saint-Victor bellowed. His eyes were popping out of his head. Edmond had trodden upon his god, had spit upon his host. He was stamping with rage. "You're crazy! How can any man . . . In the first place, there is no arguing about the Greeks. Everything about them is divine."

General tumult during which Sainte-Beuve crossed himself with the piety of an Oratorian father and murmured, "But, gentleman, Ulysses' dog . . ." while Gautier flung at Saint-Victor,

"Homer? A poem written by Bitaubé.[9] Bitaubé got him by. Homer isn't what you think. You have only to read him in the Greek. It's very barbaric."

And I said to my neighbour, "You may deny God, argue about the Pope, shout your head off about anything . . . except Homer. Literary religions are strange things."

Finally they all quieted down. Saint-Victor shook hands with Edmond, and the dinner went on.

Then if Renan didn't go off into a tale of how he was at the moment engaged in removing from his book all newspaper French in order to write in the true language of the seventeenth century, the finally and ultimately fixed French language, a language sufficient for the expression of every possible sentiment.

"You are on the wrong track and you will not succeed," Gautier told him flatly. "I will show you, in your own books, four hundred words that did not exist in the seventeenth century. You have new ideas, haven't you? Well, for those new ideas you want new words. And what makes you think that Saint-Simon did not write the language of his age? Or Madame de Sévigné? What about her?"

Gautier's great words having downed everybody's objections, he went on: "I grant you that they may not have needed any more words than they possessed in their day. But they didn't know anything: a little Latin; no Greek; not a word of art, for they said of Raphael that he was the Mignard of his time; not a word of history; not a word of archaeology. I defy you to write the article that I shall write Tuesday on Baudry, with the vocabulary of the seventeenth century."

March 19.—Bored, tired, and discouraged by our novel (*Renée Mauperin*), which is almost finished. This happens inevitably towards the end of a long task.

[9]This member of the Academy of Berlin, born at Königsberg of French parents in 1732, wrote only French and produced a translation of Homer which went through many editions. Pope was a great poet and Bitaubé was not; but the Frenchman's translation was even more elegant than the "Bacchus-in-his-glassy-prison" and "Ceres-in-her-nut-brown-cloak" product of Twickenham.

June 1.—Every candidate of the opposition party elected in Paris. To think that if all France were as enlightened as is Paris, we should be an ungovernable people! The fact is that any government which strives to diminish the number of illiterates in the country works towards its own downfall.[10]

June 8.—Coming away from a violent dispute at Magny's, my heart pounding in my breast, throat and tongue dry, I am convinced of what I here set down. Every political argument comes to this: I am better than you are. Every literary argument, to this: My taste is better than yours. Every dispute about art, to this: I have better eyesight than you have. Every squabble over music, to this: I can hear better than you can.

In political discussions the only man on our side is the silent Gautier, who is indifferent to these things as he is to all inferior things, and who refused absolutely to remember that Sainte-Beuve had met him, many years ago, walking in a procession commemorating the death of the four sergeants of La Rochelle.[11]

June 22.—Magny dinner. . . .

GAUTIER: The *bourgeoisie!* Strange things are going on in our middle classes. I have been in their houses. It's enough to make a man hide his face in shame. Tribadism is their normal state; incest is permanently installed; and bestiality.

TAINE: I know the middle classes pretty well. I come of a *bourgeois* family myself. For one thing, what do you mean by *bourgeois?*[12]

[10]"On the evening of the 31st May the crowd read feverishly the results of the voting in Paris. . . . That evening a wave of joy swept over the capital: the Government was beaten all along the line. . . . Paris cheered its revenge for the Second of December. Already it was cheering the Republic. . . . But France did not follow Paris. In the provinces, only a few towns elected republican candidates." Arnaud, op. cit.

[11]*Les quatres sergeants de La Rochelle* were four members of *La Charbonnerie,* a secret political society organized into lodges in emulation of the Italian *Carbonari,* which fomented republican uprisings at various points in 1821 and 1822. Sergeant Major Bories and three of his confederates were implicated in one of these affairs at La Rochelle and were executed on the twenty-first of September 1822.

[12]There is no satisfactory word in English. Carlyle's "gigmanity" never took; "Philistine" went out of fashion. We ought to emulate the Russians and accept the French word without italics.

GAUTIER: People who have fifteen or twenty thousand francs a year and nothing to do.

TAINE: So? Well, I can name thirty *bourgeois* women of my acquaintance, all of them pure.

A VOICE: What do you know about it, Taine? God himself couldn't be sure.

TAINE: Look here. In the town of Angers they keep such a close watch on women that there is no breath of scandal about a single one of them.

SAINT-VICTOR: Angers? But they are all pæderasts. There was a case recently. . . .

SAINTE-BEUVE: Madame Sand, gentlemen, is doing a book on a son of Jean Jacques Rousseau during the Revolution. It will be most generously written. She is full of her subject; has written me three letters about it. Wonderful organization, that woman.

SOULIÉ: You know, there is a farce by Théaulon on Rousseau's children.

RENAN: Madame Sand is the greatest artist of our time and the truest talent.

General protest.

SAINT-VICTOR: Isn't it strange that she writes on notepaper?

RENAN: By true I do not mean realistic.

SAINTE-BEUVE: Let's drink. I am for drinking. Come along, Scherer.

* * *

TAINE: Hugo? But Hugo is not sincere.

SAINTE-BEUVE: What! You, Taine, you put Musset higher than Hugo? But Hugo writes books! Under the very nose of the government that exiled him he has snatched the greatest popularity of our time.[13] His books penetrate everywhere: the women, the common people—everybody reads him. Editions go out of print between eight in the morning and twelve o'clock noon. When I first read his *Odes et ballades* I sought him out immediately with all my verse. The editors of the *Globe* called him a barbarian.

[13]Hugo was, in politics, an idealizing and courageous ass. Having protested against the coup d'état of December 1851 he escaped to Brussels, thence to Jersey, and finally to Guernsey. From Jersey he published *Napoléon le petit* and the extravagant but eloquent anti-Napoleon poems contained in *Les Châtiments*.

Well! Everything that I have done I owe to him; whereas in ten years the people on the *Globe* taught me nothing.

SAINT-VICTOR: We are all his descendants.

TAINE: Allow me. Hugo, in our time, is an immense event; but——

SAINTE-BEUVE (very animated): Taine, do not say a word about Hugo. You don't know him. There are only two of us here who know him—Gautier and I. Hugo's work is magnificent!

TAINE: It is what you nowadays, I believe, call poetry; painting a steeple, a sky; making things visible, in short. For me that is not poetry: it is painting.

GAUTIER: Taine, you are talking *bourgeois* idiocy. Poetry is not sentimentalism, far from it. Words that radiate; words of light; and rhythm, and music—there you have poetry. It doesn't set out to prove anything. Take the opening of *Ratbert:* there is no poetry in the world like it. It is the Himalayas. All of heraldic Italy is in it . . . and it is nothing but words."

NEFFTZER: Come, now. If it is beautiful, there must be an idea in it.

GAUTIER: You! Don't talk to me. You made up with the good God in order to get out a newspaper. You are on good terms with the *old chap*.

The whole table laughs.

* * *

TAINE: The Englishwoman, for example.

SAINTE-BEUVE: Oh, there is nothing more charming than the Frenchwoman. One, two, three, four, five women. Delightful. Has our lovely friend returned? And to think that when quarter day comes round, and the rent is due, one can have a crowd of ravishing ones. For nothing. The poor dears! For the wages of woman. . . . There is something that historians like Thiers never think of. There is the place to reform the state. These questions——

SAINT-VICTOR: No, there is no way women can earn a living. Little What's-her-name, at the Gymnase Theatre, who is paid 4,000 francs a year, told me yesterday——

GAUTIER: I have always said that prostitution was woman's normal state.

A VOICE: After all, Malthus——

VEYNE: Malthus is an ignominious book!

TAINE: But it seems to me that one should bring children into the world only if one is certain of being able to ensure them some sort of existence. Those poor girls who go off to be governesses in Russia!

A VOICE: Long live our wives! Long live sterile mistresses!

SAINT-VICTOR: Come, Taine. Nature! The great god Pan!

SAINTE-BEUVE (whispering to his neighbour): Every year I sell the rights to a little book. That allows me to make little gifts to women . . . in holiday season. They are so sweet; one cannot really . . .

At this point in the dinner Sainte-Beuve, cheered up by his memories, made himself earrings of clusters of cherries. Tableau!

Somehow the name of Racine fell into the general talk.

NEFFTZER (to Gautier): Look here, you committed an infamy this morning. In the *Moniteur* you extolled the talent of Racine and Maubant.[14]

GAUTIER: True. Maubant has a great deal of talent. But, with my government paper, you see how it is: my minister is idiotic enough to believe in masterpieces. I was therefore obliged to review Racine's *Andromaque*. For that matter, Racine wrote swinish verse and I said not a word in praise of the creature. And somebody let loose one Agar in the sport. You saw that, Uncle.

At our dinners Gautier never calls Sainte-Beuve anything else than "Uncle" or "Uncle Beuve."

SCHERER (horrified and staring at the whole tableful over his glasses): Gentlemen, it seems to me you are excessively intolerant. You proceed by way of exclusion. After all, what should our task be but to reform, to combat instinctive opinions. Taste is nothing. The only thing that counts is judgment. One should possess judgment before all else.

A VOICE:— on judgment! Taste and nothing else! Only taste! *Tumult.*

[14]An actor. Agar, mentioned later, was an actress.

SOULIÉ: We can hardly hear one another.

GAVARNI: We hear one another only too well.

Exeunt omnes.

Wednesday, June 24.—At the end of a path in the park at Saint-Gratien, Princess Mathilde stood in a cream-coloured foulard dress talking to someone, her hands behind her back à la Napoleon, followed by her pig-fat little dog on its four matchstick legs. She turned round.

"Ah, there is Sainte-Beuve. Come: information, quickly. What do you know about Duruy?"

"Why," Sainte-Beuve began with a vague smile; "he is very cordial. Physically attractive, which does no harm."

"We want more than that."

"Well, he wrote the outline of history that you know about; and I believe he helped the emperor with his book on Caesar."

"Yes, yes, I remember," said the princess. "The emperor asked me one day if I knew of anybody who could take Mocquard's place, Mocquard tiring very quickly these days. He mentioned Duruy. But it's a queer substitution. I only heard about it yesterday, coming back from Versailles, where I had a very amusing time. I miss Rouland a good deal. After all, we always change men and never things. I must run now."

We dined; and after dinner Sainte-Beuve complained that he was growing old. He was told he had never been so young. "That's true," the princess exclaimed. "He has broken with a lot of foolishness, given up a lot of solemn notions. I prefer what you do now. Isn't it true, gentlemen, that his articles have a freshness. . . . He's going well; he is *floundering in reality.*"

"That is probably true," Sainte-Beuve said, blushing at the compliment. "Criticism consists in saying whatever comes into one's head. That is all there is to it."

June 25.—This office which has witnessed so many dreadful things, this confidant of so many dark secrets, this official study of the prefect of police—who would believe it?—is filled with blond and amorous paintings, with roguish nudes, with many a flirtatious little phiz, all these not merely covering the hideous, bee-sown imperial paper on the walls, but lying strewn round on armchairs, desk, floors, spread in every direction. "Yes," said Boitelle, "when you spend your day as I do, seeing such ugly individuals, it is restful to be able to look at something pretty from time to time." And he took us into his intimate *caphar-naum,* the gardener's lodge in the little garden of the prefecture, which we found crammed to the roof with pictures. There, with a box of cigars, a basin of water, and sponges, he spends the happiest hours of his life, bringing back and reviving the fouled and besmirched colourings of enigmatically anonymous canvasses.

Monday, July 6.—Sainte-Beuve submitted his resignation as member of the Dictionary Committee of the Academy, giving up thus an honorarium of 1,200 francs per annum, in order to feel free to write the article he published this morning on Littré's dictionary. There is a beautiful disinterested passion in the critic's hatred.

July 12.—A commissionnaire brought us a note from Sainte-Beuve saying that he was indisposed and hoped that we would come round to talk to him about his article on Gavarni.

After we had given him certain biographical information, we began to go over the captions written on Gavarni's lithographs. What was our amazement to hear Sainte-Beuve mangle these lines through total ignorance of modern life, of every Parisian idiom. But what was really extraordinary happened when we came to look at the pictures as a whole. Concerning the actors in these scenes with dialogue he saw nothing, perceived nothing, could not distinguish which character was speaking. I swear that this is the exact truth: in one picture, containing two characters, he went so far as to take the shadow of one of them for a third character, and he was for a moment comically angry in his insistence that there were three people in the scene.

He drank in everything we told him and took notes on it all. He would grasp at the slightest technical word we let drop, scribble it on a sheet of paper, building up his article out of these landmarks strewn here and there over the paper so that it looked like a drawing of a tick, of a sort of drone magnified under a microscope. Before we left he wanted to know about genre painters of earlier times.

"Abram Bos," we suggested.

"What period?" he asked.

"And Freudeberg."

"How is that?"

"Freudeberg."

"How do you spell it?"

Thus does he snatch, bag, snap up on the fly, without digesting any of it, your ideas, notions, knowledge. And I thought, laughing in my beard, of the almost religious veneration with which numbers of people were going to read this article. Just the same, I think Sainte-Beuve would do well to give up writing about art.

July 17.—This evening I shall go to the *Closerie des Lilas.* That is the only dance hall where one can still see in the flesh the little Parisian mouse Gavarni loved to draw. There you hear real laughter, genuine gaiety, and a hubbub in which women ask passersby for the hairpins they may need, while the music of the band is sung in happy chorus by the dancers and the students who, by way of tips, shake hands with the waiters when they leave.

Monday, July 20.—Magny dinner. Apropos of a new biography of Victor Hugo, Gautier declared that it was not a red waistcoat he had worn at the opening night of *Hernani,* but a pink doublet.[15]

And upon everybody's laughing, he added, "But it is an important distinction. The red waistcoat would have meant I was a republican, whereas there was no politics in the thing. We were simply *mediævalists.* All of us, Hugo as well as the rest. We didn't

[15]The riot which took place in the Théâtre-Français on this night, the twenty-fifth of February 1830, marked it as a historic date in the struggle between romanticism and classicism. On that night Gautier wore a cherry-red satin doublet, water-green breeches with black velvet braid, and a hazel-grey coat lined with green satin. As he said on another occasion, "The costume was fairly well calculated to irritate and scandalize the Philistines."

know what a republican was. Pétrus Borel was the only republican we knew. We were all against the *bourgeois,* but for Marchangy. We represented the *machicoulis,*[16] that's all. Later, when I eulogized antiquity in the preface to my *Mademoiselle de Maupin,* it meant secession. Machicoulis and nothing but machicoulis. I admit that Uncle Beuve was always a liberal. But in those days Hugo was for Louis XVII. Yes, Louis XVII. No one can tell me that Hugo was a liberal and had all that nonsense in his head in 1828. He didn't take up with that filth until later. At bottom, Hugo is absolutely mediæval . . . and Jersey, where he now lives, is full of heraldry."

"Gautier," said Sainte-Beuve, interrupting him; "do you know how we spent the day of the first night of *Hernani?* At two in the afternoon we went along with Hugo, whose *fidus Achates* I then was, to the Théâtre-Français. We climbed all the way up into the lantern tower and looked down on the queue at the box office, all of them Hugo's troops. There was a moment when he took fright at the sight of Lassailly, who was on a newspaper and to whom he had not given a ticket. I reassured him, saying that I would answer for Lassailly. Then we went down to dine at Véfour's restaurant—in the public rooms, as well as I remember, Hugo's face not being then as famous as it later became."

* * *

"Yes, yes. I admire Jesus wholeheartedly," Renan said.

"But after all," cried Sainte-Beuve; "there are a great many stupid things in his Gospels. 'Blessed are the meek for they shall inherit the earth.' The thing doesn't make sense."

"And Sakyamuni," Gautier threw in. "Suppose we did a little drinking to the health of Sakyamuni."

"And Confucius," some one proposed.

"Not him. He's terribly dull!"

"What could possibly be duller than the Koran?"

"Ah," sighed Sainte-Beuve, leaning forward towards me. "The thing to do is to make the rounds of everything and believe none of it. There is nothing true except woman. Wisdom . . . really

---

[16] A mediæval balcony roof with holes in the floor through which the besieged let drop hot oil, missiles, and so on, upon the besiegers.

. . . wisdom is what Sénac de Meilhan put into his novel, *L'Émigré*.

"Quite right," said I. "An amiable scepticism is still the *summum* of humanity. To believe nothing, not even one's doubts. All conviction is stupid . . . as a pope."

* * *

"I admit," Gautier was meanwhile saying, confessing himself to Veyne, "I have never felt a particularly violent desire for that intimate gymnastic. It isn't that my constitution is any weaker than the next man's: I have fathered seventeen children, all of them rather good looking. There are samples to be seen. But I assure you that to give way to love once a year is quite enough. It leaves me completely self-possessed: I could solve mathematical problems while it is going on. Besides, I consider it humiliating that a trollop should think you found it necessary to leap her."

Sainte-Beuve, for his part, was informing us that when he gave his course at the University of Liége in 1849, having written much and extremely rapidly, he had been seized with what the doctors called writer's cramp, which had paralysed the muscles of his right arm a little, so that since then he wrote only notes and dictated all letters of any length.

As we rose to go, Gautier went over to Scherer, the silent member of the company, and said to him: "As for you, I hope that the next time you come, you will compromise yourself. We all compromise ourselves here, and it is not fair that you sit by dispassionately observing us."

Monday, August 17.—Coming away from the solitude of Gretz, near Fontainebleau, we returned with pleasure to the Magny gossipshop. The talk, to begin with, was all of the newly buried Eugène Delacroix, Saint-Victor sketching in a single comic sentence that ravaged bilious creature we had seen one day going through the rue des Beaux-Arts with a portfolio under his arm: "He looked like Tippoo Sahib's apothecary."

No sooner had Saint-Victor got that out than he went white

and remarked that we were thirteen at table. Positively, we were thirteen. "What of it?" said Gautier, pretending to be easier in mind than he felt; "Only Christians count, and there is more than one atheist at table." Nevertheless, he and Saint-Victor sent off for a fourteenth, who turned out to be Magny's son, a school-boy before whom heinous stories were soon being told.

August 25.—Cabourg: a singular place we find ourselves in; a sea-bathing resort for people of the theatre; a sea-bathing place whose placard, regulating the modesty of the bathers, begins— "The Mayor of Cabourg, Knight of the Legion of Honour, Com-mander of the Order of Charles III . . ." and is signed with the name of Dennery, author of *The Two Orphans.* You ask, "Who owns this Swiss cottage" and the answer is "Cognard." "And that one?" It belongs to Clairville. "And the one there being built?" "Matharel de Fiennes," they say. All stage people. The whole place seems to have been built up out of authors' passes, royal-ties, stage criticism, and farce verses. The villas look like décors, the staircases like permanent sets, the sea like the backdrop for Scribe and Delavigne's *Dumb Girl of Portici,* with music by Auber. In the midst of all these chalets stands a chocolate-coloured château flanked by four towers. It belongs to Billion, one-time manager of the Cirque, and the towers look like English privies. The whole scene is like something in a fairy show, and you almost look for Lebel to come on and exclaim in his stentorian voice: "I thought so! Now I've got the colic!"

In this undeveloped town, whose placards everywhere promise new streets, each isolated villa is the hideaway of a name once known to the stage: here La Franconi, there the widow of Adam, farther on Rosalie, the bareback rider of the Hippodrome. Cabourg is a home for disabled veterans of the wings. The elderly females behind the cashier's windows of the hotels speak in a way to remind one of voices once heard in the theatre. And the largest café of the town is kept by a publican who startles the good citizens by repeating the jokes and witticisms heard of old round the bar of the Variétés, in Paris.

September 14.—Magny dinner. Great battle on the subject of Thiers' history, with almost everybody agreeing that he is a historian without talent. Sainte-Beuve alone defended Thiers. Such a charming man! So witty! Such a great influence! And Sainte-Beuve described how he would wind the Chamber of Deputies round his finger, or seduce one of its members. Sainte-Beuve's dialectic and his method of defence are always the same. You say: "Mirabeau was a traitor," and he answers, "Yes, but he loved Sophie so dearly" and goes on to paint a picture of the man's passion for his mistress.[17] He is like this about everything and everybody.

*   *   *

Sainte-Beuve left early, the rest of us sitting and drinking the mixture of rum and curaçao he always brews for these dinners.

"By the way, Gautier; you are just back from Madame Sand's, at Nohant. Did you find it amusing?"

"As funny as a monastery of Moravian brethren. I arrived late in the day. The house is far from the railway station. They left my box in a bush. I reached the house by way of the farms, followed by dogs that frightened me. They gave me dinner. The food was good, but there was too much game and chicken. I don't like it. Marchal, the painter, was there, and Madame Calamatta, and Alexandre Dumas the younger."

"What kind of life do they lead at Nohan?"

"You breakfast at ten o'clock. On the last stroke, when the hand is exactly on the hour, everybody sits down. Madame Sand arrives with the air of a somnambulist and remains asleep throughout the meal. After breakfast, you go out into the garden. There you play at bowls, for it wakes her up. She sits down and begins to chat. There is general conversation, at that hour, about pronunciation: for example, comparison of *d'ailleurs* and *meilleur*. The talk is wildly gay, I must tell you, and the jokes are stercoraceous."

"How awful!"

[17]Strange that the Goncourts, who hated the Revolution and all who were associated with it, should refer here and later to the "perfidy" of Mirabeau, a man who did what he could to keep Louis XVI on the throne and only thus "betrayed" the Revolution. (See biographical appendix.)

"However, not one word about the relations between the sexes. I believe you would be thrown out of the house if you made the slightest allusion to sex. At three o'clock Madame Sand goes upstairs to grind out copy until six. Then you dine; but you dine a little hurriedly so that there may be time for Marie Caillot to dine. She is the servant in the house, a little Fadette[18] that Madame Sand found thereabouts to act in the theatre she has on the place. Marie Caillot joins you afterwards in the drawing room.

"After dinner Madame Sand plays patience without uttering a word, until midnight. On the second day, I want to tell you, I said that if there was no talk about literature I was going to leave. Ah, literature! . . . It seemed to bring them back from another world. I forgot to tell you that the great preoccupation of the moment is mineralogy. Each person has his hammer and never goes out of doors without it. So, I declared that Jean Jacques Rousseau was incomparably the worst writer in all French literature, and that set off an argument with Madame Sand which lasted until one in the morning.

"There is no gainsaying that Manceau did a good job at Nohant, so far as copy goes. Madame Sand cannot sit down in a room without pens springing up, and blue ink, and cigarette papers, and Turkish tobacco, and striped note paper. She certainly uses it. You've heard that she goes back to work at midnight and works until four in the morning. Let me tell you what happened to her. Something fantastic. One day she finished a novel at one o'clock in the morning . . . and immediately started another. Turning out copy is a natural function with Madame Sand.

"On the whole, she does you very well. The service, for instance, is absolutely soundless. In the vestibule there is a box with two compartments: one for letters intended for the post, the other for letters intended for the household. If you want anything, you write for it and sign your name, indicating where your room is. I needed a comb. I wrote: 'Monsieur Gautier, such-and-such a room' and what I wanted. The next morning at six o'clock there were thirty combs for me to choose from."

[18]See George Sand's novel, *La Petite Fadette.*

September 27.—We came in from the country for the Magny dinner. There was talk about Vigny, the corpse of the day. And Sainte-Beuve, of course, had his spadeful of anecdotes to toss into the grave. When I hear Sainte-Beuve, with his little phrases, touch upon a dead man, it seems to me I see a colony of ants invading a cadaver: he will pick you a reputation clean in ten minutes and leave you a well-licked skeleton where there was once a famous man.

"Truth to tell," he said with an oily gesture, "nobody can be quite sure whether he really was a nobleman or not, for no one has ever seen his family. He was a nobleman of 1814; and in those days they didn't look too closely into these matters. In Garrick's published correspondence there is a letter[19] from a Vigny soliciting a loan, but doing it very *nobly,* letting Garrick know that he had been specially selected for this honour. It would be interesting to know if our Vigny was a descendant. He was certainly an *angel;* he was always an angel, our Vigny. You never saw a beefsteak in his house. If you left him at seven o'clock to go dine, he would exclaim, 'What! Going already?' He had no notion of reality—it didn't exist for him. Every now and then he would say something superb. After he read his address to the Academy, a friend remarked to him that the address did seem a bit long. 'But I am not in the least tired!' Vigny retorted. That same day, when he was received into the Academy, he was wearing a black cravat. He met Spontini who, out of consideration for the etiquette demanded by the occasion, was wearing the imperial uniform. Vigny said to him, 'The uniform is in one's nature, Spontini.' Gaspard de Pons, who was a brother officer of Vigny's, said of him: 'There goes a man who does not look any of the three things he is—a soldier, a poet, and a wit.' He was not in the least adroit. He never understood the first thing about the arrangement that got him into the Academy; and

[19]The letter in question may be read in *The Private Correspondence of David Garrick,* London, 1832, Vol. 2, pp. 491–92. Dated from "King's Bench, in State House number 7, ce 5 Septembre, 1766", a debtors' jail, and written in French, the letter begs Garrick to lend the writer "ten or twelve guineas of which I am in as pressing need to settle humiliating debts as to live while making arrangements" for the future. It is signed "*Jean-René de Vigny, ancien Mousquetaire et Officier dans une des Compagnies de la Garde du Roi de France.*"

when it came to recommending anybody for one of the Academy prizes, he always bungled the job."

Then Sainte-Beuve talked about the only two salons now frequented by men of letters: that of the Princess Mathilde, and the salon of Mme de Païva.

Here Gautier spoke up, describing the remarkable life of Mme de Païva.[20]

She seems to have been the natural issue of Grand Duke Constantine and a Jewess. Her mother, who was very beautiful but pitted with smallpox, had had all the mirrors in the house covered with crêpe, so that the child grew up without ever seeing herself and tormented by the notion that her nose was shaped like a potato. She was married off young to a French tailor, in Moscow. Hertz persuaded her to run away with him, while he was her piano teacher. He had to leave the country in 1848, brought her with him to Paris, and then deserted her. She fell gravely ill, without a copper, at the Hotel Valin, on the Champs-Élysées. Gautier received a note from her, asking him to come to see her. He went. She said to him: "You see how things are with me. It may be I shall not recover. But if I do recover, I am not the kind of woman to earn my living keeping a shop. One of these days I intended to have—now listen to me—I intend to have the finest town house in Paris, round the corner from here. Remember that." Her friend Camille, the milliner, who was then making a great deal of money, furnished her with an arsenal of clothes for her great campaign. Gautier saw her again when she was about to leave the hotel: all her dresses were laid out on chairs, sofas, the bed. She was trying them on, one after the other, like a soldier inspecting his equipment before going into battle. Said she: "I am not badly equipped, am I? But one can never be sure. I may miss my aim. In that case—good night!" She asked him to get her a vial of chloroform to be used in the event that she failed. Gautier went off for the chloroform to an interne who was a friend of his, and brought it back to her.

[20]The tale is somewhat romantic, but my job is that of stenographer and I give it as it fell from Gautier's lips. In Gautier's words one must always look for romanticism or hyperbole; in Flaubert's, for exaggeration and a magnifying of things.—E. de G.

September 30.—This evening, at Saint-Gratien, Girardin said after dinner:

"Now that there is neither good nor evil, now that we are vaguely sure about what is right, what is honest, and there is no rigorous rule about these things, only one thing counts—Success; and the emperor ought to have a minister bearing that name. Drouyn de Lhuys was no more fortunate with the Russians than the ministers of Louis Philippe had been. Therefore he should be sacrificed. What are honesty and good intentions to me? A minister is no more than a cook who arrives with the handsomest recommendations in the world and still cooks badly for me. Do I not owe it to my guests to dismiss him?"

Going home by train we talked about Gautier's candidacy for a seat in the Academy. "He hasn't the slightest chance," Sainte-Beuve said. "He would have to spend a year in visits and solicitations; there isn't an academician who knows him. You see, the great thing is that they must have seen you about, they must know your face. An election to the Academy, let me tell you, is an intrigue. An intrigue in the good sense of the word," he added hastily. "Look"—he counted on his fingers: "Gautier will get the votes of Hugo, Feuillet, Rémusat; Vitet, I think; and even so he will have to see a lot of the last two. If he were clever he might get Cousin to vote for him; he might set La Colonna at him, and she could tell Cousin that she simply had to have a symphony in white major, dedicated to her personally by Gautier.[21] But at that, it would be absolutely essential that he never leave Cousin's side for one second, before the election. Through the princess, we might also get de Sacy."

October 30.—We were met at the railway station in Rouen by Flaubert and his brother, chief surgeon of the hospital, and brought in a carriage to Croisset—a pretty house with an Empire

---

[21]Gautier had, in fact, written a *Symphonie en blanc majeur* for Mme Kalgeris, née Nesselrode, an international beauty of the diplomatic world who, incidentally, had furnished pecuniary aid to Wagner following the failure of *Tannhäuser* and had been rewarded by an intimate recital of the second act of *Tristan und Isolde*, Wagner himself singing Tristan and Pauline Viardot Isolde, with Klindwort, a disciple of Liszt, accompanying at the piano.

façade, built halfway up the hillside on the banks of the Seine, which, at this point, is as wide as a lake. Flaubert lives here with a niece and his mother. The old lady was born in 1794 and retains the vitality of the people of that period. Visible beneath her wrinkles are the remains of what was once beauty, allied to a severe dignity. Indoors, the house is of provincial austerity, and the young girl, living between the studiousness of her uncle and the gravity of her grandmother, has friendly words and gay blue-eyed glances for the visitors, as well as a pretty grimace of regret when, at eight o'clock, after the son has bid his mother "good-night, *old dear*", grandmother takes granddaughter off to her room to bed.

November 1.—We spent the whole day indoors. This delighted Flaubert, who has a horror of exercise and whom his mother is obliged to nag in order to get him to go into the garden. She told us that often, when she came back from spending a half day in Rouen, she would find her son in the place where she left him, still in the same posture, and would be almost frightened by his immobility. He never goes out of doors; he lives in his writing and his study: doesn't ride; doesn't row a boat. All day long, in a stentorian voice and with the bellowings of an actor in a boulevard melodrama, he read aloud to us his first novel, written in 1842, out of a notebook whose cover read, *Fragments of Unremarkable Style*. The subject was a youth's loss of his virginity with an *ideal wench*. There is a good deal of Flaubert himself in the youth—his despondency, his impossible aspirations, his melancholia, his misanthropy, and his hatred of the masses. Except for the very childish dialogue, the writing is astonishingly mature to have come from a lad of twenty-one years. Already at that age he was capable of details of landscape, skilful and loving observation of nature, of the kind he put into *Madame Bovary*. The beginning of the novel, entitled *Autumn Sadness,* is a fragment which he could sign today without shame.

By way of recreation, after dinner, he went rummaging among costumes—castoff clothes, souvenirs, things brought home from his travels. He was enchanted to come upon trappings picked up in the East; and in a moment he had got into a costume and was standing before us with a tarboosh on his head, looking magnificently Turkish with his sanguine complexion, his long, drooping moustaches, and his forceful features. From the colourful heap he drew forth, sighing, a pair of shrunken leather breeches, at which he gazed with the tenderness of a snake contemplating its shed skin.

Hunting for his novel he had discovered a disordered jumble of old papers. These were documents collected because of the curious interest they presented. Among them was the holographic confession of Collet, the paederast who killed his lover out of jealousy and was guillotined at Le Havre—a confession filled with frenzied and intimate details of his passion. There was a letter written by an inmate of a house of prostitution, offering all the garbage of her affection to a bully. Among other papers was the manuscript of an unfortunate creature who had grown humped both before and behind; had contracted the scurf and been burnt with acid by quacks; had lost one leg and then both, and who now wrote without recrimination—which made it the more terrible to read—the story of his martyrdom to fate. This manuscript remains the greatest objection I have encountered in my life to Providence and the notion of the goodness of God. Plunging into the abyss of these cruel truths about life, we thought of the wonderful book that might be written out of them for moralists and philosophers, under the title, *Secret Archives of Humanity*.

November 23.—We went to thank Michelet, whom we had never seen, for the flattering things he said about us in the preface to his history of the Regency in France. He lives in a large, middleclass, almost working-class house in the rue de l'Ouest, at the far end of the Luxembourg Gardens. The door to his flat, on the third story, not being a double door, makes one think of a shopkeeper who plies his trade at home. A maid opened it, announced us, and ushered us into a small study.

It was already dark. A lamp with a low shade lit up vaguely a few pieces of mahogany furniture among which we saw art objects and mirrors with carved frames. In the penumbra, the room looked as if inhabited by a *bourgeois* who frequented auction sales. The historian's wife, a woman with a face at once grave and youthful, was sitting on a chair beside the desk, on which was a lamp. She sat with her back to the window in the slightly rigid pose of the cashier of a Protestant bookshop. Michelet was sitting propped up by embroidered pillows in the middle of a sofa that was covered with green plush.

He was like his own *History of France,* the lower parts bathed in light and the upper half hidden in twilight;[22] the face a mere shadow surrounded by the snow of long white hair; and coming out of this shadow, a sonorous, professorial, rolling, chanting and so to say strutting voice that rose and descended with the effect of a solemn and continual warbling. He spoke with high praise of our Watteau, and went on to speak of the extremely interesting history that has not yet been written, the history of French furniture and decoration. As if he were making a sort of poetical inventory, he sketched for us a sixteenth-century abode in the Italian manner, with immense staircases in the middle of the palace; then the spacious stories resulting from the disappearance of the staircases, as first built in the Hôtel de Rambouillet; then the clumsy and uncivilized style of Louis XIV; then those marvellous apartments of the farmers-general of taxation, in the eighteenth century, about which he wondered whether it was the wealth of these financiers or the particular taste of the builders which brought them about; and then, finally, the modern apartment, the richest of which is solemn, unfurnished, deserted.

"You, gentlemen, you who are observers," he exclaimed, leaving the subject of French furniture, "there is a history which you have not written and will one day write; it is the history of the personal maid. You needn't bother with Madame de Maintenon, of course; but there is Mademoiselle de Launai. And you have the Duchess de Gramont's Julie, who had such a great

[22]The point of the analogy is that Michelet was the first historian of France who described and stressed the state of the lower classes in successive ages, rather than the ruling classes—particularly in the volumes on the Middle Ages and the Revolution.

influence over her—particularly in the Corsican affair. Madame du Deffand says somewhere that there are only two people in the world who really love her—D'Alembert and her maid. The part played by female domestics in our history is strange and important, gentlemen. Menservants, now, have been less significant in our history, however."[23]

He spoke for a moment about Louis XV and the modern age. Louis XV was an intelligent man, but a nonentity, a nonentity. "The great things of our day startle us less; they escape us. We do not see the Suez Canal; we do not see the piercing of tunnels through the Alps. All we see in the railways is a little smoke from a passing locomotive; but what about the hundred leagues traversed? Yes, we fail to see our time in perspective."

A moment of reverie at the end of which Michelet went on: "I once crossed England at its widest point, from York to . . . I was at Halifax. There were pavements on the countryside; fields as well tended as the pavements, with sheep grazing in them. All this lighted by gas. It was a very strange sight."

Silence, and then he resumed:

"Have you observed that nowadays the faces of famous men are without significance? Look at their portraits, their photo-

[23]When Michelet says *femme de chambre* he often means something like "Mistress of the Robes"; it is thus, for example, that he refers to Queen Anne's Sarah, whom Macaulay taught him to detest. Mme de Maintenon (see biographical notes appended) first came to the attention of Louis XIV, who later married her and made her his principal adviser, as governess of the natural children which Mme de Montespan had by him. . . . Mlle Delaunay was the personal servant and confidante of that Duchess du Maine who was head of the pro-Spanish and pro-Stuart party against which the regent and Dubois had to struggle to keep France from falling into the hands of the Bourbon Philip V of Spain. Her memoirs are intelligent, amusing and informing—on everything except this very important incident in the history of France. . . . "Julie" was the servant of that Duchess de Gramont whose incestuous relationship with her brother, Louis XV's minister and Joseph II of Austria's great friend, the Duke de Choiseul, is one of the tidbits of eighteenth-century chatter. La Gramont ruled her brother; Julie governed La Gramont; "Julie," says Michelet, "was Queen of France." In the "Corsican Affair" she was bribed by a representative of the Genoese Republic to use her influence to place France on the side of Genoa against their Corsican vassals who, under Paoli, were in revolt against the Republic. Choiseul saw here an occasion to defraud both parties; and with the only half-hearted opposition of the English, he was able to annex Corsica to France in 1768-69.

Menservants, incidentally, have acted less but written more than maidservants: we have the curious and useful memoirs of Mirabeau's manservant, Napoleon I's mameluke, Chateaubriand's hairdresser, and Maupassant's valet, among others.

graphs: there are no handsome portraits any longer: remarkable men no longer look distinguished. Balzac had nothing characteristic about him. Would you recognise Monsieur de Lamartine if you saw him? Nothing in his face; his eyes dead; merely a certain distinction in his figure, which age has not bowed. The thing is that in our time there is an excess of accumulation. Certainly there is more accumulation than there used to be. We all contain in ourselves more of other people, and this being so, our physiognomy is less our own. Each of us is rather a portrait of a collectivity than of himself."

For about a half hour Michelet went on like that, rummaging amongst lofty ideas. We rose, and he accompanied us to the door. Only then, in the light of the lamp he was carrying in his hand, did we see for a second this prodigious historian of the dreamworld, this great somnambulist of the past, this original conversationalist; and we saw before us, crossing his frockcoat over his abdomen in a tight gesture and smiling at us with his death's-head teeth and bright eyes, a tomtit of a man with the look of an irritable old *rentier,* his cheeks swept by long white hair.

* * *

Coming away from the Magny dinner and strolling with the slow rolling gait of an elephant just off a ship and still under its influence—for this is the way Gautier now moves—the dear chap, albeit as happy and flattered as a beginner over the two articles lately written about him by Sainte-Beuve, complained a little that in discussing his poetry Sainte-Beuve had omitted to mention the poems into which he had put the most of himself—the *Émaux et camées.* He could not understand the critic's insistence upon discovering an amorous, sentimental and elegiac side to him—things that horrify him. He agreed that, in the thirty volumes which he had been obliged to turn out, he had been forced now and again to let the middle classes have the satisfaction of a sentimental episode; but the two strings of his instrument, the two truly great notes in his talent, were buffoonery and black melancholy.

"After all," he exclaimed; "in my case it was the bloody times I lived in that induced me to attempt a kind of expatriation. And this is precisely what Sainte-Beuve cannot grasp. He doesn't realise that we four are sick men; and that what distinguishes us from the rest is exoticism. The word 'exotic' has two meanings: one gives you a taste for exoticism in space—a taste for America, a taste for yellow women, or green women, and so on. The more refined exoticism is a more supreme corruption: it is a taste for the exotic in time. Flaubert's ambition would be to fornicate in Carthage; you two would like to have La Parabère;[24] and nothing would rouse me as much as a mummy."

"But how," we said to him, "how can you expect old Beuve, despite his touching desire to understand everything, to understand completely a gift like yours? His articles are very nice; they are an agreeable and extremely ingenious literary exercise; but that is all they are. With that idle chatter that he writes he has never baptised a single man; never given us the definitive meaning of a work in a word or a sentence; never struck in bronze the medal of a single reputation.[25] As for you, despite all his longing to please you, how could he possibly get under your skin? All the plastic side of your nature escapes him. When you describe a nude, he sees in it a species of onanism in which the drawing of the line is only a pretext. You said a moment ago that you were not after anything sensual; but for him the description of a woman's breast, or her leg—the nude, in short—is inseparable from lasciviousness, from a physical stimulus. In a word, he sees Devéria in the Venus of Milo."

December 2.—This evening, dining with the princess, Saint-Victor and Flaubert got unbearably on our nerves with that in-

[24]In the Regency of Philippe II d'Orléans which followed the death of Louis XIV in 1715, La Parabère, although a lady of birth, distinguished herself among the concubines and boon companions who caroused at the famous *"soupers des roués"* given by that dissolute and ruinous but not unreasonable prince.

[25]When one reflects that Anatole France wrote of Hector Malot, author of *Sans famille,* that he had *perfectionné Dostoievski,* one becomes conscious of the gulf in criticism between "the soul's adventures among masterpieces" of the past and the business of reviewing one's contemporaries. So much said, it may be added that France was sure to find Dostoievski repellent and almost certainly never read him.

tensification of *Graecomania* which has taken them these days. They have reached the point of admiring the marvelous white of the marble in the Parthenon, which, Flaubert exclaimed enthusiastically, "is as black as ebony."

December 4.—It is three days since our novel, *Renée Mauperin*, has begun to appear in the *Opinion Nationale*. It is three days that our friends abstain deliberately from talking to us about it, and we have no way of knowing what impression it is producing upon the casual people we meet. We had begun to despair a little of this book surrounded by silence when, this morning, we got a friendly letter from Paul Féval which indicates that the child is stirring.

December 16.—The princess arrived from Compiègne at five o'clock and spoke of the emperor. "What do you expect? The man is neither spirited nor impressionable. Nothing can stir him up. The other day a servant squirted a siphon of Seltzer water into his neck and he merely set his glass the other side of his plate, without a word and without the slightest sign of irritation. He never loses his temper, and the angriest word of which he is capable is, 'It's absurd.' He never says anything more than that. I believe if I had married him I should have broken his head open to see what was inside it."[26]

December 17.—Looking at those eyes, their contracted pupils as bright in the green light as two black pinheads, those strange, deep, sharp and fascinating eyes, those eyes comparable in their rings to emeralds mounted in fever, I thought how dangerous it would be to meet this woman too often—a danger composed of the immateriality of her person, the supernatural nature of her glance, the emaciation of those features of an almost psychic fineness, that something suprahuman as if belonging to one of Poe's heroines become a Parisian.

Of all the women I have ever seen this is the one whom I

[26]Before her marriage to Anatole Demidoff, the Russian Duke of San Donato, from whom she was early separated, there had been some question of the princess marrying her cousin, Napoleon III.

should be proudest to engross, the one before whom I should feel most humiliated if I were undistinguished, the one by whom I should most wish to be esteemed for my literary value. And at the same time, if I fell in love with her I should understand— assuming it came to that—love without corporeal possession, though I should require the absolute possession of everything that charms me in her, everything in her that is divorced from matter—the possession of her heart, her head, and her imagination.

It is possible that I should not be jealous of her husband's possession of her; but I should probably be jealous of her affection for her children.

1864

Undated.—A childhood impression is often responsible for the bent or the character of a whole life. I have been told that Mérimée was a man created uniquely by the fear of appearing ridiculous, and that the origin of that fear was this: When he was a child he was scolded; and on leaving the room he heard his parents laugh at the blubbering face he made during the reprimand. He swore then that no one would ever laugh at him again, and he kept his word by maintaining a harsh, curt exterior which has now become part of his profoundest nature.

Undated.—Instinctively, man does not love the truth, and he is right not to love it. Falsehood and myth show a much pleasanter face. It will always be more agreeable to imagine genius in the form of a tongue of fire than in the image of a neurotic.

January 18.—Magny dinner. Gautier extolling the asexual woman, that is to say, the woman so young that she repels all notion of childbearing, of obstetrics. Flaubert, his face flaming, proclaimed in his booming voice that beauty was not erotic, that beautiful women were not made to be physically loved but were useful only to dictate sculpture, that at bottom love is the product of that unknown element which produces excitation, which is something rarely produced by beauty. With which he elaborated his ideal, an ideal at once so Turkish and so *bemired* that the table jollied him about it. Thereupon he shouted that he had never truly possessed a woman; that he was a virgin; that all the women he had had were no more than the couch on which lay the women of his dreams.

Meanwhile, Nefftzer and Taine were arguing about the word *concrete,* filling themselves with amazement over all it contained, and letting fly at every instant words like idiosyncrasy.

* * *

From coitus the talk moved to hypochondria.[1] Taine deplored this ailment peculiar to our profession. He urged that it be fought with all the weapons of hygiene and right thinking, and fought methodically. Retort as we will that our talent, perhaps, exists only at the cost of this nervous condition, he still insists that we react against those moods of flabbiness and indolence which seem to him the sign of the centuries moving down the slope of civilisation; and continuing to protest, he sees the cure for despondency, the salvation and renovation of our decadent societies, in the childish imitation of English manners, in their life of civic zeal, in our adaptation of the patriotism and the pedestrianism of the British. "Yes," cries someone; "the alliance of talent and the militia!"[2]

We laugh, and we leave.

February 10.—Ash Wednesday. The princess is still in high spirits over M. de Morny's ball last night. Eugène Giraud had costumed her in the rags of an artist's model with a frightful wire mask behind which not a soul was able to recognise her. She spoke with delightful enthusiasm of her pleasure at meeting discourteous men, saying she was so used to seeing them smirking

---

[1]"Du coït on passe au spleen," the Goncourts wrote. The English word *spleen* was brought into the French language by Voltaire with the meaning *low spirits.* It continues to enjoy literary fortune as an elegant and intense variant of *ennui.* In a different department of life, *spider* (pronounced speeder) has been wrenched from English to give the French motorist a word meaning dicky, or rumble seat.

[2]It can be done. The most "French" (if you will allow) of English writers, Edward Gibbon, was a militia officer.

and all smiles before her; and it seems to have pleased her, too, that women told her she was old and ugly.

The painter Hébert having defended a woman whom someone else had spoken of most abusively, that experienced rogue, Émile de Girardin, whispered to him: "Good Lord! Do you want her to be torn to pieces? You must never rush to the defence of a friend in a drawing room: it is simply encouraging them to finish off the wounded victim. What you do is, quickly throw another name into the conversation."

Undated.—Respectable women often speak of the transgressions of other women as if those transgressions had been stolen from them.

March 3.—At a ball, at Michelet's, the ladies were costumed as the oppressed nations—Poland, Hungary, Venice, and so on. It was like watching the future revolutions of Europe dance.

March 14.—Magny dinner. With the sweet, Gautier said, "It's curious; I don't think of myself as a father at all. I am kind to my children; I love them; but not at all as my children. They are there, beside me; they are in my branches—and that is all. I cannot think of myself as a man old enough for them to be mine. There is a youth in me, a freshness. . . . I do not believe in my age."

Then he spoke of the profound tedium in which he lived; of the perpetual plaguing of the two selves within him, one of them saying, when his evening clothes are laid out: "Go to bed. What do you want to go there for?" and the other, once he has got to bed, saying: "You ought to have gone. You would have had such a good time."

March 21.—. . . The talk was about a mistress of Sainte-Beuve's, a Mme W——, whom he firmly believed to be Spanish and consulted about everything literary the other side of the Pyrenees, taking her advice about Calderon, and so on. She had persuaded him that she was Spanish by telling him so, but even more by wearing a dagger in her garter. Unfortunately she died in his house, of consumption; and her papers revealed that she was born in Picardy.[3]

April 9.—At bottom, what plagues us is an insatiable and rankling literary ambition, the galling bitterness of the specific literary vanity. That critic who fails to mention you, wounds you; and he who mentions other writers casts you into the depths of despair.

And, really, what have we to complain about? No sorrows. Enough to live on. No ailments thus far that endanger our lives. A modicum of literary reputation. Why, then, be miserable? Ah, why? Because we are too sensitive to be happy; and because we are wonderfully apt at poisoning our happiness as soon as a hint of it comes into our lives.

Monday, April 11.—Magny dinner. The Duke Pasquier is on the tapis.

"A pretty small man concerned with great matters," said we.

"Really, you are hard on the man," sighed Sainte-Beuve with his ecclesiastical gesture of appeasement. And thereupon the defender and champion of the dead duke's memory began to paw it and mess it about in his own way:

"I shall not exactly talk to you about him as a writer. In Chateaubriand's circle he was scarcely tolerated. When Joubert's letters were published, the editors blotted out all the derision whereby Joubert covered him with ridicule. And nobody could say anything more about him than Rémusat did, in my hearing, at Madame So-and-so's: 'Pasquier understands nothing about anything'—with which he enumerated all the things Pasquier was ignorant of, and ended by saying: 'And aside from these subjects, there is nothing he could be minister of.'[4] And then the academic eulogies; the venerable priest; everything Dufaure had

[3]The lady called herself Mme de Vaquez. Following a riotous "demonstration" against the Empire during Sainte-Beuve's lecture at the Collège de France on the ninth of March 1855, the timorous and unhappy man carried her dagger in his sleeve, for a time, whenever he left his house.

[4]The leading authority on European politics in the period of the French Restoration—I refer of course to Professor Webster—calls him "the energetic and intelligent Pasquier" in *The Foreign Policy of Castlereagh*, Vol. I, p. 211.

to say. Well, let me tell you the truth. Two hours before he died he was having read aloud to him Voltaire's tales. As a matter of fact, he spent his life quoting lines of verse out of Voltaire's *Maid of Orleans*—and getting them wrong, of course. That is the truth."

"Ah," said I to Sainte-Beuve, "if I die first, God forbid that I should be mourned by you."

The greatest and most malignant conversational wit that Sainte-Beuve possesses consists in tearing a man to pieces in the guise of defending him. A horrible poisoner of eulogies!

He spent the rest of the dinner revealing intimate confidences to me. Tedium, tedium—he lives in terror of tedium. He told me again that he had fallen back upon the philosophy of Sénac de Meilhan. So far as he was concerned, the pleasures of the senses were the only pleasures.

He has cut himself off from the social world. The only women he sees are the princess, Mme Païva, and Mme de Tourbet. He works from eight o'clock until five, then takes a stroll until six in order to *deserve* an appetite. On Tuesdays he always has his secretary and a little lady to dinner. On Saturdays he has another young woman to dinner, but in a private room, the dinner being always ordered in advance. He prefers the exhaustion of hard work to boredom, to emptiness.

Great argument about whether one felt modern or not, Saint-Victor declaring that he possessed none of this feeling, and Gautier proclaiming himself *rotten* with it.

Undated.—Spent the evening with Mme Sabatier, the celebrated "Madame President" with the glorious figure, modelled by Clesinger in his "Bacchante." A coarse nature with a base, trivial, common heartiness. This vulgar woman of classical beauty might be described as a camp follower for fauns.

May 8.—At the Clignancourt tollgate, looking for a setting to be used in our novel, *Germinie Lacerteux.* In the midst of the wretched huts and ragpickers' hovels by the fortifications, I saw suddenly a rush of people towards a young man who was standing flanked by three women in tatters. They were holding him and slapping and hitting him. We could see them break his top hat. The crowd that swarmed forward in an instant looked like people come up from under the ground. Beggarly children, laughing ferociously, were running up to see what was going on, while in the doorways of these earthen caves, these packing-box houses, stood old women so ancient that there was a kind of mould, a kind of mushroom white, on their skins.

Suddenly, in the midst of all this, a powerful man in a workman's tunic planted himself deliberately in front of the frail, weak, blond young man and began to rain blows into his face until the young man, without a single gesture of defence, fell to the ground. Like a circus audience, the onlooking plebe feasted its eyes upon this butchery without the slightest evidence of revulsion against the cowardly slaughter effected by the strong upon the weak. And thereupon the crowd melted away as it had come, like a nightmare crossing a dream.

An hour later, out beyond the fortifications, I recognised the beaten, the slaughtered young man. He was stumbling along in the chalky ruts, wandering at random and waving his arms, hatless, coatless, his shirt in ribbons flying all round him, witless, as if drunk, and wiping automatically from time to time, with his sleeve, a bleeding eye that hung half out of its socket.

May 9.—Magny dinner. The others will not allow that Mirabeau sold himself during the Revolution, that he was bought as easily as any other man who has a price. We referred our contradictors to the correspondence of M. de Bacourt. Sainte-Beuve, wrought up, exclaimed that Louis XVI was a swine; that he deserved the axe for having jobbed a genius like Mirabeau. Almost all of them upheld this theory, declaring that a Mirabeau was superior to the code of petty *bourgeois* honesty. "In that case, gentlemen," said we, "there is no morality; there is no justice in historians or history. You are setting up two scales, two standards—one for men of genius and the other for the poor devils who are not geniuses. We believe that posterity will be more democratic than you are."

"Posterity!" exclaimed Sainte-Beuve. "Why, posterity is a matter of fifty years. Posterity is simply the people who have known a man, who talk about him and tell his story from personal knowledge of him."

"Yes; when he is dead and still warm," said I to the critic who had just declared that posterity was himself.

* * *

The conversation moved round to the Abbey of Port-Royal.[5] Saint-Victor flew into a passion against those *cretins* whom he hated. "Fribourg, lay down your hates," Sainte-Beuve admonished him with a smile. The reference was to his education by the Jesuits at Fribourg. Renan, undertaking the defence of Port-Royal, delivered himself of the paradox that the great men are perhaps those who remain unknown, and confessed that he deeply admired in Port-Royal their "Invocation to the Unknown."[6] He ended by declaring that *exhibitionism* was the signal product of our literary baseness, and that there was only one true and worthy thing in the world, which was saintliness.

At this there was a general outcry, everybody talking and shouting at once; and forth from the tempest of words came Gautier's singsong voice, declaring, in his indifference to the discussion, "I am very strong. I can hit 357 on the Turk's head at the Fair, and what is more, my metaphors make sense. That is what counts."

Then Soulié told us that, during the Revolution of 1848, a man

[5]Jansenius (1585–1638), a Dutch bishop and theologian, held views on the doctrine of grace, on free will, and on predestination, which were bitterly opposed by the Jesuits. In France his views were adopted and expounded by those Jansenists who collected on the outskirts of Paris, at the Abbey of Port-Royal, in 1636. Louis XIV ordered the abbey closed in 1709, influenced thereto by his confessor, the Jesuit father de la Chaise. The most glorious name associated with Port-Royal is that of Blaise Pascal. The leader of the group was the abbé de Saint-Cyran, of whom the abbé Brémond said that "He wrote badly, but without the slightest effort." Lord Chesterfield's son studied the Greek roots in a Grammar written by *"ces messieurs de Port-Royal."*

[6]This is a mystifying reference and one not traceable in Sainte-Beuve's masterly *Port-Royal.* Is it—in the mind of Renan, then writing his *Saint Paul*—a confused association with "an altar with this inscription, TO THE UNKNOWN GOD" (Acts, XVII, 23)? That verse pursued Renan for many years; and in the *Prière sur l'Acropole* he troubled to argue again that St Paul had not understood the inscription seen at Athens, that it did not celebrate "the God of the Jews" at all, etc., etc.

walking across the Pont des Arts saw a blindman's cur bite its
blindman, whereat he rushed off to sell his government stock,
saying, "The end of the world has come."

May 23.—Magny dinner. Sainte-Beuve took Taine to task for
having submitted his history of English literature to enemies and
inferiors for comment and criticism, saying that they were only
too happy to lecture him and rap him over the knuckles. . . .
One after the other, voices began to rise, and soon Taine was declaring that the four great of the earth were Shakespeare, Dante,
Michaelangelo, and Beethoven, he calling them "the four carya-
tids of humanity."

"But all of them represent only power," Saint-Beuve protested.
"What about grace?"

"And what about Raphael?" asked someone present who could
probably not have perceived the difference between a Raphael
and a Rembrandt.

Then the talk was of the health of the ancients, of the sound-
ness of their constitutions, and thereafter of the moral hygiene
of our time and the physiological conditions of life half a century from now. This gave Taine the opportunity to assert that
the future would bring a lessening of sensibility and an increase
in activity. To which we rejoined:

"So you believe, Taine. But there is a terrific objection to your
thesis. Ever since humanity has been on the march, its progress
and its acquisitions have been in the direction of increased sensibility. Humanity grows more and more fidgety, more *hysterisized,*
so to say, every day; and as for that activity whose increase you
desire, how do you know but that it may not be directly responsible for our modern neurosis? How do you know that the
anaemic dejection of our age is not due to its excess of activity, its
stupendous effort, its frenzied production, its cerebral powers
stretched to the breaking point—its riot of creation and thought
in every domain?"

Undated.—The son of one of our cousins came to see me this
morning, having just left school. He has an assignation with a

cocotte who is to take him driving in her own carriage, to Saint-Germain. At the moment we have round us a remarkable type of high-class tart, picking up her custom amongst boys still in school and thus ensuring herself, through these children of rich parents, gentlemen who will support her in later years.

The boy gone, we mused upon the course taken by love in our three generations. The elder of us, at the age of our little cousin, had a girl who earned her living stitching slippers; I had a young girl of the town who could usually produce a few sous out of her rosewood chest; and this lad has a woman who keeps her own carriage. Here we have the three ages—Louis Philippe, 1848, and the Second Empire.

May 30.—It is very strange that it should be we, living surrounded by all that was daintiest in the arts of the eighteenth century, who give ourselves up to the most severe, the most arduous, the most repugnant, inquiries into the life of the common folk; and that it should be we, who keep women at the greatest distance, who should have undertaken the most serious and profound psychological study of the modern woman.

Tuesday, June.—We are at Gretz, near Fontainebleau. The inn-keeper's sister got married yesterday. This morning she led her cattle out to pasture. It would seem that for these peasants there was less ceremony in marriage than in having a cow covered.

At two o'clock I saw the arrival of a band of male and female relatives. They came in a carryall, and they came from leagues around. This fair company scattered through the garden. It was horrible to see it amongst the vegetation: it was like a wedding party out of a Labiche comedy, painted in a genre picture by Courbet. One of the women had a goitre as big as her head hanging in a checkered kerchief.

At four o'clock I could see, in the kitchen, the bridegroom, wearing his town clothes, struggling desperately and ineffectually with a pair of hazel-coloured gloves at least ten and three quarters in size.

Then arrived relatives dressed in clothes designed in 1814.

They looked like a troop of gorillas grown up in their first communion clothes. Formalities were dispensed with. There was no Mass here. The bride, all in white, had the tanned and softened look of a macaroon dripping in a damp spot.

This morning I met the bride in the courtyard, carrying her chamber pot with no more embarrassment over her night than over her pot.

June.—Living in the same inn with us is the mistress of a young provincial nobleman. He has come here to paint. I am studying the woman, because she represents, for me, the moral and physical archetype of the brothel girl, whether she has ever been in a house or not.

Her forehead is low, narrow and bulging. She has thick eyebrows, planted rather at random and meeting above the nose. Her nose has a fine line, but it is cheap, it has that slum-quarter tilt at the tip that gives her away. Her mouth is small, with dimples in the corners; and when she laughs she shows white teeth with gaps between as if they had been filed through. Her cheekbones look as if rouged with brick, that particular redness that tells of a bad digestion nourished by nasty food. Her skin is thick and freckled on a base of tan—a skin that has remained rustic despite all the beauty shops of Paris. Her puffed-out and pomaded hair, which is surely coarse, is worn brushed back and piled high on the head, so that she looks like one of the women in those coloured pictures, always surrounded by gilt frames, that you win at county fairs. Nothing about this woman is ugly, but everything is low in breeding, and third rate.

Mornings she wears a black skirt and a white camisole with a yellow fichu, that terrible fichu of the registered prostitute. Her feet in her slippers are often bare. She makes exactly the right errors of speech, says "Sir" humbly and politely to everybody, and calls her lover, "little man." She feels no need to impress one; no desire to touch anything; no ambition to be the object of a man's concern. There is no coquetry in her. She has that commonplace, and so to say public, amiability of the woman who does not belong to herself.

At table she asked to have a whole bottle of wine, and would drink only out of that bottle, because it reminded her of her childhood, when she used to be sent to draw wine from the cask. There are times when her mind is vacant and she makes one think of a peasant driving a cart, asleep with his eyes open. She sleeps a great deal, day and night. In the evening, as soon as she sees a lighted candle, she must go to bed; and she goes off, saying, "If I were rich, I should learn how to stay awake at night." The heat of noon always finds her at her siesta, like a cow in a field. Dawn wakens her, however, and then she wanders about her room, or sits up in bed and sews. Is she by chance out of doors when night falls, she must look up, squint her eyes at the moon, and say, "I can see the Man in the Moon." When she walks out, she climbs the cherry trees and pillages the raw peas. Salad is her only passion.

Speaking, she stares at the servant who is waiting on her. She goes instinctively towards the humbler servants and is in and out of the kitchen all day long; yet she is very respectful of nobility, of note paper with a crest, and so on. In the theatre, she believes that the great actors are those who play the part of kings. She is always agreeable, not in the least touchy, and it is only when the air is heavy and stormy that she grumbles like a child that wants its sleep.

Man is not company for her: like all women who have lived a common life with other women, she needs the company of creatures of her own sex. She is sexless. She does not invite the senses of man in any way. There is not the least molecule of voluptuousness about her. In her bold, coarse mouth there is never an allusion to anything relating to love. None of those tricks of coquetry that are so exciting in a woman. It is as if on leaving her lover's room, she left behind a tool that was her sex. No modesty. She urinates before you like an animal.

She told me her story. She comes from the Morvan, near Château-Chinon. A childhood of theft and pilfering. Her parents thought her possessed. When she did anything bad she would punish herself by going and kissing the latrines. Then she would misbehave again. She was about twelve when she came under the

influence of a fortuneteller, a one-time camp follower who happened to be begging her way through the Morvan with a sack
on her back and a basket. The little girl stole from her parents in
order to have her fortune told. Bacon, salt pork, flour—everything went to the fortuneteller. She remembered having paid
fifteen pounds of bacon to have the whole pack of cards used,
and the witch predicted that she would have seven children,
would make seven trips to Paris, and would die at the age of
thirty. But the theft of the fifteen pounds of bacon was discovered: she was whipped with stinging nettles and her bottom was
covered with welts. A few years later she was in a small town,
behind the bar of a café frequented by men from the law courts.
The king's attorney took her off to his house in Autun, where he
put her under lock and key with a servant to watch over her when
he was away. One fine day, according to her, she was able to un-
screw the lock on the door with the aid of a knife, and she ran
off with eight hundred francs to Paris, where she arrived so
green that when the coachman who drove her to a hotel asked
for his *pourboire,* she thanked him and said, "I am not thirsty."

June 20.—We arranged to get back to Paris in time for the Magny
dinner—those dinners about which the *Indépendance Belge*
wrote the other day as if they were as illustrious as Baron d'Holbach's suppers.

Taine was proclaiming that in Edmond About there was something of Marivaux and something of Beaumarchais; whereat
someone said, "Not in About. He is a descendant of Voltaire—
by Gaudissart, Balzac's bagman."

Renan was very cross and very talkative this evening. He was
inveighing against the hollow poetry of the Chinese, of all the
Orientals. There came to his support Berthelot, a very clever
chemist, a chap who spends his time decomposing and recom-
posing the ultimate substances, a sort of god in the home. Somebody said "Hugo" and in a moment it was no longer Hugo but
Heine who was on the tapis. You could tell that by the look in
Sainte-Beuve's face. Gautier sang the praises of Heine's looks,
saying that in his youth this German poet was beauty incarnate,

despite his slightly Semitic nose: "He was a mixture of Apollo and Mephistopheles." Sainte-Beuve contradicted him angrily: "Really, I am amazed to hear you speak of that fellow. A rat who learned and took everything he knew from you and put it into his wretched articles. A man who tore his friends to bits."

"I beg your pardon," Gautier said quietly. "I was his intimate friend and I always had reason to congratulate myself on the fact. He never said a word against any people except those whose talent he did not esteem."

Undated.—Trade is the art of taking unfair advantage of the need or the desire which somebody has for something.

July.—Cider is a drink which sends a man home, makes him serious, sound, and determined, cools his head and clarifies his mind, intoxicating only the dialectic of his material interests. After drinking beer a man might write a treatise on Hegel; after champagne, he might talk like a fool; after burgundy, he might act like one; but after cider he would draft a lease.

August 7.—There was a ball this evening at the Casino. She wore a gown cut very low, showing the tender hollow between her breasts. We went out together. She was half happy over her gown, like a child, and half embarrassed, like a person who felt herself almost naked. With her free hand she sought to fasten together a little jacket she was wearing, so that one might not see too much beneath it; but she was careful not to button it up altogether. As we were walking, she hailed one of her friends who was sitting in a ground-floor window, asked for a pin, and murmured, "It's embarrassing to display one's skin in the street."

While we sat at our coffee in the lounge the pin somehow came undone. She was wearing a white corsage with blue embroidery. A brassière of batiste, into which disappeared the roseate flush of her skin, confined the bit of palpitating flesh visible to the eye. A necklace of filigreed gold was twice wound round her throat and fell thence to her bosom. She had placed between her breasts a pink with purplish veins which brought out the milky whiteness of her skin and lent the pink the look of an artificial flower. She lowered her head to smell the flower, thus deepening the hollow of her bosom. Then, from time to time, her carmine-tipped fingers would stroke the dull whiteness of her skin, now revealing and now concealing it under her hand. At one moment she drew forth the pink, held it long to her flaring nostrils while she inhaled its odour, and then passed it to me as something which, almost, she had kissed, saying, "Smell it. I adore the odour. In the days when I was making artificial flowers, you know, for charity, I used always to put a clove of gilly-flower in my pinks."

It is astonishing how we men, even when we do not wish or desire anything from a woman, are made happy by the occasional resemblance of that woman's friendship to love. She was very affectionate with her husband that evening, stroking him and patting him tenderly in a way I have never known her to do in public.

August 21.—A strange person, that abbé Migne, that manufacturer of Catholic books. He has set up, at Vaugirard, a printing shop filled with renegade priests, unfrocked blackguards, escaped convicts who at the sight of a police sergeant scuttle back into the doorway, so that he has to shout to them, "As you were! This has nothing to do with you: they are after a counterfeiter."

Forth from these presses come orthodox encyclopaedias and collections of the Fathers of the Church in a hundred volumes. But the abbé has still another trade. He takes part payment for his books in certificates good for one Mass each, countersigned by the bishop. They cost him about eight sous, on the average, and he sells them at forty sous in Belgium, where the clergy is insufficient for all the masses inherited from the Spanish domination.

September 2.—When Saint-Beuve is tired and disposes himself to take a nap during the day, he says this to his housekeeper, Mme Dufour: "If the Pope calls, say I am not in; and if my dear mother comes back from heaven, ask her to wait."

He told us this story about Alfred de Musset. Véron had asked Musset to let him have a serial story for the *Constitutionnel*. Musset said he had in mind a phantasy, and that he wanted four thousand francs for it. Véron agreed, and sent the money round to him next day. That evening he went into Véry's restaurant to dine and saw the staircase decorated with the most beautiful flowers. He asked who was giving a party. "Monsieur de Musset," said the waiter with a face all smiles. Véron went up to have a look. There was a whole lupanar upstairs, upon which Musset was throwing away the four thousand francs; and by the time the women arrived, Musset was already so drunk that he could take no pleasure from his orgy.

Undated.—This evening, on the stroke of midnight, walking along the boulevard, I caught these words, flung by a man to a woman: "Good-bye, my pineapple juice."

Undated.—Reading the *Historia Augusta*[7] one is astonished that the notion of good and evil, of justice and injustice, should have been able to survive the Caesars, and that the Roman emperors did not succeed in obliterating the conscience of mankind.

September.—In the midst of our intensive work on the last chapters of *Germinie Lacerteux,* affected by the brainfag that always accompanies the final stages of such work, I dreamed that I had gone off to call upon Balzac. He was living in some vague suburb, in a house that looked half like Janin's chalet and half like a villa I am sure I have seen somewhere. I had the impression that a great battle was going on in the environs, and that Balzac's house was a sort of headquarters. This I gathered not from the fact of seeing soldiers about, but in one of those flashes of revelation that come to us in dreams. I remember now that I noticed arms stacked in the courtyard, and that there were maps lying on the floor of the room in which I waited.

[7] A series of biographies of the Roman emperors from Hadrian to Carinus (A.D. 117 –284), modelled upon Suetonius and written by a group of anonymous secretaries and librarians in the reign of either Constantine or Julian. Gibbon despised its authors, though they appear to have been men versed in both letters and law.

Balzac came in, heavy of body and monacal of face, looking like the portraits of himself. He was wearing the campaign uniform of an army chaplain. I knew that I had never seen him before, yet he received me as if I had been an old acquaintance. I told him the story of my novel and noticed that he displayed great repugnance when I came to the part about hysteria.

Then, suddenly, as these things happen in dreams, I forgot what had brought me to his house and talked to him about his books, asking him what he was working on. In my dream he was deaf. I was obliged to shout into his ear, and he, like all deaf people, spoke in a low voice, so low that I could hear only part of his replies. I asked if he had finished his military novels. He shook his head to signify no, and added: "No, no. Ah, my lad, I know what you're alluding to!" And I understood that he was referring to the houses of prostitution on the Vincennes Road. "I have seen them, yes; but I have never lived there, I have never lived there," he said sadly.

Here there is a gap like one of those in Petronius's *Satyricon*.

Balzac said further: "It's a shame, you know. The other day Heine, the famous Heine, the all-powerful Heine, the great Heine, came to call on me. He wanted to go up without being announced. After all, I am not exactly a nobody; but when I found out who it was, I gave him my whole day. If I had known your address I should have written you. It is most unfortunate that I did not know your address."

October 24.—Since Balzac, the novel has nothing in common with what our fathers understood by "novel." The novel of today is written with the help of documents narrated or taken from nature, just as history is written out of documents preserved in archives. Historians tell the story of the past; novelists tell the story of the present.

1865

Undated.—I was wondering how justice came to be in the world when, walking by the river, I saw a group of children at play. The biggest boy was saying:

"Let's organize a law court. I'll be the court."

January 18.—There is one thing for which the princess deserves great praise, it is that talking with silly women, with stupid men —that boredom, in short, bores her. And what is more curious is that it turns her complexion livid, like the colour in a painting by Guercino. Nothing could have been funnier than the crucified face she turned towards us this evening while we were talking with that great and fascinating scientist, Claude Bernard, and she was having to listen to two chattering women.

February 1.—Dinner this evening with the princess and a table-ful of men of letters, including Dumas the elder. A sort of giant with negroid hair turned pepper-and-salt, the tiny eye of a hip-popotamus, bright, cunning, and watchful even when veiled, and an enormous face with features like those vaguely hemispheric lines drawn by caricaturists to show you the inhabitants of the moon. There is something about him that makes one think of a bear-leader or a *calender* in the Arabian Nights.

He talks fluently but without brilliance, without the bite of wit and without colour or nuance: his speech consists only of facts, curious facts, paradoxical facts, *flabbergasting facts,* that issue forth in a hoarse voice from the depths of an immense memory. He told us, for example, that an article written by him about Mount Carmel had brought the monks 700,000 francs. He drinks no wine, takes no coffee, and does not smoke: the sober athlete of the *feuilleton* and of copy.

Lesseps, the piercer of isthmuses, with eyes so black beneath his silvery hair, just arrived from Egypt, dined this evening and told us in confidence—this man of implacable will—that often in his life he had been dissuaded from doing things by a fortune-teller in the rue de Tournon, successor to Mlle Lenormand.[1]

After dinner, in the smoking room, Nieuwerkerke related that Bénédict Masson, having been engaged to paint the history of France round the Cour des Invalides, had thought of symbolising the reign of Louis Philippe by a barricade during the Revolution of 1830. Nieuwerkerke pointed out to him that this symbol was not in particularly good taste, and suggested that in place of the barricade he paint the Return of the Ashes of Napoleon I.[2] Was this not really a sensitive suggestion to come from the director of fine arts of the Second Empire?

February 8.—Dined at the Charles Edmonds' with Herzen, the Russian revolutionist. A Socratic ugliness, with the warm, transparent skin of a portrait by Rubens, a red mark between the eyebrows, as if scarred by a hot iron, and greying hair and beard. From time to time, while he is talking, a kind of ironic catch rises, falls, and rises again in his throat. His voice is mild and mournfully musical with none of the harsh sonority that one might expect from this massive, bullnecked man. Any idea he expresses is intelligent, accurate, acute, sometimes subtle; and while one has to wait for the words that explain and cast light

[1]For many years, Parisians went to hear their future told by Marie Anne Adelaïde Lenormand (1772–1843) as feverishly as "the biggest men in Wall Street" were said to have run to Mme Evangeline Adams—before October 1929, of course.

[2]It was in 1840, while Louis Philippe was king of the French, that the *"Retour des Cendres"* took place.

upon the idea, when the words come forth they have that happy turn of phrase characteristic of a delightful foreign mind expressing itself in one's own language.

He spoke of the anarchist Bakunin, of the eleven months he spent chained to a wall in a dungeon; his escape from Siberia down the Amur River; his wanderings through California; his arrival in London where, after having heaved a sigh for a moment in Herzen's arms, his first words were, "Do they have oysters here?"

Russia, Herzen believes, is threatened with dismemberment before long. He said the czar had the mentality of a drill sergeant, and he cited a number of traits which made him appear to us a sort of Christ of the drill manual. Many Russians will tell you that the czar took poison after the disastrous defeat of Russia in the Crimean War. Herzen described how, after the taking of Eupatoria, the czar, walking at night in his palace with his tread of stone, his footfall of the commander's statue in *Don Juan*,[3] stepped suddenly up to a sentry standing guard, and, tearing his musket out of his hands, exclaimed to him, "On your knees! Let us pray for victory."

Then, concerning the manners of the English, whose country he loves as the land of liberty, he told us curious stories. A servant, for whom Turgenieff had found a place in the Viardot household, being asked later by the novelist why he had left the Viardots, made this wonderful reply: "They are not respectable people. Not only Madam, but the master himself spoke to me while at table." Another story was of a rich English friend whose whole staff—butler, coachman, groom—all but the housekeeper, left him on the same day. He asked the housekeeper why, and she answered, "If I hadn't been with you half a century I should have gone too. Let me show you how impossible the kitchen is." And she led him into the vast kitchen, in the middle of which stood a spotless table. "Look here, sir: this table is round. Sometimes it's the coachman and sometimes the groom who sits beside me. If the table were square, the butler would always have been able to sit where he belongs—beside me." And as we sought

[3] Molière, *Don Juan, ou le festin de pierre,* Act V, sc. vi.

to distinguish between and define the natures of the two peoples, French and English, Herzen said, "An Englishman summed them up pretty well in this sentence: 'The Frenchman eats his cold veal hotly; the Englishman eats his hot beef coldly.' "

March 27.—As we were leaving the dining room—that room whose grooved columns, wound with ivy, lend it the antique air of a true dining hall of a cousin of Augustus—the conversation turned on love. Someone having said that after reaching a certain age one ought to bid farewell to love, the two eldest amongst us protested—Sainte-Beuve and old Giraud of the Law Faculty. Sainte-Beuve advanced the theory that a man should never ask a young woman to love him, but ask merely the charity of her love, in such wise that the young woman tolerate him and do not grow to hate him. "That," he said with a sigh, "is as much as one is entitled to."

"But have you ever been really in love, Monsieur Sainte-Beuve?" the princess asked him.

"Let me tell you, princess, that I have in my head, here, or here"—he tapped his cranium—"a drawer, a pigeonhole, that I have always been afraid to look squarely into. All my work, all that I do, the spate of articles I send forth—all that is explained by my desire not to know what is in that pigeonhole. I have stopped it up, plugged it with books, so as not to have the leisure to think about it, not to be free to come and go through it. You don't know what it is," he went on animatedly and in a tone of black despair, his words coming forth from a heavy heart; "you don't know what it is to feel that one will never be loved, that the thing is impossible, for the unavowable reason you mentioned a moment ago—that one is old, and it would be ridiculous, because one is ugly."

"And you, now?" the princess said, turning to Giraud.

"Oh, Princess, I have never had only one love: always two or three. It is the only way to live in peace and to avoid trembling for fear that you may lose one of the two."

"Indeed. And what kind of women are these?"

"Entirely possible women, Princess."

"Princess," Sainte-Beuve interrupted; "you don't know this, but ask our friends, the Goncourts: in the eighteenth century there were particular groups in society which provided such women: there were *groups of the moment.*"

"Yes," Giraud agreed. "Now assume the existence of people today descended from those groups, people who, at first sight in a drawing room, recognise and greet and understand one another in the twinkling of an eye."

"Look here," the princess exclaimed. "You are disgusting! Ah, the filthy beast!"

Old Giraud knelt before the princess with the eyes of a satyr humbling himself, the three wirelike hairs rising on his bald head like a caricature in *Punch*. He kissed a hand which the princess instantly withdrew and made as if to rub against her gown.

April 9.—Called on Gavarni. Our friend is becoming unsociable. He refuses to dress, to wear new boots, to put on starched shirts, saying that they hurt his neck. Impossible to draw him forth from his solitude and overcome his aversion for society. But his conversation remains the same; he is still able to formulate views about people and things which sum them up and define them in a brief rapid phrase like those captions written on his lithographs. Today he said that what was wonderful in Proud'hon's paintings was "the clarity of the expression and the obscurity of the thought."

April 14.—I wrote recently to the manager of the Vaudeville Theatre, asking him to appoint a time when I might read to him our play, *Henriette Maréchal*. This morning Banville writes me to say that Thierry, of the Théâtre-Français, whom we do not know and have seen only once in our lives, is very interested in our play, not as theatre manager but as man of letters, as our colleague. To what end, in sooth? The play is impossible for his theatre, with a first act so unconventional as to take place during an Opera Ball and a windup so monstrous as to consist in a pistol shot actually fired on stage!

April 21.—A letter from Harmand, of the Vaudeville Theatre, promising that we may read the play to him after he has put on Feydeau's play, which opens in a few days.

April 27.—Left our manuscript last Saturday at the Théâtre-Français without the slightest hope of its being accepted. Thierry was to have sent it back yesterday; we wrote for it, and got it back this morning with a note asking why we would not offer it formally to his theatre. This evening we went to see him. He spoke of the play absolutely as if it had a chance of being performed and dazzled us by the cast he suggested for it: all the great names of the Théâtre-Français—Mme Plessy, Victoria, Got, Bressant and Delaunay.

We went down his stairs in a state, intoxicated with happiness.

May 4.—A strange table, that at which we dined at Gautier's. It was like the ordinary in the last caravanserai of Romanticism and the Tower of Babel, a mixture of people of all nationalities, for the master of the house has such people in habitually and takes some pride from the fact. He told us that the other day he had twenty people at his table speaking forty different languages: you could have gone round the world with them and not have needed an interpreter, he said.

This evening, beside Flaubert and Bouilhet, there sat a real Chinese with almond eyes and a raspberry-coloured robe. He teaches the Chinese language to Gautier's daughters. Next to him was an exotic painter with eyes stolen from a jaguar and boots up to his belly. Below the painter sat Reminy, the Hungarian violinist with a face as hairless as that of a priest or a devil, flanked by his accompanist, a fat, feminine little man who looked like an Alsatian and had blond hair that hung in curls straight from the part in the middle of his head. He wore the frock coat of a German seminary student with a sprig of fading white lilac at the opening: a plump, mild, and slightly disquieting chap. Farther along, accompanied by her son, sat the wife of a god, the widow of the Mapah—Mme Ganeau.[4]

[4]For the story of the "Mapah"—a word composed of *maman* and *papa*—see "Ganeau" in the biographical notes appended.

Throughout the dinner Gautier seemed to be acting in an Italian improvised comedy with the waitresses, threatening to *strangulate* them for an unwiped plate or a soured sauce, while the younger of his daughters was sticking to her cheek a beauty spot made of I know not what, and using the handle of her fork for mirror.

Saturday, May 6.—Very early this morning there was a ring at our door. We ignored it. At ten o'clock a letter was brought up with the message that an answer was to be returned. It was an appointment for our reading at the Théâtre-Français on Monday next.

I rushed to the theatre and was taken in to see M. Guyard, who asked me to come back this afternoon, because Thierry would be studying the matter of directing our play this evening. Full of confidence, with notions of direction and performance of the successive scenes already in our heads, we went back promptly at five o'clock—to have our hopes doused by Thierry's icy words. He said that he had not been able to win the co-operation he had looked for from Got, who, having just played the role of an old man in Laya's *Duke Job,* now wanted to play a young man, and that Got felt himself, besides, greatly indebted to Laya for the great and successful part given him in *Duke Job,* so that he really belonged to Laya, held himself in reserve for Laya's next play. All this in a discreet and confidential tone which said he was telling us only the half of it and made us extremely fearful of the untold half. At the close of our visit there were phrases which seemed designed to absorb the shock of a rejection to come, seemed to console us in advance in the event the play was not accepted, phrases concerned with other plays we might write in the future.

We left Thierry's office without exchanging a word, our hopes dashed. Half our beautiful dream had crumbled, and I could feel the stirring of my bile, ready to swamp me and giving me already a feeling of uneasiness, as if I were about to be seasick.

Sunday, May 7.—Thierry handed us a list of the principal actors of the Théâtre-Français, advising us to pay a call upon Got, whom we had met at dinner at Charles Edmond's. Your actor is a country lad, a rustic, or at best a dweller in suburbia. To get at him you want the railway, for he is sure to live at Courcelles, at Passy, at Auteuil, in one of those summer places where you find the delightful houses of this sort of chap set against a background of greenery. It was in such a place that we found Got, booted and spurred, and living in the midst of a cool clump of vegetation all his own.

May 8.—We were sitting at a green baize table on which stood a reading desk and something to drink. On the opposite wall hung a picture representing the death of Talma. Ten people, besides ourselves, were in the room, serious, impassive, mute.

Thierry began to read. He read the first act, the Opera Ball, to the accompaniment of laughter and general glances of friendliness sent in our directon. Then he went through the second act and began the third. During this reading our minds were void of ideas; deep down we felt an anxiety which we strove to suppress and to evade by listening to our play, to the words, to the sound of Thierry's voice as he read. The small audience grew grave with that implacable and secret seriousness that impels one to wonder, to seek to guess what people can be thinking. When it was over, Thierry led us into his office.

We sat in that office with its padded muslin curtains through which the daylight sifted as white and discreet as in a bathroom, and our glances went to the mythological scenes in the ceiling as if in prayer to our dear eighteenth century. Then, as happens in moments of great emotion, we fell into the heavy, dull process of mechanical contemplation, our eyes going from the point of the nose of a terra-cotta bust to its pedestal and back again.

The minutes were eternal. Through one of the double doors which alone was shut, we heard the sound of voices out of which arose the voice of Got, of whom we were afraid. After a while there was a gentle succession of metallic sounds that marked the balls clicking into the lead box. My eyes were on the clock, which told the hour as three thirty-five, so that I did not see Thierry come in; but I felt both my hands taken and heard a soothing voice which said, "Your play is accepted, and enthusiastically accepted." Thereupon he began to talk to us about the play, but after a couple of minutes we begged to be excused and flung ourselves into an open carriage in air that we cut with our hatless heads.

May 9.—Flaubert said to us yesterday, as we left Magny's, "When I was young my vanity was such that if I found myself in a brothel with friends, I would always choose the ugliest girl and would insist upon lying with her before them all without taking my cigar out of my mouth. It was no fun for me at all; I did it for the gallery."

Flaubert still retains a little of this vanity—which explains why, with a very honest nature, what he tells you he feels, or suffers, or loves, is still never perfectly sincere.

May 20.—This afternoon we went through a little gate in a wooden enclosure hung with verdure beyond which was a large house in the rue de Vaugirard, the home of Tournemine. A cheerful ground floor filled with sprightly water colours, small pictures of friends, and Oriental weapons. There were glass cases containing delightfully coloured silks of various kinds—the jackets and vests of Turkish women, with rows of gold buttons and amongst them a mounted pearl. A little museum of the East.

The painter of Asiatic Turkey had been good enough to let us have, for the novel we plan to write (*Manette Salomon*), the letters which he had written to his wife; and she soon came forward with a packet of these thick long letters, rendered almost venerable by a dozen postage stamps on each envelope. She began in a happy frame of mind to reread them aloud, to live again through the joy of receiving them, sitting where her prominent forehead and plump cheeks, her gentle eyes and kindly face, were lighted up by a pair of lamps. At certain passages memories would rise in the painter's breast and make his heart jump, and he would beat with his fist on the divan and, seeing it all again, with the glow of Paradise in his face, he would exclaim: "Ah, how beautiful it was!"

During this reading that exhaled the East, a table inlaid with mother-of-pearl was brought out, and, in their silver-filigreed holders, tiny blue cups were filled with Turkish coffee brewed in coffeepots from Constantinople.

At that moment, gathering her skirts about her for fear of upsetting the little table, a tall young girl crossed the room and sat off in a corner where she spent the evening sending smiles to her father from her lovingly relaxed face each time the letters told of the dangers he had run or the bugs he had killed. The coffee was replaced on the table by four pots of Turkish sweets made of bergamot pears, of orange blossoms, of rose leaves, and of a sort of white mastic which sent into the mouth the land one had in one's ear. A delightful evening that went on until two in the morning, in which we sensed all the charm of family life mingled with the titillations of the exotic.

May 22.—There is left in our life nothing but one consuming interest—*the passion for the study of reality.* Apart from this there is only tedium and emptiness for us. Indeed, we have galvanized history as far as it was possible to do so, and galvanized it with the truth, a truth truer than that of other historians, and we have rediscovered reality. But now the true that is dead is no longer of interest to us. We are like men for whom, following years of drawing from a wax model, the academy of the living has suddenly been revealed—or, rather, life itself, with its entrails still warm and its tripe still palpitating.

May 25.—To lunch at Trianon in a group with the Princess Mathilde. Life is strange. We never thought, in the days when we went there to get materials for our sketch of Marie Antoinette, that we should one day be lunching in the same place with a Napoleon, in a cottage designed for the queen by Hubert Robert.

All meals attended by women end with the conversation running on sentiment, on love. The princess asked each guest what he would best like to possess to remember a woman by. One said a letter, another a lock of hair, a third a flower: I said a child, and was all but thrown out of the cottage. At that moment

Amaury Duval, with that sparkling eye and beating heart habitual to him when he speaks of love, said that what he had always loved and desired from a woman was her glove, the imprint and mould of her hand, the shape of her fingers. "You don't know," he went on, "what it is to ask your dancing partner for a glove and be refused it. An hour afterwards you see her at the piano. She has taken off her gloves to play, and you stand staring at the gloves. She gets up and leaves both on the piano. You won't take them, for a pair of gloves is not a glove. She comes back and picks up . . . one glove. Imagine your happiness at this pennant flown for you alone."

Amaury Duval got this off very prettily.

Undated.—A long conversation with Fromentin, one of the greatest talkers about art and spinners of aesthetics I have ever listened to. He was interesting on himself, saying that he knew nothing, not the first word, about painting; that he had never painted from nature, had never drawn preliminary sketches, in order to force himself to look at things simply; and that things came back to him only years later, in painting as well as in literature. He said that his books on the Sahara and the Algerian littoral known as the Sahel were written out of the reappearance of things which he believed himself never to have seen, and that his particular truth was devoid of accuracy—for example, he had really seen the chief's caravan and dogs which he wrote about, but not at all in the locality in which he describes it in his book, and not in the course of the journey narrated. He said also that his great misfortune, as it was the misfortune of all the painters of our time, was not to have lived in the heroic age of painting, in an age when people knew how to paint big subjects; and he let slip the regret that he had not painted in a tradition, that he had not been an apprentice dauber in the studio of some van der Meulen.

June 6.—We feel a disgust, almost a contempt, for the Magny dinners. To think that this is the meeting place of the freest spirits in France and that nevertheless, despite the originality of their talents, there is such a paucity of original ideas, of opinion born of their own nerves, their own sensations. And what an absence of personality, of temperament! What a *bourgeois* fear of excess in them all! This evening we were all but stoned for saying that Hébert, the founder of *Le Père Duchène*—which incidentally nobody at table had read—was a man of talent. Sainte-Beuve maintained that the proof of his having no talent was that none of his contemporaries had acknowledged that he had it!

They are all servants of current opinion and of the prejudices which have the force of law; domestics either of Homer or of the principles of the Revolution of 1789. For this reason we no longer say much at the dinners; we repress our personal ideas and disdain to amaze them by what is characteristic of our thoughts.

July 3.—Magny dinner. Renan told us this evening that Boccaccio says somewhere that he worshipped the cover of a Homer in his library, not a word of which he could read. He was in ecstasy over the name inscribed on the back of the folio. Literary religions are like other religions. There is in almost everyone an admiring respect for the particular beauty that does not speak the language of the admirer. Man insists upon *paraphagarmus.*

August 8.—Thierry told us that Ponsard, before the reading of his play, *Le Lion amoureux,* had attended a performance of *Le Supplice d'une femme,* and that after the play he said, "There is life in that play and there is none in mine." Thereupon he had begun to weep like a child. Poor chap, those tears are the best thing that he will leave to posterity.[5]

Undated.—The material description of things and places in the novel, as we conceive it, is not description for the sake of description. It is a means whereby the reader is transported into a certain atmosphere favourable to the moral emotion which should arise from these things and places.

[5]Posterity, indeed! *Le Lion amoureux* was a smash hit.

Sunday, August 13.—We arrived in several carriages to spend a few days with the princess at Saint-Gratien. Round the table at lunch were collected the Count and Countess Primoli, Nieu-werkerke, Eugène Giraud, the painter, and his curly-haired son with the fine features of a Mephistopheles, Baudry, Marchal, Hébert in whom there is something of a humbug of idealism, Saintin, Soulié, and Alfred Arago, whose anaemia has for the moment muted his amusing banter. The talk is of Girardin's *Les Deux Sœurs,* which opened last night and was a complete fiasco, and which the princess, out of a feeling of benevolence for Girardin, insists tenaciously, against all of us, was a success.

After lunch we went into the verandah, and there old Giraud was hitched to the caricature album. The princess, on the arm of the sofa where Giraud sat drawing, was the first to laugh, look-ing over his head, at the caricature of Arago, dragged down by the weight of an enormous Cross of the Legion of Honour, and Baudry with his nasal apparatus, and Marchal with his broad face, and the two of us in profile, bound by a single pen.

Coming back from rowing on the lake we found the two newly decorated men of the day who had been summoned by telegraph—Protais and Boulanger, whom the princess put on her left and right at dinner, after having pinned on each of them the little diamond cross which, habitually, she presented to friends who had been decorated by her influence.

In the great drawing room after dinner we went through large albums and portfolios filled with sketches by Giraud which were a sort of intimate and burlesque history of the house, seeing on one page the princess posing for Carpeaux while embracing her dog, Chine, and on another the enormous bottom of the abbé Coquereau in baby's drawers, etc.

Monday, August 14.—At lunch the princess spoke of the people she wanted to marry off, Taine amongst others, saying that she had found him a match which would bring him a dowry of 400,000 francs and 800,000 francs of expectations.

We went into the studio with its Algerian portieres, its velvety garnet wallpaper, its great inlaid cupboards, and its wall hung

with immense crossed palm leaves. Giraud, standing, was painting the sky of a panel which formed part of a decoration containing portraits of people of distinction under the Directory of
1795–99; it is to adorn the staircase of the château.

Two Italian women came in through the shuttered door from
the garden, and the princess began to paint one of them. She
was at it about two hours with scarcely a few minutes of rest
for the model. Near by the Countess Primoli sat reading the
memoirs of Mlle de Montpensier, while behind the princess
Hébert stood doing a water colour of the same Italian model.

The model was charmingly sculptural. In her straight profile
and in the graceful bronze nape of her Florentine neck, she displayed a distinction of blood and that style of the Etruscan coun-
trywomen which bespoke a great past; for these women, peasants though they be, are nevertheless the queens of nature. She
was as motionless and as blank as marble most of the time, but
occasionally, on a word spoken in Italian by the princess or by
Hébert, her face would light up and come alive with pretty intelligent smiles, and she would reply briefly in a most musical
voice.

Giraud would toss into their work from time to time a joking
word which the princess would chide and rebuke with laughter.

The maid brought in a knot of diamonds that her mistress had
recently ordered, and while the princess showed off its water
against the black of her painting smock, Giraud took the maid
by the chin and said in the voice of a stage marquis, "Let us
tease the soubrette a little." Upon which the princess exclaimed,
"Come, you dotard. Leave off! You disgust me." And the work
went seriously and doggedly on, interrupted by the arrival of
yellow telegrams which the princess tore up and rolled into small
pills. These hours of painting and sketching give off something
like the charm of the studio of a princess of the Italian Renaissance, enlivened by the presence of a wit.

The carriage was at the steps. The princess laughed to see her
reader, Mme de Fly, hesitant about leaving her with us. "But
what does she think we are up to?" she asked. On the Montmorency Road she described to us the house of her dream: an

immense studio on the ground floor, lighted from overhead, and all about the central edifice a colony of a dozen of us lodged in little houses.

During dinner, apropos of a word let fall by someone, the princess went off into a diatribe against antiquity in general and classical tragedy in particular, declaring that she could only love or sense or understand that which was modern, seeming to hate everything classical with all the horror of a schoolboy set a distasteful task. Chesneau came in afterwards to thank the princess for the award of his Cross. She had asked me during the day if Flaubert had been decorated, and when I replied that he had not been, she said, "I really did not know that. Had I known, I should have asked for it myself; but I knew it so little that only the other day Charlotte and I wondered about it."

At half-past eleven the men went up to chat and tell stories in Giraud's room until two in the morning. It is one of the habits of the house.

August 15.—Eugène Giraud took us off to a little rustic house he owns at Saint-Gratien, a sort of grange which he has rebuilt and decorated out of mediæval remains, its wild vines and untended ivy zigzagging all over the architectural odds and ends of the walls. It is the perfect cottage, the true nest, for a romantic honeymoon. Giraud never lives in it. People have wanted to buy it and have offered to pay whatever he might ask; but he has always refused to sell. A strange man, a true artist, an eccentric who spends his life in follies like the purchase of this place, or the purchase of the large house he owns in Paris, and somehow grows rich out of them without intending to. He is an old haunter of the wings, a respectable night owl of the boulevards, who sleeps in the same bed with his wife in patriarchal fashion, their son sleeping on a cot at the foot of their bed.

Back at the château we found the princess home from a *Te Deum* sung in honour of the emperor's birthday, which she had had the tact not to mention to the rest of us. During luncheon there was talk about the awards of the Legion of Honour reported in the *Moniteur*. Giraud opined that certain people had not been decorated who ought to have been, and, driven by the princess, finally named Carpeaux, declaring that those who most deserved the Cross were the last to get it. The princess, in the agitated voice and with the strident laugh of a person who has been irritated, lost her temper, and said rather angrily that people of talent could afford to wait, that they ought not to be spoiled, that recognition put them to sleep, that they ought always be left with something to hope for; but Giraud would not be denied and maintained his position sharply, bravely and squarely. When one hears him talk like this one is filled with esteem for this man who is reputed to be a courtier and who, at the princess's table, retains all his independence of spirit and is constantly able to let the voice of truth be heard under cover of banter.

It was raining. Giraud left. The princess set to work in her studio on an unfinished crayon portrait of the Countess Primoli. Hébert, standing behind the princess, but not touching a crayon, presided over her work with little admonitory and counselling phrases: "Touch that up lightly . . . Sketch it in this way . . . Tone it down a little there . . . I know well enough that you are afraid to smudge your fingers." "Not true," the princess answered. Meanwhile, the three dogs snored in their basket and telegrams kept arriving, and the princess worked away on this holiday as if she were earning her living by painting and would be given her dinner in payment for the portrait. This went on till half-past six, when we all dressed for dinner.

At dinner the talk was of painting and orders for paintings. Hébert asked the princess's advice about some work La Païva wanted him to do. The princess waxed indignant at the thought that a painter of Hébert's quality might do anything for a woman of that sort, saying, "A vile woman like that patronizing the arts! Why, you couldn't take your mother to her house to see your pictures there."

"Don't take it seriously," Hébert defended himself weakly.

"So far as I am concerned the matter is very simple," said the princess. "For that sort of woman you may do anything you please, so long as you do it for nothing. But the moment you take money from her . . . Don't you think I'm right?" she suddenly asked Soulié. He maintained cynically that Raphael would have done a job for any pretty woman of his time and ended by affirming that he himself had no principles.

This declaration brought the princess to her feet, and as she turned to leave, and we were bidding her good night, she said, "Really, your indulgence is such that if I were ever to be born again on earth, you would make me wish, gentlemen, to come back a lustful drab."

We went up to Hébert's room, where he spoke of Rome and the Academy and the rolling countryside of the Campagna, in the loving and emotional voice of a man talking of the homeland of his talents and his tastes and his happiness. While we were chatting, a lackey brought me from the princess a salve for my cold. The princess is often sweetly attentive in these little ways that tell you she is thinking about you.

Wednesday, August 16.—In the omnibus that took us back to Sannoy we went over our three days and formulated our opinion of the princess. We agreed that few commoners would be as little stiff in their friendliness as she was. The princess as hostess was more thoughtful of her guests, and more sensitively concerned to put them at their ease and draw them out, than almost any lady we had hitherto met. We thought of her easy ways, the charm of her abruptness, her passionate speech, her colourful choice of words, the immediacy of her attack upon everything stupid, that fusion of virility with little evidences of feminine thoughtfulness, of the sum of her qualities, and even her defects, all of them of our time and all novel in a Highness—and we said to each other that she was the archetype of a nineteenth-century princess, a sort of Marguerite of Navarre in the body of a Napoleon.

August 28.—30, rue du Petit-Parc. M. Bressant? A servant introduces us into a sitting room, Bressant comes in, begins by declining to play the part we offer him, says that the other parts are magnificent and he would be thrown into the shade, that he hasn't acted in a long time and means to create something when he does, and that our part seems to him merely that of a sort of confidant. As we rise to go, and express our regrets, he exclaims that he would really like to be of service to us, that he had perhaps read the part hastily, he would reread it and would let us know. I begin to see that these actors are actors at home as well as in the theatre. Habitually they begin by saying no, for they want to be begged.

Rue du Petit-Parc, number 32, at Delaunay's. Thierry had told us that the thing was settled, and we were come, out of courtesy, to thank him for agreeing to do his part. No sooner have we begun to pronounce a word of thanks than he pretends astonishment and says he is at a loss to understand, that Thierry has not said a word to him about our play, that others in the theatre had told him a young lover had been engaged and he assumed it was for the part now in question. We stressed the importance of the part, and he said that he had paid no attention to that when the play was being read, his mind had been on the play as a whole, it was impossible that he should play the part of a youth of seventeen. There we were, forced to beg, and he was good enough to say he would think it over. We left, completely bewildered.

What strikes us about these people, these men who represent love the other side of the footlights, is their ugliness, their grey skins, their features coarsened and magnified by the grimaces of the stage, their great, dilated nostrils.

At four o'clock we went to report to Thierry. That almost ecclesiastical diplomatist allowed us to perceive a dull anger rise in him as we related the farces we had witnessed. His unctuous voice almost quivered with rage as he spoke: "What! Delaunay said that? But I rearranged his holiday for the express purpose of having him in your play. There is not a word of truth in it. What you were told is not true. Even the lies you were told are not true. I tell you, none of it is true."

Magny dinner in the evening. Sainte-Beuve and Soulié both confirmed a report in the *Independance Belge* that we were to have been decorated on the fifteenth of August. The princess had asked the emperor directly, without a word to us, and had invited us to spend the holiday with her in order to surprise us with the Legion of Honour. We were truly very touched and truly grateful to the princess for this mark of her affection about which we should have known nothing if our friends had not been indiscreet. Our Crosses have been put off until January, when we are to be decorated in the company of Flaubert and Taine.

August 29.—Still at table, we talked about ourselves. I have not the same aspirations as has the other of us. He, if he had not been what he is, would have inclined towards home life, towards the *bourgeois* dream of a blissful communion with a sentimental wife. He is tenderly and pensively passionate; I am pensively materialistic. I can sense in myself a bit of the eighteenth century abbé and even a little of the cruelty of the sixteenth century Italian—not that I do not dislike bloodshed and the physical suffering of others, but that I am malicious in spirit.[6] Edmond, on the other hand, is almost goody-goody. He was born in Lorraine and is Germanic in spirit. Edmond sees himself, in another age, the perfect military man with no distaste for a fight and a love of musing. I am a Latin and a Parisian. I see myself involved in the business of a chapter of prebendaries, in the diplomacy of monasteries, with a great vanity about playing on men and women for the irony of the thing. I wonder if there may not be in us a natural predestination—as there used to be a social one—of the elder and the younger in the family? We discover this now for the first time.

Summing up, the strange thing about us is that we are absolutely different in temperament, in taste, in nature, and yet we have absolutely identic ideas, likes and dislikes as regards people, and the same intellectual perspective.

August 30.—Decidedly, it is harder to cast a play than to organize a cabinet of ministers. What seems to dominate in the actor is

[6] I publish this note just as it was written by my brother after having been uttered by him; but I owe it to him to declare that he exaggerates by painting himself as uglier and me as more attractive than we were.—E. de G.

not a desire to get a good part, but an urge to prevent another actor from getting one.

September 3.—The princess was terribly revolutionary this evening. With a tableful of academic guests to dinner, she asserted roundly and loudly that she much preferred a Japanese vase to an Etruscan vase. We came back by rail with Carpeaux, who was overflowing with aesthetic passion. Beauty, to him, is still nature —beauty of the past as well as beauty to be created in the future. He maintains that handsome specimens of the human body today are just as beautiful as the wonderful models of the Greeks. There are still athletes in our time, he says. For Carpeaux, as for all men of talent of our age and the future, there is no idealization of beauty, there is only the encounter with beauty and the recognition of it. In a word, he is the sort of artist who is capable of making a sketch in an omnibus—as was remarked by an imbecile member of the Institute who was present and thought to tease Carpeaux by saying as much.

This Carpeaux is all nerves, transport, exaltation; an unpolished countenance, its muscles constantly working, and the eyes of a labourer in anger—the fever of genius in the envelope of a stone-cutter.

September 11.—Rereading of our play to the cast. Now that Got has decided to play Bressant's part and Mme Plessy has agreed to do the part of a mother (her first); now that in order to persuade this cast to perform there have been more solicitations, errands, and diplomacy expended than for the drafting and signature of a peace treaty, here is Delaunay—the character round whom the whole play is built—refusing his part, not in complaint that the play is bad or the part distasteful, quite the contrary, but because he deems the character too young for him. Unfortunately, the *Constitutionnel,* that very morning, had said he was too old to play Damis;[7] and like all those who are cast for lovers, his coquetry is reversed, he aspires to older men's parts, to the role of Molière's misanthrope. At bottom, he seems to want to

[7] In Molière's *Tartuffe.*

have his hand forced, to be covered by an order from the Ministry of Fine Arts.

However philosophical one may be, and however one may try to explain these things to oneself, this unceasing stream of exactions, claims, vanities and self-importances on the part of actors ends by irritating one to the point of disgust. And the minor actors are just as importunate as the rest. Little Dinah Felix asked me rather sulkily the other day to add ten lines to her part, while Lafontaine is annoyed because the character he is to play was at one time of his life a mere labourer.

September 14.—Delaunay has positively refused the part, this apparently rendering the whole project impossible. The production is disintegrating; as Thierry said, "This link gone, the whole mesh falls apart." We spent the day wandering about in despair, dragging our feet through the dead leaves in the Tuileries Gardens, blind to things and people, a taste of gall in our mouths.

September 15.—"Well, old friend! We had been told you were ill."

"Ah, you know, a man can make a fool of himself!"

And there came forth from him, unhurriedly, a hazy succession of sentences muddled by little choking spells and by a rising emotion that brought tears into his eyes and into his watering and mumbling voice. Then, as if trying to make fun of himself: "I warned her: There are more ways to kill a man than with a pistol shot, I said. . . . Every time I think of it, these two months past, it's like a needle sticking into me, here." He touched his breast over the heart. "I have just come from seeing the doctor. I told him everything. You realize that in these matters, it's better to tell him everything. Ah, that was a dreadful shock I had! You see, it was so sudden. I had left her on Tuesday. She wrote to me Wednesday. And on Sunday her banns were put up. Nothing had happened between us, the last time. Only, just as she was leaving, she made me admire her new hat. The hat she was to be married in, I suppose. Good Lord, whenever she happened to talk about marrying, I always advised her to do it. But this was too abrupt. Then, those last days, too, she said to me—I remember, I was struck by it—'I thought I was only so many years old, and I am so many years old.' She had found out her age from her baptismal certificate; and she had sent for that because she was going to be married, you see."

And so he went on, clinging to every smallest memory, savouring the bitterness, talking in a voice that lost itself in emotion while his skin grew yellower with every word.

In the evening, after dinner, he said: "The So-and-so's had gone back to Italy. I had nobody in the world. My son was away at school. I used to pray God in my empty dreams that he would send me a woman to give some sense to my life. When I got her letter, my dream was answered. We saw each other every fortnight, in a hotel, never at my house nor at hers. I had forbidden myself to go to her house for fear of becoming jealous. I didn't want to be jealous, didn't want to know anything of that side of her life. Every fortnight I was the first to arrive. You know how women are: they always keep a man waiting. There would be a fire in the grate. They would bring up my newspaper. I would read and wait for her. She would come along; take off her hat. I'd say to her, 'What have you been doing since I last saw you? Tell me everything.' And she would; at great length. Then she would ask my advice about things she dared not mention to others. I gave her books to read. We would talk about what she had read. She often said to me, 'You don't know how much—I won't say I love you, but how fond I am of you.' We would lunch together. She would stay four or five hours. Then, when she left, I would watch her go down the stairs. . . . What has become of all that? It is two months since I had a letter from her." He went through his pockets, looking for a letter. "Here: here is the telegram telling my son that I am dead."

"Poor old friend!"

"It's too much for me. I can't get over it."

He is an old friend of the family, an old man of seventy-six, telling us this story in the voice of a man mortally wounded, telling us of a life broken by the loss at one fell blow of a habit of fifteen years, a family, a daughter, and a mistress. There was something tragic and funereal and touching in the passionate desolation of this aged man who seemed not to want to have the strength to live and for whom desertion had been like a knife in the heart. When I spoke to him of going abroad for a change of scene in the company of his old valet, whom we had baptised Leporello,[8] the old man murmured half sadly and half ironically, "A wretched Don Juan I should make."

Sunday, September 17.—Mérimée came to stay with the princess at Saint-Gratien. Heavy features, thick black eyebrows, and the stocky build of the wits of the reign of Louis Philippe, with the general air of a headmaster of a provincial school. He is trying to persuade the princess to buy a villa at Cannes and he brought drawings of the place done by himself: shrieking water colours reminiscent of the eruptions of Vesuvius framed in black.

September 26.—They came to tell us that our old friend was dying. Already! We went to see him. He had asked that the last sacraments be administered this morning. A priest had come from St Augustine's Church, but he had refused to receive that particular priest because it was he who had officiated at the marriage of the woman our old friend loved. How strange and how like the inventions of a novelist are these dramatic coincidences of life itself! We went into his room. He recognized us. He shook hands with a hand that was almost still alive. Shutting his eyes, which he had momentarily opened, he said with a last sigh of his vanished gaiety, "Castor and Pollux." Nothing could be as harrowing as this ultimate smile of a man beginning to be a corpse.

September 28.—Thierry told us today that it would be impossible to produce our play at the moment and that he must put it off until after Ponsard's play. "There is a wind of rebellion blowing through the French theatre," he said. It is our bad luck—unprecedented at the Comédie-Française—to have our play cast and the parts accepted by the best actors of the troupe, the décor built and set up, and to be stopped by the stubbornness of a single actor who had himself voted for our play and was acting

[8]The name—a stroke of genius—found for Don Juan's valet by Lorenzo da Ponti in his libretto for Mozart's *Don Giovanni.*

parts in plays by Musset, every evening, just as young as the part whose youth is his pretext for not playing it. As a matter of fact, we know fairly well what is at the bottom of all this. Delaunay said he would play the part, would begin rehearsals, whenever the minister of fine arts gave him what he was demanding. What is that, except rank in the troupe equal to Bressant's? In a word, our play is killed by his refusal.

November 1.—In the doorway of the princess's private sitting room, a white shape in camisole and petticoat. A cry. The yapping of dogs. It is the princess in dishabille, fleeing with two women in black. The two women are the Princess Murat and her daughter Anna, whose engagement to the young Duke de Mouchy her mother has just announced.

After dinner Sainte-Beuve spoke of his great irritation during the Thursday sessions of the Academy when his nerves are always raw and his temper is on edge as the result of writing his weekly article for the *Constitutionnel*. He confessed that one day he had gone so far, in the course of a little altercation with Villemain, as to call him a vile name and raise his umbrella against him—for there is always an umbrella in all of Sainte-Beuve's great actions.

Mérimée arrived in the evening, and for the first time we heard him talk. He talks listening to himself, slowly, word by word, drop by drop, broken by deadly silences, as if he were distilling his effects, letting a glacial chill fall round everything he says. No wit, no flash, but a seeking after effect, the procedure of an old actor taking his time with the impertinence of a spoiled conversationalist and an affectation of contempt for all illusion, modesty, and social convention. Something indescribably offensive to healthily constituted people comes out of this curt and malignant irony, laboriously elaborated in order to amaze and dominate women and weak men.

Undated.—The provinces exceed anything that could be put into a novel. Never will a novelist invent the incident of the wife of a major of *gendarmerie* putting into verse the vicar's sermons.

November 5.—I am buried in the eiderdown of the provinces. My aged cousin flings a letter on my bed. I open it. It is from Thierry, announcing that Delaunay has agreed to take the part, that I must come back to Paris, that the play will open on the first of December.

The theatre is really a terrific box of surprises.

November 10.—At last our play is being rehearsed on stage, where we sit beside the prompter at his little table. We were still terrified at the first rehearsal, because Delaunay did not turn up for his entrance. He was sent for and finally appeared.

What strikes us most is the long hemming and hawing of the actors before they get their lines. They begin by repeating and reciting, the way children do. One feels that they have to have the words dinned into them, have to work themselves up, warm to their job. They fumble the intonation, muff the business. Constantly, they speak their lines in such a way as to suggest the opposite of what the author meant. And how long it seems to take them to get under the skin of the part!

From these strictures we must except Mme Plessy, who alone of them all possesses a truly literary intelligence. From the first word, she understands and she delivers. She showed immediately that she understood what we had observed and what was true in the part of Mme Maréchal; and her comprehension is so spontaneous that the translation into acting is instantaneous, always intelligent, and sometimes noble.

November 18.—At bottom, there is something austere about the theatre. Women are not women on the stage. They arrive for rehearsal dressed as for housework. One has the feeling that their fine clothes and their smiles are reserved for the audience. No coquetry; practically no sex; nothing in them of the novels written about stage life; not the least intention of finding in the theatre a lover or a whim. The play is their whole concern.

Life is turned wrong end to by these rehearsals. You spend the daylight hours in darkness, in a twilight illumined by a pair of gas lamps. Life, the sun, the hours marked by the sun out of doors, is abolished. Leaving the theatre at four in the afternoon, as the day begins to decline, you emerge into the street dazed and disoriented, hardly sure it is not all a dream. It is a thrilling life, though, with its creative inventions and ingenuities of all sorts, its infinitely delicate details, and all the undreamt-of art of the thing. There is the search for and the discovery of a gesture that shall be the very gesture of the words spoken by the actor; the grouping of people on the stage; the communications established or broken between the characters; all the emphasis upon certain words here and there to be fixed; the business of getting up and sitting down perfectly naturally, which has to be rehearsed a dozen times in each scene—all these trifles that are so absolute, so positive, of a reality so flagrant that the moment the right note is struck everybody cries out, "That's it!" and a little stir of joy goes through one like a warm current. Nobody outside the theatre has any notion of the work, the perpetual *mastication,* necessary before the actors get into their parts. They require a daily infiltration for a month.

Mme Plessy's only defect is that her spontaneous intuition never jells. She understands so rapidly that she understands something new every day. From one rehearsal to the next, bit by bit, she goes through the whole play in magnificent fashion, but each day she is magnificent in a different place and never in that same place again.

November 20.—The life of the theatre is a perpetual flutter. Today, when everything seemed to have been settled, Thierry told us that the government censor was very excited against our play, and that it might still be interdicted.

November 25.—Rehearsal today with the prompter in his box. The play is beginning to be performed admirably. Mme Plessy is almost continuously sublime; yes, sublime, I am not afraid to use the word. What a great dramatic artist we have set to work! As for Delaunay's voice, it is the most beautiful music that an author can wish for his prose.

Mme Plessy told us that she had seen Scribe, in his later years, chew a handkerchief to bits during a bad rehearsal.

November 29.—Thierry showed us a letter from Camille Doucet in which the prime minister, Rouher, and Marshal Vaillant do us the honour of seeking and finding a way to end our play. Rouher wants the daughter to be wounded, merely, and that there remain *the hope of a marriage with her mother's lover.* Marshal Vaillant found another ending in about the same taste; but fortunately he does not insist upon his ending, and being a soldier, he has no great objection to our pistol shot at the end.

December 3.—Dress rehearsal today. Coming into the green-room I found there, bounding gaily, that adorable Rosa Didier costumed for the part of Bébé, her fine eyes shining under a blond wig, and a mad cloud of muslin flying about her. It seemed to me that all the old portraits hung in this grim room, all the ancestors of noble tragedy and grave comedy, the Orosmanes[9] in their turbans and the daggered queens, were frowning down upon this carnival sprite. In the passage I ran against Delaunay, whom at first I did not recognise, so rejuvenated was he by some magical preparation and so truly did he seem to be the age of the seventeen-year-old youth he was to play.

Looking on as these people moved about speaking one's own words and playing the lives oneself had created; watching that scene that was one's own and that one felt belonged to oneself—the stair, the music, the actors, the supernumeraries, and even the sceneshifters and firemen, one was filled with an immense joy over the possession of all this. The audience, meanwhile, were very curious. Worth and his wife were present, for without their inspection Mme Plessy never goes on; and they had brought with them all the well-known dressmakers and milliners of Paris. The effect of the play grows stronger with each rehearsal. The actors themselves are amazed and express their admiration of each other. Everybody looks forward to a great success, and

[9]Orosmane, the central figure of Voltaire's *Zaïre,* is the Othello of the French classical theatre, the hero unjustly jealous who murders his beloved.

the thing they all say is, "It is twenty years since the Théâtre-Français has seen a play produced and performed like this one."

December 5.—Slept well. Left cards on the critics. Called on Roqueplan and found him at lunch. He was all in red and shod with a pair of slippers that looked like great embroidered moccasins—half headsman and half Ojibway Indian. He talked of the hygiene of men of letters, saying that in our trade "we are forced to fight against nervous waste." He said he had just eaten two beefsteaks; that there was an art of testing the stomach, training it. When we complimented him on his health, on the way he bore his years, he sighed and said, "Oh, everybody has his ailment. I too have my dustbin. Mornings, I hawk up my phlegm. It cleans me out for the day."

We called on Janin, who no longer leaves his house and has become, with his gout, a theatre critic in the home. He said his wife was dressing to go to our play. Despite everything between us, despite his ferocious attack upon our *Men of Letters,* we remember our first visit to him and his first article about us.

Time came to dine and we went to Bignon's restaurant, where we ate and drank enormously—thirty francs' worth, absolutely as if we had a hundred performances ahead of us. Not in the least nervous. Perfectly serene. Convinced that even if the audience does not think our play perfect, at any rate it will be so wonderfully acted that the actors will make it a success. We called for the theatre paper, *L'Entr'-acte,* and read and reread the names of the cast.

We reached the theatre. All about it the street seemed to be stirring, lively. We went like conquerors up those stairs which we had so often climbed in a totally different mood. We had promised ourselves earlier in the day that if we saw, towards the end of the play, that it was received with great enthusiasm, we should slip out before the end in order not to be dragged in triumph before the curtain.

The passages were crowded. A rumble of volubility was running through the crowd, and we caught certain remarks on the fly as we went by. "The railing in front of the box office has been broken by the queue." Guichard, still in Roman costume, came into the greenroom, rather upset. He had been booed in *Horace et Lydie*.[10] Bit by bit we found ourselves breathing in a stormy atmosphere. Got, against whom we ran, said that the audience was wearing a singular smile: "They are not very loving tonight."

We went to the peephole in the curtain and tried to look at the house, but in the dazzling light all we could see was a mob of faces. Suddenly we heard music. The rise of the curtain; the three knocks announcing the beginning of the play—these solemn moments for which we had been waiting with beating hearts, had totally escaped us. Then we were amazed to hear one catcall, more catcalls, still more catcalls, and a storm of hisses answered by a hurricane of bravos. We were standing in the wings, and it seemed to us that as the supernumeraries passed by, they sent us pitying glances. The hissing and the applause went on.

When the curtain was lowered we went out of doors without putting on our coats. Our ears were burning. The second act began. The hissing started up again, accompanied by animal cries and imitations of the actors' intonations. Still they hissed until interrupted by a word of silence from Mme Plessy. Then the battle continued between the actors, supported by a part of the stalls and almost all the boxes, which were applauding, and the whole of the gallery, which was trying with shrieks, interruptions, catcalls and angry vulgarities to force down the curtain.

"Blowing hard out there," Got said two or three times. The pistol shot was fired. The final curtain went down in the roar of a riot. I saw Mme Plessy stride off stage with the wrath of a lioness, raging with abuse against the audience that had insulted her. And from behind the curtain we listened for a quarter of an hour to ferocious vociferations that would not permit Got, as is the custom at the end of a first performance, to pronounce the names of the authors of the play.

[10]*Henriette Maréchal* was performed on a triple bill with Ponsard's one-act *Horace et Lydie* and Molière's two-act comedy, *Le Dépit amoureux.*

We made our way through the *tumultuating* groups that filled the lobbies of the theatre and went to take supper at the Maison d'Or with Count d'Osmoy, Bouilhet and Flaubert. We stood up pretty well, despite a nervousness that made us want to vomit each time we took up a morsel of food. Flaubert could not resist saying that he thought we were superb, and we went home at five in the morning more infinitely weary than we had ever been in our lives.[11]

December 6.—The chief of the *claque*[12] told me that since Hugo's *Hernani* the theatre had not witnessed a tumult like that of last night.

Dined with the princess, who went home last night with her gloves torn and hands burning as the result of her applause.

My stupid mistress attended the performance. She told me to-night that she had scarcely dared go out into the street this morning, for she felt that she had last night's applause written in her face.

December 9.—Augier, who was present at the first perform-ance, was astonished that the management had not quieted the whole house by the simple expedient of throwing out ten or a dozen agitators. Once again, as when this has happened before, the actors are wondering why the police tolerate such things. As I was leaving tonight, Coquelin told me that when the catcalls

[11]The Goncourts nowhere explain that the attack upon their play was political. In 1865 the Second Empire was still the "authoritarian Empire", part of which we gather from the fact of the censorship of which these Journals speak. The emperor's authority had been weakened by an economic crisis, and the republican opposition was mani-festing itself with more and more audacity. This opposition—and other quarters as well—believed that the Goncourts' play had been accepted by the official Théâtre-Français ("the Players-in-ordinary to the Emperor," as the troupe then was), and that the censor had been dissuaded from interdiction, only through the influence of their friend, the Princess Mathilde. Therefore they who were totally without political opinion, and whose relations were, in fact, almost altogether anti-Bonapartist, were deemed by the town Bonapartists; and as Bonapartists they were to be booed off the stage. Incidentally, the riot seems to have been touched off by one character's hurling at another this un-qualifiable insult: "Subscriber to the *Revue des Deux Mondes!*"

[12]In France at both opera and theatre, and in England and America only at opera, men are hired by the house or by individual performers to applaud either the production or the particular performance.

made it impossible to hear anything that was said on stage, several men sitting in the lower-tier boxes went out to the police sergeant and informed him that they had paid for their seats and had brought their families to hear the play, and they wanted to hear it. The police sergeant had replied that he had no instructions in the matter.

These painful hours that we have to live through anew each evening cut off one's appetite and constrict one's digestion. When we go to the theatre, we always take English peppermints with us. Speaking of this, Dumas the younger told us the other day that early in his career as playwright Labiche had said to him:

"Well, is your digestion out of order yet?"

"No."

"Wait until you've done a play or two. You'll see."

December 15.—Thierry came to see us this morning. He showed us a copy of the *Gazette de France* in which there was an attack upon us and a strange appeal to the taxpayers whose money went to produce *Henriette Maréchal,* to join in insisting that the play be stopped. On the score of this, Thierry requested that we agree to withdraw our play. We refused, saying that he knew very well it was not the play that was hissed, and that we were resolved to go on until the government stopped us.

This evening, thanks to the warmth of anonymous supporters which the unreasoning and mad enmity has won the play, the performance was a triumph. At the first catcall, the whole audience rose and demanded that the interrupter be thrown out. After this success we begged Thierry to allow one more performance, which he said he could not promise us.

Eugène Giraud told us backstage that the princess had received frightful anonymous letters as the result of our play, promising that her house would be the first one burned down.

I have already observed that my birthday is always marked by some fatal occurrence in our lives; today it is the closing of our play; ten years ago it was our arrest on the score of an article published on the fifteenth of December.

1866

Undated.—Travelling in France, it is a misfortune to be a Frenchman. The chicken wing at table always goes to the Englishman. The reason is that the Englishman does not look upon the waiter as a man, and that every servant who feels himself considered a human being is contemptuous of the person who regards him as one.

Undated.—The genius of Japan lies in its imaginative preoccupation with the monstrous, in its art of painting both man's waking fears—the ferocious and the reptilian—and his fears in the night—the ghostly apparition. The Japanese have a particular faculty for incarnating these panics of vision and illusion, lending shape to them in the construction of articulated and almost viable beings.

Japan created and infused life into the *Bestiarium* of hallucination. Forth from the nightmarish brain of its art, one can almost see the rushing flight of a world of animal demons, a creation carved in the turgescence of deformity, beasts as twisted and convulsed as the roots of the mandragora, an excrescence of gnarled branches in which the flow of the sap has been arrested, beasts of confusion and of bastardy, a mingling of saurian and mammifer grafting the toad on the lion, cutting and slipping the sphinx on the cerberus, beasts swarming and ghastly, liquid and fluent, squirming out their lives like earth-worms, creatures crested and shaggy of mane rolling their eyes and grinding their teeth at the tip of a stem, beasts of dread bristling and menacing and blazing with horror, dragons and chimaeras out of the Japanese Apocalypse.

We Frenchmen, we Europeans, have not this wealth of invention; there is but one dragon in our art, and that is over and over again the dragon that figures in Theramène's monologue in *Phèdre* and in the painting by M. Ingres, where he threatens Angélique with a tongue of scarlet flannel.[1]

In Japan the dragon is everywhere. He is the adornment and almost the furniture of the household. He is the flowerpot and the incensepot. The potter, the bronzeworker, the draughtsman, the needleworker—all these sow him in the path of the daily life of the Japanese. With furious nails he grimaces angrily on the garments worn in every season of the year. In that world of pallid women with painted eyelids, the dragon is the habitual, the familiar, the beloved, almost the caressing, image of their lives, quite like the statuette on our mantelshelves; and who knows but that he may be the ideal of this nation of artists?

[1]*Phèdre,* Act V, sc. vi:

> L'onde approche, se brise, et vomit à nos yeux,
> Parmi des flots d'écume, un monstre furieux.
> Son front large est armé de cornes menaçantes;
> Tout son corps est couvert d'écailles jaunissantes;
> Indomptable taureau, dragon impétueux,
> Sa croupe se recourbe en replis tortueux;
> Ses longs mugissements font trembler le rivage.
> Le ciel avec horreur voit ce monstre sauvage;
> La terre s'en émeut, l'air en est infecté. . . .

Etc. This appears to provide an occasion to quote what P. Valéry wrote of dragons in literature (see "Adonis" in *Variété*): "Pour effrayant que soit un monstre, la tâche de le décrire est toujours un peu plus effrayante que lui. Il est bien connu que les misérables monstres n'ont jamais pu faire dans les arts qu'une figure ridicule. Je ne vois de monstre peint, chanté ou, sculpté, qui non seulement nous fasse la moindre peur, mais encore qui laisse notre sérieux en équilibre. . . . Voyez cet extravagant composé animal qui transfixe Roger tout armé d'or, aux pieds de la délicieus Angélique de M. Ingres; figurez-vous ce dugong ou ce marsouin dont les brusques ébrouements et les jeux brutaux dans l'écume de la mer viennent effaroucher les chevaux d'Hippolyte; entendez braire dans sa caverne le cornard et lamentable Fafner,—ils n'ont jamais pu obtenir de personne l'aumône d'un peu de terreur. . . . Le complément nécessaire d'un monstre, c'est un cerveau d'enfant."

January 15.—Taine declared this evening that all men of talent were the product of their environment. We maintained the countrary. Where will you find, we asked him, the root of Chateaubriand's exoticism? It is a pineapple growing in the courtyard of a barracks! Gautier upheld us, saying, for his part, that the brain of an artist in the time of the Pharaohs was no different to what it is today. As for others than artists, those *bourgeois* whom he called *fluid nonentities,* it may be that their brain has changed, but that is of no importance.

Undated.—In the reading room of the Imperial Library I saw, as I went by, a man engaged in reading a book while holding the hand of a young woman seated by his side. I passed the same way two hours later. The man was still reading and he was still holding the young woman's hand. It was a German couple. I mean, it was Germany.

Undated.—That which, perhaps, hears more silly remarks than anything else in the world, is a picture in a museum.

Undated.—The newspaper has killed the salon, and the successor of society is the public.

Undated.—God made woman to be the nurse of man. Her devotion does not rise above disgust; it ignores it.

February.—How little we live, we who write! Taine, putting himself to bed at nine, rising at seven, working till noon, dining at a provincial hour, paying calls, running to libraries, spending the evening with his mother and his piano. Flaubert, chained like a convict to his work. Ourselves in our cloistered incubations, neither bothered nor distracted by family or society, with the exception of a fortnightly dinner with the princess and an occasional and inquisitive meandering stroll along the quays.

October 7.—Magny dinner. Once again the immense and gossipy memory of Sainte-Beuve. The Duke Pasquier told him that he would never return to public life, that the emperor would never forgive him his remark when, Louis Napoléon Bonaparte having been brought into Pasquier's office a prisoner and having stood there, his hat on his head, the duke had said, "Officer, remove the prisoner's hat!"[2]

Then Sainte-Beuve jumped from Pasquier to Louis XVIII and to what he had once said at a meeting of his Cabinet: "Gentlemen, there will be no Cabinet on Tuesday: the king plans to take his pleasure."

Mme du Cayla had succeeded the king's earlier mistress, Mme de Mirbel, whom one assignation had sufficed to disgust. On that Tuesday, everybody fearing a fainting fit on the part of the king, the whole court had gathered in an anteroom to have news of the outcome of his physiological experiment. Soon afterwards, Baron Portal took the king's pulse, and they could hear him say, "Slow, very slow."

From Louis XVIII the conversation moved on to Chateaubriand, Sainte-Beuve insisting that in 1817, when a warrant for his arrest was issued, the author of *The Genius of Christianity* was discovered, at six o'clock in the morning, in bed with two prostitutes.[3]

Veyne confided to us about Gavarni that from the time of his separation from his wife, in 1848, he had had no commerce with women. The man who, up to that moment, has divided his life between women and work, suddenly broke off; and Veyne added that Gavarni had once said to him, about Mlle Aimée, whom

[2]This occurred in 1840 when Bonaparte landed at Boulogne from England and sought to foment the overthrow of Louis Philippe and put himself on the throne. But is the story true? Louis-Napoleon is said to have met Pasquier at Falloux's and to have spoken thus: "Sir, I have thus far had the pleasure of meeting you only twice: be assured that I have forgotten our first meeting." This is surely more in keeping with his nature.

[3]A pretty dubious story. Chateaubriand was not arrested and dragged out of bed. His political pamphlet, *Considérations sur la monarchie selon la charte,* was suppressed by the Decazes Ministry, against which it was directed, on the seventeenth of September 1817, twelve days after Decazes dissolved the *"Chambre introuvable."* The seizure took place in the printing shop, where the author turned up and protested with emphasis. He was stripped of all his dignities except that of Peer of France and the annual honorarium of 12,000 francs attached thereto, but he was not otherwise molested.

In this book Chateaubriand had referred to the Duke Decazes, an ex-Bonapartist, as a man "whose feet have slithered in blood."

everybody thought his mistress, that it was a pity he had never got a child on her, for that might have saved her.

October 15.—This evening there were very few of us in the drawing room. The princess, her eyes a little tired, was not at her needlework, and she let herself go in reminiscences. She talked about her marriage, about Czar Nicholas I greeting her with the words, "I shall never forgive you for this!" when she arrived at his court married to Demidoff. It had been his dream to marry off his son to a member of Napoleon's family. This very woman, who sat talking to us, had missed two imperial crowns. It was therefore natural that in her moments of melancholy there should come into her mind the memory and the shadow of the two crowns that had grazed her forehead.

"Nicholas," she went on, "was rather an ogre, but tempered by sweetness towards his family. An excellent father and relative. He went every day to see the little princes and princesses, sat with them while they ate, was present when the children were punished, inquired about their diet, and was always on hand when they were put to bed, if their parents were absent. I must say, he was extremely kind and paternal to the members of his family. He had friends, like one commoner, for example, Kisselleff, who was allowed to come into the empress's room familiarly at any hour.

"In justice to him it must be said that part of his severity was due to the thieving, blackguardly people he had round him. He used to say to the czarevitch, 'You and I are the only two honest men in Russia.' For he knew well enough that all the posts in his government were trafficked in. Therefore, there was nothing astonishing in his affecting a certain theatrical pitilessness." And the princess spoke of his being his own police officer, going through the streets in a little carriage, he a head taller than any man in his realm. "And as handsome as a cameo," she added. "A Roman emperor!

"He was a little mad, I agree; but how easy it is to understand when you think of what I have seen in Moscow. For example, when he rode to the Kremlin, moujiks would touch his boot and make the sign of the Cross with the hand that had touched it.

"There was always something recalcitrant in him. When one of his sons married the illegitimate Princess of Hesse, he whispered into my ear, 'After all, it is the pig ennobling the sow.'

"One day the grand duchess told me that he was furious because he had read in Custine's book that he was beginning to develop a paunch.[4] She must have been mistaken, because when the czar came to see me he said, 'You haven't asked me why I am in such a bad temper.' And then he told me that he had just been reviewing his troops. It was a winter day, and after the review he had seen a colonel, freezing though the weather was, force his soldiers to take off their breeches and sling them over their shoulders to save the wear and tear on them. . . . Very given to gallantry, he was, with a singular habit of kissing all the pretty women he saw in the neck, or on the shoulder. Yes, very addicted to actresses. But the czarina was extremely old, with a doddering head. His last love was a lady-in-waiting who refused the money left to her in his will and went into a convent near where they buried him.

"He was always extremely kind to me. He had his mind fixed on the emancipation of Siberia, repeating that it would have been a great event in history, done in the name of a Napoleon. As for Monsieur Demidoff, he would not even utter his name and never did utter it. He would come in unannounced at dinnertime without his guards, without an escort, and the dinners would be frightful, for he would never even give Monsieur Demidoff a glance. Finally a day came when the czar said to me, 'Why won't you tell me this evening what is on your mind?' And as I refused to speak, he added, 'Whenever you need me I shall be there. Let me know directly through Count Orloff.' "

The princess let all this slip from her dreamily, broken by silences in which it seemed as if she was not going to go on, touching with an idle hand this object and that upon the table,

[4]The Marquis de Custine (1790–1857), a friend of Stendhal, wrote *La Russie en 1839* in four volumes, translated as *The Empire of the Czar* and published in London in 1843.

letting her glance drop and stray over the carpet. Talking, she had not noticed the time, she who invariably retired early, and she was suddenly astonished to find that it was a quarter to twelve.

Ah, history, history! I was thinking of the terrible portrait of the czar drawn for us by Herzen. Perhaps both portraits are true.

Monday, October 22.—Magny dinner. Immediately, this evening, the talk went to hypotheses concerning whether or not the planets were inhabited. Like a half-filled balloon, the conversation tossed about in the realm of infinity, and from infinity it was naturally led to the subject of God. Formulae defining Him rained upon the table. Against us who, as Latins concerned with form, could conceive God (if He exists) only as an ancient with a human face, a sort of kindly God by Michaelangelo with a long beard, Taine, Renan and Berthelot countered with Hegelian definitions, showing God as a vast, vague diffusion whose worlds were so many atoms, so many bubbles.

Renan, his imagination heated, fumbling for the words that would express a living whole, after profound digging into his brain and a long silence that bespoke the labour pains of genius; Renan, as seriously and religiously as a man could pronounce himself in this world, ultimately was able, before the gaping table, to compare his particular God with—guess what?—with an oyster and its vegetative existence. Oh, an oyster on a grand scale, mind you!

This comparison finally sputtered forth, the whole table went off into a gale of laughter in which, after a moment of bewilderment over what he had himself said, Renan very good-naturedly joined.

Whether or not it was this Homeric laughter that brought Homer to mind I cannot say, but in any case Homer was on the tapis. And in an instant all these great destroyers of faith, these demolishers of God, burst out into the most disgusting latria. With a single voice, every one of these critics proclaimed that there was a time and a country, at the beginning of humanity, when a work was written in which everything was divine and was above all discussion and even all scrutiny. They began to swoon over quotations.

"Cloud-marshalling Zeus!" Taine cried out enthusiastically.

"The unharvestable sea!" exclaimed Sainte-Beuve, his little voice swelling prodigiously; "the grapeless sea! Could anything be more beautiful?"

"As a matter of fact," Renan broke in; "the thing doesn't make sense. The Germans have discovered that the words have a different meaning altogether."

"Which is what?" Sainte-Beuve asked.

"I don't remember," said Renan, "but it is wonderful."

"You, there!" Taine called out, addressing us; "You who wrote that antiquity was created to be the daily bread of schoolmasters: what have you to say?"

I did not want to say anything, remembering very well the scene that had taken place at another of these dinners when I had spoken my mind about the ancients; but what with one after the other ragging me, I said as calmly as I could that I took more pleasure from reading Hugo than from Homer—using Hugo's name in order to fend off Saint-Victor's lightning. Nevertheless, at this blasphemy Saint-Victor became positively wild with fury and began to bawl and shriek in the tinny voice of a madman that this was too much; it was impossible for him to listen to such opinions; we were insulting the religion of all intelligent people. I began by retorting that it was very strange that at a table where one was free to discuss any subject in the world I should not have the right to my opinion of Homer. Saint-Victor shouted and flew into a passion, whereat I shouted louder and flew into a greater passion, carried away by the exasperation which I had long felt concerning this talented man who has not an opinion of his own and is always the humble servitor of received opinion, and whose bass voice and raging anger become weepy whinings as soon as he finds himself up against a determined opponent.

Sainte-Beuve, whom this quarrel had upset, insisted that I move to a seat beside him where he sought to calm me by stroking my arm, and to effect a reconciliation by proposing to my adversaries that they found a Homer Club, meanwhile massaging me on the other side. Little by little our anger died down, and Saint-Victor, on leaving, shook hands with me. I should have preferred that he had not held out his hand.

October 28.—Today Flaubert presented Bouilhet to the princess. I cannot imagine what unfortunate inspiration that poet had at lunch, for he stank like an omnibus in a Mediterranean town. Going upstairs afterwards, Nieuwerkerke said with a shudder, "There is a writer below who reeks of garlic."

December 5.—A visit from Felicien Rops, who is to illustrate our *La Lorette.*[5] A chap with dark hair brushed back and rather curly, little, black, paintbrush moustaches, a white silk muffler round his throat, and the face of a sixteenth-century duellist or a Spaniard born in Flanders. His speech is vivid, enthusiastic and precipitate, with the vibrant *rr-ra* of the Flemish accent running through it.

He told us that he was stricken all of a heap when, arriving from Belgium in Paris, he had his first sight of the trappings, the getup, the almost fantastic rig, of the Parisian woman, who seemed to him like a being from another planet. He spoke at great length of his desire to depict nature in its modern aspects, of the sinister character he saw in it, of the almost macabre emanation thrown off by a cocotte named Clara Blume in the dawning day after a night of gambling and pawing of the woman—a picture he intends to paint and for which he has already made eighty sketches of prostitutes.

December 21.—Days spent reading pamphlets published during the Revolution, for a play we are doing on the period. Our play will not say what we felt in the course of our reading; we shall try to be as impartial in the play as the theatre demands. But our true and intimate impression of the period is one of disgust and

[5]*Lorette* was a name invented in 1840 by Nestor Roqueplan to characterise the light o' loves who, at about that time, had gathered in new flat buildings erected in the neighbourhood of the Church of Notre-Dame de Lorette. This was the most popular of the Goncourts' books during their lifetime and went through many editions. Gavarni did a frontispiece for it; Rops never got round to the job.

contempt. If one's mind is at all fastidious, it is the mind even more than the heart that is sickened by these pages, for they record even more ineptitudes than crimes. The stench that rises from this pool of murders is the reek of stupidity. Try as it may to appear terrifying, at bottom the true characteristic of the Revolution was its stupidity. Had there been no bloodshed it would have been merely silly; had there been no guillotine, it would have been ludicrous. Take away from those great men, Robespierre and Marat, their halos of the headsman, and the first is no more than a windy professor of rhetoric while the second is a maniac, the exaggeration of a madman. Yes, without its bloodshed, you would say about the Revolution, "This is too stupid!" if you were to read the heap of cannibalistic imbecilities and anthropophagous rhetoric that we have been through. It must be read to be believed: there is otherwise no crediting that this thing could have happened in France less than a hundred years ago, this reign, this homicidal dictatorship, of the base, of the porter's lodge, of the servant's pantry, of the informer, of all the jealousies and spite of the lower orders.

What a terrible argument against Providence these years represent! If Providence exists, it must be only with the aim of tolerating all this, and God, during the Revolution, was a sort of Lafayette, sleeping through all the Sixths of October.[6]

And what hypocrisy, what lies, this Revolution was made up of! The mottoes, the walls, the speeches, the stories—everything was then a lie. *The Humbug of the Revolution:* there is a book to be written! For where can you read an opinion about it founded on the truth? Who has ever read the documents? Is there one fact about the Revolution that patriotism and party passions and journalism have not turned into legend? Everybody talks about that famous sabre stroke of Lambesc,[7] but who

[6]On the fifth and sixth of October 1789 the people of Paris marched on Versailles, where they are said to have been advised to eat cake. Soon after, Louis XVI and his family moved from Versailles into the Tuileries Palace, in Paris, under duress.

[7]Lambesc, colonel of a cavalry regiment known as *Le Royal allemand,* charged a mob in the Tuileries Gardens and killed an old man with a sabre stroke. This occurred on the twelfth of July 1789, two days before the taking of the Bastille, and is remembered as a sort of "murder at Sarajevo."

has read his justification of it and knows the truth about that scene? And out of all the gulls and simpletons in society and in the streets who have their catechism of the Bastille by heart, how many know the number of prisoners that these horrible and devouring dungeons actually released to the light of day? Three, wasn't it? or was it four?

1867

January 2.—Dined at the princess's with Gautier, Octave Feuillet and Amédée Achard, a wilted man of fashion, a mind without emphasis, an expressionless voice—the archetype of nonentity.

Ponsard pulled to pieces by Gautier and ourselves, the princess arguing against us. When we had finished, someone asked Gautier why he did not write the things he had just said. "Let me tell you a little story," Gautier replied with perfect self-possession. "One day, Monsieur Walewski[1] told me that I was to stop being indulgent to writers, I had his authority to write exactly what I thought of all the plays produced. 'But,' said I, 'it is So-and-so's play that is opening this week.' 'Indeed?' said he. 'In that case, suppose you begin the week following.' Well, I am still waiting for the week following."

Undated.—A sign of the times—there are no chairs in bookshops any longer. France was the last bookseller in whose shop one could sit down and waste a little time between sales. Books are now bought standing: the customer asks for a book and is told the price—and that is all. This is what the all-devouring activity

---

[1]Count Alexandre Walewski (1810–68), the natural son of Napoleon I and the Countess Walewska, was minister for foreign affairs of Napoleon III. Gautier wrote for the government organ, the *Moniteur Universel.*

of trade has done to bookselling, a trade that was at one time a matter for loitering, loafing, and chatty and familiar browsing.

Undated.—We feel that we are as antipathetic to Girardin as if he respected us.

January 16.—We were talking of love, caprice, sentiment, when a slightly plump woman, already past her youth but still very desirable, said jokingly that she could easily fall in love with a man of fifty years. Everybody laughing at this avowal, she went on: "I have always been rather inclined towards older people and have never appreciated young men. They are so empty, so silly; and besides, they are always doing something violent—dancing, or riding, or running about. As I have always been a little fat, I preferred sitting still in a comfortable armchair, or on a sofa, with men who enjoyed staying put and chatting."

Undated.—The Universal Exposition, the final blow levelled at the past, the Americanization of France, industry lording it over art, the steam thresher displacing the painting—in brief, the Federation of Matter.

Undated.—I believe we shall end by dying with the conviction that nobody has ever read a book or looked at a picture.

February 3.—They say that during one of Ollivier's interviews with the emperor, the emperor asked him to tell him very frankly what people were saying about him; to speak as if he were not addressing his sovereign. Ollivier having said finally that people thought his faculties were declining, the emperor remarked impassively, "That is consistent with the reports that have reached me."

The story is like him, and in his impersonality he attains a certain grandeur.

Undated.—Why does a Japanese gateway charm me and please my eye when all the architectural lines of Greece seem to my eye tedious? As for people who pretend to feel the beauties of both these arts, my conviction is that they feel nothing, absolutely nothing.

Undated.—At the moment we are buying a great many memoirs, autobiographies, collections of letters, all human documents—the charnel house of truth.

March 6.—The princess has a charming smile, a friendly, human smile, full of meaning. One must have seen that smile on her lips when she said, this evening, to Sainte-Beuve, "If, one of these days, people read our letters, Monsieur Sainte-Beuve, they will see that we have shaken hands with not a few rogues."

March 16.—Opening night of *Les Idées de Madame Aubray,* by Dumas the younger, the first I have attended since *La Dame aux Camélias.* A special audience, not to be seen on any other occasion. It is not a play that goes on, it is the celebration of a kind of mass in the presence of a pious congregation. There is a *claque* which seems to be officiating, rather than applauding, and there are gasps of ecstasy and swoonings of "Adorable!" at every line spoken on stage. An actor says, "Love is the springtime; it is not the whole year," and there are salvos of handclapping. He goes on, underscoring the invention: "It is not the fruit; it is the flower:" gloves are split. And so all through the play. Nothing is judged; nothing is weighed; everything is applauded with an enthusiasm ready in advance of the speech.

Dumas has great talent. He knows how to write for his audience, for this first-night audience. He is its poet, and to these men and women he ladles out, in a language they can understand, the ideal of the commonplaces of their hearts.

March 17.—I spew up my contemporaries. Today, in the world of letters, in the highest world of letters, judgment grovels on the ground, and conscience and opinion have crumbled. Life, the sky, the fortunes of our time, is so base, the air is so filled with cowardice, the enervating habit of compromise is so universal, that at the first contact with society, the first rubbing up against people in power, even the frankest and most irascible and most plethoric of men lose their feeling of revolt and are hard put to it not to think every success a thing of beauty.

April 2.—We are off to Rome.

April 6.—Cività Vecchia. Ten in the morning. At last we see tortuous streets, lively, swarming, filthy markets, a populace dressed in rags, buildings ready to collapse, things picturesque and artistic, a town without the visible hand of municipal councillors, and streams of colourful slops. I am overcome by a strange happiness; my eyes are bright at the thought that I have run away from that American France, that Paris towed along in the path of the *now*.

These towns in the Papal States seem to me the last towns in which the poor are still at home. There is a compassion, a mercifulness of nature, almost a familiarity, in the attitude of the middle classes towards the poor, the ragged, the miserable, that astounds a man come from one of those countries that are so hard on the penniless and where philanthropy is the subject of university courses. It is almost with a caress that the publican here gently urges a mendicant out of his place.

April 9.—The woman of the South speaks only to the senses: the impression she makes goes no deeper. She addresses herself exclusively to the masculine appetite.

In the evening, after having passed in review all the types of brilliant or savage beauty to be seen in the streets of Rome, in the Pincio, on the Corso, it seems to me that only an Englishwoman or a German woman can give a man the feeling of affection, the stir of tenderness.

Undated.—Ah, what a fortunate people, this people gay with the gaiety of bright skies, with its felicities so cheaply bought, able to get first-rate meat for a dozen coppers and wine for nothing, so to speak; with no military conscription, no onerous taxes, no bitterness in poverty, living amidst so many charitable institutions and where the hand of the less poor is ever in the pocket, ready to help the poorer.

When I compare these people with the peoples of progress and liberty, branded with the mark of the sinister *busyness* of our age, struggling daily with its budget, massacred by taxation including the tax on human life, it seems to me really that we pay dearly for our catchwords.

April 20.—This journey that we were fearful of making and did embark upon only out of literary conscience, to verify certain scenes of our novel (*Madame Gervaisais*) turns out to have brought us a sense of relief, of release, almost of cheerfulness, of which we had no expectation.

One feels in Rome that nothing has been done about antiquity —except archaeological research—and that what is missing is a *resurrection* of this antiquity such as Michelet performed for the history of France. What a wonderful task for a young man sick of Paris, a man repelled by our contemporary scene, to bury himself in Rome and write a series of monographs to be called *The Pantheon, The Coliseum;* or better still, if he had the power, to write a great fat book in which he would reconstruct ancient society with the help of the museums and the whole world of insignificant things and objects surrounding the life of ancient man, showing him as he has never yet been shown—using that strigil, hanging in a glass case, as something with which the reader could actually touch the bronzed skin of ancient Rome.

This evening, an unforgettable picture at the Pellegrini hostel: files of wild-looking, veritably lousy peasants seated on benches beneath a gas lamp which threw their heads into the shadow and made a single white spot of their shirts open at the throat, and, stripping off their stockings and washing their feet in buckets, the Brothers of the Trinity, pilgrims dressed in red with white jabots and aprons and with napkins under their arms, like waiters, a fraternity made up of cardinals, princes, young noblemen, with varnished boots peering under their servants' costumes and their carriages standing in wait for them on the square. And when these filthy feet are washed and dried the brethren bend over, bring their lips near the feet, and kiss them in two places.

This ruthless reminder of equality raises in us a certain emotion. The Catholic religion is after all a great source of humanity, and it irritates me to see intelligent men go down on their knees before the religion without bowels of the ancient classics. Everything that is tender, that is sensitive, that is movingly beautiful in modernity, comes from Christ.

April 21.—The last echoes of the Pope's words of benediction were still floating in the air when three women—this was the first thing I saw—three women began to rip each other's faces with their nails in the midst of a hilarious crowd that stood by rubbing its hands in glee.

April 23.—Dined at our Embassy last night and sat beside the wife of the United States minister to Brussels, an American woman.[2] Watching the play of this free and victorious grace, the indomitable spirit of this young race, this potential coquetry that retains the charm and domination of flirtatiousness in these young girls become spouses, and remembering meanwhile the activity and *go* of certain Americans I know in Paris, I said to myself that these men and women seemed destined to be the future conquerors of the world.

May 3.—In Rome, after a time, the poetry of life calls up in a Frenchman a certain yearning for *Parisianism;* he finds himself strolling at twilight on the Corso and turning over on his tongue some cynical enormity of one Parisian comedian or another by way of winning back the healthy reek of the Paris gutter.

Undated.—The great modern question—dominant and threatening, and now particularly acute—is the deep antagonism between Latin and German. The German is bound to devour the Latin, and yet, take a sample out of each of these two masses of human beings, and the higher individual intelligence will always be on

[2]If the lady was in fact the wife of the American minister resident in Belgium, then she was Mrs Henry S. Sanford, of Connecticut, *née* Miss du Puy of Philadelphia.

the side of the Latin—of the Italian, for example. But is not this intelligence like the purely artistic sky of Rome, which gives birth to flowers, and not to vegetables?

I am struck by the degree to which the character of the Frenchman is denationalized abroad, how rapidly and naturally the country in which he lives overpowers him and makes him one with it to the depth of his being. In France, the foreigner takes on a slight veneer; he never becomes steeped in the country.

May 4.—Raphael's "Transfiguration." The most disagreeable impression of badly painted paper that the eye of a colour-loving painter can possibly receive. It would be impossible to find a jangle, a more crying discord of ugly blues, yellows, reds and greens than these tones; one green, in particular, an abominable serge green; and all these tones associated in shrieking juxtapositions, heightened by galvanized high lights that are invariably out of tune with the tonality of the stuffs, and that fall in a glazed yellow on violet shades and in a glazed white on green.

But there is no need to dwell upon the man as colourist: let us study this masterpiece of drawing and composition, the *Sursum corda* of Christianity. A Christ who is a vulgar *frater,* sanguine, pink, painted—as the scholiasts of the picture say—in colours intended for the glow of another life than ours, rising heavily into the sky on the tips of his model's feet; a Moses and an Elijah rising with him, their fists on their haunches, like dancers, the picture empty of the flashing radiance, the glory, which the least imaginative of painters would try to get into his painting of the heaven of the blessed. Beneath is a Mount Tabor, a hill as smooth as the top of a patty on which lie flattened, and as it were boned, three puppet apostles, true caricatures of bewilderment; and at the bottom of the picture an incomprehensible medley of academic drawing, faces filled with those expressions which students are set to copy, and a flourish of human arms as by student players in a school show on St Charlemagne's Day,[3] and eyes as if a conscientious drawing master had forced the gleam of light straight into the pupil.

[3] January 18, St Charlemagne's Day, a school holiday on which plays used to be given.

In all this there is not an atom of feeling, such as one finds in Simone Memmi, Filippo Lippi, Botticelli, Piero di Cosimo—that feeling which even the least gifted of primitive painters were able to introduce into these scenes, lending them an expression of devotion, of compunction, of placid and saintly astonishment, *angelising,* so to say, the eyes of those who beheld this miracle. In Raphael, the Resurrection is purely academic, shot with a paganism which is particularly apparent in the foreground where a woman, a bit of antique statuary, kneels like a heathen for whom the Gospels have never spoken.

This, Christian! I know no picture which disfigures Christianity in a more grossly material way, and I know no canvas depicting this scene in a commoner prose, a more vulgar beauty.

Undated.—After long seeking, I have today found what it is that is inferior in the Italian race: it is that they have no nerves. The thing is visible in something entirely insignificant—the absence of any impatience with the slowness with which everything here gets done.

Friday, May 24.—Théophile Gautier, who is at the moment *maestro di casa,* introduced us to La Païva and her legendary town house on the Champs-Élysées. An old courtezan, painted and plastered, with a smile as false as her hair and the general air of a provincial actress.

We were given tea in the dining room. Despite all its luxury and the excess of its Renaissance decoration in the worst taste, and despite the ridiculous sums spent on its marbles, its wainscotting, its paintings, its enamels, and the workmanship of its candelabra of solid silver come from the mines owned by the Prussian protector who was also present, this room remains the luxurious private cabinet of a public restaurant, a hideaway for millionaires.

The conversation dragged on and was properly as embarrassed as if we were all out of place here. Gautier, despite his native imperturbability, could not put himself at ease in this house. Turgan, whom we were meeting here for the first time, brought out his little effects most laboriously. Saint-Victor crushed and kneaded his hat in his effort to find a few sentences to utter. We could feel the fall upon this magnificent table, lighted by flaming sconces, of that chill that characterizes the houses of tarts playing at being ladies, that chill made up of tedium and uneasiness which, in the palaces of prostitution and the Louvres of strumpetry, freezes the natural spirits and wit of all who find themselves in such places.

All this was the more marked for the fact that the protector is a German personage, mute and handsome, a swell out of Borussia, dominating our little feast with a straight part in the middle of his head and a diplomatic smile, while La Païva's effort to be gracious was visibly hampered by something disquieting born of the fact that she was a business woman and her thoughts were, you would have sworn, not on her table but on the two little strongboxes in her chamber where she keeps her jewels, so that one felt the presence of something terribly implacable behind her smile, a past that was a little frightening.

May 27.—We are in a vast room over the *okel* of the Egyptian exhibit. The sunlight filters in through the lacelike design of the Arabic shutters at the windows and falls in luminous rose patterns upon the mummy boxes and sarcophagi. Each of them has tacked to it a bit of paper bearing the Egyptian name of its inhabitant and the genealogical line. All about us, on plain wooden shelves, are dried heads, skulls tied with bits of rag and of every colour, some green with the patina of bronze, others oozing bitumen and naphtha in the sunlight; still others black and stuck over with little squares of gold leaf, and yet others with the beautiful ivory pallor of old bones and great hollows of shadow in the empty eye sockets. In the heap, amidst all these receding foreheads, a brow swollen with thought and wisdom, a nobly Socratic head, and beside it a fleshless skull of a woman whom one imagines to have been beautiful, covered with a luxuriant mass of hair, reddened and carmined as is the hair of the others, a great braid, half crumbling, blinding her eyes.

Thrown crosswise on a table is the mummy about to be *de-*

banded. All round the table stand frock coats with decorations in their buttonholes. Soon begins the interminable unwinding of the cloth in which this stiff package is swaddled. This is a woman who was once alive—two thousand four hundred years ago—and the redoubtable and distant past of a being upon whose form we are about to gaze, and whose infinite slumber we, in our curiosity about history, are about to violate, seems to put the whole roomful of people, and their avidity to see what is before them, into a kind of religious state.

They unwind, unwind, unwind, and still unwind, with no apparent diminution in the size of the package and no feeling, as it were, of approaching the body. The band seems to grow as they work and to threaten never to come to an end, while the attendants continue their interminable unwinding. At one moment, in order to get along faster and to hasten the stripping of the creature, the mummy is set up on its feet, which knock as if at the end of a pair of wooden legs, and the thing begins to twirl and gyrate and waltz horribly in the hurrying arms of the attendants: the package stands up, Death in a bundle.

The thing is laid down again and the unwinding continues. The yards and yards of cloth pile up, rise mountain high, cover the table with the charming rusted-saffron tone of this never-bleached stuff, and strange smells begin to rise, warm and spicy emanations of funereal myrrh and aromatics—the odours of black volptuousness of the bed of the antique corpse.

At last, with this persistent unwinding, a vaguely human outline begins to be discernible. "Berthelot! Robin! Look here!" cries Mariette; and with the help of a knife he digs out of the armpit something that is passed round and seems to be a flower with a pleasant odour: a little bouquet planted by Egypt in the moist armpit of its dead.

The last of the band has been unwound, the cloth is at its end, and here is a bit of flesh—black! a fact almost astonishing, so far had one been on the way to expect that beneath a band so well preserved there must live a corpse guarded through eternity in its original state. Du Camp rushed forward with a sort of frantic nervousness as the neck and head were unwound. Suddenly, in the blackness of the bitumen coagulated at the base of the throat, there gleamed a little gold. "A necklace!" someone exclaimed. And with a chisel, digging into the stony flesh, Du Camp brought up a small gold plaque bearing an inscription written with a *calamus,* a reed, and cut out in the shape of a sparrow hawk. Thereafter a little Horus and a large green scarab were detached. Mariette, who took charge of the bit of gold, said that it bore a prayer by this woman for the coming together of her heart and entrails with her body on the Day of Eternity.

Feverishly, pincers and knives went down the length of this desiccated corpse which gave off the sound of pasteboard, denuding the deformed, sexless chest and belly whose blackened surface was furrowed with red clots of dried blood. They stripped the arms that were stuck to the torso, and the hands which, in a gesture of stiffened modesty—the very gesture of the Medici Venus—were lowered over the pubis with the gilded nails of their fingers.

A last band stripped away from the face disclosed suddenly an enamel eye in which the pupil had run over into the white, an eye at once alive and sick, so that it was frightening. Then the nose appeared, flattened, broken and clogged by the embalmer, and the smile of a gold leaf appeared on the lips of the tiny head on which were ravellings of short hair that seemed still to bear the moisture and sweat of the hour of death.

There she was, this woman who had once been alive—two thousand and four hundred years ago—there she was, lying in full view on a table, stricken and outraged by the light of day, all her modesty bared to the sun and the glances of men. We stood about chatting, laughing, smoking. The poor profaned corpse, so well veiled and buried, once so secure in the promise of repose and of a secret and eternal inviolability, which the hazard of archaeology had flung here like a pauper's corpse on a dissecting table—there it lay, and not a soul, except the two of us, feeling the slightest dejection about it!

In the evening, accompanied by Gautier, we wandered round that great monster called the Universal Exposition. In this Babel of industry we felt as if walking in a dream in which an engineer was displaying to a Paris inundated with people collected to celebrate the fraternization of the Universe, a cork model of all the monuments on earth. Little by little, things round us began to wear a fantastic look. The sky over the Champs-de-Mars became filled with the tints of an oriental sky; the outlines of the confused medley of buildings, seen against the violet evening sky, were like a bit of a landscape painted by Marilhat; the domes, the kiosks, the minarets, with all their colours, brought into the Parisian night the reflected transparencies of a night in an Asiatic city. At times it seemed to us that we were walking in a picture painted in Japan round an infinite palace, beneath a roof projecting as do the roofs of Buddhist monasteries, lighted up by globes of unpolished glass that gave off the same glow as the paper lanterns at a Japanese celebration. Or we seemed, walking under the billowing standards and flags of all the nations, to be wandering through the streets of the Middle Kingdom as depicted by Hildebrand in his *Tour du monde,* with the flapping zigzags of their signs and their pennants.

Friday, May 31.—"Forgive me for being late. It's because of the centrepiece for the table, which only arrived at six o'clock, and the count insisted upon bringing it up himself." La Païva was talking. She had on a muslin dress which she said had cost only thirty-seven francs, but there were pearls at her throat and round her arms that cost half a million.

We moved into the dining room and sat down. There the centrepiece was shown off, and in the most middle-class fashion possible we were invited again and again to admire it. The price was not mentioned, but we were told that at such-and-such a silversmith's it would cost 80,000 francs. Each of us, his hand clutching his throat in disgust, had to deliver himself of a compliment, and however broad the compliment, it was still not enough. Meanwhile, I kept my eyes on the mistress of the house and studied her a bit. White skin, good arms, beautiful shoulders, bare behind down to the hips, the reddish hair under her arms showing each time that she adjusted her shoulder straps; large round eyes; a pear-shaped nose with heavy wings and the tip thick and flattened, like a Kalmuck's nose; the mouth a straight line cutting across a face all white with rice powder. Wrinkles which, under the light, look black in the white face; and down from each side of the mouth a crease in the shape of a horseshoe meeting beneath the chin and cutting across it in a great fold bespeaking age. On the surface, the face is that of a courtezan who will not be too old for her profession when she is a hundred years old; but underneath, another face is visible from time to time, the terrible face of a painted corpse.

After our coffee we sat in a small walled garden with tapestry designs in the grass like a garden in Pompeii. The men were frozen by the cold evening air, but she sat there almost naked giving off the chill of marble and displaying her lack of upbringing, of amiability, of form, of tact, possessing none of the gentleness of charm, none of the grace of courtesy, none of the affability of womanhood, not even endowed with the excitation of the tart, and invariably silly—but never stupid, and surprising one constantly by a remark born of her experience of practical life or of business, by original notions, by those axioms which seem to be the experience of Fortune, by a curt and antipathetic eccentricity which appears to have its source in her religion, her race, the heights and depths of her prodigious existence, the contrasts inherent in her destiny as an adventuress of love.

June 10.—We went to spend a few days this week with Count Lefebvre de Béhaine, who told us something of his mission to Vienna following the crushing defeat of the Austrians by the Prussians at Sadowa. "That Bismarck," said he; "what an astonishing man! I went to see him at Brunn, on the fifteenth of July at two o'clock in the morning, and found him in bed. On the table beside him lay two revolvers. Candles were lighted, and he was reading . . . what do you suppose? Paul Féval's cape-and-sword novel, *L'Hôtel Carnavalet.* Absolutely!"

After telling us at length of his adventures with the Prussian army, going from camp to camp and outpost to outpost, and reading to us the long letters he had written to his wife, and even a charming letter addressed to his six-year-old son, he spoke of things the public were unaware of: for example, that Russia, frightened by the rising power of Prussia, had twice offered to ally herself freely with France, on condition only that there be no more talk of creating a Polish kingdom; offering a full alliance and declaring that only through this union of the two great Powers could equilibrium be restored in Europe, even though this alliance might last no longer than the treaties signed at the Congress of Vienna in 1815, but hoping for fifty years at any rate, a lapse of time long enough to make glorious the names of two sovereigns who should have effected such an alliance. But the Russian agent in Paris had required an immediate answer from the Tuileries. Had this solution been accepted, the destiny of Europe might have been reshaped, but it was repulsed and flung into the abyss of great things buried by the temporizing nature of the emperor, retractile as he is to great decisions.

June 17.—Berthelot was saying at the Magny dinner that not only is France the country in which the fewest children are born, but it is also the nation with the largest proportion of old people, having one hundred of these for every fifty-eight in Prussia.

June 24.—Roqueplan, whom I stopped in the street and complimented upon his health and his physical resistance, said: "Ah, yes; because I have never drunk bad wine. One has to pay a great deal of attention to what one takes and what one throws up."

This evening two streetwalkers sat near me on the chairs along the Champs-Élysées, chatting. "Oh, cut it," said one of them. "It's like this: you make eight hundred francs: you live on three hundred: you put five hundred in the savings bank." The lower orders of prostitution are like careful little shopkeepers.

Undated.—Apropos of *Hernani*. Sad to think that it takes forty years, almost half a century, to be applauded as vigorously as one has been hissed.

Undated.—There are two great currents in the history of humanity: baseness, which makes conservatives; and envy, which makes revolutionaries.

October 8.—Oh, the intolerance of the party of tolerance! I think of what Duclos said: "They will end by making me go to Mass."

October 16.—Dined with Hébert. He spoke of one of his pupils, a young sculptor who was the brother of Barrias, the painter, and who had long been tormented by a mad yearning to go to Greece and do a bust or a statue which he could sign at Athens. Hébert had just had a despairing letter from the young man, saying that in the land of Phidias there was no model to be found, nor any modelling clay, and that another sculptor, whom he had finally unearthed, had told him that when anybody in Greece wanted to create a work of art he went off to Rome; that in Athens sculptors worked only from pictures.

Hébert comes from the Dauphiné, like Berlioz. They both grew up in houses in the mountains, the one a little higher up than the other. He had seen Berlioz that very morning, and the composer had told him that at the age of twelve he had fallen in love with a girl twenty years old. Since then he had been in love many times, romantically, madly, dramatically, but at the back of his memory there had always been that first love—to which he had passionately returned on finding his young girl again in Lyons, now seventy-four years old. He wrote to her daily. His letters were filled with the memories of his twelve-year-old heart, and his sole nourishment was this flame out of the past.[4]

October 27.—Bellevue, at the little *bourgeois* palace which Charles Edmond has just built for himself.

We went with him to call upon Berthelot, who lives near by, and found the chemist's family at home. A small house in the woods. A garden full of children. A sitting room full of women. Mme Berthelot's beauty remarkable, unforgettable; an intelligent beauty, profound, magnetic, a beauty of soul and of spirit, like one of those unearthly creatures of Edgar Allan Poe. Hair dressed in wide bands almost loose and forming a nimbus round the head; a calm, high brow; great eyes filled with light in the

[4]The lady would be a mere seventy-two, Berlioz having been born in 1803 and being himself only sixty-four years old at the time of this story—which, indeed, is to be read in all its extravagance in his *Mémoires*.

shadow of their rings; the body rather flat beneath a dress that might have been worn by a slender seraphim. The musical voice of an ephebe; a certain distance in her courtesy, and the friendly manner of a superior woman. A child, her eldest, came and sat beside her, as beautiful as if made in heaven.

Berthelot with us, we beat the woods of Sèvres and Viroflay all day long and came back in the evening to dine with Charles Edmond and his wife.

November 14.—Sainte-Beuve gave a dinner this evening for the princess. His little cook, Marie, showed us into the dining room, where the table was laid as by a parish priest receiving his bishop, and through the dining room into the ground-floor sitting room, all white and gold with brand-new yellow furniture looking like the decoration selected by an upholsterer for a cocotte.

The guests arrived: the princess, Mme de Lespinasse, old Giraud of the Institut de France, Dr Phillips, and Nieuwerkerke. The princess looked very cheerful; she was entranced in advance as for a bachelor party. At dinner she insisted upon serving everything, carving everything. Her father always carved. He had very pretty hands. He would eat even salad with his fingers, and when he was told that it was not proper, he answered, "In my day if one ate otherwise one would have been scolded; we should have been told that we had dirty hands."

Sitting at the head of the table, Sainte-Beuve looked like a butler at a wake, at his own funeral feast. He looked to me broken, old, twaddling, afraid to complain of how hard he found it to go on living, making senile grimaces and shutting his eyes in a way that said, "There! I feel myself going"; with gestures of woebegone compunction and those words that are complaints in a vacuum. He ate nothing, got up two or three times during dinner with the remark that we were to pay no attention to him, came back to table like the ghost in the house, like the shade of an ancient, anxious not to disturb anybody.

Everybody exerted himself to say something. We tried to whip up the champagne, but the laughter was forced and icy.

The princess became grave and looked ill. In the drawing room Sainte-Beuve, sitting at one end of the yellow sofa and leaning with his two fists on the silk, tried to smile and went off into tales of his gloomy youth, his friendless life with the people of the *Globe*—Cousin, Vitet, and others, people who gave him nothing but their wit and their kindness, nothing more, and often disconcerted him by what they said, as when Cousin, to his astonishment, once called Louis XIV a coxcomb.

He spoke of his service as interne in the Hospital of Saint-Louis in 1827; of his room on the top story in the rue de Lancry, "Where I lived alone for seven months without a caller, except that my mother came up once." It was because of those lonely days that he had rebounded in the other direction and found himself perpetually requiring people about him, women in his house, cats. He cited the example of Saint-Évremond surrounding himself, as he grew older, with animals, and men, too, in order to feel life going on round him. "If only I had had a master there, at the hospital! But the chief was Richerand, a charlatan."

Thereupon Dr Phillips, with his great sunken head, his protuberant eyes, his stiff bones, began to talk surgery, operations, speaking of Roux, that artist in bandaging who killed his patients by the prettiness of his bandages. The princess interrupted him and flung into his face the barbarism of surgeons, their insensitiveness, the little emotion they must feel. . . . "Not quite," Phillips broke in; "I feel a great deal of emotion, but only for children. The poor little things! One can't make them understand that it is for their own good. That is horrible!" Then, after a silence, "You see, in my trade you get so that science is all you think about. It is so beautiful. It seems to me that I should stop living if I couldn't operate. It is my absinthe."

This distressing conversation, in this mournful house, combined with the thought of the nearing end of the host who was receiving us, threw all the guests into a gloomy reverie.

November 25.—At Bar-sur-Siene. In the country with our relatives for a change. We leave behind, in Paris, our novel, *Manette Salomon,* a great success.

December 26.—To see Thierry and ask that he arrange a reading of our five acts on the Revolution. Thierry's civilities made us quake.

December 29.—Called on the princess this morning. In sound of the bell that rang during the Mass served for her in the next room, Alfred Arago made humourous remarks and Vimercati told us the story of the strange departure from this life taken by one of his friends, who bore the last name inscribed in the register of nobles in Venice. This gentleman, who had an income of a hundred thousand a year, one day said farewell to his friends and acquaintances and told them that he was going off to die in the mountains. He had a little house built and got a sort of gardener to stew up his meals for him morning and evening, and, refusing to see a soul, he spent seven years on a mountain top in a white tie, waiting for the moment of his flight into eternity.

*   *   *

At four o'clock we went to find out how Sainte-Beuve was doing. He sent word that he would like us to come up. We climbed the narrow stairs, followed the landing, and went into that bare and yet encumbered bedroom with its curtainless iron bed and its general air of a camp pitched in the middle of a chaotic library. From the bed two warm soft hands were stretched forth. Vaguely we could see a head wrapped up, a body which pain and a kind of horizontal crouching had almost deprived of human shape.

"Badly . . . it's going badly." These were his first words.

"Still, the doctors . . ."

"Who? What doctors?" he retorted with a note of anger in his voice. "I have no doctors any more. They have deserted me. Alton-Shee sent me Johnston. Phillips has been very nice, but he is a surgeon. I may come to that tomorrow, for I can't go three hours any longer without being probed. And then I get on the vase and I spend minutes twisting and having spasms of the bladder. Oh! It's horrible!"

He went into all the technical details of his horrible ailment as if by stressing his disgust with himself he hoped to disarm the disgust of others. He seemed to us despairingly resigned. At one moment he drew a breath and said, "I still have myself read to, but off and on, you know; I can't collect my ideas." A silence fell, then the word "Good-bye", and he held out both his hands and turned his face to the wall.

1868

January 2.—Day before yesterday fair copies of our play on the Revolution were finished. Instinctively, we are almost afraid of it, as if out of it were to come the infernal anguish of emotions about the theatre.

Undated.—One of the proud joys that a man of letters can feel— if that man of letters is an artist—is to feel that he has the power to make immortal, at his pleasure, anything he chooses to immortalize. Mere mortal though he be, he is conscious of possessing the attribute of creative divinity. God creates life; the man of imagination creates fictional lives which at times, in the world's memory, persist more profoundly, more vividly, than any others.

January 3.—La Païva dislikes a grate fire. She came into her drawing room dripping with emeralds all over the flesh of her shoulders and arms. "I am still a little blue with cold. My maid has just done my hair with the windows wide open," she said. Out of doors it was snowing, and the night was so cold that, coming here, we shivered for the ill-clad poor of Paris. This woman is not built like the rest of humanity. She lives in icy air and water like a kind of boreal dragon in a Scandinavian myth.

At table she developed a theory of will power that was frightening, saying that everything was the result of the exercise of the will, that there were no circumstances, that one created one's own circumstances, that people who were unfortunate were so because they wanted to be so. And when Taine—dining with her for the first time—corroborated her thesis by a little speech on the power of concentration, citing Newton as usual and saying that the great physicist used to concentrate so fixedly that in his periods of meditation he seemed like an idiot, La Païva spoke of a woman who, to accomplish a certain unrevealed purpose, cut herself off from the world and lived three years alone, scarcely eating a morsel and having to be reminded of food, walled up within herself and given over wholly to the plan she was developing. And, after a moment of silence, La Païva added, "I was that woman."

February 11.—A large party at Arsène Houssaye's. Almost the first time that our success actually reaches our ears and that a billowing of curiosity is audible when we come into the room. There were people present almost as unknown to us as to the public, who told us of their admiration.

In the midst of this crowd was a handsome young man wearing a heart-shaped waistcoat, a frilled shirt, a dress coat with velvet lapels and a white camellia, and scent that stank—a bastard mixture of young centrist deputy under Louis Philippe and Second Empire coxcomb. This was Marcelin, otherwise known as Planat, editor of the *Vie Parisienne*. There were introductions, and two hours later we were supping together at the Café Anglais. He needed to utter only four or five sentences, in that lofty tone of the fashionable journalist the world over, for me to see in him an exasperating reflection of his paper. He was the Parisian with *chic* opinions, the superficial amateur, the fellow who is a friend of Worth, the dressmaker, and quotes Heine. This was enough to make him unpleasant, but he became positively odious to me when, speaking of a fake Rubens he owns, he said "It's so honest!" So honest, indeed! I loathe that sort of word in praise of a picture.

February 14.—At La Païva's. Wonderful thing, money. Makes one forgive everything. Nobody who comes to this house appears to notice that it is the most uncomfortable house in Paris. At table it is impossible to drink a glass of water because the mistress of the house has whimsically acquired, by way of water pitchers, cathedrals made of crystal which it would take a water carrier to lift. In the conservatory, where we smoke after dinner, one is either frozen by draughts or strangled by the puffs of heat that blow up from the registers. There is a magnificent tea service, but ask for anything not on the programme and the hubbub could not be more dismaying in the smallest and wretchedest house.

Gautier, in this most inhospitable of houses, sitting beside this woman who, in middle-class fashion, moves hastily out of the way for fear his cigar will burn her dress, Gautier delivers himself inexhaustibly of paradoxes, lofty ideas, original notions, and marvellous phantasies. What a conversationalist! Far superior to his books, however great their value, and invariably better in the spoken than in the written word. What a feast for artists is this speech in two registers, the *timbre* of Rabelais sounding so often with that of Heine, the lusty enormities of the first mingling with the tender melancholy of the second.

February 24.—Exactly twenty years ago today, towards one o'clock, from the balcony in the rue des Capucines where we then lived, I saw the boilermaker across the way run up his ladder and, with hurried hammer strokes, beat out the words "to the King" which followed the word "Coppersmith" on the sign over his shop. We had gone thereafter into the Tuileries Gardens and had seen, near the Clock Pavilion, the hacked-off head of a roebuck lying near the basin on the ground, and an equestrienne from the Hippodrome caracoling on her horse. The statue of Spartacus had a revolutionary bonnet perched on its head and a bouquet of flowers in its stone hand. And on the great balcony of the palace, one of the victorious revolutionaries, in Louis Philippe's dressing gown, looking like a caricature by Daumier, was mimicking the king in a speech beginning with the poor chap's conventional gambit: "It is with ever grateful pleasure that once again I . . ." Today, going through the rue des Capucines, I raised my eyes by chance to the sign and saw that it read, "Coppersmith to the Emperor."

March 6.—So many annoyances, so many disappointments, a sort of despair of life born of its pitiless plaguings, have put us in a philosophic state in which we shall be well able to bear the rejection of our play: it will be merely one more cause for bitterness among the many to which we are subjected.

Rops, who had sent us a drawing of a prostitute in a most artistically macabre style, below which he had written "To MM. Edmond and Jules de Goncourt, after *Manette Salomon*", came to see us today. A strange, interesting and likeable lad. He spoke intelligently of the blindness of painters to what is there before their eyes, saying that they see absolutely only those things which custom has taught them to see—a juxtaposition of colour, for example, but none of the *ethics of modern flesh.* He was truly eloquent when painting the cruelty inherent in the woman of our time, her steely glance, her ill will towards man, which she takes no pains to hide, does not dissemble, but flaunts in all her person.

March 4.—This evening the princess said, "I enjoy only those novels of which I should have liked to be the heroine." Could there be a more perfect expression of the literary standard by which women judge novels?

March 7.—This morning, a terror of the headache. We hadn't one, but the irritation induced by noises in the house and the successive annoyances that we have suffered for so many days past have absolutely shattered our stomachs. Meanwhile, we realize in advance that there is no hope for our play; we have no illusion on that score. He of us who was to do the reading was overcome by a sickish feeling in the street which made him fear that he would be unable to read. We went into a café, swallowed a rum toddy, and went on to the theatre.

Despite the discouraging atmosphere—the question put by

several actors whether "it was going to be very long", their attitude as they disposed themselves in armchairs and on sofas for
the boredom of the reading—we determined that, though the
play be condemned in advance, still we would do all in our
power to fix it in their memories. Perfectly self-possessed, perfectly the master of my effects, as calm as if I were reading in my
own room, with a complete and superior feeling of contempt
for my audience, I read quietly on while Coquelin, drawing
caricatures, nudged Bressant with his elbow to make him look
at them. The others, I must say, Got, Régnier and Delaunay, listened to the play and seemed interested in it. For these people,
who knew the Revolution only from Ponsard's melodramas,
there was of course something stupefying in our Revolution, written out of the quick of history and displaying its reality.

The play ends on a terrible cry which I am free to call sublime
because I found it in one of the documents: it ends on the cry
of an old woman climbing into the tumbril that will take her to
the guillotine: "We're off, scum!"[1]

The double door to Thierry's office is opened, locked, and
without a word of discussion or debate, without the sound of a
single voice raised in our favour, we hear the clicking of the balls,
after which, through a door half open on the passage, we see all
the committee disappear on tiptoe as if running away. Almost
immediately Thierry's door opens and he comes silently in, more
full of compunction than a prison chaplain going into the death
cell at five in the morning, and says in a snuffling voice, "Gentlemen, I regret to announce that your play has been accepted subject to changes." And he adds: "Oh, it isn't that your play lacks
talent; but it seemed to all of us highly dangerous.[2] We broke
into his condolences and asked that our manuscript be sent back
to us.

March 23.—If people only knew the kind of thing it is that in-
duces Sainte-Beuve to write a book! We found him today all in

---

[1]The untranslatable original reads, "On y va, canaille!"

[2]It must be acknowledged that it was hard for M. Thierry to put on another of our
plays so soon after the failure of *Henriette Maréchal*.—E. de G.

a dither over a plan to do a book on Mme de Staël and her circle, to serve as a pendant to his famous work on Chateaubriand, with the same vipers' nests as footnotes; and this, not out of interest in Mme de Staël, not because he had been fascinated by certain new materials, but simply in order to annoy the De Broglies,[3] whom he detests. At bottom, there is a malicious monkey in Sainte-Beuve.

Undated.—I read today that black snow has fallen in Michigan— exactly the snow that should fall in Poe's native land.

April 5.—"A woman who has never been pretty has never been young." I read this in a book picked up by chance in a lending library; and read, written in the margin in a woman's hand, "How sadly true!"

April 15.—At the princess's, rue de Courcelles, the party was very lively this evening. Two ghosts among the dinner guests: Gautier, very pale, his lionlike eyes more sunken than ever; Claude Bernard, with the face of a man dug up out of his grave. The talk was of modern marriage, this marriage without court-ship, without even flirtation, this brutal, cynical form of marriage that we called "rape in the presence of the mayor with the en-couragements of the parents." Someone speaking of the embar-rassed modesty of a bride flung into her husband's bed, one of the women present said that she possessed a curious manuscript —instructions posted by an absent mother to her daughter.

May 4.—M. de Marcellus, the Christian nobleman, took com-munion in his château only with consecrated wafers stamped with his arms. One day the officiating priest observed with terror that the stock of stamped wafers was exhausted, and he took the risk of holding out to the devout and noble communicant a com-

---

[3]Mme de Staël's daughter married, in 1816, Prince Achille de Broglie, who sought to save Marshal Ney from execution in 1815 and was minister in the reign of Louis Philippe. Of all the surviving families of the *ancien régime,* this one has most dis-tinguished itself in the past century and a half. Two of the greatest living physicists are the present Duke de Broglie and his younger brother, the Prince de Broglie.

mon wafer, excusing himself with this admirable remark: "Pot-luck, eh, your lordship?"

Since, of two poets who were candidates for a seat in the Academy, one called Autran and the other Théophile Gautier, the Academy elected Autran, I am convinced that its members are either cretins or dishonest men: they may take their choice.

Undated.—The persistent fatality of books! We whose racial and family sympathies incline us to favour the Pope, who have no feeling against any man who is a priest, we find ourselves writing, urged on by some irresistible force in the air, a book harmful to the Church. Why? But who knows the why of what he writes?

May 18.—Magny dinner. The conversationalist with ideas is at the moment Dr Robin, who is full of novel views, discoveries, finds, that go from the highest to the least significant facts of medicine. This evening, after speaking of the brain, he talked about the calf of the leg, calling it the pure product of civiliza-tion and remarking that it was as lacking in the savage as in the rural postman and for the same reason—that the rebuilding effected by nourishment and sleep was, in them, not equal to the waste of tissue that went on.

What a pity, what a loss, that so intelligent an observer and physiologist should not write the book, of which he gave us so interesting a bit this evening, on the moral effects of diseases of the chest, a book of which no one has yet written the first line, a book which would be a medico-literary clinic on the particular diseases (of the liver, the heart, the lungs) that are so contiguous to and bound up with the sentiments and notions of the patient, a book that would display all the revolutions of the soul in the sufferings of the body.

May 20.—At the princess's this evening we heard for the first time the wit of Dumas the younger. A coarse but constant mettle, slashing retorts without the slightest regard for good breeding, an assurance that is almost insolence and lends happy inspiration to his speech, and, crowning all this, a kind of cruel bitterness;

but incontestibly a very personal wit, a biting, cutting, trenchant wit that I think greatly superior to the wit he puts into his plays, for it is so much more concise, it has an edge so sharp, this spontaneous wit of his.

He told a story by way of illustrating his contention that the feelings and impressions of every man without exception depended upon the state of his digestion; an argument with which we were in full agreement. The princess, as if we were depriving her of that which she held dearest in life—her illusions, the ideal she clings to in respect not of men, precisely, but of things human—the princess cried out in horror at this skeptical, this materialistic declaration. Her face became convulsed with disgust and with a sort of childish and fearful repugnance over the idea. In such a moment she flies out of her mind, she is beside herself, she is the prey of a real despair that is almost comic in its sincerity; and she could throw a lamp at your head with pleasure.

May 25.—At Renan's. Fourth story in the rue Vaneau, a small airy, middle-class flat furnished in green plush with portraits by Ary Scheffer on the walls and shelves of bric-a-brac in the room, among them the cast of a shapely woman's hand. Through a door one can see the library with its plain deal shelves and the disorder of heavy books lying in heaps on the floor, the tools of an Oriental and mediæval erudition, quartos of all kinds, among them the fascicles of a Japanese lexicon, and, sleeping on a little table, the proofs of his book on St Paul. Out of the two windows an immense view of those forests of vegetation hidden among the walls and stones of Paris, the vast Galliera gardens, and that undulation of treetops dominated by the tips of the domes, belfries and other religious edifices which lend this scene a little of the horizon of Rome.

The better one knows Renan and the closer one comes to him, the more charming and more affectionately courtly does this man appear. He exemplifies the finest type of moral beauty combined with physical ugliness. There is in this apostle of doubt the lofty and intelligent amiability of a priest of science.

He gave us a copy of the life he wrote of his beloved sister.

When we got home we began to read these pages aloud, and they went so straight to our fraternal hearts that sobs rose in our throats and we had to stop reading.

May 27.—Fontainebleau. In a moment of despair over our health we said, "Let us embrace each other; it will give us courage," and we kissed without another word.

May 31.—The dining room of the hotel at Fontainebleau. Among these horrible couples of starched *bourgeois,* these foppish stock-brokers and affected nonentities, we see an old English couple. Rarely do French people possess this nobility in the declining years, this breeding in old age, this Franklin-like beauty of the *grand seigneur* with its crown of white hair, its blissful eye, its well-cut mouth, and its fine, human glance—in short, this example of a full and honourable life, a conscience at rest, a limpid soul. In the distinguished Englishman there is something of the aristocracy of the beautiful and kindly dogs of his country.

June 1.—Magny dinner. Curious details concerning those German scientists, X and Y, who are not better scientists than certain others but upon whom the fashion for Germanism in science has forced ironic destinies. One of the guests at dinner knew Y when he was poor, humble, seedy, and, like all Germans, played a piano in his garret. When our guest saw Y again he was wearing a handsome cravat and the most startling clothes, the clothes of a German scientist turned dandy. "You find me changed, I dare say," the German said to him. "Well, I discovered that hard work, application and the rest were all nonsense. Haase told me that the only way to get on was through women. Look at Longpérier: if he hadn't begun frequenting drawing rooms . . ."

They met another time and Y dragged our guest over to a corner of the room and asked him anxiously if he thought that a German like himself would ever be able to talk smuttily to women, saying that he had tried, but what he said was too coarse, somehow it became filth that he himself hesitated to utter.

What a comic sign of the times! Science employing vile expressions in order to be successful; science represented by two gross natives of the land of artlessness, trying to succeed by the grace and lightness of touch of French corruption.

Two chaps to be castigated in a novel.

June 19.—This musty chamber of the family solicitor, at the end of a couryard in the rue Saint-Martin, has seen, in its day, practically all of our family business transacted. Grey and dim, with white wainscotting. The files of documents are kept in wire-screened cupboards with green curtains showing through the screens and bronzed plaster busts standing in the arched niches of the room. Missing from this otherwise typical private room of the Parisian solicitor of yester-year are the two immemorial Carcel lamps which stood on the mantelshelf in old Buchère's day.

We had gone there in the matter of the sale of our farms at Les Gouttes, that bit of family pride, that great landed estate of our grandfather, that venerable, respected and sacred ground to which, despite the modesty of their income, our father and mother had stubbornly clung in the face of magnificently tempting offers, thinking thus to preserve for their children the sorry advantage and dubious influence of *property,* that assurance of position and income which only land could furnish in the eyes of an old family during the reign of Louis Philippe. Finally, after eight months of negotiation, of correspondence, of title searching, we succeeded in getting rid of this chief nuisance in our life.

The purchaser, a cunning, thickset peasant from the Upper Marne, with little pig eyes, was there accompanied by his village-idiot son and his wife, she in that rusty black peculiar to undertakers' draperies, clutching the purchase money, incubating it in the leather bag she held snuggled between her thighs. The money came forth all warm from the woman, accompanied by a savage darting of her eyes and a look of grave consternation in the face of the son, while at the thought of being parted from it for ever, the lobes of the father's enormous ears quivered with regret.

The notes were counted by the clerks, and then the gold coins were freed from their curly paper wrappings and stacked in piles. Everything was counted and counted and counted again in dead silence, after which the mocking voice of the chief clerk announced that one pile lacked a hundred francs, another ten francs, and a third twenty francs. The rustic trio feigned total stupefaction and sat mutely gazing, gazing at the table as if, by staring, they might add to the piles of gold the missing coins. In the end their long resistance won out, and though the coins failed to appear, we surrendered our receipts for the full amount.

July 23.—At Saint-Gratien. Théophile Gautier, who came down for a few days, talked Opéra dancers. He described their white satin ballet slippers, saying that each slipper is re-enforced by a bit of wadding at the point where the dancer feels that her weight is concentrated; and that an expert could tell you, from a glance at the wadding, the name of the dancer. This work, incidentally, is done by the girl herself.

July 28.—Théo spent a week with us down here, and from morning until the inspiring hours of the night he regaled us with the flow of his conversation. The pleasure he took from his surroundings and from the people round him, as well as the stimulus of what he calls so delicately the *voluptuous friendliness* of the princess, whipped up his verve and brought out the old sixteenth-century courtier in him, and he unbuttoned in an enormous eloquence. His conversation was monstrously daring, but the things he said were redeemed by those charming graces of language and modulations of the voice which characterize the entrancing conversation of this great, fat fellow. And in this princely drawing room everybody forgot to be shocked, and was instead enchanted by a rare and strange pleasure at hearing these tales, these paradoxes, these crude narratives of his travels told in the dual voice of Rabelais and of Diderot.

During the day, dragging his leg as we strolled in the shade of the trees, the poet talked to us intimately, reciting his *lamento* over the chore of his journalism, the grind of routine, his exuberant and overflowing muse imprisoned within the confining limits of the *Moniteur,* condemned to paint mere walls—"and even then," he said, "not allowed to refer to the fact that a dirty word may be scrawled on the wall."

He went on: "Who knows but it may be the mere fact of daily bread that has prevented me from being one of the four great names of the age? Why should not I have achieved the place that Hugo has? There are days when the thought *melancholifies* me. I've always had to think about the nose bag. I've been filling it for thirty years: father, sisters, children—I've had to feed them all. Money? Well—I don't need to talk sob stuff to you chaps; but I've got three twenty-franc pieces in my pocket and a hundred and forty francs to keep us at home. If I had the bad luck to fall ill for a fortnight, we could still get along by moving out of the house. But if it lasted six weeks I should have to go to a charity clinic like anybody else."

Lying outstretched in a skiff in the princess's boathouse, Théo continued his monologue. "Really, there is something mysterious in my life. I am very well liked. Generally, people take to me. I have no enemies. My talent is taken for granted. Will you explain to me, then, why I cannot get what others seem to get so easily? They say it's because I don't ask for things: that isn't it. There is something else, and I don't know what it is. For instance —and of course I am speaking merely theoretically—for example, what has Sacy done to be made a senator? and Mérimée? I have as much talent as he has, wouldn't you say? Same thing as regards the Academy: you saw that. A post of some kind: have they ever dreamed of appointing me to a post? In their museums, it is again the same thing. Yet I have written on art. Why is it? Do you know why?"

Then he talked about hashish, visions, the cerebral excitations in fashion in 1830, telling us that he had written *Militona* in ten days, thanks to the pills he took, five grains in the morning and five in the evening, which gave him a marvellous lucidity of mind.

August 4.—We stood on the stone steps of the house in Auteuil we so much desired to own. The sun was still shining, and the lawn and the leaves of the shrubs were glittering under the rain of the garden hose.

"Eighty-two thousand five hundred francs," said my brother; and our hearts pounded in our breasts.

"I'll write to you tomorrow," the proprietor said; "probably I shall accept the offer."

"Eighty-three thousand and an immediate answer?"

The proprietor thought it over five eternal minutes and then let fall drearily, "Done!"

We left, absolutely intoxicated.

August 7.—Yesterday the princess gave Flaubert a terrible wigging because of his visits to a certain notorious kept woman. This morning, speaking as a woman of rank and respectability, she complained reasonably that it was with such women she had to share the company and the ideas of her friends, of men like Sainte-Beuve, Taine, Renan, who would, dining with her, steal twenty minutes of her time in order to present them to that strumpet. She declared her opposition to the dominion enjoyed by these women, whose houses were honoured by the frequentation of philosophers, men of letters, scientists and thinkers, deploring the power that lay in the hands of sluts who hadn't even the excuse of an art or a talent or a name, or the genius of a Rachel, and in whose houses the purest of men were to be found eating the truffles of the kept woman.

Undated.—While we were staying with the princess Arsène Houssaye was good enough to write for my permission to propose to the minister of education and fine arts that I be awarded the Cross of the Legion of Honour. I replied to him immediately that he is to do nothing about it, telling him what has always been our view, that a man of letters has the right to accept, but not to solicit, an honour.

Undated.—When France begins to have an itch to beat up its own constabulary, any government of whatever colour, if it is in the least intelligent, will turn its mind towards beating up a foreigner.

September 16.—Auteuil. We are not quite sure that this is not a dream. All this ours? this great plaything of taste, these two drawing rooms, that sun in the greenery, that fan-shaped cluster of trees against the sky, this happy garden spot and the flight of birds overhead?

September 17.—Yes, house and garden are ours; but in this house —and we fled here from the roar of Paris—in this house there resounds the clumping of a horse in a stable invisible but belonging to the house on our right; and the whining cry of children reaches us from the house on our left; and in front of us the rumbling, whistling sound of the passing train makes us toss in insomnia.

September 21.—The first quill sharpened in our house was used to sign the receipt for the fascinating Japanese fountain, with its bronze dragon, for which we were mad enough—considering how little money we have, particularly after buying the house— to pay what the emperor or a Rothschild might have had the whim to pay—two thousand francs.

October 29.—The English are sharpers as a nation and honest as individuals; the French are honest as a nation and sharpers as individuals.[4]

Undated.—We were the first to introduce the taste for Chinese and Japanese objects. Who more than we felt, preached and propagated this taste, which has now descended to the middle classes? Who fell in love with the first Japanese prints and had the courage to buy them? In our novel, *In the Year 18—* we described a chimney piece covered with Japanese knickknacks, and on the score of this, one critic, Edmond Texier, insisted that we should be locked up in the lunatic asylum at Charenton, because our taste proved us mad. But go back farther into old family memories. When the elder of us was fourteen years old, we had

[4]Cp. Joubert: "Englishmen are honest in their personal affairs, but faithless in the affairs of their nation."

an old country aunt, an enormously fat woman with bones so small that she weighed nothing at all, who adored him. And the only quarrel that ever arose between them came about because she thought the Chinese were a people who lived on screens, and had never seen one except in a drawing: to her they were a comic invention. My brother, full of notions gathered in school, loved the Chinese and would instance to her their invention of the compass, gunpowder, printing, and so on, all of which our aunt would persistently pooh-pooh, snapping her fingers and saying, "That for your Chinese!" And in her day, "that" was what people thought of the Chinese.

Undated.—This evening, coming down the princess's staircase after having been appointed librarian to the princess, Théophile Gautier said to me, "But tell me, has the princess really a library?" I replied: "Take my advice, Gautier, and act as if she had not."

November 26.—Apropos of religious education, one thing intrigues me. The children I see in the street who are in the care of a board school usher look like a dreary band of little prisoners, while those I see in the charge of priests from the parochial schools always look happy, as if on an outing with older schoolmates.

December 14.—Our admirer, Zola, came to lunch today. This was our first meeting with him. Our immediate impression was of a *Normalien* with something of Sarcey's thickset build, though at the moment looking a bit done in. When we looked closely, however, we saw that the sturdy young man's head was rather finely modelled, that there was something of a rather fine porcelain in his features, in the line of the eyelids and the fierce planes of his nose. In brief, there was something chiselled about all his person; he was like one of those vivid characters in his books, those complex beings who are occasionally a little feminine in their virility. Then, what is striking about him—given his build—is that there is something ailing, puny, ultra-nervous in him that gives you a sharp feeling, from time to time, of being in the company of a rebellious and unhappy victim of some ailment of the heart. In a word, a restless, disquieted, profound, complicated, evasive man, hard to read.

He talked about how hard his life was, how much he needed and would like to find a publisher who would give him thirty-six thousand francs at the rate of six thousand a year, so that he might be assured a livelihood for himself and his mother and thus be able to write the "history of a family" which he had in mind, a novel in eight volumes. For he wants to do "big things" and not—as he exclaimed in a voice expressing indignation with himself—"those squalid, ignoble articles I have to write for the *Tribune,* for people whose idiotic opinions I am forced to take. For there is no question about it, this government, with its ignorance and indifference to every living talent and product, flings us, poverty stricken as we are, into the opposition press, because only there can we earn enough to be able to eat. That's the truth; that is absolutely all we earn." Then, after a moment of silence: "I have so many enemies! And it is hard to become known." He repeated to us, and repeated to himself, that he was only twenty-eight years old; and out of the bitterness of his recrimination there would burst forth occasionally a vibrant note of acrid wilfulness and raging energy.

Finally he said, "Yes, of course you are right; my novel does go off on a tangent. I should have had only three characters. But I'll take your advice. I'll do my play that way. We are the younger generation, you know; and we know that you—you and Flaubert—are our masters. Even your enemies admit that you invented your art. They think that is nothing; but it is everything!"

December 21.—Dined at Sainte-Beuve's with the princess, Pongerville, Viollet-le-Duc, and old Giraud of the Institute. The whole dinner was spent trying to find a way to get M. de Pongerville to tell us the two stories (there are only two) in his repertory—his interview with Louis XVIII and his interview with Millevoye. And all this in order to get him to vote for Gautier at the Academy!

December 24.—A pleasure to see Flaubert again, and the three of us, unsociable bears and shy hermits, relieved ourselves of our contempt, our indignation, and our feelings generally about the baseness of our time, the disintegration of character, the decadence and domestication of our fellow workers in the field of letters.

1869

Wednesday, January 6.—I told the princess that I had called on Sainte-Beuve and had found him weary, despondent, distracted. She said nothing, but crossed in front of me and beckoned me to follow her into the first drawing room, the gallery of her intimate conversations and confidential twosomes. There she burst forth:

"I shall never see Sainte-Beuve again! He has behaved with me like a . . . It was because of him that I quarrelled with the empress. He owes everything to me. The last time I was at Compiègne he wanted three things, and I got two of them out of the emperor for him. And what did I ask in return? I didn't ask him to give up a single conviction. All I asked was that he keep away from those people on the *Temps,* that he sign no contract with them; and even that request was merely something I transmitted from the government. I offered him everything. If he had gone to Girardin's *Liberté,* I could have understood; after all, that is his circle. But the *Temps!* The personal enemy of our house! Where we are insulted every single day!"

She stopped, then went on: "Oh, he is a wicked man! As long as six months ago, I wrote to Flaubert, 'I am sure that one of these days Sainte-Beuve will play some trick upon us.'" And with a kind of hissing bitterness, she added: "He wrote to me on New Year's Day that it was to me he owed all the comfort and well-being that surrounded him in his illness. No: a man has no right to behave like that."

She was suffocating, stifling, fanning herself with the bertha of her embroidered frock, waving it in her two hands while tears rose in her voice and her emotion strangled her speech from time to time.

"Understand, I am not speaking as princess, but as woman. As woman!" she emphasised, shaking me by the lapel as if to thrust her indignation into my very breast: "Look here, Goncourt; don't you think it is revolting?" And her eyes, filled with her heart's anger, plunged the question straight into my eyes.

She strode over the carpet, waving behind her the long train of her white gown, and came back to face me: "As woman!" she said again. "I have dined at his table. I have sat in the very chair in which Madame X—— has sat. As a matter of fact, I told him in his own house. 'But,' I said to him, 'your house is a house of sluttish women, a house of ill fame. Except for you, I wouldn't come here.' Oh, I let him have it! 'What are you, after all?' I said to him. 'An impotent old man! You can't even look to your own needs. What possible ambition can you have in any other direction? Let me tell you, I could wish that you had died a year ago, so that you might at least have left me the memory of a man who was my friend.'

"I came away from that quarrel sick," she ended with a shudder.[1]

January 11.—Brown, the painter of horses, told us this amusing story. He was sent for by M. Pointel, the Christian editor of an

[1]It must be added that once the princess's righteous anger was expended upon us and one or two other friends, she promptly forgot her grievances against the old familiar of her house and remembered only the charm of his conversation, his wit, his sociability, and became once again the wholehearted friend, so that, after he died, she would warmly defend Sainte-Beuve's memory against everybody, including ourselves.

A word should perhaps be said at this point concerning the portrait of Sainte-Beuve painted here by my brother and me. What we have written has certainly not been prompted by any shabby or contemptible feeling, particularly since, as regards the critic's attitude to us, there is room for self-congratulation rather than for com-

illustrated paper published by Dalloz, and asked to do some
woodcuts for the paper. What, Pointel asked him, did he paint?

"Why, horses," Brown answered.

"Horses!" Pointel strode feverishly twice round his office and
came back to Brown:

"Horses! Horses lead to whores. Whores lead to the death of
the family. I cannot allow horses in my paper."

February 5.—Midnight. Corrected the last batch of proofs of
Madame Gervaisais. We thought of the secrets of the birth and
the development of this true child of ourself, a creature born
of thought and in its miracle and its mystery truly parallel to the
creation of the life of a human being. Probably readers will
assume that it was pure imagination which made this woman die
at the moment of crossing the threshold into a room where she
was to have been received by the Pope, yet this is very close to
what actually happened. The woman, the relative, whom we
studied in this novel, died as we make her die, while dressing
to attend an audience at the Vatican, except that we put off her
death two hours.

We reread the bit on consumption, this bit that would not exist
if we had not seized it, animated it, written it, as it came forth
at the end of one of the Magny dinners, delivered into the world
by our midwifery from Dr Robin's foggy speech, from his cloudy
and yet lightning-flashing brain. That to which we have lent
clarity of outline and character could never have issued forth
from the scientist with the style and the daring which it possesses, except for our pen—for at the sight of the blank page he
would have felt the drooling timidity and awkward correctness

plaint. We have simply been stung by the bee of analysis, by the urge to probe deeply
into the psychology of a very complex personality, exactly as a naturalist, in love with
science, might dissect and redissect an animal whose anatomy had seemed to him to
have been inaccurately or incompletely defined by his colleagues. I take a certain pride
in proclaiming that love of truth alone prompted the researches and explains the
ambition of these journals, and that we have permitted none of our personal rancour
or our resentment against criticism to filter into the portraiture of the people here
depicted. Thus, it will be found that men who were ferociously critical of us are well
treated in these pages, while others who have praised us, but who seemed to us devoid of talent or deserving of contempt, are here literally executed.—E. de G.

which he indited in the margin of the proofs we sent for his inspection.

February 19.—Went to call upon Sainte-Beuve, whom we found despairing over the state of his health, the state of literature, and the state of politics. He talked about the abasement of the Academy, the jobbing over votes that went on, the cliques, and Guizot's underhand dealings. He recited to us this dialogue between the Duchess de Galliera and Lebrun, reported to him by Lebrun with all the indignation and bitterness of an old humanist.

"Well, Monsieur Lebrun," the great lady called out to him as he walked into her drawing room; "the first seat has been awarded. Yes, to Monsieur de Haussonville. That much is settled."

"I was unaware of that," the academician said with a bow.

"As for the second, it will probably go to Monsieur de Champagny!"

"Really?"

"And the third, I think, to Monsieur Barbier."

It was five in the evening; the day had begun to decline, and in the melancholy twilight, with its threat of a lonely evening to come, Sainte-Beuve began to complain in a weak voice of all the privations he suffered, the impossibility of getting about and mingling with other people, an inhibition that led to a total lack of interest in action and in the world. Night fell softly and the old man's voice became more and more a voice of chiaroscuro, a voice nearing gradually the great silence.

Undated.—This evening our very young cousin celebrated the first sprouting of his moustache by what is called a little party in a private room at Voisin's. Two enormous bouquets of violets on the mantelpiece gave notice of the prompt arrival of two ladies. The first was one of those hetaerae with five horses in the stable and a town house, one of those women kept at the rate of three hundred thousand francs a year and who are always short a hundred francs—a blonde Alsatian with a mole on the most beautiful bosom in the world, bared in a square-cut bodice. She was accompanied by a pimply woman of Württemberger origin who jabbered the French of Balzac's German bankers,[2] a procuress whose specialty was the furnishing of simili-nuns to a Croesus of Jewish banking; a repository of all the secrets and scandals and horrors of Paris, one of those deep and sputtering creatures which the Rhine exports to France armed with all the ruse and gift of underground intrigue of a Metternich in skirts.

The pleasures of these three young people were both noisy and violent. They got drunk; they knocked each other about, chased each other through the upstairs rooms, and carried on like sophomores down for the holidays, so that in the end the bill, which came to four hundred francs, included seventy-five centimes for the arnica required by the Württemberger who had bruised her coccyx by running into a door.

April 1.—Sat in an omnibus beside a young peasant girl, a little hot-water bottle in a blue bonnet who looked as if she had just arrived in Paris to go into service. Try as she would to appear unconcerned, to cross her arms in perfect immobility, it was impossible for her to sit still. It was as if, in this vast and crushing city, she felt a kind of restless embarrassment, a shy and agitated disquiet, that sent her head back, time and again, against the glass behind it. Like a goat rubbing itself against a branch, or as if she still carried in her shirt the fleas of her province, she kept straightening herself against the back of the seat, her haunches already agile and lascivious and prepared to put themselves into the limp service of a streetwalker in a great city. Absent minded, now worried and now flustered, biting her nails, she would mutter to herself and then yawn prodigiously with weariness.

April 3.—Assizes. The Firon Affair. Murder in the rue Monthabor. On walking in we saw the doomed profile of the defendant,

[2]Specimen: *"Afec sa leddre, vis affez tan ma messon eine grétid ki n'ed limidé ké bar lais pornes te ma brobre vorteine."* Key: *Avec sa lettre, vous avez dans ma maison un crédit qui n'est limité que par les bornes de ma propre fortune.*—Baron de Nucingen to César Birotteau.

a high cheekbone casting a shadow on the cheek. In the box he answered the Court's questions, swaying perpetually on his feet, hands crossed behind his back as if they were tied together, lashed already in preparation for the guillotine. At the sight of the kitchen knife with which he had killed his wife, there came into his face the indefinable expression of an eye veiled by an albino's lashes, the sly expression of a winking glance that prefers not to be caught looking. When the presiding judge asked him to tell what had happened, he rubbed his forehead, and his grey lustreless face suddenly reddened. Then, after a few nervous jerkings of the shoulders, he spat on the floor, wiped his lips with a handkerchief, and began to speak in a faltering voice, still passing his hand over his face and opening his mouth to breathe, as if emotion was beginning to strangle him. Suddenly he began his tale, and as if the recital of the murder had revived his homicidal fever, he repeated in the air the terrible and proud forward sweep of the blow, saying, "She did not fall when I struck her; I held her up."

He sat in his place with his hand over his face and his fingers in his hair while the testimony of witnesses was taken. When the presiding judge asked, at one moment, "You had gambled that evening, with incredible luck, according to the witness?" he answered, "Yes, with incredible luck," in a singular voice, as if it seemed to him that the crime had brought him luck at play.

The testimony of one witness fell into the charged silence of the courtroom; it was that of his mistress, a poor, ugly actress from the Batignolles theatre, all scrawny in her black rehearsal clothes and confessing in a brave, modest voice her love of the man sitting surrounded by the court attendants—a miserable little stage person elevated by the grandeur which the sorrows of woman take on in this tragic theatre.

The barrister for the defendant was Lachaud, that licenced acquitter of murderers, a low actor lending to his client's case a false emotion, a false sensibility, and a gesticulating and ambulatory declamation.

Day began to fall. The summing up came forth from the judge's toothless mouth as out of a black hole. The Court withdrew. The jury retired to deliberate. Finally the terrible bell rang to announce the return of the jury, and they filed down the lighted stairs, their shadows announcing and preceding them in almost fantastical fashion. As they took their seats there appeared behind the defendant's bench a police officer in a three-cornered hat. The lighted lamps sent strips of light over the table with its papers and codes, and a reddish glow on the ceiling. Through the windows came the pallid blue of the beginning of night.

The middle class faces of the jurors took on the severity of great judges. The atmosphere was concentrated, silent, almost religious. The foreman of the jury, who happened to be white-bearded Giraud, the princess's painter, rose, unfolded a bit of paper, and in a voice grown suddenly husky, read out the verdict, which was "Guilty!" Then Giraud sat down again.

For a moment nobody breathed; then the word "death" ran in a murmur through the courtroom. In the sinister surprise born of this unexpected "Guilty!" without any recognition of attenuating circumstances, there was the chill of a great terror, and the sweeping quiver of the crowd rose in a wave of emotion that dashed itself against those cold executors of the Law.

The accused was brought back into the box, and by one of those strange reversals of emotion everybody now sought to devour his anguish, standing upon chairs to stare at him. He, for his part, seemed calm, determined, and stood with head erect awaiting sentence, stroking his goatee. In an atmosphere of great solemnity, the presiding judge read him the verdict of the jury in that biting and ironical voice that characterizes old judges in every court. The court rose, conferred a few seconds, after which the presiding judge read in a low voice to the accused the articles of the criminal code, so that one heard only vaguely the word, "beheaded." At this word there was a cry and a sound as of something knocking against wood: it was the swooning of the condemned man's mistress. He, meanwhile, took the sentence without flinching, and once the reading was finished sprang up on a near-by bench, turned in the direction of the woman's cry, touched his heart, and sent forth, in one violent, supreme gesture, a kiss in the direction of her who had screamed.

April 7.—Magny dinner. They were saying that Berthelot had predicted that a hundred years from now, thanks to physical and chemical science, men would know of what the atom is constituted and would be able, at will, to moderate, extinguish and light up again the sun as if it were a gas lamp. Claude Bernard, for his part, had apparently declared that in a hundred years of physiological science man would be so completely the master of organic law that he would create life in competition with God.

To all this we raised no objection, but we have the feeling that when this time comes in science, God with His white beard will come down to earth, swinging a bunch of keys, and will say to humanity, the way they say at five o'clock at the Salon, "Closing time, gentlemen."[3]

April 16.—Stopped at a nurseryman's to buy a magnolia plant. There we felt ourselves stung by a new taste for rarities, the taste for nature's objects. We went in totally ignorant and it was all completely new to us, this appreciation of the beautiful line of a plant, the distinguished quality of its leaf, its aristocratic quality, so to say; for nature, like humanity, has its preferred and pampered creatures, those which it endows with a special and superior beauty. Thus, in complete ignorance, we fell in love with the two most costly trees in the nursery.

Wednesday, April 28.—Rue de Courcelles. By way of furnishing an agreeable surprise to the emperor, who will call on her tomorrow, the princess has suddenly decided to ask that unfailing improvisor, Gautier, to turn into verse a bit of prose written by the emperor on the return of the ashes of Napoleon I to France. Today, Gautier's galloping muse ran through ninety lines, and this evening he recited them to general applause, after which a discussion arose in one corner of the drawing room over whether

[3]This otherwise unimportant passage is included only because it records an aspiration voiced not in the age of fable but in the age of science. Voltaire (*Dictionnaire philosophique,* art. "Job") had 100 years' better excuse for the particular imbecility he expressed as follows: "There is not a single little book on physics which, today, is not more useful than all the books of antiquity." This is the sort of stuff that delights the half educated, who are always ready to believe that engineers are economists, biologists are philosophers, and water-closet manufacturers are purveyors of human happiness.

the emperor was better characterised as *dreamer* or as *thinker,* ourselves meanwhile going up into the smoking room with Chesneau.

When we came downstairs we found that imprudent Gautier telling Sacy, whose vote he is sure to need at tomorrow's Academy election, that one of the women he loved most in his life was a panther woman, as spotted as the name indicates, who worked in a side show; and at the general "oh's" and "ah's" which rose round him, Gautier merely said suavely, "But I assure you that a skin like that can be very pretty." And he was off, while Sacy, that poor puritanical fellow, out of deference to the princess and her protégé, stood listening to the colourful tale of this animal love.

Gautier's son sighed soberly and said to me, "My father is at it again." I said, "Why don't you go across and pull him by the sleeve?" And the boy answered: "But you don't know him. He is capable of turning and shouting a dirty word at me, the way he does when I wake him up in the theatre."

April 29.—We arrived at half-past eleven. The imperial ceremony was over. Gautier, who lost his election at the Academy today, and with whom we shook hands cordially and commiseratingly, said, "What does it matter? My thingumabob here went off very well. The emperor wept." I must say I should have preferred a seat in the Academy for Gautier to the tear of an emperor who spent part of the evening talking to Ricord about pineapple growing while the empress talked with Dumas the younger about his repentant Magdalenes.

April 30.—Frightfully funny it is, that Claude Bernard's reception at the Academy keeps being put off for the reason that Patin, who is to receive him and eulogize him in the customary speech, does not know what to say. Every day poor Patin forgets at the bottom of Bernard's stairs the bit of physiology taught him a moment before by the great physiologist in his study.

July 7.—This evening we dragged ourselves painfully out to Saint-Gratien, where the princess's drawing room suffers somewhat from the political unsettlement of the moment. Dr Phillips was there. He talked about certain specifically modern ailments, nervous maladies such as those which are born of certain mechanical work, of the same motions gone through again and again, second after second, for seven hours, instancing the sewing machine; and then of a disease of the spinal cord particular to stokers and resulting from the constant quivering of the machine being stoked; and also of the necrosis of the lower jaw that attacked girls working in match factories.

August 1.—Saint-Gratien. Prince Napoleon dined this evening and was in a most amiable mood. His conversation gave evidence of a remarkable ethnographic memory, recalling the names and the look of every place he had ever been to. Travelling, he said, was the only pleasure left to him in the world; and he added that it was the sole resource of those who could no longer enjoy amorous activity; that he had replaced love by locomotion.

I wrote not long ago that princes did not like people who were ill: for that, I must apologize. The princess took us both aside and begged us most affectionately, with positively a commoner's friendliness, to come out of our shell more often. She pooh-poohed very prettily the distaste I expressed at the thought of showing my dreary face in her house, the shame that overcame me at the thought of being ill away from home, saying many sweet and charming things which came from the heart. She refused to let us return to Paris tonight, in the rain; and the next morning, while I was still in bed, she sent me by Eugène a sweet pencilled note asking how I felt and urging me to take her Catinat house and bring my servant, Pélagie, with me.

August 25.—Yesterday, in the course of a discussion about Franck, the Jewish member of the Institut de France, the princess hurt me by something she said concerning my liver complaint. Today at lunch I was still a little wounded, and as she was still eulogizing Franck there escaped from me, in a moment of sickly peevishness over which I had no control, these words: "Well, Princess, you ought to turn Jew!" There was a silence, and every guest went white. The outburst was impolite, ill bred and coarse; and I could have bitten my tongue out.

When we got up from table I made my excuses, told her how fond I was of her, and said that in this beastly nervous state the words had come out in spite of myself. As I spoke tears dropped from my eyes on her hands, while I was kissing them, and she, seized by the contagion of my emotion, took me in her arms and kissed me on both cheeks, saying, "Come, come! Of course, I forgive you. You know very well how fond I am of you."

1870

January 19.—The doctor at my hydrotherapeutic institute was asked if Troppmann, the murderer, had been beheaded. "Yes, he must have been," said the doctor, "for a tombstone cutter, whose wife I attended quite a long time ago, came to see me, drunk as an owl, and said that since I had been very nice to her, she wanted me to have a window in their house, which is on the corner of the square where the guillotine has been set up. The wine dealer below him had sold three casks of wine the night before last."

Undated.—How strange and bizarre nervous diseases are! Here is Vaucorbeil, the composer, in absolute torment whenever he is about to dine in a house for the first time, for fear that the dining-room chairs may be covered with velvet and he be unable to sit on them.

* * *

After months, many months, I take up the pen fallen from my brother's fingers. At first I had in mind closing these journals at his last entry. Why, I asked myself, continue this book? My career is at end, my ambition is dead. I still feel, today, as I did then, but I feel also that there may be a certain consolation for me in telling myself of those months of despair that I have lived through; and perhaps I also want vaguely to capture what was

so lacerating *for the future friends of my beloved brother's memory. Why? I do not know, but it is a kind of obsession. I resume
these journals, then, with the help of notes written during my
nights of anguish, notes comparable to those cries by which we
relieve the pain of great physical suffering.*

E. de G.

* * *

Night had fallen and we were walking in the Bois de Boulogne. Neither of us spoke. He was sad that evening, sadder than
usual. I said to him, "Look here, old chap. Let us assume that
you need a year, say two years, to get on your feet again. What
of it? You are young. You are not forty yet. You will still have all
the time you need to turn out books." He looked at me with the
astonished stare of a man whose secret thought has been divined
and said, stressing each word: "I feel that I shall never be well
enough to work again. Never again." And the only effect of
what I said was to introduce a note of anger into the despairing
phrase that he repeated over and over again.

That scene hurt me cruelly. All night long I could see the
somber and concentrated despair in his face, his voice, his attitude. Poor lad! I understood, now, why he had been possessed
by that rage for work during October and November, and why
I could never get him out of that chair in which he sat day and
night relentlessly driving his pen, repelling rest: he was in travail
of the last book he was to sign. The writer in him was hurrying,
hastening, stubbornly and obstinately fighting for time, refusing
to lose a moment, using up the last hours of a mind and a talent
about to go under.

I think of that last paragraph in the book on Gavarni which,
one morning at Trouville, he came to read aloud to me while I
was still abed. He had written that paragraph during a night of
insomnia. It is impossible for me to convey the profound sadness
into which I fell while he declaimed with solemn concentration
that little paragraph which we had not worked upon together
and that was not to have been written just then, but later. I felt
that in mourning Gavarni he was mourning his own death, and
the little phrase "*. . . he sleeps near by us in the cemetery at*

Auteuil" became, without my being able to explain it, a thing fixed and as it were droning in my memory.

For the first time I had an idea which had never occurred to me until then, I had an idea that he might die.

February.—For some time now—and it grows more noticeable every day—there are certain letters that he pronounces badly, *r's* he elides, *c's* which become *t's* in his speech. I remember, when he was a little boy, how sweet and charming it was to hear his childish, halting pronunciation of these two consonants, when he was *angwy* with his *stoolmistwess.* To hear it again, to hear that childlike voice come out of the distant and forgotten past, the memory of which is a memory of things long dead, frightens me.[1]

April 8.—One day—I do not know what day—he was incapable of identifying a certain point on the boulevards where I had asked him to wait for me a moment. Another day he struggled unavailingly to spell the name of Watteau, which after all was as well known to him as his own name. It costs him an effort to distinguish between the dumbbells of different weight and size with which he does his exercises. And yet, the faculty of observation persists in him, and he astonishes me from time to time by a remark, a word of comment, that could only come from a true novelist.

Over this beloved face, in which there was intelligence, there

---

[1] Oh, I know very well that there are people who will say I did not love my brother; that true affection is not *descriptive.* But the charge leaves me indifferent, for I also know that I loved him more than any of these people can ever have loved any one. Nor will they fail to add that when we love a person we are particularly careful not to reveal the secret of those mental falterings and stumblings which are the accompaniment of illness. There was a moment, I confess, when I was hesitant to publish this section entire, when the thought of making public certain words, certain sentences, was to me heart-rending; but I repressed this sensitiveness deliberately; I said to myself that I owed it to the history of literature to write the agonizing chapter of the death struggle of a writer killed by the practice of his art and the injustice of criticism. It may be asked whether I am myself a private person or a public character; whether my own sorrow and despair are properly the subject of literature? When these journals are made public in their entirety, it will be seen that in 1874, at a time when I was suffering from an inflammation of the lungs and thought myself dying, I still took notes upon myself.—E. de G.

was irony, there was that fine-grained and mischievously witty expressiveness, I see creeping minute by minute the haggard mask of imbecility. I suffer more, it seems to me, than any loving human being has ever suffered before.

Almost never does he answer a question put to him. If you ask him why he is sad, the answer is, "Well, I shall read Chateaubriand this evening." His mania has become the reading aloud of the *Mémoires d'outre-tombe* of Chateaubriand; he persecutes me with it from morning till night, and my face must indicate to him that I am listening as he reads.

April 16.—What is horrible in the diseases of the mind is that they do not attack only the intelligence, but work in subterranean fashion to destroy the sensibility, the tenderness, the attachment of the beloved person whom they undermine. That sweet friendship which was the great prize of our life, which was my very happiness, exists no longer. I feel that he no longer loves me, and this is the worst torture of all: nothing I can say to myself about it serves in the least to soften the blow.

An obsession these several days past, a temptation, that I do not wish to record here.

Most irritating is his stubborn hostility towards everything pertaining to reason. His mind, in which the chain of ideas has been broken, seems to have taken a fierce dislike to logic. If you talk reason to him, in however affectionate a tone, you can get nothing out of him, no promise that he will do anything that you ask in the name of reason. He shuts himself up in a stubborn silence; an evil cloud comes over his face and he turns into a different being, a sly, inimical person you have never seen before.

His face has gone humble, abashed: his eyes evade one's glance as if he thought one was spying upon his enfeeblement, his humiliation. It is a long time since his face lost the power to smile, since he forgot how to laugh.

April 24.—He was reading and he interrupted himself, tried to find where he had left off, and after worrying the book with his hands for a long time, he said to me timidly, "Where was I?"

May 2.—This evening—I am ashamed to put it down—because of something I wanted him to do for the sake of his health, and that he refused to do . . . It is because I am so unhappy that I am angrily peevish and not always in control of myself. . . . Well, I said to him.that I was going out and he was not to wait up for me, because I did not know when I should be getting in. He let me leave with entire indifference. I beat the woods in the darkness, hacking away at the weeds and the leaves with my stick, running away from our roof, when of a sudden I saw an apparition of him among the trees. Finally, very late, I came back.

I rang the bell, and when the door opened I saw at the top of the stairs my beloved little brother, who had got out of bed in his nightshirt, and heard his tender voice asking all sorts of affectionate questions. It is impossible to convey the almost stupid joy I felt at this evidence of the existence of a heart I had thought long vanished.

June 11.—This evening I was miserably unhappy. We were finishing our dinner in a restaurant. The waiter brought him a bowl. He began to eat clumsily. His clumsiness was unimportant, but people were looking at us, and I said to him a little impatiently, "Do be careful; we shan't be able to go anywhere." With which he burst into tears and exclaimed, "It's not my fault; it's not my fault," and his trembling and spasmodically contracting hand sought my hand across the table. "It's not my fault," he said again; "I know how unhappy I make you; but *I often want to and can't*" (verbatim). And his hand squeezed mine with a heart-rending "Forgive me!"

Thereupon the two of us began to weep into our napkins in the sight of all the astounded people about us.

* * *

I could not get over it; I could not believe my eyes or my ears. Quite unexpectedly, just back from Italy, Édouard Lefebvre de Béhaine dropped in to ask us to lunch. At the sight of this childhood friend Jules became entirely transformed, as if life had suddenly awoken in him. He began to chat, his memory recovered names and incidents out of the past which I had thought gone for ever. He talked of his books, and listened with so much attentiveness and pleasure to what was said that he seemed to have escaped for ever from his *dark being*. We listened to him, looked at him, stupefied, both of us. I accompanied Édouard to his carriage and he did not hide from me the astonishment he felt at seeing Jules so well, after what his mother's letters had led him to fear. We were so confident about his resurrection that we talked only of convalescence and recovery.

This lasted but a brief moment. I had left him in the garden, and when, happy and animated by the words of hope exchanged between Édouard and me, I came back, he was sitting, straw hat over his eyes, in a posture of frightening immobility, his eyes fixed upon the ground. I spoke to him: no answer. What sadness! It was not any more the sadness of these recent days with their implacability freezing my affection little by little; it was an immense, stricken sadness, sorrowing, infinite, the sadness of a soul experiencing its Passion, the sadness of the agony in the Mount of Olives.

I sat with him until night fell, lacking the energy to speak or to make him speak a word.

In the night of June 18–19.—It is two in the morning. I have got up to take Pélagie's place at the bedside of my poor dear brother, who has not spoken a word nor recovered consciousness since Thursday afternoon.

The day before yesterday—that is, Thursday—he was still reading aloud to me out of the *Mémoires d'outre-tombe,* which was the poor boy's single interest and sole distraction. I noticed that he was weary and reading badly. I begged him to stop reading and come with me for a stroll in the Bois de Boulogne. He resisted a little, then gave way. As he got up to leave the room with me I saw him sway and fall into an armchair. I picked him up and carried him to his bed, where I asked him how he felt and sought to force an answer from him, being anxious to hear his speech. But he was exactly as in his first attack—able only to mumble sounds that were not words. I was out of my head with distraction and asked if he recognized me. He answered with a great burst of mocking laughter, as if to say, "What a fool you are to think such a thing possible!" There followed a moment of calm, of tranquillity, while he looked at me with a gentle smile. I was thinking that this attack was like that of last May when, suddenly, flinging back his head, he let out a raucous, guttural, frightening scream that made me shut the window. Instantly his face was seized with convulsions which deformed his features unrecognizably, while terrible twitchings ran through his arms as if they were being twisted in their sockets and his grimacing mouth sent forth a foam of spittle tinged with blood. I sat on the bolster behind him and pressed his head against my heart and into the hollow of my stomach, feeling the sweat of death dampen my shirt and run finally down my thighs.

This spasm was followed by minor convulsions in the course of which his face took on again the features I knew, and soon after he fell into a delirious calm. He would raise his arms above his head and appeal to a vision, with kisses, to come to him. He would fling himself about like a wounded bird, while over his tranquillized face, in the bloodshot eyes, across the pale fore-head, and on the half-open and palely violet lips, there spread an expression that was no longer human, the veiled and mysterious expression of a Leonardo da Vinci. Ever and again he would be seized with fits of terror, his body would seek to flee, he would huddle into the bedclothes and hide as if from an apparition fixedly staring at him from the curtains of his bed and against which he would fling incoherent words while he pointed with his finger at the spectre and cried out once very distinctly "Go away!" There was a flow of truncated sentences, spoken with his head held high, with that ironic tone, that lofty intellectual con-tempt, that particular indignation characteristic of him when he heard a stupid remark or heard someone eulogize an inferior article. At times, in the unceasing agitation of fever and delirium, he would go over all the actions of his life, making the gesture of putting on his spectacles, raising and lowering the dumbbells with which I wearied his last months, and plying his craft, going through the gestures of writing.

There were swiftly passing moments when his roving, darting eyes would meet my eyes, or Pélagie's, and would seem to recognise us while they stared obstinately at us and a faint smile ran over his lips; but soon they would be off again in the direction of the horrible or radiant apparitions of his hallucination.

Last night Dr Béni-Barde told me that it was all over, that a disintegration of the brain was going on at the base of the skull, at the back of his head, and there was no hope whatever. He added—although I had stopped listening—something about the effect being to injure certain nerves in the chest and produce the terrible ravages of phthisis. On the first day when I knew him to be irrevocably stricken, my pride, the pride I felt for us both, had said to me, "Let him rather die." But today I ask that he be preserved to me, no matter how lacking in mind or how paralytic in body he come forth from this attack; and that I ask on my knees.

What is this expiation of which we are the victims? This is the question that comes into my mind as I go back over this life that has only a few hours left to it and that gained for its pains in literature and in the laborious seeking after fame only contempt and insult and injury; this life that for five years has struggled daily with physical suffering and is about to end in physical and mental torment; this life throughout which I see a sort of flight from a murderous Fatality.

Ah, Divine Providence, Divine Providence! How right we were to doubt its existence!

Monday, June 20, 9:40 a. m.—He is dying, he has just died. God be praised! He died after two or three gentle sighing breaths, like a baby falling asleep.

How frightful is the immobility of this body under the covers, rising and falling no more with the light movement of respiration, dispossessed in its bed of the life of slumber.

*   *   *

The Magny dinners were founded by Gavarni, Sainte-Beuve and ourselves. Gavarni is dead. Sainte-Beuve is dead. My brother is dead. Will Death content himself with the half of us? Or will he soon be calling for me? I am ready.

June 22.—Thinking and thinking about it, I am convinced that he died of the labours of art, the *travail of style*. I remember now, after the hours without rest spent over his retouches and corrections of a draft, after those efforts and that expenditure of brainwork in order to attain perfection, to force the French language to convey everything it could possibly express, after those stubborn, obstinate struggles into which there would enter the irritability and anger of his powerlessness; I remember now the strange and infinite prostration with which he would let himself sink down upon a divan, and the silent and completely crushed fit of smoking that would come upon him.

*　*　*

I saw him disappear into the vault in which lie my father and my mother, and where there is still room for me. When I got home I went to bed. I covered my bed with pictures of him, and his image was with me until night fell.

BIOGRAPHICAL REPERTORY

BIOGRAPHICAL REPERTORY

IN EVERY CIVILIZED SOCIETY *there are men who leave nothing of significance to posterity, but whose talents as commentators, or conversationalists, or* animateurs *were a precious leaven in the society of their time. There are other men who write, who publish, who are seen at the right cafés, so to speak, and who, while they accomplish nothing of consequence even for their contemporaries, turn up in the diaries and memoirs of others, along with references to dentists and bad plays and the general nuisances attendant upon life. Both sorts of men are here, provided they could fairly easily be traced. In this repertory will be found, also, notes about figures whose names, beyond doubt, are universally known, but whose works do not ordinarily form part of the reading of the generally cultivated person in the English-speaking countries. Balzac, Flaubert, Hugo, the two Dumas, for example, are omitted, but Sainte-Beuve, Renan, Taine, are here; Voltaire is out, but Diderot is in. Nothing is said about other painters than those who were contemporaries of the Goncourts, mainly because I have no particular eye for pictures and no competence in these matters. Not that the notes on historians, poets and novelists are critical: they are more often than not anecdotal: but I have frequented them somewhat and feel no uneasiness in speaking about them.—L. G.*

ABOUT, Edmond (1828–85) wrote a novel, *Le Roi des montagnes,* which is still reprinted and read with pleasure, but the dash and brilliance of his polemical books are as completely forgotten as, fortunately, are forgotten certain insipid novels and dreary phantasies which this gifted writer also turned out. About's great early success was a series of *Letters from a Proper Young Man to his Cousin Madeleine,* written to controvert the then powerful Bishop of Orleans' *Warning to Fathers of Families* against the materialism of the times. M. Marcel Thiébaut has recently proved that About served as official pamphleteer for Napoleon III. In later years his paper, *Le XIXᵉ Siècle,* enjoyed considerable influence. It is customary to recall about him that he entered the École Normale Supérieure de Paris in the same year as Taine, Sarcey and Prévost-Paradol (the glorious Class of '48).

ABRANTÈS, Laure, Duchess d' (1784–1838) was the widow of the Napoleonic General Junot, Duke d'Abrantès. She rallied to the Bourbons at the time of the Restoration, dissipated the fortune they bestowed upon her, wrote lively memoirs for a living, had a salon, and died in poverty. Balzac was very fond of her and owed to her many tales of life under the First Empire which he worked up in his novels. A bond which united them was that each was extremely vain of an imaginary ancestry.

ACHARD, Amédée, (1814–75) wrote as many novels—of a kind—as perhaps anyone who ever lived. Readers gobbled them up.

ALEMBERT, Jean Le Rond d' (1717–83) was born of a vexed mother and an indifferent father. His uncle was the Cardinal Archbishop of Lyons. His mother, the Marquise de Tencin, presided over a salon in which the Jesuit party planned its campaign against the Jansenists. Mme de Tencin loved nothing better than intrigue, but her role was, as Michelet puts it, a little disturbed in the spring of 1716. "She became unexpectedly embarrassed. There she was, one morning, with child. A heedless fellow, a military man, who knew her ever so slightly and had fallen in love with her during the carnival, had played her this scurvy trick. It was most ill-timed. Just at that moment she had two promising intrigues well started."

The fruit of this fortuitous union was picked up, a foundling, near the Church of Saint-Jean-le-Rond by the wife of a glazier named Rousseau. His foster parents called him Jean Le Rond; he added D'Alembert later. He is one of the most sympathetic figures of *la nation des gens de lettres* (to use his own happy phrase)—a self-taught but gifted mathematician and a humanist who translated Tacitus and wrote on the sciences and their relation to geography, on music, and on literary subjects. His association with Diderot in the production of that immense liberating work, the *Encyclopédie* (1751–66), is well known, and his introductory discourse to the encyclopaedia continues to be read. He declined Frederick the Great's offer of the presidency of the Academy of Berlin, as well as Catherine of Russia's proposal that he become tutor to her son and bring with him to St Petersburg as many of his friends as he might wish to make her guests. David Hume held him in high enough esteem to leave him £200. D'Alembert was deeply in love with Julie de Lespinasse (see Mme du Deffand infra) and never got over the double shock of her death and the revelation that she had a desperate passion for two other men under his very nose. Diderot found him hard to work with, apparently largely on the score of D'Alembert's caution—though he did get into trouble with the Calvinists of Geneva on the one side and the Jesuits on the other, as befits a true humanist.

ALLAN–DESPRÉAUX, Louise Rosalie, (1810–56) is the full name of the actress to whom Alfred de Musset owed the performance of comedies more like Shakespeare's than any others written in French, and the Goncourts their first palpitations about the theatre. She was so fat that Augustine Brohan, who got on none too well with her, used to discipline her little son by threatening to "make you run all the way round Madame Allan" if he did not behave.

ALLEGRAIN, Christophe Gabriel (1710–95), a favourite sculptor of Mme du Barry, praised by Diderot, chiselled the "Diana" of which Jules de Goncourt is minded by the sight of Maria's beautiful legs (p. 62). He was the son of an academic painter and the grandson of an excellent landscape artist and engraver.

ANTONELLI, Giacomo, (1806–76) Cardinal, secretary of state to his Holiness P. P. Pius IX and prime minister of his first constitutional ministry following the Roman revolution of 1848, restored absolute government in the Pope's favour in 1850 and obtained Napoleon III's help against Garibaldi in 1867. On his death it was discovered that the papal finances were in great disorder and that His Eminence had left an immense fortune—to his family, not to the Church.

ARAGO, Dominique François, (1786–1853) physicist and astronomer, member of the Academy of Sciences at the age of twenty-three years, is referred to as one of the "glories" of French learning in the last century. His other glory is that he was a *Quarante-huitard,* an unrepentant republican of 1848, serving the Second Republic for a time as minister of war and minister of marine. It is to the credit of Napoleon III that he absolved this great man from the general oath of fealty (which Arago, then astronomer to the Bureau of Longitudes, refused to take) out of regard for the renown reflected upon France from his European reputation. Twentieth-century despots are made of sterner stuff. That Alfred Arago, by the way, whom the Goncourts met in the 1860's at the Princess Mathilde's, was of course not the physicist.

ASSELINE, Louis (1829–78) a forgotten man of letters who edited the works of Diderot and wrote a history of Austria.

ASSELINEAU, Charles, (1820–74) a friend of Baudelaire, wrote a history of the sonnet, a history of the ballade, and, in 1869, the first biography of Baudelaire.

AUBRYAT, Xavier (1827–80) was a journalist who wrote all over the place and entitled one of his books *Les Idées justes et les idées fausses*. A fortunate man, to be able to distinguish neatly between them.

AUGIER, Émile, (1820–89) the author of *Le Gendre de Monsieur Poirier*, also wrote an admirable play called *Le Fils de Giboyer*. In an age when only the French had a living theatre, and when every journalist in Paris turned out dreadful and often successful melo-dramas and farces, Augier wrote solidly and soberly, with a self-respect and a rejection of compromise that won the regard of even so difficult a critic as Jules Lemaître.

AUSSONDON, Hippolyte was born in 1836, was a pupil of Horace Vernet and of Flaubert's friend, Gleyre, and sent canvases to the Salons.

AUTRAN, Joseph (1813–77) who defeated Gautier for a seat in the Academy, wrote verse in celebration of peasant virtues and the hero-ism of common soldiers and found readers for it.

BACCIOCHI, Félix (d. 1866) was principal chamberlain to Napoleon III. This family were connections of the Bonaparte, Elisa Bonaparte, sister to Napoleon I, having married a Bacciochi.

BAKUNIN, Mikhail, (1814–76) a fuddled, sentimental, undisciplined, and yet somehow serene gentleman, most idealistic of anarchists, who, amongst other things that he did, fell in love with George Sand. Early a leader in the First International, he was contemptuously and ruthlessly driven out of it by Marx and Engels, who despised his incapacity for method, his ignorance of dialectic and economics, and his warmth of heart.

BALLUE, Théodore, (1817–85) painter and architect, specialized in the restoration and preservation of the churches of Paris.

BANVILLE, Théodore de, (1823–91) a delicate and fluent poet who has achieved a place in most French anthologies chiefly for his felicitous practice of the rondeau and the villanelle. He wrote that stand-by of the nineteenth-century European and American theatre, *Gringoire,* and he had the wit and the discernment to call Arthur Rimbaud *"l'enfant Hugo."* It was Mme de Banville who was one of the "frail-fingered, silver-nailed" ministrants to Rimbaud celebrated in the boy's miraculous *Chercheuses de poux.*

BARBEY D'AUREVILLY, Jules (1808–89) posed as a sort of Catholic Viking of ancient lineage, rarely had two coppers to rub together, talked marvellously, and was an excellent example of what the French call a *dandy*—an elegant nonconformist. He was a colourful and imaginative inventor of tales of horror and voluptuousness, writing with a kind of distinguished extravagance. Oscar Wilde made a translation of his worst novel, *Ce qui ne meurt pas,* which Wilde signed "Sebastian Melmoth."

BARRIÈRE, Jean François (1786–1868) wrote historical notes and criticism for the *Débats* for thirty-five years and was co-editor of a forty-seven volume collection of memoirs relating to the Revolution, as well as of other eighteenth-century documents.

BARTHÉLEMY, Auguste Marseille (1796–1867) was a versifier with a satiric gift under the Restoration and the reign of Louis Philippe. Writing in a time when, despite political censorship, people read other things than legends under photographs, he enjoyed himself greatly; and in his life prison sentences and fines alternated with the receipt of government bribes in payment for his intermittent silences.

BAUDELAIRE, Charles (1821–67) is one of those great poets who are deemed of second rank because their total output fills few pages and they never essayed the larger forms. I wonder, had we nothing of Beethoven but the piano sonatas and the quartets, would he be placed lower than Tchaikovsky and Sibelius? So, and for something like this reason, do the schools rank Catullus, Theocritus, Villon, Ronsard, Louise Labé, the Metaphysicals, Coleridge, Leopardi, Heine —the list is familiar enough. There is perhaps some reason for this in England, where, after 1820, there was almost no poetry worthy the name for a hundred years;* but in France, whose nineteenth century witnessed such an efflorescence of poetry as the country had not known since the dozen great decades preceding 1670, one would expect better judgment.

Baudelaire is read in the English-speaking countries only by professional men of letters and by adolescents in search of a thrill. The obvious retort is that few people read a foreign poet anyway; but the true explanation may be that, between memories of the nineties and the fact that Protestants have lost all notion of sin, people read into the title of Baudelaire's poems, *Les Fleurs du mal,* an insistent decadence which has the effect of making the poems appear "bohemian", frivolous, something likely to corrupt the reader's manners. Clearly, where Evil connotes uniquely sexual lapses, where Humility is uncivic and Pride is an aldermanic virtue, where the immortal soul is dismissed as a mere convention and ignored as a source of torment and joy, Baudelaire must be misread. In such quarters a poem like "Une Charogne" will seem to be literally a poem about carrion, and not a poem about this corruption which must put on incorruption. The wonderful heartrending cry at the close of "Un voyage à Cythère,"

> Ah! Seigneur! donnez-moi la force et le courage
> De contempler mon cœur et mon corps sans dégout!

will seem a bewilderingly distasteful form of exhibitionism—something excessively Gothic, uncomfortably lacking in consolation, not so easily admired and dismissed as *In sua volontade è nostra pace.* Much more readily swallowed—though still alien to the alderman— would be this line out of the poet's notebooks: "L'homme qui fait sa prière, le soir, est un capitaine qui pose des sentinelles. Il peut dormir." The misgivings that might have been induced in Matthew Arnold by the poetry would be stilled by the prose.

A far cry from Bohemia, from hashish, Negro mistresses, and the gloomy Paris of Meryon's etchings, which, in official France and the rest of the world, seem still to be thought the content of Baudelaire's poems! Strange that though the commonest anthologies include "Recueillement", that very great sonnet which opens,

> Sois sage, ô ma Douleur, et tiens-toi plus tranquille.
> Tu réclamais le Soir; il descend; le voici . . .

---

*E.g., compare the last three hundred pages of *The Oxford Book of English Verse* with the first seven hundred. *Vous m'en direz des nouvelles!*

it is so little recognised that the poet knew where peace was to be found. Even more strange is it that a poet so thoroughly identified with the *frisson nouveau* (how Hugo's label sticks!) should more eloquently than any other modern poet have clarioned the spirit's victory:

> O Mort, vieux capitaine, il est temps! levons l'ancre!
> Ce pays nous ennuie, ô Mort! Appareillons!
> Si le ciel et la mer sont noirs comme de l'encre,
> Nos cœurs que tu connais sont remplis de rayons!

There is a Baudelaire I care less about, the quasi-mystical poet of "Correspondances" and "Harmonie du Soir", for example. But in all of his poems he is harmonious and pure, and his metaphor creates in the reader that little explosion of recognition and delight without which there is no poetry. It is present in the Racinian

> C'est un cri répété par mille sentinelles;

in—may I say it?—this Shakespearean metaphor,

> Le doux relent de mon amour défunt;

in a vision of the ocean which probably Rimbaud and certainly Valéry read:

> Quel démon a doté la mer, rauque chanteuse,
> Qu'accompagne l'immense orgue des vents grondeurs,
> De cette fonction sublime de berceuse;

in this daring and majestic invention:

> . . Vois se pencher les défuntes Années,
> Sur les balcons du ciel, en robes surannées;
> Surgir du fond des eaux le Regret souriant;
>
> Le Soleil moribond s'endormir sous une arche,
> Et, comme un long linceul traînant à l'Orient,
> Entends, ma chère, entends la douce Nuit qui marche.

He had this in common with John Donne, that his preferred subjects were death and love, and, like Donne's, his poems begin with a great stroke of the bow and do not always end as thrillingly:

> Je suis belle, ô mortels! comme un rêve de pierre
> > ("La Beauté")
>
> O toison, moutonnant jusque sur l'encolure!
> > ("La Chevelure")
>
> Mère des souvenirs, maîtresse des maîtresses!
> > ("Le Balcon")

[297]

Like Coleridge, Baudelaire was a remarkable thinker in the domain of aesthetics. Those interested will wish to read his *Curiosités esthétiques* and his *Art romantique*.

BAUDRY, Paul, (1828–86) a portrait painter and muralist to whom was entrusted the decoration of the Opéra in Paris which, from the name of its architect, is still known as *Les Folies Garnier*. Nobody with a notion of decorum would wish to hear Italian opera in a different setting.

BEAUMARCHAIS, Pierre Augustin Caron de (1732–99) began life as an inventive watchmaker, continued as teacher of the harp to the sisters of Louis XV, exploited a litigation from which he emerged a polemist of enviable talent, and then became a secret political agent for the king. In the course of his hazardous and accidented career he furnished aid to the American revolutionary cause and lined his pockets in the trade of gunrunner. Meanwhile, this fantastic man wrote for the theatre two deathless masterpieces of comedy which were powerfully influential as political and social satire. One, *Le Barbier de Seville,* served as libretto for the opera of a highly gifted composer (Rossini); the other, *Le Mariage de Figaro* (which Napoleon I called "the revolution in action") was seized upon for the same purpose by a surpassingly great artist (Mozart). Goethe told Eckermann (tenth of April 1829): "I have in my *Clavigo* whole passages lifted out of Beaumarchais' *Mémoires.*"

BEAUVOIR, Roger de could not of course be anybody's real name. This obscure signature was signed from time to time to thundering melodramas and novels by Eugène Roger de Bully (1806–66).

BELLOY, Marquis de (1815–71). The Goncourts' Belloy is of an age to have been that Marquis de Belloy who, with Ferdinand de Gramont, was paid 400 francs, as provided in a contract between Balzac and the publisher, Souverain, to make "corrections of style &c" in the matter of the publication of Balzac's juvenilia as the *Complete Works of Horace de St Aubin* in 1835. They actually wrote the finishing chapters of two of these works, which Balzac had left incomplete in manuscript. (See the notes appended to Bouteron and Longnon's admirable edition of Balzac, published by Conard, Vol. X, pp. 417–18.)

BÉNI–BARDE, Alfred, born in 1834, a specialist in hydrotherapy and in the treatment of nervous disorders, was chief of the hydrotherapeutic establishment at Auteuil where Jules de Goncourt was treated before his death.

BÉRANGER, Pierre Jean de, (1780–1857) whose first patron was Lucien Bonaparte, represents history rather than poetry. His jingles were sentimental, patriotic, anticlerical, and occasionally libertine; they are now scarcely readable, though to be found in all French anthologies. In their day, nevertheless, they were a powerful force against reaction everywhere in Europe. Two terms as political prisoner under the Restoration, and his presence on the barricades in 1830, combined with the popularity of his songs to make Béranger one of the great names in the first half of the nineteenth century, and he had the grand old age of an Anatole France, all the world doing him homage. Béranger was no Burns, for his personal emotion was thinner than the Scotsman's; he was no Heine, despite an instinct for form.

BERGERAC, Savinien Cyrano de, (1619–55) universally known for his nose, wrote imaginary tales of journeys to the sun, the moon, and round the skies generally—which explains again the Goncourts' coupling of his name with that of Arago.

BERLIOZ, Hector, (1803–69) whom Mr W. J. Turner considers a *génie méconnu* on whose altar he would have us immolate that *génie trop connu,* Richard Wagner, was the soul of honour and the despair of every friend he had. His incapacity for orderly living, for moderation in personal relations as in orchestration, in feeling as in expression, argues a being in whom genius was never subjected to any form of discipline. There was in this widely travelled man, this man who was a public figure, who lived in the world and wrote and performed for the world, something deeply innocent and unworldly, something that posterity is better able than contemporaneity to bear. He wrote a half-dozen books, both technical and literary, and as music critic of the *Débats* for quarter of a century he wielded a power which was never exercised in his own interest. He loved almost every woman who was kind to him and sympathetic with his ideals, and married two of them, apparently to no good purpose.

BERNARD, Claude (1813–78) was a physiologist, but like Charles Darwin he was also a gifted writer and he wrote one book, *L'Introduction à l'étude de la médecine expérimentale,* which has made his name familiar to all Frenchmen. Some fifteen years ago, when that excellent actor Jouvet, in the part of Jules Romains' Dr Knock, announced to the audience his axiom, *"Tout homme bien portant est un malade qui s'ignore,"* he was able to get a second laugh by adding, *"épigraphe que j'ai attribuée à Claude Bernard."*

BERTHELOT, Marcelin (1827–1907) is described as a genius in the field of organic chemistry. He was editor of the *Grande encyclopédie* (1885–1901) and served in two Cabinets, once as minister of education and again at the Foreign Office. As a boy of fifteen he strongly influenced Renan by introducing the young seminarist into the world of the natural sciences.

BISCHOFFSHEIM, Raphaël Louis, was the son of an Alsatian banker and philanthropist to whose generosity the study of astronomy in France owed a great deal.

BESSON, Faustin, (1821–82) painter and son of a painter, worked most successfully in the field of decoration.

BLANC, Charles, (1813–82). brother of the revolutionary Socialist, Louis Blanc, an engraver and writer on art, served as director of fine arts under both the Second and the Third republics, but not under the Second Empire.

BOIGNE, Countess de, (1789–1866) an intimate friend of Louis XV's eldest daughter, Mme Adélaïde; a witty, chattering, attractive woman who wrote gossipy memoirs that are of some worth and very easy to read, was the wife of a soldier who collected a large fortune as general of the troops of a Mahratta prince but was (unfairly, one feels) neglected and despised by the lady he married.

BOISSIEU, Alphonse de, (1807–86) grandson of an eighteenth-century painter and engraver, was an erudite antiquarian.

BOREL, Pétrus (Pierre Joseph Borel d'Hauterive, 1809–59) wrote various volumes of verse and short stories in a language so extravagant that it has saved his name from oblivion.

BOSSUET, Jacques Bénigne, (1627–1704) Bishop of Condom and later of Meaux, dubbed "the Eagle of Meaux", one of the great names of French literature and the Church, and not an insignificant name in French history. The prince of sacred orators, his sermons would still not rank with Donne's even if we had them in finished form; his funeral orations, however, which we possess as written, are of unequalled grandeur. Hear him, for example, on the Cardinal de Retz (in the oration on Michel Le Tellier, Chancellor of France): "Mais puis-je oublier celui que je vois partout dans le récit de nos malheurs, cet homme si fidèle aux particuliers, si redoutable à l'État, d'un caractère si haut qu'on ne pouvait ni l'estimer, ni le craindre, ni l'aimer, ni le haïr à demi. . . . Mais pendant qu'il voulait acquérir ce qu'il devait un jour mépriser, il remua tout par de secrets et puissants ressorts; et après que tous les partis furent abattus,"—and now a phrase as good as Tacitus—"il sembla encore se soutenir seul, et seul encore menacer le favori victorieux [Mazarin] de ses tristes et intrépides regards. La religion s'intéresse dans ses infortunes, la ville royale s'émeut, et Rome même menace. . . ." He thundered marvellously, but he was fond also of the "dying fall" and knew how to handle it. Thus, a church: "Asile inviolable, où les querelles des hommes ne pénètrent pas." Or: "Je réserve au troupeau que je dois nourrir de la parole de vie, les restes d'une voix qui tombe et d'une ardeur qui s'éteint."

Bossuet was tutor to the dauphin; he sought in vain to persuade the Calvinists of their error. He was the leading apologist of the notion of the divine right of kings, which he defended in his *Politique tirée de l'Écriture Sainte;* but his greatest service to the court and to France consisted in the drafting of the "Déclaration des Quatres Articles" in which he asserted (though more moderately than Louis XIV desired) the independence of the temporal power and in which, also, the doctrine of Gallicanism, subordinating the authority of the Pope to that of the episcopal body united with him, to the general Councils, and to the canons of the Church, was first codified. (This doctrine was condemned by the proclamation of pontifical infallibility by the Vatican Council of 1870.) Like Jeremy Collier, he wrote against *"la Comédie,"* but he wrote rather more odiously, attacking the memory of Molière then twenty years dead. Voltaire was among those who believed they had evidence that his Grace was a married man, a subject upon which the opinion of that great churchman, Monsignor Dupanloup, was,*"ceci regarde la miséricorde de Dieu."*

BOUILHET, Louis Hyacinthe (1822–69) is a name that remains because it was that of a schoolfellow and intimate friend of Flaubert. Bouilhet had the quaint notion of employing science as a subject for poetry. He also wrote a few respectable historical plays.

BOULANGER, Gustave Rodolphe, (1824–88) a painter of oriental and classical subjects, celebrated in his day.

BRESSANT, Jean Baptiste Prosper, (1815–86) was a leading actor of his time and the professor at the Conservatoire of Mounet-Sully.

BRETON, Louis, born in 1827, exhibited with great success in 1857 his "Bénédiction des blés" and painted many popular rustic scenes.

BROGLIE, Albert, Duke de, (1821–1901) eldest son of Achille, Duke de Broglie, a French Lord Acton who described himself as "a penitent Christian and an impenitent Liberal", had the courage to pour withering scorn upon the Second Empire as early as 1856, in the formal address delivered on the occasion of his reception in the French Academy. Speaking of his predecessor in the Academy chair, he said, "It was not given him to die in time. He lived long enough to see the great of the nation persecuted, proscribed, fled." The Empire of Napoleon III, he said, was "the government that the poorer classes had desired and the rich deserved." This philosopher and historian was ambassador to London in 1871 and prime minister in 1873.

BUFFON, Georges Louis Leclerc, Count de, (1707–88) whom Flaubert quotes, wrote a *Natural History* in forty-four volumes which seems to have been the first attempt to synthesize and co-ordinate the various elements of this vast subject. His inaugural address to the French Academy, the *Discours sur le style* (1753) is, as everybody knows, the source of that oft-repeated and oft-mutilated axiom, "le style, c'est l'homme même." Anatole France once declared that he considered Buffon the best of all writers of French. A specimen of his style is this superb picture-book sentence on the tiger: "Lorsque le tigre leur fend et leur déchire le corps, c'est pour y plonger la tête et pour sucer à longs traits le sang dont il vient d'ouvrir la source, qui tarit presque toujours avant que sa soif ne s'éteigne." A schoolmaster, incidentally, would give you a black mark if you did not omit that *ne*.

BULOZ, François (1803–77) took over the *Revue des Deux Mondes* from its founders, Ségur-Dupeyron and Mauroy, in 1831 and made it in a very few years into the leading literary and political review of Europe. Sainte-Beuve, Vigny, Musset and George Sand were among the most illustrious of its many contributors in every domain, and, for all its respectability, it published Baudelaire's poetry. The story of the review has been excellently told by Buloz's granddaughter, Mme Marie Louise Pailleron, in *François Buloz et ses amis*.

CALAMATTA, Mme, the lady whom Gautier found visiting George Sand (p. 162), painted and exhibited portraits and religious subjects. Her husband, Luigi Calamatta, was an Italian engraver.

CALVET–ROGNIAT, Pierre Paul (1812–75) was a rich politician whose electoral methods gave rise to considerable talk, particularly when he gave away whole calves in exchange for votes.

CARPEAUX, Jean Baptiste, (1827–95) a pupil of Rude strongly influenced by Donatello and then by Michaelangelo, is called by the Goncourts "the greatest French artist of the second half of the nineteenth century." "Where experts are agreed, the contrary opinion cannot be held to be certain," wrote Bertrand Russell (more or less).

CAYLA, Zoé Talon, Countess du, (1784–1850) presented to Louis XVIII when he was well past sixty, was the enchantress of his old age and the confidante of the political ideas that remained to him. She was said to have been placed in this David's . . . path by the "Ultras", the reactionary party, through the intermediary of Viscount Sosthène de la Rochefoucauld, and to have served as their agent.

CHALIER, Joseph, (1747–93) known as the "Marat of Lyons" and chief of the Montagnard party in that city, was a rich merchant of Piedmontese origin who had been moved by his commiseration for the poor to place himself at the head of the revolutionary movement there, winning fame as an orator and death in the course of the reaction against his rule, when that took place.

CHAMFORT was the name taken by Sébastien Nicolas (1741–94), son of a grocer who lived by literary hackwork, won an Academy prize for a eulogy of Molière, and exchanged his brilliant conversation (and perhaps at times his handsome person) for board and lodging in a number of the most fashionable houses of France. He was twice attached to the court of Louis XVI, but the life seems to have irked him. Of his many plays there is nothing to be said, but his *Maximes et Pensées,* while not so unfailingly significant in matter nor so flawless and untouchable in form as La Rochefoucauld's, stand immediately below them and well above any other Frenchman's. I like, for example, "Un homme sans élévation ne saurait avoir de bonté; il ne peut avoir que de la bonhomie." "Weak men are the light brigade of the army of evil" is rather neat; but the fact that it can be translated seems almost to judge it. There is also, "The tragic stage is open to the great moral objection that it lends too much importance to life and death." Characteristic of his time is this: "Reason now and then makes us as unhappy as our passions do; and when a man is in this pass we may say of him that he is a patient poisoned by his doctor." The celebrated maxim on love, which the Goncourts quote in part, goes as follows: "L'amour, tel qu'il existe dans la société, n'est que l'échange de deux fantaisies et le contact de deux épidermes." At the house of the Prince de Beauvau, towards the close of 1788, Jacques Cazotte, author of *Le Diable amoureux,* prophesied the fate of each of the assembled guests. To Chamfort, the report goes, he spoke as follows: "You, M. de Chamfort, will open your veins with twenty-two slashes of the razor, but you will not die till several months afterwards." Such indeed was the manner of Chamfort's death.

CHATEAUBRIAND, François René, Viscount de, (1768–1848) the most highly considered man of letters in France between Voltaire and Victor Hugo, might deserve to be called the French Byron if he had written verse and not prose, had had a club foot and not a swollen head, had been tormented instead of smug, had despised the world of politics instead of cutting a great figure in it, and had practised incest and not merely written about that divine malediction. It is impossible to exaggerate the esteem in which he once was held, the avidity with which his dreariest and soupiest books were gulped down, sighed over, cherished. He is still taken to be one of the most eloquent of French writers, but with the exception of parts of his masterpiece, the *Mémoires d'outre-tombe,* I find him unreadable, a stew of rolling periods in which bad Lytton Strachey might be said to be stirred up with the worst pomposities of Edgar Allan Poe.

He travelled to America in his early twenties (some say never landing on the continent) and found there matter for his messy *Vie de Rancé* and for *Les Natchez,* written twenty years later. An émigré in London during the Revolution, he was ambassador there during the Restoration and was minister of foreign affairs in 1822–24. I like what the aged Talleyrand said of the aged Chateaubriand when it was reported that the noble viscount was deaf: "He thinks he is deaf because he no longer hears himself talked about." Chateaubriand appears to have been just as solemn as he was irresistible to women—a fact of which I make a free gift to misogynists.

CHENNEVIÈRES, Charles Philippe, Marquis de (1820–99) wrote short stories and art criticism while pursuing a career as inspector of museums under the Second Empire and curator of the Luxembourg Museum, later director of fine arts, under the Third Republic.

CHESNEAU, Ernest, (1833–90) a journalist who wrote on art and published a long list of small works on the subject, producing also a novel and some "reflections" on the state of the press and of literature.

"CLAIRVILLE" was the pseudonym of Louis François Nicolaie, who turned out innumerable libretti, farces, revues, pantomime shows, and thus served a certain purpose.

CLAUDIN, Gustave, born in 1823, embalmed his journalism in a volume of anecdotal memoirs (*Mes Souvenirs, les boulevards de 1840 à 1871*). Like most other chroniclers of the press in his day, he wrote novels and tales.

CLÉSINGER, J. B. A. Stello (1814–83) began his career as sculptor by making portrait busts and ended it by fabricating statuary on classical and historical subjects. In 1848 he ran off with George Sand's daughter, who was sitting for him. They married.

COLET, Louise (1810–76) wrote verse, tried her hand at plays, and published several novels, of which *Lui* remains faintly interesting as a *roman à clef* in which are portrayed a number of her contemporaries. Not only Flaubert but also Victor Cousin was among her admirers. She seems to have been a pest. There is a story I have not taken time to run down, but which I remember to have read or heard long years ago, that Colet was awarded an Academy prize for a poem which Cousin (or Flaubert) had written for her . . . by copying out something of Vigny's, or Musset's which had already been published when her manuscript was submitted to the august jury. Compare Lebrun, "Sur une Dame poète,"

> Eglée, belle et poète, a deux petits travers:
> Elle fait son visage, et ne fait pas ses vers.

COLONNA di Castiglione, Adèle d'Affry, Duchess (d. 1879) was a female sculptor who signed her work "Marcello."

CONSTANT, Benjamin (1767–1830) was born in Lausanne and educated at Oxford and at Erlangen, residing subsequently for a time in Edinburgh. The two most important influences in his life were Mme de Charrière (the lamented Geoffrey Scott's "Zélide") and Mme de Staël. *Sola inconstantia constans* was his device. Mme de Charrière, twenty-seven years his senior, was his mistress for nine years, until he became intimate with Mme de Staël in 1796. With the latter he spent ten tempestuous years, the most notable literary product of which was *Adolphe,* a short novel of the torments of love that certainly makes as painful reading as any in literature. (A diary, known as *Le Cahier rouge,* confirms much that is in the novel.) In *La Muse du département* Balzac makes *Adolphe* the Bible of his unhappy heroine: "Elle l'étudiait; car pardessus toutes choses, elle ne voulait pas être Ellénore." Constant was prominent in French politics under the Revolution, was excluded from the political scene under the Empire through Napoleon's quite comprehensible detestation of that pushing bluestocking, Mme de Staël, and was a formidable opponent, both as journalist and as parliamentarian, of the Restoration. He wrote a five-volume work on religion of which M. Marcel Arland has spoken respectfully; I doubt that anybody else has opened it in our day. *Adolphe,* however, is in the major line of the French novel, that marvellous line of truth and sensibility that began with the beautiful *Princess de Clèves.*

COQUELIN, Benoît Constant, (1841–1909) remembered as Coquelin *aîné,* made his debut at the Comédie-Française in 1860 and was a full-fledged member of the troupe, a *sociétaire,* as early as 1864. He remained there until 1892 and then continued on the boulevards the most successful career of his time on the French stage.

CORNEILLE, Thomas (1625–1709) was the younger brother of the great Pierre Corneille. He had the honour of writing a play, *Le Baron de Fondrières,* which is said to have been the first play ever hissed off any stage. It is said also that he was the first French poet to make use of a rhyming dictionary. He translated Ovid, produced a large dictionary of history and geography, and did other respectable work in the domain of letters, meriting his succession to his brother's seat in the Academy.

COTTIN, Marie Sophie (1770–1807) had wonderful notions about the Crusades, Siberia, and the world in general, all of which went into a series of extravagant novels.

COUSIN, Victor, (1792–1867) an eclectic philosopher and great bonze of the university, about whom librarians are taught that he wrote *Du vrai, du beau et du bien* when it would be so much more useful if they were allowed to know that he invented the phrase *l'art pour l'art,* which perhaps Whistler translated as "art for art's sake." That restless man of politics, letters, music and nature, Édouard Herriot, sums up Cousin as follows (in *Normale*): "What will you have? Plato? Schelling? Hegel? A theory of energy? A doctrine of liberty? Pantheism? Monotheism? Eclecticism is the department store of the mind: M. Cousin suffices for everything." Cousin's *Report* on the state of education in Germany was translated (in the U. S. A.) by a Mrs Sarah Austin in 1834 and was frequently reprinted, the legislatures of New Jersey and Massachusetts distributing it gratis. Later Cousin said, "Nothing has touched me more than the title of member of the American Institute for Education." To his own students at the Normal School Cousin would say, "Gentlemen, now that you have won your appointments I hope you will call on the bishop and assure him of our conviction that religion is essential to the common folk. . . . Do not read Malebranche; it is a disease." To write more about Cousin would be to write too much.

CRÉBILLON, Claude Prosper Jolyot de, (1707–77) son of Prosper Jolyot de C., the playwright, and therefore known as Crébillon *fils,* after an excellent education at the hands of the Jesuit Fathers, became a novelist whose titles and plots are more *alléchants* than these fictions are readable, largely because of the wearying hyper-refinement of the style but also because, to put it vulgarly, his heroes and heroines take a frightfully long time getting to the point. The title of *La Nuit et le moment,* for example, promises much, but, as summarized by a recent historian (Crane Brinton, in *The Lives of Talleyrand*), this is what you get: "A gentleman suddenly appears in his bathrobe in a lady's bedroom and eventually attains the lady's bed. One hundred and fifty pages describe their conversation, in neat, witty, very self-conscious French. It is true that the dialogue is now and then interrupted by action; but the participants seem even more interested in the dialogue than in the action, and they certainly never forget to be witty and polished." As truly as Mr Aldous Huxley or Mr Sinclair Lewis, Crébillon mirrored the society in which he lived: compare, for example, Lord Chesterfield's one hundred and thirty-eighth letter to his son (fifteenth of April 1751, O. S.): "I am assured that Mme de Blot, although she has no great regularity of features, is notwithstanding, excessively pretty; and for all that, she has been scrupulously constant to her husband, though she has now been married over a year. Surely she does not reflect, that woman wants polishing. I would have you polish one another reciprocally. Force, assiduities, attentions, tender looks, and passionate declarations, on your side, will produce some irresolute wishes, at least, on hers; and when even the slightest wishes arise, the rest will soon follow." I like that touch of indignation against the heedless Mme de Blot: "Surely she does not reflect, that woman wants polishing.". . . And this picture of the society of the time is but corroborated by the fact that, reading Crébillon's fictions, an English lady of distinguished family, Henrietta Maria de Stafford, fell in love with their author sight unseen. She sought him out; and in 1748, two years after having had a child by him, married him. The single book of Crébillon *fils* that is still read on occasion is *Le Sopha* —not an article of furniture, but our friend the Sophy of Persia, one of the exotics brought from the Near and the Far East into European literature at this time (cp. Montesquieu's *Lettres persanes*).

CRÉMIEUX, Hector, whom the Goncourts sneer at because he was well paid for the musical-show verses he wrote, collaborated with Ludovic Halévy on the libretto of Offenbach's *Orphée aux enfers*.

CROZAT, Pierre, (1661–1740) whose house is the scene of one of Watteau's drawings (see entry, December 9, 1859), was banker to the Realm and therefore its creditor. Except for a certain discretion which he possessed, he might have become the Cecil Rhodes of Louisiana— but he left that sort of thing to the genius of John Law. He was a celebrated collector under the Regency, and his possessions were catalogued between 1729 and 1742 in what is known as the *Cabinet Crozat*.

DAMAS–HINARD, Albert de, born in Madrid in 1805, was librarian of the Louvre and secretary to the Empress Eugénie. There are translations made by him of a number of the writings of Cervantes, Lope de Vega, and Calderon.

DECAMPS, Alexandre Gabriel (1803–60) travelled in the East in his youth and painted oriental life and scenery with a boldness and freedom from conventional notions that puzzled contemporary critics. Extremely fond of all animals, he had a special affection for monkeys and sketched them with great sympathy and humour.

DEFFAND, Marie Anne, Marquise du (1697–1780) is celebrated in England for her letters to Horace Walpole, admirably edited in multiple volumes by Mrs Paget Toynbee, in which she displays an epistolary gift, a concern with the ideas then in the air, and a tolerant affection for and comprehension of human foibles and grandeur, quite as ingratiating and meritorious as her insistent docility and unflagging tenderness in the face of Walpole's neglect are tiresome. Her salon was in the main aristocratic rather than literary, but she received Voltaire, Montesquieu, Fontenelle and D'Alembert, as well as that button-nosed, bottom-cheeked genius, Edward Gibbon. It was she who said, apropos of Cardinal de Polignac's account of St Denis' miraculous march of two miles with his head in his hands, "Il n'y a que le premier pas qui coûte." She was the aunt of that even more passionately eloquent letter writer (the French "opposite number", I suppose, of Dorothy Osborne), Julie de Lespinasse, who lay dying for love of Señor de Mora in the bed of M. de Guibert—whom of course she also loved.

DELAAGE, Henri (1825–82) wrote a number of forgotten works on magnetism, occultism and kindred stimulants of the imagination by which some of the meek are, in every generation, consoled and made insolent.

DELACROIX, Eugène (1799–1863) is maligned by the Goncourts in but one sentence, but this is enough to make so great a man the most maligned figure in their diaries. Emerging in the Salon of 1824 with the "Scène des Massacres de Scio" he sprang at a bound into the leadership of the Romantic School—and he hated romanticism all his life, as his absorbing *Journal* again and again reveals. His subjects, indeed, were "romantic"—Dante, Shakespeare, Ariosto, Goethe, Byron, furnished themes for his pictures. But, as Baudelaire pointed out in a wonderful essay, he had a mind, a wide culture, a habit of reflection. Hugo he considered lacking in simplicity; Berlioz was in his view an "heroic mess"; Mozart, on the other hand, was his notion of genius. He refused to believe that—as the romantic poets were then writing —lovers wasted their time gaping at the moon and sobbing over nightly farewells. It was simply not true: "Ce vague, cette tristesse perpetuelle, ne peignent personne." In sum, he was romantic as Stendhal was romantic—and remark that Stendhal, besides writing the adorable *Chartreuse de Parme,* created the first "modern" hero in fiction, Julien Sorel, the gifted youth of humble origin determined to "make good" and accompanied throughout life by an irrepressible *Minderwertigkeit.*

DELAROCHE, Hippolyte, *called* Paul, (1797–1856) a romantic painter of historical subjects, engravings of which still hang in thousands of homes, e.g., "Charles I taunted by the Children of Cromwell," "Death of the Duke de Guise," &c.

DELAUNAY, Louis Arsène (1826–1903) made his début at the Comédie-Française in 1848 as young Dorante in Corneille's *Menteur* and continued to play young-lover parts until he was past sixty. His chief successes were in the comedies of Alfred de Musset.

DELÉCLUZE, Étienne Jean (1781–1863) painted first, then wrote and published memoirs which (it is said) contain "interesting details" of his period.

DEMBÍNSKI, Wcyl., (1791–1864) a Polish general and adventurer who fought in Russia and Germany under Napoleon I, was a leader in the Polish uprisings of 1830–32 against Nicholas I of Russia, and took part in Kossuth's Hungarian revolution against Austria in 1848.

DENNERY, Adolphe (1811–99) collaborated in the writing of about two hundred plays, his "masterpiece" being *The Two Orphans,* written with Eugène Cormon. He turned some of his plays into novels, a trick not to be performed again until it began to be done with "screen plays."

DEVÉRIA, Joseph, (1805–65) a friend of Victor Hugo, early enjoyed an immense momentary success as painter and lithographer. He did portraits of Edmond and Jules de Goncourt, among others.

DIAZ de la Peña, Narcisse Virgile, (1809–76) a French painter of the Barbizon School, rather better than most.

DIDEROT, Denis (1713–84) is an interesting case. The richest, the most abundant and variously gifted and attractive figure of one of the great ages of European civilization—the pre-lachrymal French eighteenth century—is apparently a product not made for export. On the English side, I dare say, the same is true of Dr Johnson. Diderot was Generosity made man: Grimm's *Correspondance* (written for a fee to his royal and princely subscribers) is filled with contributions freely made by this most harassed writer and editor; and not only the reviews of the salons of painting (which have long been known to be Diderot's), but also reviews of plays, of pamphlets, notes "that I have scribbled on the ruins of Greece", etc., etc. "Do with this chatter whatever you please," he wrote to Grimm; "but above all do not use my name." As the Goncourts often write of Gautier, so Marmontel wrote of Diderot: "He who knows Diderot in his writings does not know him at all. . . . When he grows animated in talk and allows his thoughts to flow in all their abundance, then he becomes truly ravishing."

With all his friends and his talk, with his papers thrown off for Grimm and his hundreds of occasional pieces of every sort, Diderot (with D'Alembert as co-editor, but often obstructing progress) was bringing out that Encyclopaedia that was to liberate Europe and the text of which had constantly to be hidden from the police, moved from one house or one shop to another. Exploding at every instant with ideas, with inventions of intrigue, with re-creations of life and commentaries upon life, Diderot threw off masterpieces about which he could never take the time to know whether they were of consequence or not. The beautiful *Neveu de Rameau* was to him "a little satire"; of *La Religieuse* he wrote, "There will be true things in it, pathetic things, and even powerful things if I set myself to it. But I cannot take the time. I let my pen run on and am therefore not my own master." It was the same with his essays, his plays (which, in truth, are better forgotten) and the rest.

He was fifty years old and still grinding out copy when he scribbled to a friend: "I love reading madly, which is as much as to say very clearly that I no longer love to think. . . . I enjoy moralising—another proof of decrepitude." Without Diderot's *Paradoxe sur le Comédien* the ungrateful Lessing would never have been able to write his stimulating *Hamburgische Dramaturgie;* the *Essai sur la peinture* so illuminated the subject for Goethe that he thought of translating it; his encyclopaedia piece on Beauty shows that he had mastered the metaphysics of aesthetics. As for his *Correspondance littéraire,* it is essential for an acquaintance with the ferment of ideas and idealisms that animated the *philosophes.* Goethe said of Voltaire very shrewdly: "Few would have wished to make themselves so dependent for the sake of becoming independent." This could not have been said of Diderot: his only substantial (and passing) patron was the Empress Catherine of Russia; his existence was throughout noble and disinterested.

DINAH, see FÉLIX.

DORVAL, Marie, (1798–1849) one of the great actresses of the Romantic period, had the honour of possessing Alfred de Vigny's love, thought and spirit. In *La Colère de Samson* we get a hint of the source of his torment over her: "La femme aura Gomorrhe . . . Les deux sexes mourront chacun de son côté." If there is anything in this —and I know no confirmation of it—then there is no harm in adding that she was a more powerful figure than Proust's Albertine, and that Vigny had not Saint-Loup's epicene gift for armour. Two of her great parts were Marion Delorme, in Hugo's drama, and Kitty Bell, in Vigny's *Chatterton,* in which her fainting spell and birdlike fall down a flight of steps constituted the *clou* of the evening.

DOUCET, Charles Camille, born in 1812, wrote comedies in verse and was elected to the Academy. As "perpetual" secretary, his reports on the annual award of Academy prizes were appreciated for their skilful and noncommittal grace.

DROUYN DE LHUYS, Edmond, (1805–81) a career diplomatist, was four times minister for foreign affairs under the Second Empire. At the time of the Crimean War he attempted to obtain Napoleon III's consent to an alliance with Austria and a strong front against Russia, and failed.

DUBOIS, Guillaume, Cardinal (1656–1723) is one of the most curious figures in French history. Until he was sixty years of age his career was without distinction except for the fact that he had been tutor and pander to the nephew of Louis XIV, the young Duke de Chartres. But when that duke became Philippe of Orleans and regent of France, Dubois, with his simple tonsure, became his minister. Saint-Simon says of him that he had all the vices: "Perfidy, avarice, debauchery, ambition, flattery, battled within him for mastery." Michelet, who, God knows, was as full of moral indignation as an atheist, wrote more judiciously of Dubois: "A rogue; ambitious; devoted to the cause of England (which paid him a million francs per annum); a flatterer of Rome (for he was avid to wear the cardinal's hat); untrustworthy in every way, he nevertheless possessed an ideal which was a burning passion; by unworthy means he pursued a great, a splendid aim—the foundation, the sound establishment, of the peace of the world." After Louis XIV had made a mess of the Spanish succession, Dubois gained the friendship of England and warded off the dominion of Spain over France, crushing out, at the same time, the last breath of the Jacobite pretension to the British throne. Incidentally, he got his hat. On a single day in January 1720 he was ordained subdeacon, deacon and priest. Three months later, on the third of April, he was made Prince-Archbishop of Cambrai, the richest see in France. Michelet, again, says: "The new prelate, knowing not a word of the Mass, had trouble enough learning it. He worked at it. He held farcical rehearsals at the Palais-Royal in the course of which his blunders, his *lapsus,* his exasperation, and his curses scattered among the prayers, amused the Regent and sent the onlookers into gales of laughter." How like (in one aspect) that Byzantine prelate of whom Gibbon wrote, "The new archbishop, accidentally recommended by an easy temper and venerable aspect, was obliged to delay the ceremony of his consecration, till he had previously despatched the rites of his baptism."

DU CAMP, Maxime, (1822–94) journalist and novelist, wrote relatively discreet memoirs. He was an intimate friend of Flaubert's for about ten years, and they visited Egypt together; but when he (and Bouilhet) advised Flaubert to throw into the fire his first version (1849) of *La Tentation de Saint-Antoine,* and when Du Camp's success in journalism went to his head, Flaubert began to write of him as "young Du Camp" and otherwise rather disdainfully. In the *Bulletin du Bibliophile* for November and December, 1930, M. Parturier points out curious resemblances between the Mme Dambreuse of Flaubert's *Éducation sentimentale* and the Viviane of Du Camp's *Forces perdues,* revealing that the model for both characters was Mérimée's friend, Valentine Delessert, wife of Louis-Philippe's prefect of police. (It was Delessert, by the way, who issued an ordinance probably unique in police annals, instructing that misspelled and ungrammatical shop-signs in Paris were to be corrected.)

DUFAURE, J. A. Stanislas, (1798–1881) a better lawyer than poli-tician, held ministerial posts under Soult in 1839 and under Thiers in 1871–73 and was elected leader of the Paris Bar, as well as a member of the French Academy.

"DUMANOIR" was born Philippe François Pinel (1806–65). He wrote plays, as every other journalist of his day seems to have done, but he is mentioned here only because his name, Pinel, was that of the seventeenth-century schoolmaster who taught divine Molière his letters and therefore deserves to be remembered.

DUPANLOUP, Philbert, (1802–75) Bishop of Orleans, one of the handsomest and most powerful orators of the Church in France, as noble in charity and elevated in mind as he was liberal in his social views, was nevertheless an adversary of the spirit of his time as repre-sented by Taine, Renan and other powerful agnostics. There is a touch of irony in the fact that when Renan was a fifteen-year-old seminary student, already showing extraordinary attainments, Monsignor Dupanloup singled him out and found a place for him in the School of St Nicholas du Chardonnet, which he had founded in order to bring together the children of the nobility and the most gifted semi-narists of humble origin. It was Monsignor Dupanloup, also, who negotiated—there is no other word, since it involved a sealed docu-ment—the ministration, and finally administered, the last rites of the Church to the Prince de Talleyrand, one time Bishop of Autun.

DURUY, Jean Victor (1811–94) was a brilliant student at Normale, had served as secretary to Michelet, had taught for over a quarter of a century in the Collège Henri IV, and had published a series of popu-lar textbooks in history when, out of the blue, Napoleon III chose him to be his *teinturier,* or ghost writer, in the matter of a book on

Julius Caesar which the emperor was engaged upon. His appointment as minister of education astonished the country, which had never heard of its new minister; but it turned out excellently, Duruy effecting numerous reforms and ameliorations. The leading authority on the period, Pierre de la Gorce, says that on first appearing before the emperor, Duruy displayed "that happy awkwardness which is so pleasing to princes as a change from the courtier's grace."

EDMOND, Charles, (Charles Edmond Chojecki) born in Poland in 1822, served as lieutenant colonel of Omer Pasha's troops in the Crimean War; was secretary to Prince Jerome Bonaparte; librarian to the Senate; contributed to Girardin's *Presse;* and wrote plays that were praised in their day.

EGGIS, Étienne, (1830–67) a hypersensitive Swiss poet, passionately devoted to his craft, gave up a post as tutor to a Bavarian prince in order to come to Paris, where he brought out volumes entitled *Chatting with the Moon* and *Journey to the Land of the Heart,* and died an impoverished consumptive.

ÉNAULT, Louis, born in 1824, was an art critic and man of letters who translated Mrs Beecher Stowe's *Uncle Tom's Cabin.* He wrote a great many novels, travelled widely in Europe and the East, and wrote a number of books of travel that took in the world from the North Cape to India.

FALLOUX, Pierre, Count de (1811–86) began as a Legitimist, went over to the Republic of 1848, and then became a supporter of the Second Empire. This facile turncoat is remembered for the *Loi Falloux* which placed primary education in the hands of the parish priests and, in the higher studies, exempted them from the normal scholastic requirements in the way of diplomas and degrees demanded of lay professors. In 1872 he succeeded in offending all parties equally, and it is satisfying to relate that in 1876 he was excommunicated by the Bishop of Angers.

FÉLIX, the family name of the great Rachel (Élisa Rachel Félix, 1820–58) the lesser Lia, and the inconsequent Dinah, all ladies of the theatre and daughters of an itinerant Jewish pedlar and his gypsy wife. Rachel possessed from childhood a particular genius for the declamation of classical French verse, a genius comparable say to that of certain Russian-Jewish boys for the violin. She was not beautiful; she was uniformly unfaithful to her lovers; she was notoriously avaricious; but she seems more than any other person to have been the cause of the revival of public appreciation of classical tragedy in the forties and fifties of the last century, when romanticism was still alive; and she became thus a kind of storm centre and great public figure. Anecdotes concerning her pullulate, but there is none that deals altogether kindly with her. The most agreeable of them relates that the Prince de Joinville (a son of King Louis Philippe and more cavalry-man than cavalier) seeing her play one night, sent back a card on which he had written: "Où? Quand? Combien?" to which she replied on the spot: "Chez toi. Ce soir. Pour rien." She detested Dumas *père,* but seems to have fallen in love with Dumas *fils,* and proposed that he marry her. His reply was: "Je n'épouse pas mes maîtresses, comment voulez-vous que j'épouse celles des autres." It is to her credit that they remained friends. Dining one evening at the Count Duchâtel's, she admired a silver epergne, which her distinguished host immediately offered to her, Spanish fashion. He was a bit taken aback when she accepted instantly. Later, on his proposing to send her home in his carriage, she asked if she might take the table decoration with her. "Naturally, mademoiselle; but you *will* send me back my carriage, won't you?" M. J. Lucas-Dubreton, who knows everything about the period, has published an attractive little book on her, from which these bits were lifted.

It is Lia Félix who is the heroine of the drama at the Porte-Saint-Martin reported on pp. 76 et seq.

FEUILLET, Octave, (1821–90) long a contributor to the *Revue des Deux Mondes,* wrote novels and comedies which enjoyed great success. The *Jeune homme pauvre* that Flaubert rails against is pretty smug, but it is lively and well written. Feuillet was a favourite of the Empress Eugénie, before whom several of his plays were performed in advance of their public showing. This ought to account in part for the enmity with which other writers heard his name.

FEUILLET DE CONCHES, Félix Sebastien (1798–1887) was a worker in the field of history. He made a specialty of the publication of the letters of Louis XVI, the king's sister, Mme Élisabeth, and his queen, Marie Antoinette. Whether it was the style or the substance of the queen's letters that he disliked, nobody remembers; but it is recalled that as editor of them he was a bungling forger.

FÉVAL, Paul (1817–87) wrote romantic and exaggerated novels of pseudo-history and of crime, one of which, *Les Mystères de Londres,* he published under the pseudonym "Sir Francis Trolopp." His stuff was very popular.

FEYDEAU, Ernest Aimé (1821–73) wrote a novel called *Fanny* with the Parisian demi-monde for subject. Most of the charges against Sainte-Beuve that he was a poor judge of his contemporaries arise from the fact that he took this novel seriously. Feydeau composed several plays and is the author of a work in three volumes on what the ancients did about funerals and burials.

FIORENTINO, Pier Angelo (1806–64) was a journalist and story writer in his native Naples before he was brought to Paris by Dumas *père* (who had met him in Italy) and made a fiction-machine in that great man's factory, where he is thought to have written a half dozen tales signed by Dumas, and to have had a hand in the composition of *Monte-Cristo*. In Paris he became an active journalist, particularly as music critic and drama critic, making such a good thing out of the bribes he took for his praise that he was publicly disgraced by the Société des Gens de Lettres.

FLORIAN, Jean Pierre Claris de (1755–95) wrote epistles in verse, comedies, and romantic tales; but all that survives of his work is a selection from his Fables printed in school texts. He is said to have made a commendable translation of *Don Quixote*.

FORGUES, Paul Emile D. (1813–83) had the second most *angliche* pseudonym in the world: he called himself "Oldnick." (The winner is Jouvet's fellow actor, M. Jim Gerald's—apostrophe and all.) Hail to Forgues! He was of the tribe of translators and is therefore forgotten. The man who translated into French the writings of Borrow, O. W. Holmes, Wilkie Collins, Mrs Gaskell, Goldsmith, Mrs Radcliffe, Macaulay, is totally forgotten!

FOULD, Achille, (1800–67) four times minister for finance under Napoleon III, was a Jewish banker who welcomed the coup d'état and the Second Empire, opposed free trade, and displayed himself a careful manager of the nation's finances and an art collector of much taste. Among the objects he collected was an old guitar, sold to him by his *co-religionnaire,* Rachel, for 20,000 francs, after she had told him that she could not bear to part with it because it was with this same instrument that she had begged in the streets, as a child. The broken and useless instrument, in truth, had been spied by the tragedienne in a friend's house not long before and brought home to bait the very trap Fould fell into.

FOURNIER, Édouard. (1819–80) got through an enormous amount of work as critic, composer of comedies in verse, editor of seventeenth and eighteenth century texts, and historian of innkeeping, street lighting through the centuries, etc., etc.

FROMENTIN, Eugène. (1820–76) was a dexterous and brilliant painter of the African scene and desert who wrote two masterpieces —a study of the Dutch painters (*Les Maîtres d'autrefois*) and *Dominique,* an autobiographical novel, one of those breviaries in which youth—French youth, at any rate—seeks to recognize itself and to learn the truth about its experience of ideal love in adolescence.

GALIANI, Ferdinand (1728–87) was an economist and wit who wrote a treatise on money which displayed him to be a member of the mercantilist school. He made his reputation with a book he wrote in French under the title *Dialogues sur le commerce des blés.* Voltaire was one of those he delighted. In addition to his *Correspondance,* which was published in 1818, reference is made by biographers to a series of parodies of Neapolitan writers which were much appreciated in their day in Italy.

GALLIERA, Marie, Duchess, (1812–88) the daughter of a Sardinian nobleman, married Rafael Ferrari, a railway contractor upon whom the Pope conferred the title Duke Galliera. She was a sort of Lady Houston of her day; her public bequests were enormous, as befitted a contractor's wife in the great age of railway building.

GANEAU, whose widow the Goncourts found at Gautier's table, was decidedly a card. From gambler and dandy, he became a phrenologist *très à la mode,* a fantastic feminist, and finally *Le Mapah.* His feministic doctrine was called *Èvadisme* (from *Ève-Adam*),

[318]

which was intended to signify perfect equality of the sexes. His personal designation was a contraction of the words *maman-papa.* To Pope Gregory XVI he wrote a manifesto dated "from our apostolic pallet, this first day of the first year of the Era of Evadah" in which His Holiness was notified that the Papacy had run its course and that it was he, The Mapah, who was called to take the place of the Sovereign Pontiff. This done, he sent off a note to Victor Hugo, inviting him to become Deputy God. He wore a sort of Armenian costume, printed and distributed his apostolic pronouncements, and seems to have been a fascinating talker. Influenced by Louis Blanc and Félix Pyat, he exchanged his magician's robe for a workman's smock, and during the Revolution of 1848 his handsome beard waved in the storm over the barricades. His sort is to be found among the minor characters of Flaubert's most beautiful novel, *L'Éducation sentimentale;* he himself figures in the recently unearthed *Mémoires* of Théophile Thoré, published in 1935 in the *Nouvelle Revue Retrospective.*

GATAYES, Joseph Léon, (1805–77) one of the great harpists of Europe, a first-rate writer on music questions, and sporting correspondent for a number of newspapers.

GAUTIER, Théophile (1811–72) was one of the youngest of the Romantics who met on Sundays at Charles Nodier's and called themselves *Le Cénacle.* By all odds the most attractive figure in these diaries, he did everything flawlessly within the limited emotional compass of his temperament. We may say of him what Gibbon wrote of one of his emperors: "In every art that he attempted, his lively genius enabled him to succeed." His *Émaux et camées* are poems which, in their fluidity and chiselled perfection, have not been surpassed; his studies of seventeenth century writers (*Les Grotesques*) repay reading; his short stories rank with Mérimée's; his voluptuous and picaresque novels, *Mademoiselle de Maupin* and *Le Capitaine Fracasse,* are the best of their kind; he was unapproached as *feuilleton* writer and he wrote some of the liveliest of all travel books; his scholarship, as well in Egyptology as in French literature, has been admired by the learned; Balzac went out of his way, in *Une fille d'Ève,* to call him *un des plus remarquables poètes de ce temps* and to quote from his work.

Gibbon, on his emperor, continues: "But, as his genius was destitute of judgment, he attempted every art except the important ones of war and government." Gautier, it is true, possessed judgment; but his indifference to everything except plastic beauty, while it makes him infinitely sympathetic as artist, also has the result of making the reader more indifferent to his writings than one should be in the presence of an artist of the first rank.

GAVARNI was the name signed to his drawings and lithographs by Sulpice Guillaume Chevalier (1804–66), the wittiest and most mordant satirist of the reign of Louis Philippe, and among satirists one of the most gifted artists of Europe. He was as popular as he was gifted, and a vignette, a single sketch, by Gavarni in a new book sufficed to sell it. A keen intelligence and a wide culture—not merely a skilful pen—made him an apt and at times a powerful illustrator of the works of Balzac, Eugène Sue, E. T. A. Hoffmann, and many others. Lucky the man who possesses old copies of *Charivari* or *La Mode* that contain his work. Incidentally, there is one of Gavarni's drawings that reproduces most faithfully the atmosphere and the tone of voice in which Gautier so frequently pronounced that horrid word *bourgeois:* it shows a man in rags leaning against a lamppost, smoking a pipe, and, near by, a middle-class couple on their Sunday stroll. "Bounder!" exclaims the burgher as he receives a cloud of pipe smoke in the face. "Bounder I may be," the fellow retorts; "but at least I am not a grocer." (For more on the *bourgeoisie,* see Guizot, infra.)

GENLIS, Stéphanie Félicité, Countess de, (1746–1830) became lady in waiting to the Duchess of Chartres in 1770 and was governess first of her daughters and then of her sons. Possessing ingenious notions of education, she developed them for the benefit of the royal children in a series of volumes which included comedies specially written for purposes of instruction. She used magic-lantern slides to teach history and employed a trained botanist to explain vegetable life to her charges on their walks. Mme de Genlis wrote a long series of historical romances, as well as a clever volume, *Les Dîners du Baron d'Holbach,* directed against the *philosophes.* Talleyrand said of her that in her day she surrendered instantly to the men who courted her, because she did not wish to be thought a coquette.

GIRARDIN, Émile de (1802–81) was the by-blow of General Alexandre de Girardin and a Mme Dupuy, wife of a Paris advocate.

More than half a century before Northcliffe, he inaugurated the penny press, published an *Almanach de France* in a million copies, and had several hundred thousand subscribers to his "useful knowledge" paper at four francs per annum and his *Journal des Instituteurs primaires* at one franc fifty a year. The book mentioned on p. 116, *Questions de mon temps,* was one of a series of volumes which Girardin published under this title, made up of pieces written for his papers. He was practically alone in his silly clamour, in 1869, that France must have the left bank of the Rhine, even if it meant "giving Europe a bath of blood."

GIRAUD, Charles Joseph Barthélemy, (1802–81) the Goncourts' "old Giraud of the Institut de France", had an honourable career as university professor and administrator and was for a short time minister of public instruction in 1851. He refused to lend his support to the dictator after December 1851 and was not molested; indeed, he was made dean of the political science faculty. He wrote much on Roman and early French law, and a great deal on literature and history.

GIRAUD, Eugène, (1806–81) the familiar of Princess Mathilde and her neighbour at Saint-Gratien, is said to have been a better engraver than painter.

GLEYRE, Marc Charles Gabriel, (1806–74) the painter in whose company the Goncourts heard a reading by Flaubert of *Salammbô,* was of Swiss origin, travelled in the Near East, and composed somewhat "literary" pictures. Among his pupils were Renoir, Monet, and Sisley.

GRAMONT–CADEROUSSE, whom the diarists saw at the theatre in the company of Marguerite Bellanger, the emperor's mistress and mother of a child by him, was a son of the Duke de Gramont-Caderousse. He seems to have led a pretty wild life after dark in Paris, and eventually exiled himself to the Orient, where he died. (Dans l'Orient désert quel devint mon ennui!) He left his fortune to a Paris doctor and a fashionable actress, a circumstance which gave rise to an entertainingly scandalous lawsuit.

GRANGÉ, Eugène, (1810–87) produced a stream of dramas, farces, comedies, and libretti in the course of nearly half a century of writing, all of which, and his name with it, are completely forgotten.

GRASSOT, Jean Antoine (1800–60) was the favourite comic actor of the day—a skinny, bony-faced, hoarse-voiced eccentric. Was it his wife, or his daughter, who had that wonderful imperfect of the subjunctive to use in a line in which, discharging a servant in I forget whose play, she complains, "Et puis, vous dévoriez notre sucre sans que nous le sussions!"

GUÉRIN, Maurice de (1810–39) was educated for the Church and would undoubtedly have taken Holy Orders had he not attached himself to Lamennais (q.v. infra) and been discouraged by the episcopal displeasure which fell upon that undisciplined genius. After his premature death George Sand arranged for the publication in the *Revue des Deux Mondes* of *Le Centaure* and *La Bacchante,* two short prose works in which the poignancy of a deeply sensitive and pantheistic nature is conveyed in language of great purity. There is a mood in which this sort of thing can be extremely moving. It is usual to mention with him his sister Eugénie, who left letters and a diary of an elevated tone that are the subject of an essay by Matthew Arnold.

GUICHARD, Victor (1803–84) was a politician against whom nothing was ever said. As rare as Nerva among the Roman emperors.

GUIZOT, François (1784–1874) had a great career as historian and as politician; but whereas in the first rôle he is admired by the learned, in the second he is remembered without great esteem. Nevertheless, he ruled France in the 1840's, and his name belongs to history. Of Protestant origin, a "Doctrinaire" (see Royer-Collard, infra) demanding a constitution (but a strong king), a liberty-loving people (but an obedient one), he was one of the most determined foes of democracy in Europe and one of the most unpopular men in the history of French politics. If the reader will reflect that the 1840's were an era of industrious, insolent, pious, "get-rich-quick" speculators, stone deaf to the genuine and increasing grievances of a growing proletariat, and that Guizot was the leader of this section of the middle classes, he will have a good notion of the public figure he cut. Privately, as his correspondence with Mme Laure de Gasparin reveals, he was capable of affection and expansiveness, and even displayed on occasion a bucolic nature totally at variance with his public evidences of invariable severity, insensibility, and an almost fanatical conviction that he alone possessed the truth. All very Protestant, if I may be allowed to say so. Scholars owe him a great debt for his editing of the *Documents inédits sur l'histoire de France* in emulation of the colossal *Monumenta Germaniae Historica;* and he wrote histories of the rebellion in England and of civilization in Europe—which Taine characterized as lifeless and Sainte-Beuve as lacking in *"la vibration populaire",* though others have called them "classics of historical research." In his younger years he translated Gibbon.

GUYS, Constantin, (1805–92) born in Holland, drew life under the Second Empire—and particularly the life of fashion—most charmingly and was the subject of one of those penetrating and appreciative essays which Baudelaire wrote on a number of his contemporaries who were despised by the then Academy and are pointed to as respectable models by the Academy of today—Delacroix, for example. Incidentally, Baudelaire says that Thackeray *"parla un jour de M. Guys dans un petit journal de Londres";* Guys, despising publicity, *"s'en fâcha comme d'un outrage à sa pudeur."*

HALÉVY, Ludovic, (1834–1908) a member of a distinguished French-Jewish family, practised every branch of writing without much success until he met Henri Meilhac (1831–97) and began that collaboration which gave France and Europe, in the 1860's, those delightful and imaginative satires: *La Belle Hélène, Barbe Bleue, La Grande Duchesse de Gérolstein,* and *La Périchole.* Later, Halévy wrote alone two entertaining fictions on the "Cardinal family", as well as that French "Vicar of Wakefield", *L'Abbé Constantin.*

HÉBERT, Antoine Auguste Ernest, whom the Goncourts saw so frequently at the Princess Mathilde's, was born in 1817 and sent paintings to successive Salons from 1839 onward.

HÉBERT, Jacques René, (1757–94) was lucky to live as long as he did. This notorious journalist of the Great Revolution—for in France one must distinguish between revolutions—was a violent advocate and supporter of the massacres of September 1792 and exercised for a time enormous influence. (For a specimen of his style see the footnote on p. 127, supra.) When he tried to organize a "worship-of-reason" movement against Robespierre's theism, he and his partisans were arrested and guillotined.

HEINE, Heinrich (1797–1856) need not be discussed here as poet. He turned up in Paris after the July Revolution of 1830 and became thereafter Henri Heine, French journalist and essayist, supported out of the secret funds of both the Thiers and the Guizot ministries, supplemented by occasional help from his family and stock-market tips from Rothschild. ("J'ai assez de gloire," he wrote, "pour pouvoir perdre un peu d'honneur.") In 1835 he warned the French against the Germans in these terms: "I advise that you be on your guard. Whatever happens in Germany, whether it is the Prince of Prussia or Dr Wirth who comes into power, see that you are armed, stay at your post, musket in hand. I wish France well, and I was seized with fear the other day when I heard that your ministers intended to disarm France." And this friend of Marx and of Lassalle wrote also: "When the terrible wheel begins to turn, we shall see emerge, this time, the most frightful of all the antagonists that have ever attacked the reigning order. . . . Communism is the name of this terrible antagonist, [of this] sombre hero to whom will fall the great role in the tragedy of modern times." Balzac wrote of "the great and powerful Heine." Sainte-Beuve, despite his private opinion, said that Frenchmen should "love him as one of our most fervent and outspoken allies." Of himself, Heine wrote: "What am I? A plate of sauerkraut into which there has fallen a bit of ambrosia." Concerning his chances of immortality, he had this to say: "Wit is only momentarily amusing. Posterity, which is the judge of the literature of an era, will lend small importance to Monsieur Heine, but will rather award the laurels—and properly so—to those men of character and principle who inculcate into the younger generation the love of country and of duty. Talent passes; character remains." (Cp. Goethe: Es bildet ein Talent sich in der Stille, Sich ein Charakter in dem Strom der Welt.) It appears that Heine could be a bad prophet, as well as a good one.

HERZEN, Alexander Ivanovich (1812–70) is best known for his valuable and extremely interesting memoirs. Under the timorous despotism of Nicholas I he was arrested and condemned to five years in Siberia on suspicion of being acquainted with certain university students who had been guilty of singing a political ditty against the régime. Sentence was commuted, but it was not until 1842 that he was allowed to reside again in Moscow. By then he had begun to write and publish critical work in a review edited by the leading

Russian critic, Bielinsky. Those who have written about him say that it is in his short stories that Herzen's concern with social reform, as well as his literary gifts, are best seen. Following the death of his father, he was allowed to travel abroad, and he left Russia in January 1847. The next year found him an excited and enthusiastic spectator of the wave of revolution that swept over Europe. In Paris he became an independent republican, contributing to the Left press of the time. Summoned by the court to return to Russia, he refused, and the estates he had inherited from his father were confiscated. He was driven out of France by the authoritarian government of Napoleon III and went to Switzerland, where he became a citizen of the Confederation and devoted his life to revolutionary propaganda until his death in 1870. It is clear from his memoirs that he was an individualist and a liberal, the enemy of violence and of all forms of doctrine.

HOLBACH, Paul, Baron d', (1723–89) born in Germany of an obscure family but with a great fortune, is remembered as the host of Diderot, D'Alembert, Buffon, Condillac, Turgot, Helvétius, the brothers Grimm, Hume, Garrick, Sterne, and in general the *philosophes* and wits of the middle of the eighteenth century. He was a conscientious materialist with that fervent faith in science which is repeatedly mistaken for scepticism. An upright man and loyal friend, he is said to be the model of Rousseau's virtuous atheist, Wolmar, in *La Nouvelle Héloïse*.

HOUSSAYE, Arsène (1815–96) wrote novels, art criticism, historical sketches, literary criticism, etc., etc.—in short, he was a journalist: had he lived in 1915 he would have written on strategy and tactics; in 1930, on the gold standard. Like many men of letters since his time, he was managing director of the Théâtre-Français (commonly called the Comédie-Française), an appointment he obtained through the influence of the actress Rachel.

JANIN, Jules (1804–74) was a great force in his day. He wrote now-forgotten novels which had a certain influence upon Jules, though not upon Edmond, de Goncourt. His career was, in the main, that of critic of literature and of the theatre, but the subjects of his "copy" were a matter of indifference to him, and it was apparently only in his verve that his readers were interested. Janin, travelling in Italy, bought a lottery ticket and won a country house near Lucca.

JOSEPH II, (1741–90) to whom Sainte-Beuve refers approvingly on p. 137, is one of the most instructive figures of history. The eldest son and greatest trial of the pious and strong-minded Empress Maria Theresa, succeeding her on the throne of the Holy Roman Empire, he was a close student of Voltaire and the Encyclopaedists, a bitter enemy to the Jesuits and generous friend to religious tolerance, and a passionate believer in the reasonableness of his own reason, in his personal power to give his people happiness. Once on the throne he went the whole hog—emancipation of the peasantry; secularization of the Church; submission of the clergy to the state; spread of free education; and all of this, undertaken simultaneously, combined to produce unrest, chaos and bewilderment throughout his lands. In foreign affairs he displayed a clumsiness which offended all his royal neighbours, and his great minister, Kaunitz, refused for two years even to see the emperor. This enlightened and desperately well-meaning autocrat died an unhappy, disappointed and embittered reactionary, leaving no children. But Vienna, in his day, with Haydn, Mozart, Metastasio, and the Prince de Ligne among its adornments, must have been an enchantment.

JOUBERT, Joseph (1754–1824) was a civil servant who published nothing in his lifetime but left a collection of papers which his executor, Chateaubriand, brought together under the title *Pensées*. The book proved that he spoke only a fraction of the truth when he said of himself, "Like Montaigne, I am incapable of sustained discourse." This is the sort of thing he was epigrammatic about: "Reason can make us temperate; piety alone can make us chaste." For myself, I prefer a sentence in his private correspondence, written upon the death of Pauline de Beaumont, whom he loved and who loved Chateaubriand: "I shall say nothing to you of my sorrow: it is not extravagant, but it will be eternal." He loved books, particularly small ones: Paul de Raynal found him one day in his library, a waxed glove on one hand, polishing an Elzevir. Matthew Arnold wrote of him with high regard in the first series of the *Essays in Criticism*.

KARR, Alphonse (1808–90) was a critic, pamphleteer, novelist, editor of *Le Figaro*. To him is attributed the first utterance of the phrase, Plus ça change, plus c'est la même chose, and it was he whose comment on a proposal for the abolition of capital punishment was, "Je veux bien que messieurs les assassins commencent." Like A. B.

Walkley or Churton Collins (to mix the *genres*) in England, or like William Winter or Frank Moore Colby in America, the Karrs, the Janins, the Aurélien Scholls make a great noise in their day and achieve no place in history.

KOCK, Charles-Paul de, (1793–1871) the son of a Dutch banker established in Paris, was the most widely read novelist in Europe during the 1820's and 1830's. Major Pendennis remarked that he had not read a novel in thirty years, "except Paul de Kock," and Karl Marx read him avidly. His novels, which contain wonderful pictures of lower middle-class life in Paris a century ago, in particular of the shopkeeper's life, were sold in England and America under the cloak, as pornography; and in Ireland Mrs Leopold Bloom ran her tongue over her lips when, hearing his name, she thought of the stuff he doubtless wrote. His collected works were published in ninety-seven volumes.

LABICHE, Eugène. (1815–88) advanced from the writing of broad farce into the domain of comedy with a series of plays in which shrewd observation and fertile invention (his own and that of his many collaborators) won him a deservedly large following. That school text, *Le Voyage de M. Perrichon,* is his.

LA BRUYÈRE, Jean de (1645–96) became tutor to the Duke de Bourbon, grandson of the great Condé, on the recommendation of Bossuet. This sage and unprepossessing young man, of whom Boileau said that he "would be lacking in nothing if nature had made him as attractive as he would like to be", translated Theophrastus and wrote *Les Caractères ou les Moeurs de ce siècle,* a series of reflections interspersed with "characters" which Gide deems the "most French" of all books. A number of contemporaries saw or professed to see themselves in certain of the sketches, in consequence of which their author was honoured by some very distinguished enmities—and his accession to a seat in the Academy was for a number of years delayed.

La Bruyère's book is composed of paragraphs and not of formally elaborated essays, but this does not by any means signify that he is merely one of the writers of maxims and *pensées* in the line that goes from La Rochefoucauld to Chamfort, Rivarol, and the court wits. This admirable writer (who reformed French prose, tightening the language and making it crisp and incisive where it was once discursive and meandering) was a precursor of Montesquieu, of Voltaire, of Diderot, a critic of society even more than an analyst of types or a dissector of human motives. And yet there is in everything he wrote such penetration, such accuracy of delineation, such elevation without priggishness, that had he written only of the human psyche, he would still make the flawless La Rochefoucauld seem a little too much the man of the world, and the moving and eloquent Pascal himself a little too fevered. He will not seduce as does La Rochefoucauld by the extreme polish of the *Maximes,* nor enrapture with the Pauline mingling of metaphor and dialectic to be found in the *Pensées.* He is French sense, French realism, French reflection upon the world immediately round him; and as he does not know how to be extravagant, there are many passages in his book which will seem commonplace when read as men normally read—with a wandering mind.

Compare La Bruyère with the psychoanalysts of the inferiority-feeling school: they arrive two hundred and fifty years late, know no more than he knew, and are still without his reasonableness because of their confinement in the clinic and ignorance of society:

> Our vanity, and the excessive esteem in which we hold ourselves, make us suspect in others a hauteur towards ourselves which sometimes is there and often is not. Modest people do not possess this delicacy of feeling.

> Even as we must defend ourselves against that vanity which makes us imagine that others look at us with interest and talk to each other only about our merits and in order to sing our praises, so we must possess that certain confidence which shall prevent us from believing that they murmur into each other's ears only in order to speak ill of us, or laugh together only to ridicule us.

His chapters on The Court, on Woman, on Conversation, wonderful though they are, are still what one would expect to come out of the second half of the seventeenth century in France. Where La Bruyère is truly powerful and original, is a precursor, is in such chapters as those on Riches and on The Sovereign. A reader of the twenty or twenty-five pages on riches and those who gain them, is bound to be constantly astonished, not only by what La Bruyère says, but because the mere fact that he has these things to say tells us something about the seventeenth century which no historian is able to make real for us. One knew there were rich men in the France of

Louis XIV, but one saw them bewigged and feudal, mitred and ducal, not in the semblance of the company director that this suggests:

> What with making new contracts and seeing one's money pile up in the strong-box, one ends by believing oneself intelligent and quite capable of governing.

Anybody can philosophize (as it is called) about the rich and the poor; but only a philosopher finds the enriched man an object of curiosity.

> It wants a sort of mind to get rich, and especially very rich: not a good mind nor a fine one; not a great, not a sublime, not a powerful nor yet a fastidious mind. I do not know exactly what sort of mind is wanted, and I am still waiting for some one to teach me.

> Not so much intelligence as habit, or experience, is wanted to make oneself rich. One thinks of it too late, and when at last one determines to do it, one begins by making mistakes which one has not always the time to repair—and that, perhaps, explains why fortunes are so rare.

No less pertinent to our times is the chapter on sovereignty:

> There is no fatherland under a despotism. Other things take its place —self-interest, glory, the service of the prince.

> What boots it that the Prince place the boundary-stones of his empire beyond the lands of his enemies, making of their realms the provinces of his kingdom; that he be happy and showered with glory and my country powerful and redoubtable; if, sad and disquieted, I live in oppression or in indigence; if, in the horror of night, I have less fear of marauders and assassins in the tangled forests than at the crossroads of the town; if, weak and alone on my farm, I am forced to suffer from the presence of a neighbouring lord. . . .

Thus, directly as well as indirectly, La Bruyère showed the way to those who were to be known as the *philosophes* and who were, by the power of ideas, to make men of a peasantry he described in this unforgettable and hardly translatable dry point:

> L'on voit certains animaux farouches, des mâles et des femelles, répandus par la campagne, noirs, livides, et tout brûlés de soleil, attachés à la terre qu'ils fouillent et qu'ils remuent avec une opiniâtreté invincible; ils ont comme une voix articulée, et quand ils se lèvent sur leur pieds ils montrent une face humaine, et en effet ils sont des hommes.

Ils se retirent la nuit dans des tanières, où ils vivent de pain noir, d'eau et de racines; ils épargnent aux autres hommes la peine de semer, de labourer et de recueillir pour vivre, et méritent ainsi de ne pas manquer de ce pain qu'ils ont semé. . . .

If one were asked whether such writing had its uses, one might reply that La Bruyère wrote in the seventeenth century, while a Herzen or a Turgenieff wrote a century and a half later, in the 1840's; and that this is the measure of the distance between the status of the French peasant and that of the Russian serf by the time the year 1840 had come round.

I find it hard to stop quoting my author, but with this paragraph I take leave of him:

> It must be confessed, the present is for the rich and the future for the virtuous and the talented. Homer exists and will remain: the tax farmers, the Party men, the publicans, are no more. What has become of those important personages who despised Homer, who sought only to avoid him on the public square or returned not his greeting, who deigned not to ask him to meat and saw in him a man who was not rich and was writing a book?

It is the luck of the French that *Les Caractères* happens to be a work which the Ministry of Education takes seriously and school children are obliged to study.

LAMARTINE, Alphonse de (1790–1869) preceded the generations of Romantic poets by ten years or so, an interval sufficient, perhaps, to explain why, romantic though his poetry is, it does not belong to the fake-Gothic, chromo-historical, *révolté* school but rather participates in the bucolic and innocent sentimentalism of the *Hermann und Dorothea* sort of thing. He travelled widely, wrote a great quantity of prose (both tales and histories) and was for a time in the diplomatic service. Drifting into politics, he found himself momentarily at the head of affairs during the Revolution of 1848, which he had the bad taste and worse judgment to call a "servile" revolt—a word he applied to people who, in their material misery, still raised on the barricades placards that read, *"Respect aux propriétés, mort aux voleurs!"* What *do* such people as Lamartine want of the plebe? Anything rather than self-respect, seemingly.

LAMENNAIS, Robert de (1782–1854) received the tonsure in 1811 and early concerned himself with the religious regeneration of

France. His *Essai sur l'indifférence en matière de religion,* published in 1817, one year after his ordination, affected Europe as no work on religion had done in a century. It denounced toleration and the right of private judgment and advocated a Catholic restoration of belief. But Lamennais was born to be *"mal vu à l'archevêché"* and even this first volume of a work continued in three others, displayed a stubborn individualism repugnant to the doctors of the Church. Active in politics, first with the reactionary minister Villèle, and later with Chateaubriand, Lacordaire and Montalembert, Lamennais moved away from the Royalist party and dreamed of a theocratic democracy. He was condemned in the encyclical, *Mirari vos,* in 1832; his newspaper, *L'Avenir,* ceased to appear; and his propaganda organization, *L'Agence générale pour la défense de la liberté religieuse,* with its network of denunciators, was broken up. Having now the entire Church against him, the harassed and fervent idealist published his *apologia,* the *Paroles d'un croyant,* of which the Pope said it was "a book small in size but immense in its perversity." Thereafter, Lamennais conceived of himself as the apostle of the people: he endured imprisonment, became the collaborator of the Socialist Louis Blanc, and the path he followed led to Communism.

LA ROUNAT, Charles Rouvenat de, (1818–84) a left-wing republican in the Revolution of 1848, turned producer of farces and finally became manager of the Odéon Theatre, where he put on plays by Augier, About, George Sand, et al.

LAVALÉE, Théodore, (1804–66) in his day a distinguished geographer and historian.

LAYA, Léon, (1811–72) playwright and son of a playwright, wrote a long list of comedies and dramatic works which were brilliantly successful—say as Noel Coward or George Kaufman is successful. He committed suicide.

LAZOVSKI, Claude, dubbed *"Le Foudroyant"*—literally, the hurler of thunderbolts—was a savage leader in the massacres of September 2–4, 1792, when some thousand people incarcerated in the several prisons of Paris were guillotined, including three hundred priests, fifty members of the King's Guard, and the Princess Lamballe, a devoted friend of Marie Antoinette. Lazovski was particularly notorious for his attack upon the Sulpician Seminary at Issy, where Talleyrand had been put to school and where, later, Renan was to be educated for the priesthood.

LEBRUN, Pierre Antoine (1785–1873) wrote odes in celebration of the victorious armies of Napoleon I and a play called *Marie Stuart* which still forms part, it is said, of the repertory of the Comédie-Française. He was a member of the French Academy, a senator, a peer of France, etc. Not to be confused with the poet Écouchard Lebrun, who wrote:

> On vient de me voler!—Que je plains ton malheur!
> Tous mes vers manuscrits!—Que je plains le voleur!

LECOMTE, Jules François (1814–64) was a naval officer turned publisher of maritime reviews and finally man of letters (criticism, plays of course, historical works, and novels, one of which was happily entitled *Les Smoglers*).

LEFEBVRE DE BÉHAINE, Armand Édouard, (1807–64) a cousin of the Goncourts, was the son of a Napoleonic general, a career diplomatist, and author of a *History of European Cabinets during the Consulate and the Empire.*

LEMAÎTRE, Frédérick, (1800–76) a boulevard actor who was as highly praised in his day as, say, Charles Laughton in ours. Even Heine called him "a sublime mummer", though when he played London *The Times* of January 19, 1835 was less kind to him: "He is by no means a good actor . . . but he is clever, and although coarse, is striking . . . too gross for our notions of theatrical decency" but his acting "gave a kind of rage to the performance."

LENCLOS, Ninon de, (1615–1705) the daughter of a gentleman, was the centre of the most fashionable and unconventional society of the seventeenth century. Among her lovers were Gaspard de Coligny, the great Condé, La Rochefoucauld, and Saint-Évremond. Queen Christina of Sweden called on her; Anne of Austria, widow of Louis XIII, was powerless against her. Among the friends of her later years were Mme de La Fayette (author of one of the gems of European literature, *La Princesse de Clèves*) and La Maintenon. Voltaire was presented to her as a boy and was left by her 2,000 livres with which to buy books. Her letters to Saint-Évremond and the testimony of many of her contemporaries bear witness to a charming mind and a civilized affability of nature. Among the apocryphal stories about her is that she put off an importunate and acceptable lover until—out of a coquetry understandable in the circumstances—her eightieth birthday.

LIA, see Félix.

LIGNE, Charles Joseph, Prince de (1735–1814) seems to have been the best-liked man of his time. He was an intimate friend and counsellor of Joseph II of Austria and of Catherine II of Russia, and he distinguished himself in the Seven Years' War as a soldier and in most of the European capitals as a man of the world and of scholarly attainments. It was he who said of the Congress of Vienna, "Le Congrès danse, mais ne marche pas," thus furnishing a title to the movies. He was a patron, in Casanova's cranky old age, of that bright, amiable charlatan and trustworthy historian of eighteenth-century society, and was uncle to that Waldstein whom Casanova served as librarian at Dux.

LITTRÉ, Émile (1801–81) edited the works of Hippocrates, translated a whole chant out of the *Iliad* into thirteenth-century French verse, compiled a dictionary of medicine, and produced French versions of Dante, Schiller and Strauss's once-scandalous *Life of Jesus,* among other writings, before he began work in the 1840's on his monumental *Dictionnaire de la langue française.* He framed as follows the rule by which he guided himself in this work: "To guess at nothing; to know nothing intuitively and by anticipation, as it were; to constrain myself to learn everything that the work demands." Perhaps what distinguishes men of affairs from men of learning is their incapacity for a becoming humility.

LOUIS XVII, second son of Louis XVI and Marie Antoinette, was born in 1785 and imprisoned with his parents and their immediate entourage on the tenth of August 1792. Their prison was the Temple, a structure built in the twelfth century by the Knights Templar, torn down in 1811 after long serving as a monastery. He was kept in prison after his parents were beheaded (on the twenty-first of July, 1793) and was proclaimed titular king of France by the émigrés.

Visited from time to time (by Barras in July 1794; by Commissioners representing the Committee of Public Safety in December 1794), it was reported in May 1795 that he had fallen ill, and on the eighth of June 1795 the report was given out that he had died. In the years that followed, there sprang up the legend that it was not he but another child who had died and been buried; that he had been rescued and was still alive. At various times between 1815 and 1830 some forty pretenders presented themselves, each with a more ingenious story than the last. The mystery was sufficiently absorbing to engage some people's interest for many years, and as lately as in 1905 a monthly review was founded in Paris called *Revue historique de la question Louis XVII*. Having no Shakespeare-Bacon game to amuse them, and being inapt for the fascination of such elevated intellectual problems as what became of the Lost Tribes of Israel, the poor French have to fall back upon vanished dauphins and mythical men in iron masks.

LOUIS PHILIPPE, (1773–1850) king of the French from 1830 to 1848, was seen by Mrs Trollope in 1835 strolling on the boulevard des Italiens with an umbrella under his arm, two commonly dressed men walking at a little distance behind him. Her astonishment (and feeling of superiority) can only be compared to that of Walter Map, the twelfth-century English bishop, when he saw the simplicity that surrounded Louis VII and heard the monarch say, "We at the French court have only bread and wine and gaiety." In 1848 Louis Philippe refused to hear what was rumbling outside his windows and persisted in limiting his reading to *The Times,* a habit he had formed during his years of exile. Summoned to surrender his throne, he spoke these sublime words: "I shall never abdicate—at least not until I have consulted my wife." An amiable gentleman, and in his youth a valiant soldier of France.

MAINTENON, Françoise d'Aubigné, Marquise de, (1635–1719) widow of the comic writer Scarron, governess to the king's get by Mme de Montespan, morganatic wife of Louis XIV from 1685 to his death in 1715, is by all odds the most unbearable woman in French history. It is not that she lacked qualities. Her language was pondered and pious; her care of her charges was unremitting and must have been skilful, since both the Duke du Maine and Mlle de Nantes loved her; doubtless she had a kind of character, for she was able to persist in favour without an unbecoming show of either eagerness or servility; the king, at any rate, believed she had judgment, for he would ask what "your solidity" thought about matters of state; she must have had an air of distinction, as well as a powerful will, else the king had not married her. But there is in her no trace of kindness, no gentleness, no grasp of the affairs in which she meddled, no ardour except the flame of ambition, no passion other than to dominate. She taught the half-royal children nothing, and the wards she later gathered together at Saint-Cyr turned out, on the whole, no better than the bastards. There seems to be no question but that in public affairs she was as irresolute as she was persistently intrusive, and as dangerous to the peace of the realm as she was influential. "Liselotte," the king's sister-in-law, that Duchess of Orleans who was called "Madame Palatine" because her father was the Bavarian Elector, wrote of the Protestant-born Maintenon as follows: "Before the old girl came into power the French Church was very moderate. She it was who ruined everything. When reasonable men appeared, the old girl and the [king's] confessor had them imprisoned or—not poisoned, there is no need to exaggerate—or exiled. These two are the cause of all the persecutions [of the Protestants]. Father La Chaise, with his long ears, began the beautiful job, and Father Tellier finished it. In every way possible, this is what has ruined France."

Mme Palatine was "the old girl's" enemy; but Mme de Maintenon is one of those figures of history who cannot show a friend, and the best that can be said for her is that as calculation, as an example of a career deliberately carved out by power of ruse and will, her emergence from a dubious domestic rank and rise to the conjugal bed and council chamber of the then greatest king in Europe, is a masterpiece. The revocation of the Edict of Nantes was only one of its repellent and immeasurably costly achievements.

MALTHUS, Thomas Robert, (1766–1834) who argued in his *Essay on the Principle of Population* that misery must result from the tendency of the population to increase faster than the means of subsistence, has endowed the world with an adjective which, like Machiavellian or Jesuitical, may seemingly be used in any context whatever. E.g., the writer of the Money Market leader in the *Statist* of January 20, 1937, speaks of "The old fear of somewhat Malthusian character that the discovery of new gold was bound to lag behind the rate of normal economic development . . ." It was in Malthus, incidentally, that Darwin found that useful phrase, "the struggle for existence."

MANTZ, Paul, (1821–89) for a time on the staff of *Le Temps,* wrote well-documented art criticism and a history of the French goldsmiths' craft, and collaborated with Eudore Soulié in the editing of eighteenth century memoirs. His *Holbein* and his *Boucher* are said to be authoritative monographs.

MARAT, Jean Paul, (1743–93) of Sardinian extraction, studied medicine and optics and practised in London after obtaining an M. D. from St Andrews. He wrote, in English, a *Philosophical Essay on Order* which, one of his biographers says, displays a remarkable acquaintance with European philosophy. Returning to France, Marat became eye specialist to the court and carried out experiments that enchanted Benjamin Franklin, who used often to visit him. He was known to Goethe and translated Newton's *Optics.* Politics began to interest him only as late as 1788, but in 1789 he founded his celebrated paper, *L'Ami du Peuple,* and launched himself on the sea of the Revolution, which he was to do a good deal to make blood red. Never joining club or party, an object of suspicion to them all, frequently denounced, Marat was often in hiding in the Paris sewers. From the first, he hammered away at the moderate Girondins, refusing to hear of a foreign war as something which would merely bring about the invasion of France by foreign anti-revolutionary powers and the reaffirmation of the Bourbons on the French throne. At the same time, when Louis XVI was on trial, he defended the king's advocate, Malesherbes, as a *"sage et respectable vieillard."* His Girondin enemies almost got him on the score of his part in the awful September massacres, but he had by then become the idol of the Parisian populace, who drove them to take refuge in Normandy. Suffering from a serious skin disease, he was sitting in his medicated bath when a girl was admitted to him on pretext that she had urgent news from Caen, where the escaped Girondins were trying to rouse Normandy against Paris. That girl, Charlotte Corday, stabbed him to the heart.

MARCHAL, Charles François (1826–77) hung a picture in the Salon of 1852 and became a popular painter of Alsatian scenes, though almost totally devoid of talent.

MARCHANGY, Louis Antoine François de, (1782–1826) chief prosecuting attorney under the Restoration, a violently eloquent advocate, pursued the *Charbonnerie* (republican emulators, in France, of the Italian Carbonari) and obtained the conviction of the four sergeants of La Rochelle (p. 152). His extreme and denunciatory pleadings won him such fierce hatred in the country that the government was after a time unable to employ him in the courts.

MARGUERITE of Navarre, more properly Marguerite of Angoulême, (1492–1549), married first Charles, Duke of Alençon and then, after her widowhood, Henri d'Albret, titular King of Navarre. She was, in her day, the chief patroness of French letters (Rabelais and Clément Marot were among those she protected) and the principal refuge and defender of the Protestants. To Marguerite is attributed the *Heptameron,* which may have been the joint product of this great and generous woman's entourage. She was passionately devoted to her brother, François Ier, and wrote a moving and eloquent poem, *Le Navire,* on his death.

MARIE ANTOINETTE, in the matter of the Necklace (p. 147). The Affair of the Necklace (1784–86) is a mystery about which everybody knows something, but nobody, seemingly, knows the truth. Its bare bones are as follows: an adventuress, Mme de Lamotte, persuaded the Cardinal de Rohan, whom Marie Antoinette hated and who sought her favour nevertheless, that the queen coveted a diamond necklace which the jewellers, Boehmer and Bassenge, were holding for 1,600,000 francs. The cardinal signed bills for this amount and turned over the necklace to the intermediary. When he was unable to honour his bills, he was arrested, the arrest taking place in the Royal Chapel just as he was about to officiate at a Mass on Assumption Day, 1785. The Lamotte was whipped, branded with a hot iron, and imprisoned; her husband seems to have got away to London with the bauble—but what became of it is not known. The jewellers maintained that they had communicated with the queen before delivery of the necklace, but whether the queen was in truth ready to accept the necklace, or whether, as has been said in mitigation of the part she played, she intended out of hatred of Rohan merely to entangle him in a ruinous scandal, is still a matter of debate. In any case, she was bespattered with the filth of this case and it was one of the causes of the hatred which the French people later manifested towards her.

MARIETTE, Auguste Édouard, (1821–81) one of the great Egyptologists of the past century, founded the museum at Bulak, in Cairo, now moved to the Giza Palace, where a statue to Mariette was unveiled in 1904.

MARIVAUX, Pierre de (1688–1763) began his novel *Marianne* in 1731, nine years before the publication of *Pamela* and fifteen before *Clarissa Harlowe.* Very like a heroine of Richardson, Marianne was a voluble, moralizing and reasoning creature, constantly falling into and out of the hands of wicked gentlemen, poor but virtuous, ever ready with a retort that ran to five pages, and impossibly recalcitrant in the matter of that which she could only lose once. Though the novel was never finally finished, it is still a mystery that *Marianne,* a much sprightlier book than any of Richardson's, and just as idiotically eloquent, never succeeded in taking Europe by storm, as Richardson's in no way superior creations did.

There is a world of liveliness to oppose to its dullness, of movement to set off against its relative immobility, in another department of Marivaux's career, in those dazzling comedies, *Le Jeu de l'amour et du hasard, Le Legs, La Double inconstance,* written in a style whose elegance almost conceals its preciosity and whose artifice is ignored in favour of its sparkle (even the chambermaids are wits), so that *marivaudage* has entered the language as a substantive useful these two and one half centuries to characterize the language of "high comedy." One of the many engaging things known about Mme de Pompadour is that, anonymously, she gave Marivaux a handsome pension.

MARMONTEL, Jean François (1723–99) wrote tragedies, articles for the *Encyclopédie,* libretti, and the celebrated *Contes moraux* which furnish a charming if over-elaborate picture of French society in the time of Louis XV. His *Mémoires d'un père* are the literary history of two important reigns and contain a long gallery of portraits.

MARS, Mlle, was born Anne Boutet (1779–1847) and was celebrated for her intelligent and spirited performance of the great rôles in the comedies of Molière and Marivaux. Vigny refused her the leading part in his *Chatterton,* despite King Louis Philippe's intercession, in favour of Mme Dorval, the love of his life.

MASSILLON, Jean Baptiste, (1663–1742) Bishop of Clérmont, member of the French Academy, one of the great sacred orators of France, whose sermons were praised by the Encyclopaedists for their persuasiveness and beauty of form. Voltaire (*Dictionnaire philosophique,* art. "Guerre"), not ordinarily an admirer of churchmen, excepts Massillon's sermons from the common run in the following terms: "Out of five or six thousand declamations of this type, there are at the most three or four, composed by a Gaul named Massillon, which a gentleman can read without disgust."

MATHILDE, Princess, (1820–1904) daughter of King Jérôme of Westphalia, niece of Napoleon I, married in 1840 the immensely rich and sadistic Anatole Demidoff, who, on one occasion, when his wife was trying to persuade him to do something for her impoverished father, rang for his steward and shouted, as the man came through the door, "See this niece of Napoleon begging me on her knees to send money to her father!" Another time he slapped his wife's face publicly in a ballroom. They separated. From 1850 to her death she lived in the rue de Courcelles, in Paris, and at Saint-Gratien, surrounded by those who were the choice of her heart (Nieuwerkerke, Giraud, the painter, perhaps Flaubert and Gautier, and not impossibly the younger Goncourt) and of her mind (Sainte-Beuve, Renan, and many others not named in this book). In her old age Marcel Proust used to urge her to write her memoirs, and even offered to serve as her secretary to this end. It is unfortunate that she thought him too young for the job, the more so as the fragments she left make pretty dull reading.

MAUBANT, Henri Polydore, born in 1821, became a participating member of the Comédie-Française in 1852 and played in both classical and contemporary drama.

MAURY, Jean Siffrein, Cardinal, (1746–1817) was a famous preacher and author of a classic treatise on pulpit oratory. Active in the States General of 1789 and afterwards, he defended the old régime with energy and the clergy with enlightened moderation, frequently at great personal risk which he was always able to turn away by his sane and ready wit. He emigrated in 1792; was made a cardinal in 1794; became Louis XVIII's ambassador to Rome in 1795 (during the exile). Returning to France in 1806, under the first Napoleon, he was appointed—there is no other word for it—Archbishop of Paris by the emperor in 1810, quite without reference to the Vatican. To have got on with Napoleon I was no recommendation under the Restoration: when the Bourbons returned, the cardinal was banished.

MERCIER, Sébastien, (1740–1814) whose praise of Diderot the Goncourts recall, was the author of sixty plays which are no more remembered today than his stout maintenance of the notion that the earth is a flat circular plain round which the sun revolves. He was particularly hostile to the eighteenth-century enlightenment, his praise of Diderot having regard exclusively to the latter's only unsatisfactory productions, his anti-classical comedies.

MÉRIMÉE, Prosper (1803–70) owes his celebrity in the English-speaking world to the accident—or more justly the admirable taste and dramatic sense—which prompted Meilhac and Halévy, men of wit and distinction in their own right, to make a libretto for Bizet of Mérimée's *Carmen*. No one would guess, from all the solemnities written about him, that he had the sense of fun to publish as frontispiece to his *Théâtre de Clara Gazul* (which includes that *Carrosse du Saint-Sacrement* Copeau used to mount in the rue du Vieux-Colombier) a portrait of himself, coiffed and veiled, as the "lady authoress." Another hoax, *La Guzla,* "translated from the Illyrian" (as Ring Lardner's *Upholsterers* was "translated from the Bukowinian"), took in Pushkin as well as Sir John Bowring, a well-known Slavic scholar.

Across half a century of time a bond between Mérimée and Marcel Proust existed in the person of Mme de Beaulaincourt, whom young Proust used to call on in the rue de Miromesnil in 1895–96, who served as model for his Mme de Villeparisis, and to whom Mérimée wrote just before his death and just after the necessary tragedy of Sedan, on the thirteenth of September 1870, as follows: "All my life I have sought to be free of prejudices, to be a citizen of the world before being a Frenchman; but all these cloaks of philosophy are of no avail. I bleed today from the wounds of these imbeciles of Frenchmen, I weep for their humiliation; and ungrateful and ridiculous though they be, I still love them." His definition of politics is perhaps not well enough known to be omitted from this note: *"L'art de scier du côté de l'arbre, la branche sur laquelle on est perché."* This great man, this sympathetic friend of the great and adorable Stendhal, is one of the Goncourts' failures.

MICHELET, Jules (1798–1874) brings to mind the saying that every Frenchman is a natural son of either Louis XIV or the Revolution. Perhaps there is no such saying: in any event, Michelet was decidedly the spiritual son of the Revolution. His notion of a great man was Calvin; of a great woman, Jeanne d'Arc; of a great deed, the defeat of a bully by a weaker man (e.g., Jarnac v. La Châtaigneraie). He hated Napoleon ("the tyranny of Napoleon, his fatal victories at Austerlitz and on the Moskowa, which made of war a national thing"), the Guise family (because they persecuted the Huguenots), and the Spanish emperors (who sought for two hundred years to swallow up France and hand her over to the Church). The Church was the Enemy; the Revolution, the Saviour: "Shall we show obedience to unjust powers? Yes, replies Christianity. No, replies the Revolution." In the sixteenth century "the clergy summoned *the foreigner*" to invade France in order to put down the Calvinists: the old Jacobin bristles: the Clemenceau within him (by anticipation) growls.

Never was there a more prejudiced historian—necessarily, for never was there an historian more "humanitarian." The accusation he levels against Schiller, that he displayed "a deplorable effort at impartiality between good and evil", cannot be charged against Michelet: he *knew:* he was not to be fooled. This innocent man saw injustice everywhere, which of itself is probably good history. He saw it with an indignation and castigated it with a virile eloquence that make his thirty volumes on France (eldest daughter of the Church) the national history of the French people, despite their Protestant bias. One must be wary reading him (apart from his prejudices he had whimsies; e.g., he saw incest everywhere), but one reads him with absorption. There is nobody like him in French literature for *accidental* beauty, for heedless magic of language, figure, metaphor; there is no writer so little artful, so little concerned with "style", as this man whose prose flows in so effortless and abundant a stream of image and characteristic epithet. He could not compose a paragraph; he gave no thought to the proportions of a chapter, or even a page; but from line to line his eloquence is so great, his sympathies and grasp of character are so varied, that if one were to ask, *toutes proportions gardées,* "Who is the Shakespeare of France?" the answer might as readily be Michelet as Balzac. I take space for a few specimens of his untransltable art.

Of two members of the bloody Convention of 1792:

> Ces fouines à museau pointu, propre à tremper dans le sang.

Of the Cardinal Dubois:

> Cette ordure romaine, par les canaux, fentes et fissures que fit partout en terre une main astucieuse, filtra, souilla, infecta toute la politique du temps.

Of the young French troops at Waterloo:

> Dernière levée de la France, légion imberbe, sortie à peine des lycées et du baiser des mères.

Of Mme de Maintenon and the king's eldest bastard:

> Le lien entre elle et le roi, image burlesque de l'Amour, était le petit boîteux, le duc du Maine, avorton de malheur, rusé bouffon, de Scapin fait Tartufe. Lui-même se chargea de chasser sa mère de Versailles et mérita par la bassesse sa monstrueuse grandeur.

Of the Duke of Burgundy's victory over the people of Ghent (1462):

> Ce fut le lendemain une scène à crever le coeur, lorsque les pauvres femmes vinrent retourner tous les morts pour reconnaître chacune le sien. Le duc en pleura. On lui parlait de sa victoire: "Hélas! dit-il, à qui profite-t-elle? c'est moi qui y perds; vous le voyez, ce sont mes sujets."

MIGNE, Jacques Paul (1800–75) started his religious press in 1836 and produced an incalculable quantity of theological books at popular prices of which the *Patrology* (edited by the learned Benedictine, J. B. Pitra), containing 85 volumes of Latin texts and 165 volumes of Greek, is the most enduring part, but only a part.

MIGNET, François Auguste Marie, (1796–1884) the Orleanist historian of the Revolution of 1789, came up from Aix-en-Provence with his school friend, M. Thiers, to make his fortune in Paris. Unlike his companion, he was a scholar. His work on the Revolution was a sort of hors d'oeuvre, the bulk of his writings treating of the Middle Ages, Spain and the Reformation.

MILLEVOYE, Charles (1782–1816) experimented successfully with the amatory elegy in the manner of Ovid and Tibullus, and wrote a number of simple and touching poems which were published in an edition annotated by Sainte-Beuve. Of his tragedies there is nothing kind to be said.

MIRABEAU, Honoré Gabriel Riqueti, Count de, (1749–91) a name immortal in the annals of French statesmanship, was forty years old before he began to cut a figure in politics and died after a career of only two years. His earlier record is one of escapades for which the unconscionable severity of his father must be accounted largely to blame. Twice imprisoned under *lettres de cachet* procured by parental influence, he escaped the second time to Switzerland with Marie Thérèse de Monnier, that "Sophie" of whom the Goncourts resent the mention by Sainte-Beuve (p. 162). Seized in Holland by the French police, he went to prison again in May 1777, and it was there, in the Vincennes fortress, that he wrote the legendary indecent love letters to Sophie, as well as a little obscenity entitled *Erotica biblion*. Released in 1782, he got instantly into further trouble by attacking the ruling powers and was forced to fly to England, where he was handsomely received in Whig society and became an intimate of the then prime minister, Lord Shelburne (first Marquess of Lansdowne). He had already written on political subjects when, returning to France in 1785, he brought out a controversial pamphlet and obtained some celebrity by defeating, in a joust of this sort, that other famous pamphleteer, Beaumarchais. Following a German venture (with more writing too violent to win him advancement), he got himself elected delegate of the Third Estate (though a nobleman) from Aix-en-Provence to the States General of 1789.

This marked the beginning of his career, and once in contact with great affairs he proved himself a political thinker of superior judgment and an orator without peer. He was sought out, on behalf of the king, by the Count de la Marck, and wrote for the court a *Mémoire* of counsel and guidance which, had his advice been taken at Versailles, might yet have preserved the monarchy while reforming it. From May 1790 until he died in April 1791, Mirabeau was in the service of the court and was the greatest figure at the National Assembly then in session. His position has always been described as equivocal because of what has seemed his divided loyalty between the National Assembly and the court; but that in the circumstances, and

merely because he allowed the king to pay his debts, he can be called a
a traitor is at least open to question. It was well known that he was an
"unofficial" adviser, a sort of unavowed minister, to the king; and
as such he certainly need not have thought of himself as the recipient
of bribes from Versailles. In that age, moreover, a man of politics lost
no caste by accepting money at the hands of those who were his clients
or admired him: one of the successive series of the debts of Charles
James Fox was settled in 1793 by "respectable" friends in an amount
which his latest biographer, Edward Lascelles, says "must have been
enormous." The City of London—which, translated into the American idiom, means "the financial community"—offered Pitt a testi-
monial of £100,000 in 1788, "to provide for him out of office" at a
moment when he was thinking of resuming the practice of the law;
and though Pitt found it "embarrassing" and did not accept, the
tender was not deemed evidence that Pitt had governed corruptly
in the City's favour.

MIRBEL, Aimée Zoé Rue de, (1796–1849) wife of a well-known
botanist, was a miniature painter and hostess to the world of art. It is
usually assumed that the interest displayed by the aging King Louis
XVIII in her work and person was not without responsibility for the
fashionable success she enjoyed.

MIRÈS, Jules, (1809–71) a Jewish banker, was a truly Balzacian
figure. Owner of financial and general newspapers; one of the in-
ventors of the holding-company trick; married off his daughter to
the Prince de Polignac—nothing is missing from this career, not even
the scandalous lawsuit which sent the great man to prison and broke
his life in the middle when he was scarcely fifty years old.

MOCQUARD, Jean, (1791–1864) principal private secretary to
Napoleon III, had a variety of talents—and allegiances. He began as
diplomatist, became a liberal lawyer, courageously defending the
four sergeants of La Rochelle, got a subprefecture under Louis Philippe,
worked shrewdly for the election of Louis N. Bonaparte to the French
presidency in 1848, and was most useful to the dictator on the night of
the Second of December. Dabbled in the history of crime and in the
theatre.

MONTALEMBERT, Charles Forbes, Count de, (1810–70) born in
London of an émigré father and an English mother, is remembered in

parliamentary history for his eloquent defense of the Swiss Catholic cantons, the *Sonderbund,* during the troubles of January 1848. He was the spirited leader of the militant Catholic party and a determined opponent of Napoleon III. Condemned in 1858 for exceeding the "freedom" of the press in an article in which he had compared British liberty with French servitude in parliamentary debate, he rejected the clemency which the emperor offered him. It was this high-principled adversary of tyranny who said there was "but one receipt for making those who are not proprietors believe in the sanctity of property—it is to make them believe in God, in the God who dictated the ten commandments and who prescribes eternal damnation for thieves." In his *Histoire des moines d'Occident* he sought to demonstrate that a large degree of political freedom was enjoyed during the Middle Ages. He extolled Gothic architecture and was influential in reviving European appreciation of its beauties.

MONTALIVET, Marthe Camille, Count de, (1801–80) a "liberal" under the Restoration, was minister of education and again of the interior under Louis Philippe, repressing the Legitimist royalist outbreaks of 1832 as readily as the republican insurrections of the same and later years, and securing the repeal of certain reactionary measures earlier promulgated by Guizot. As remarked in a note on p. 104, he was most energetic in attempting to prevent the confiscation of the personal fortunes of the Orleans family in 1848, and to persuade Louis Napoleon that they should be restored in 1851.

MONTÉGUT, Émile (1825–95) wrote, among other critical works, a series of articles in the *Revue des Deux Mondes* on English and American novelists between 1851 and 1857. He also translated Shakespeare.

MOREAU, Louis Ignace, (1807–81) librarian of the Mazarin Library, published curious works on phrenology, a biography of Louis Claude de Saint-Martin, the theosophist, and various translations, including one of St Augustine's *Confessions.*

MONTESQUIEU, Charles Louis de Secondat, Baron de, (1689–1755) the political philosopher and historian, satirized the France of his day in the brilliant and still entertaining *Lettres persanes* which, published anonymously at Amsterdam in 1721, initiated the libertarian movement that culminated in the Revolution of 1789. His essay on the decline and fall of Rome, which followed, was equally a pioneer work. After it came Montesquieu's masterpiece, the *Esprit des lois,* of which Saintsbury said that it was ". . . an assemblage of the most fertile, original, and inspiring views on legal and political subjects, put in language of singular suggestiveness and vigour, illustrated by examples which are always apt and luminous, permeated by the spirit of temperate and tolerant desire for human happiness, and almost unique in its entire freedom from doctrinairism, from visionary enthusiasm, from egotism, and from undue spirit of system." It is in the *Esprit des lois* that is to be found this simple and thoughtful definition of civil liberty: "La liberté politique, dans un citoyen, est cette tranquillité d'esprit qui provient de l'opinion que chacun a de sa sûreté; et pour qu'on ait cette liberté, il faut que le gouvernement soit tel qu'un citoyen ne puisse pas craindre un autre citoyen." A party man would say that the only defect of this definition was that it could be quoted by each party against all the others. Precisely!

MORNY, Charles Auguste Louis Joseph, Duke de, (1811–65) by very much the most engaging figure in the entourage of Napoleon III, was the natural son of Hortense de Beauharnais, wife of Louis Napoleon, king of Holland, and the Count de Flahaut, himself presumed to be a natural son of Talleyrand. Morny was thus half brother to Napoleon III. After taking part in the Algerian campaign of 1834–35, Morny set himself to exploit the beet-sugar industry in France and engaged in various speculations from which he emerged with a large fortune while still a young man. This concern with finance was not forgotten when he entered politics, and the Bourse had only to hear that Morny was "in" something for quotations of that something to be marked up. He sat as deputy in the Legislative Chamber as early as 1842, and it was his purposefulness and organizing genius, as Arnaud relates in *Le Coup d'état du deux décembre,* that made Louis Napoleon Bonaparte dictator and then emperor. Following a period as minister of the interior, Morny was made president of the Legislative Assembly in 1854. "The great cleverness of M. de Morny was that, appointed by Napoleon III, he rapidly made himself the man, not of the Emperor, but of the Assembly. With consummate art, he identified himself with its spirit and bent his energies to the preservation of its dignity and the defence of its privileges against every influence, from that of the State Councillors* to the Emperor himself," wrote P. de la Gorce. In *La Deuxième république et le second empire* Arnaud says of him: "He knew how to talk to each deputy, discussing agriculture with this one, and industry with that one, and showing himself the man of the world with them all. Conversationalist rather than orator, affecting a certain disdain for eloquence, he presided 'lying back in his chair with a bored and weary air,' as Alphonse Daudet depicts him in his *Souvenirs d'un homme de lettres.*"

This dandy, this artistocrat and man of fashion, was liberal in his political instincts and even more emphatically in his political intelligence and judgment: "He was afraid of the future; he saw that political life in France was reviving, that the working classes were wakening out of their long slumber," says Arnaud; "and that if the Empire was to last, it must make itself resolutely liberal." But he began to act only in 1860, and it was not until 1863 that he disposed of real power. It was then too late: Morny died within two years, before his dream could be made reality.

MURGER, Henry (1822–61) was made a world figure by Puccini when the Italian composer used a libretto of his *Scènes de la vie de Bohème.* He wrote other novels and tales, but no one seems to have read them these seventy-five years past, and it is by his middle-class picture of French youth cutting up—in the art studio rather than on the football field—that his name perseveres.

MUSSET, Alfred de (1810–57) early drew attention upon himself by his genius for verse, his translation of De Quincy's *Opium Eater,* and his *Contes d'Espagne et d'Italie,* in which a verse parody of the Romantic school gave great delight. The failure of his first play, *La Nuit vénitienne* did not put him off playwriting, but, as already remarked, it delayed for fifteen years the production of those masterpieces of Shakespeare-like comedy, *Les Caprices de Marianne, On ne badine pas avec l'amour,* and *Il ne faut jurer de rien.* His several *Nuits* are among the most precious and tender and unforgettable discoveries that French youth can make in the domain of poetry.

*The *Conseil d'État,* possessing powers analogous to those of the United States Supreme Court, which it used in the interest of the emperor, had the right of veto over private amendments offered in connection with bills brought in by the government.

NADAR, the *nom de guerre* of Félix Tournachon, born in 1820, served for a brief time as secretary to Ferdinand de Lesseps, wrote a great number of tales, drew an immense quantity of caricatures that were famous all over Europe, and was one of the leading balloonists of the nineteenth century. He was a fantastic practical joker (frightening the Prussians in 1848, for example, by pretending to be a spy while travelling in Prussia), a staunch republican (exiling himself to Brussels when Bonaparte sprang his dictatorship in 1851), and a celebrated figure along the boulevards. Nadar was the original of Dumas's "Michel Ardan" in the novel entitled *Autour de la lune.*

NANTEUIL, Célestin, (1813–73) Roman born, was a painter and illustrator of distinction. We get from a remark of his a good notion about when romanticism died. Asked by a group of enthusiasts to form part of the anti-classical *claque* at the first performance of Hugo's *Burgraves,* he replied, "Jeunes gens, allez dire à votre maître que la jeunesse est morte." This was in 1843.

NEFFTZER, Auguste, (1820–76) a Protestant divinity student born in Alsace, became a journalist first at Strasbourg and then in Paris, founded the *Revue germanique* in 1858, and then, in 1861, founded *Le Temps.* Not Nefftzer, but Adrien Hébrard, the paper's first editor, made it the most powerful anti-Bonapartist newspaper of its day. Because of what it was three quarters of a century ago, the *Temps* is still called, in Paris, a "liberal" journal, though in truth the crabbed, puritanical, admirably written and edited sheet, is absolutely reactionary.

NERCIAT, Andrea de, (1739–1800) a soldier born in Dijon who became librarian to one German princeling and then commissioner of public works for another, emigrated to Naples during the Revolution, and was later imprisoned in Rome by the first Napoleon's troops there. He is said to have written licentious novels: if *Les Galanteries du jeune chevalier de Faublas*—the only one I know—is the liveliest of them, then they are no longer read simply because they were exceedingly dull.

NERVAL, Gérard de, (Gérard Labrunie, 1808–55) a writer of limpid and fluid idylls in impeccable prose (*Les Filles du feu*) and of impressionistic sketches of Cagliostro, Restif and others (*Les Illuminés*), author of a free translation of Goethe's *Faust,* was a manic depressive who enjoyed eight lucid years out of the last twelve of his life before he hanged himself in 1855. Nerval was a precursor of Baudelaire in the fusion of vaguely occult notions with impeccable verse. His *Aurélia* leads directly to the *surréalistes* and the literature of the unconscious. One line of his verse was brought to the attention of palpitant young sensibilities in England and America when T. S. Eliot made use in *The Waste Land* of *"Un prince d'Aquitaine à la tour abolie"*, out of *El Desdechado*. That his suicide made no impression on the Goncourts is not inconsistent with the concern for any artist evinced by his brothers-in-arms.

NIEUWERKERKE, Alfred Émilien, Count de, (1811–92) "the too-handsome Nieuwerkerke" who seems never to have left the side of the Princess Mathilde, was greatly criticised during his term of office as director of national museums, and of fine arts. He did some sculpture, on occasion.

NOAILLES, Paul, Duke de (1802–85) was a member of the French Academy but otherwise not burdened by distinction. The reader may wonder how such things can be: less than twenty years ago the composition of the Academy was explained to me by M. Francis Delaisi in more or less these words: "The Academy exists for the dukes—so we have, at the moment, the Duke de la Force, and the Duke de Broglie. Now, a ducal family has its guard—which explains the presence in the Academy of Marshal Foch and Marshal Joffre. It has, necessarily, its chaplains—in this instance Mgr Baudrillart and the abbé Brémond. Being ancient, it must have its historians—wherefore M. de la Gorce. Possessing estates, it wants stewards, legal advisers—who better than M. Poincaré? There must be some one, also, to determine what its daughters and maiden aunts may read—and could there be a more fitting choice than M. René Doumic? Finally, since, after all, the Academy has for function the compilation of an authoritative dictionary (though in a hundred years it has been unable to match, not to say supersede, Littré), a man of letters and of culture is now and again elected—at the moment in the person of M. Anatole France."

OLLIVIER, Émile (1825–1913) poor man, was prime minister under Napoleon III when that fatal woman, the Empress Eugénie, rashly declared war upon Prussia in 1870. Ollivier was said at the time to have announced that he "accepted with a light heart" the responsibilities attaching to the declaration of war; and he has not had a good name in his country since then. His record, prior to what his colleagues of the Left deemed apostasy, had been that of an earnest, industrious and honourable leader of the liberal opposition.

OSMOY, Charles Le Boeuf, Count d', (1827–79) sat in Parliament, served as senator, collaborated with Flaubert and Bouilhet on a fairy spectacle, and saw several of his plays produced without success.

PASQUIER, Étienne Denis, Duke (1767–1862) was Baron Pasquier under the First Empire and Napoleon I's prefect of police. Under Louis XVIII he served as minister of the interior, being dubbed "The Inevitable" because he was a member of every possible combination of ministry. He refused to join any government whatever in the closing years of Charles X's reactionary reign; but he became active again when Louis Philippe reached the throne, and that king revived the chancellorship of the realm for him and made him duke and president of the Chamber of Peers.

PATIN, Henri, (1793–1876) an eminent classicist and philologist, was the only member of the French Academy who received Baudelaire graciously when that ill-advised genius, having determined to present himself for election to the Academy, made the required round of ceremonial visits. This scholar fought valiantly for authenticity in the classic theatre, e.g., against the wearing of Roman costumes in Greek tragedies. Apropos of Ismene's costume, in a production of the *Antigone,* he wrote as follows: "Let it be said in passing that this truly classic hat, worn elsewhere by Orestes and Pylades on their arrival home from a journey, whose wide brim has been described by Callimachus precisely in relation to the passage in the tragedy here discussed, in verses preserved to us by the scholiast; this hat which can be clearly distinguished hanging from the neck and down the back of certain classic sculptures carved in low relief; this hat annoyed Brumoy [the actress], who substituted for it—a parasol." I have done, in English, what I could for the syntax of Professor Patin's review of the play; it is still not hard to understand why Sainte-Beuve was perturbed by the illustrious scholar's presence on the Dictionary Committee of the Academy.

PEYRAT, Alphonse (1812–91) was a political journalist so brilliant that his first contribution to a Paris newspaper, *La Tribune,* in 1833, caused the issue containing it to be suppressed and the manager to be fined 10,000 francs and condemned to three years imprisonment. Peyrat went straight onward and upward, and wrote for Girardin's *Presse* from 1844 to 1863, doing literary criticism when the political situation was unusually ticklish. He sat in the Senate as an extreme Left republican.

PHILIPPE ÉGALITÉ (Louis Philippe Joseph, Duke of Orleans, 1747–93) a great-grandson of the regent of France and equally sensitive, passionate and undisciplined, handsome and athletic, courageous in battle and gifted for leadership, was largely "conditioned" by Queen Marie Antoinette's dislike of him, the queen seizing multiple occasions to insult him and withhold honours due him. Visiting England, he returned to France strongly influenced by English ideas as well as fashions, and sided with the Paris Parliament against the Court. During the severe winter of 1788–89 he distributed charity among the poor, albeit with some ostentation and perhaps with the notion of making himself personally popular. He was a delegate to the States General of 1789, and something of an Orleanist party grew up round him through popular esteem, so that if Louis XVI had abdicated when the Revolution first declared itself, this duke would very likely have been made lieutenant of the realm. But the Revolution moved too fast for the Orleanist group, and he was shipped off to London on a mission. Back again in Paris, he shocked the Feuillants (constitutional monarchists) and was accused by them of treachery to the royal cause. He left them to become a Jacobin (extreme republican) and then went farther to the Left, having Danton and the Cordeliers to dine with him. In September 1792 he asked permission of the Provincial Council of Paris to take another family name than Orleans, and was formally authorized to call himself Louis Philippe Joseph Égalité. Whether out of personal fear, desire for vengeance upon the queen, or revolutionary conviction, he voted in favour of the execution of his royal cousin, Louis XVI; but this done, the Convention turned against him as a potential pretender to the throne. On the sixth of November 1793, after six months under arrest, he was tried as a conspirator against the unity and indivisibility of the Republic and guillotined. Choderlos de Laclos, author of the beautifully written and freezingly immoral *Liaisons dan-*

gereuses, one of the greatest novels of French literature, was at one time his secretary.

PIXERÉCOURT, Guilbert de (1773–1848) wrote one hundred and twenty plays and was called "the Shakespeare and the Corneille of the Boulevard." His plays were of every sort, but he seems to have practised melodrama with most skill.

PLANAT, Henri, (1830–87) known as "Marcelin", was a draughts-man and paragrapher who founded *La Vie parisienne* in 1862, edited it till his death, and meanwhile published a volume of disparate memoirs. Taine was a schoolfellow of his.

PLANCHE, Gustave (1808–57) through Vigny met Buloz (see supra), of the *Revue des Deux Mondes,* and wrote essays for that great fortnightly from 1831 to 1857. Balzac, who had quarrelled with Buloz, admired Planche and called him, in *La Muse du départe-ment,* "the only critic the *Revue des Deux Mondes* ever had." In *Béatrix* Planche was Balzac's model for "Claude Vignon." Hugo, on the other hand, deeply resenting Planche's anti-romanticism, called him "a poisoned mushroom waiting confidently to be bitten."

PONGERVILLE, Sanson de (1792–1870) was a mediocrity who succeeded where Molière failed, i.e., he actually finished, as Molière did not, a translation in verse of *De natura rerum.* He gave the world French versions of other Latin poets than Lucretius, none of which the world opened. A classicist does not need to write for the world: he has colleagues.

PONSARD, François (1814–67) wrote a good many plays and seems to have smelled what was in the wind, for he was the first playwright to react against romanticism before the public were aware that they had tired of it. His dramas were as certainly timely as they were not timeless. When, in 1813, he produced the "classical" *Lucrèce,* Dumas *père,* seated beside Hugo, whispered to that god, "These people must really hate us to applaud this sort of stuff." It was not all sour grapes.

PONSON DU TERRAIL (Pierre Aléxis de Ponson, 1829–71) wrote more books than anybody has taken the trouble to count. He is said to have produced seventy-three volumes in two years. Ponson invented the gentleman-criminal, Rocambole, and endowed the French language with that adjective *rocambolesque,* which has troubled so many translators. Raffles might have been his offspring. Among the gems of his hasty writing (which one read with Nick Carter in one's youth), I recall a sentence that said "the town hall clock had been striking midnight for twenty minutes", and another which went something like this: "He took both her hands in his; they were as icy as those of a snake." Terror, like love, can do wonderful things.

PROTAIS, Paul Alexandre, (1825–90) still another painter—this time of military scenes, many of which had been sketched during campaigns.

PUVIS DE CHAVANNES, Pierre Cécile (1824–98) painted canvases which, when first exhibited, excited bursts of laughter and were later bought—or things like them were bought—by committees of Bostonians.

QUINET, Edgar (1803–75) began his career as historian by translating Herder's *Philosophie der Geschichte* and later contributed greatly to the "scientific" examination of the texts of the *chansons de gest.* He was, as Sainte-Beuve says (p. 139) intimate with Michelet, and it is possible that the latter may have got from Quinet notions for his *Génie des religions,* but both were violent anti-Jesuits and anti-Ultramontanists, and it is more likely that they fed one another. Including several dramatic poems, an objective history of the Revolution, and many scholarly essays, his collected works run to twenty-eight volumes.

RACHEL. See "Félix" above for a note on this great actress and her raffish and triumphant family.

RAMBOUILLET, Catherine de Vivonne, Marquise de (1588–1655) rebuilt her town house in 1618 in such fashion as to provide suites of small rooms in which visitors could easily group themselves, in contrast to the single great drawing room of the time. Until 1650 every notable figure in French society and literature frequented the Hôtel de Rambouillet; and if the salon had an inventor, it was this handsome, open-minded, generous woman. Conversation as an art was bred for the first time in her house, and memoirs began to be written because people met one another, exchanged notions with one another, observed an existing society in this great house. *Les Précieuses,* whom Molière ridiculed and Tallemant des Réaux characterized with amusing inaccuracy, surrounded Mme de Rambouillet; a few of them deserved the ridicule, but all of them liked being called *précieuses.*

RÉCAMIER, Juliette (1777–1849) is best remembered for the chaise longue in which David painted her. ("There sat I, so deep, so fatal, so glamorous," Mrs Mabel Dodge Luhan would say.) It is a little comic to see a book about her, published in 1936, in a series called "Les Grandes Pécheresses," remembering that both before and since Dr Potiquet's *Secret de Madame Récamier* little doubt has existed on the score of her peculiar impenetrability—a condition which would normally remove her from the number of *grandes pécheresses.* The mystery is that she was the most persistently courted and perhaps the most deeply loved woman of her time: among her admirers were La Harpe, Brillat-Savarin (whose tastes were not exclusively culinary), Ampère, Adrien de Montmorency and his brother Mathieu, Prince Augustus of Prussia (whose love she returned), Benjamin Constant (who loved all women dearly, to their cost), and the volatile, the irresistible, Chateaubriand, who gave her two or three years of happiness during his quarter century of presidency over her ultra-respectable salon at L'Abbaye-aux-Bois. A singularly bloodless and snobbish woman, I have always felt, whose ultimate distinction was to serve as the subject of an excellent monograph by that cultivated man of politics, Édouard Herriot. M. Récamier? . . . R. I. P.

RÉMUSAT, Charles François Marie, Count de, (1797–1875) son of that Mme de Rémusat who wrote brilliant memoirs of the First Empire, was one of the "golden mean" supporters of the measures restricting popular freedom in the detestable reign of Charles X. He wrote much on philosophy and philosophical history, including essays on St Anselm of Canterbury, Abelard, Channing, John Wesley, and Lord Herbert of Cherbury.

RENAN, Ernest, (1823–92) historian of religion and therefore of human aspirations; orientalist who translated the Hittite inscriptions brought back by Doughty from Arabia Deserta; author of essays concerned with the perturbations of his age (*L'Avenir de la science*) and of dialogues whose subjects are timeless (*Drames philoso-phiques*); man of honour who, when his chair at the Collège de France was suppressed by Napoleon III after a single lecture, and he was offered a compensatory appointment as librarian, expressed his rejection in a note to the minister of public instruction which read simply: "Pecunia tua tecum sit"—which a lesser Calverly might render, "Take your pieces of silver and sit on them."

As a divinity student the young Renan, fresh from the mists and legends of his native Brittany, was worried by the fact that the grammar and the history of the Pentateuch were clearly posterior to Moses; the Book of Daniel was certainly apocryphal; the world of science into which his young friend Berthelot had introduced him spoke of verities that clashed with the data and the beliefs offered by the Bible. The Bible, nevertheless, was his subject; the "higher criticism" was in the air, and if the Germans were its initiators, Renan was to be its poet. That was three quarters of a century ago. Today, I imagine, his history of Israel and his *Origines du Christianisme* are read as literature more than as the works of a profoundly erudite and audacious exegete. Although one volume of the work on Christianity is that famous *Vie de Jésus,* in which scholarship and emotion and a slightly sentimental scepticism are perfectly fused in the alembic of a fluid and pellucid style, his most moving writing is still to be read, I believe, in that masterpiece of autobiography, the *Souvenirs d'enfance et de jeunesse;* and I am not sure but that the last of the "Christianity" volumes, that on Marcus Aurelius, contains Renan's most valuable intuitions about the ancient world.

The story is told that Taine one day took a page of Renan and held it up to the window against the light, saying, "On ne voit pas avec quoi c'est fait." The answer is in Renan's memoirs, where he says, "I spent a whole year eliminating style from my life of Jesus."

It would not have offended Renan to hear that his life of Jesus could be bought in American drugstores for forty-nine cents: he possessed as much grace of heart as of style. It used to be said that he had always to walk to his lectures because he was too courteous to step into an omnibus ahead of anybody else. Hoping each time that there would be room for him the next time, he would make his way from bus stop to bus stop until he reached his destination on foot.

To the reader seriously interested in Renan is recommended the *Jeunesse d'Ernest Renan* of the lamented humanist, Pierre Lasserre.

RESTIF DE LA BRETONNE, Nicolas Edme (1734–1806) was the subject of an exposition at the Musée Carnavalet in 1934, on the occasion of the bicentenary of his birth. This only goes to show how immoral the French are, for if he was a fluent, and an absorbing, and under certain aspects a serious writer, he was also a licentious one. He wrote, altogether, some two hundred volumes, many of them printed by his own hand, on the life of various levels of French society in the years preceding the Revolution. As for what they contained, to put it as delicately as possible, his *Monsieur Nicolas ou le cœur humain dévoilé* is one of the favourite exhibits in Dr Havelock Ellis's clinic. Of this great book one must say that it can only be sold in the place where its scenes are set—under the cloak. Tilly says of Restif, in his witty *Mémoires,* "One would compromise oneself if one were to praise him highly; and yet it is easy to be unjust to him." How very good that is!

RIVAROL, Count de (Antonio Rivaroli, 1753–1801) was the eldest of sixteen children of a Piedmontese innkeeper, who arrived young in Paris to make his fortune. Good looking, sprightly, well mannered, he was readily received in the somewhat equivocal world of fashion obtaining just before the Revolution, drew down a prize from the Academy of Berlin with his *Discours sur l'universalité de la langue française,* and published a translation of the *Inferno.* With Champcenetz for collaborator he produced the *Petit Almanach des grands hommes,* an alphabetical catalogue of very satisfying malice and not infrequent malignity, and his wit made even the aged Voltaire envious. Not all of his sallies were wounding, however; some were pretty. Thus: "Animals may be divided into people of intelligence and people of talent: the dog and the elephant, for example, are people of intelligence; the nightingale and the silkworm are people of talent." That silkworm gives me pleasure. Again: "A tool is a bit of reasoning which, in our workshops, has taken shining and visible form." More in the vein of other epigrammists is this one: "Reason is a historian; but the passions are actresses."

ROBESPIERRE, Maximilien (1758–94) forms a pendant to Joseph II (see supra) in that he affords another example of the havoc wrought by an idealist turned man of action. He had a kind of culture; his personal life was severely above suspicion; he dressed carefully and most neatly; he had no sense of humour, no practical gifts, no liberal views, and a singularly sweet and sympathetic voice. Although he was the idolized leader of the Jacobins, he played no part in the overthrow of the monarchy on the tenth of August 1792, and he sought to avert the September massacres which followed. But "The Incorruptible", as he was by then called, was an implacable republican: "Louis must die in order that the Nation may live," he said at the king's trial in December, and he swept aside the middle-of-the-road Girondins, formed the Committee of Public Safety, and gave France, in April 1793, the first strong central government of the Revolution. How far he was responsible for the two major actions of this Committee—the initiation of the Reign of Terror within and the heroic stand against a Europe in arms without—seems still to be the subject of debate. He destroyed the Dantonists and the Hébertists because they were not idealists, because Danton stood in the way of his politico-religious projects—for he was a religious man, a Deist who loathed the notion of a "goddess of reason." On the eighth of June 1794 he held the Feast of the Supreme Being; two days later this dictator turned his Revolutionary Tribunal into a simple court of condemnation by refusing to allow witnesses to be heard; between the twelfth of June and the twenty-sixth of July his Tribunal sent 1,285 people to the guillotine—Robespierre was weeding out the wicked, creating a Republic of Virtue. But the Convention had had enough of Robespierre, Saint-Just, and their Virtue: on the ninth of Thermidor, i.e., the twenty-seventh of July, they were seized and beheaded, and the Reign of Terror, which had lasted fourteen months, subsided.

ROBIN, Albert Édouard Charles, born in 1847, society's pet doctor, made a special study of the application of chemistry to pathology, his biographers say.

ROPS, Félicien, (1833–98) one of the foremost of nineteenth-century engravers and etchers, possessed a fertile imagination and a bold, incisive "bite" which he best exercised as illustrator of books. His range was narrow, but his craft immense.

ROQUEPLAN, Nestor (1804–70) played a great part in the Parisian life of journalism and wrote one very engaging book, *Parisine*. He was for a time managing director of the Opéra in Paris. As noted on p. 230, it was he who first used the word *lorette* to identify those certain ladies whose generous hospitality consisted, as Anatole France used to say, in the exchange of *"deux jambons pour une andouille."*

ROUHER, Eugène (1814–84) entered parliament immediately after the Revolution of 1848 and supported every repressive and reactionary measure introduced by the government of Louis Napoleon. In railway extension and trade treaties he did some solid work. From 1863 he was Napoleon III's chief spokesman, and when Émile Ollivier called him, one day, "Vice Emperor without Responsibility" the emperor promptly sent Rouher the Grand Cross of the Legion of Honour set in diamonds, to mark his faith in the man. Rouher (and Eugénie) held the power against all comers, including the emperor's earliest adherents (Maupas, Persigny, Fleury, Walewski, Morny) through July 1869.

ROULAND, Gustave (1806–78) was lawyer, politician, governor of the Banque de France, cabinet minister, vice-president of the Senate, but otherwise inconspicuous.

ROUSSEAU, Jean Jacques (1712–78) spent the first thirty years of his life in a state of vagabondage and total irresponsibility in which, to say it in Irish, there appears nothing to his credit except failures, moral, physiological and material. Settling in Paris in 1745 he copied music for a living, composed a bit, and frequented the encyclopaedists. An essay in which he argued the superiority of the savage over the civilized state won him a prize offered by the Academy of Dijon, and wide celebrity. He continued to lead a bohemian existence until Mme d'Epinay fitted up for him the Hermitage, where he wrote *La Nouvelle Héloïse,* a long-winded discourse which suited his weepy and heart-conscious age as perfectly as *Main Street* suited the beauty-conscious wives of America. Already Rousseau had started something. His "noble savage" essay, written eighteen years before Voltaire's *Ingénu,* became responsible for a spate of books on the wickedness of society and the purity of life in the woods that culminated in *Paul et Virginie.* The Héloïse business was at the bottom of the lofty tearfulness and moralizing that we get in Goethe's prose fictions.

In 1762 Rousseau produced both *Le Contrat social* and *Émile,* subtitled *De l'éducation.* The first was decidedly anti-monarchical and the second succeeded in irritating both the *philosophes* and the

Church; the first became the Bible of the revolutionists and the second eventually created the profession of pedagogy and those schools in which children are subjected to no discipline and are taught nothing except what their parents "always wish they had learned themselves"—which rarely means mathematics and the humanities.

Those who had to live with him early found that self-torment and the torment of others were Rousseau's most active characteristics, and it would not be too much to say that he is the first sharply recognizable neurotic, the first pathological case of a now common kind, in the history of literature. There is no better evidence of this than his own *Confessions,* a book which boasts of its honesty and succeeds in impressing the reader most of all with its masochistic exhibitionism. In this autobiography of a genius I enjoy remembering the sentence shouted after Jean Jacques by a Venetian tart with whom he had failed to show himself a man: "Lascia la donna e studia la matematica," she cried with great sense. His *Rêveries d'un promeneur solitaire,* a reasonably tranquil book on the beauties of nature, can be recommended, particularly in the edition containing an introduction by François Mauriac.

ROYER–COLLARD, Pierre Paul, (1763–1845) philosopher and orator, began as a Girondin, became a Legitimist in 1798, withdrew to study moral and political philosophy until the Restoration, and was the leader of those "Doctrinaires" who met at the house of Duke Achille de Broglie (who had married the daughter of Mme de Staël). Their "doctrine" was the doctrine of the golden mean (*le juste milieu,* a phrase first used by Montesquieu). They were constitutional royalists whose aim was "to nationalize the monarchy and to monarchize France." They "accepted" the Revolution as a "fact" which was the consequence of "historic evolution." The advent of the House of Orleans to the throne, in the person of Louis Philippe, constituted their triumph; and with Guizot as their spearhead, they held the power for many years.

SABATIER, Aglaé, Gautier's *"La Présidente"* whom the Goncourts found common (p. 179), was a beautiful, lively, rather full-blown widow of independent means who had a graceful weakness for erotica and received to dinner on Sundays. Baudelaire was brought to her in 1852; and he who had always protested himself fascinated by scrawny, darkly passionate, morbid women, fell in love with this light-hearted Rubens. For five years he wrote letters and verses to her without getting more than a meal and a smile in return. Eventually, his *Fleurs du mal* having been pursued in the courts as indecent, the libertine lady reflected that with the author of such a book she would certainly enjoy "complications of sensuality, a whole carnal casuistry", as Porché puts it in his intelligent little life of Baudelaire. On the thirtieth of August 1857 she surrendered. Was it the enervating heat? Was it excess of suspense? Whatever the cause, Porché believes the adventure was one of those things Stendhal used to call a fiasco; and though they never ceased to be friends, their correspondence became formal and embarrassed, and they saw less of one another.

SACY, Samuel de (1801–79) son of the famous orientalist, Silvestre de Sacy, wrote political articles in the *Journal des Débats* from 1821 until the change of régime in 1851, after which he wrote chiefly on literature (although in 1855 he dared complain that "liberty has been subjected to laws made for the repression of license"). He was curator of the Mazarin Library, member of the French Academy, and editor of the works of St Francis de Sales, Fénelon, and Mme de Sévigné.

SADE, Marquis de, (Count Donatien Alphonse François de Sade, 1740–1814) first began writing in the asylum at Charenton when he was past fifty years old. As a boy of fourteen years he was ensign in a regiment of light-horse. At the age of twenty-six he married a woman whose vein of sympathy and forgiveness took a quarter of a century to become exhausted. He seems first to have been arrested at Arcueil in 1768 for beating a woman severely. In 1771 he seduced his sister-in-law and took her off to Italy. In June 1772 he organized an orgy at Marseilles in the course of which two ladies of the town died of the cantharides he administered to them. September 1772 found him in Chambéry, arrested for sodomy and poisoning, his wife helping him to escape into Italy. Thereafter he began to spend his time indoors: he was in the Vincennes prison in 1778–84, in the Bastille in 1784–89, and in the Charenton asylum from 1789 to 1792—released in good time for the September massacres. The Revolutionary authorities seem to have found him a fit citizen of the First Republic, for it is not until 1803 that we hear of his recommitment to the asylum, and there he died eleven years later. It would be interesting to know what he thought about life; his very dull books, *Justine, La Philosophie dans le boudoir, Juliette,* tell of other things. He left plays in manuscript, and a vague diary of the years 1777–90.

SAINTE–BEUVE, Charles Augustin, (1804–69) the most devoted, the most painstaking, the most probing, and the most universally informed writer who ever gave his life to literature as civilization and as the manifestation of genius—I do not except George Saintsbury—requires no note here to celebrate his fame. A word, nevertheless, is necessary to redress the balance which swings unfairly against him in the Goncourts' account.

They saw in him a vicious old man, broken in health and repellent in his feeble sensuality; they did not see the man who had spent his life in search of a faith, going from Lamennais' theocracy to the "golden mean" doctrinaires of the Restoration, then to the communism of the Saint-Simonians, and even to the puritanical Catholicism of Port-Royal, in his vain search for God—and thrown back upon scepticism because his reason would allow him to abide nowhere else. The princess herself was more discerning in this instance than the Goncourts: *"Un croyant sans religion,"* she said of him. Nor was he nearly so *intéressé* as our diarists maintain. There is their own story of his resignation from the Dictionary Committee in order to feel perfectly free to review Littré. There is his protest in the Senate against the suppression of Renan's lectures at the Collège de France, a protest delivered despite the fact that he had accepted the toga uniquely for the income it comported and in order to be free of material cares. There is his prompt resignation from the *Moniteur* as soon as it became the official organ of the Empire and his contributions began to be "edited."

So much in general; and as regards, in particular, his attitude to the emperor, he wrote to the princess in 1862 (seven years before her outburst to Flaubert and the Goncourts): "I had idealized the Empire. I could have wished each day that the Emperor would do something new and good, something unexpected. This was my programme, and whenever it was not adhered to and fulfilled, I suffered like a playwright whose actors were ruining his lines and distorting his characters." On a lower level, doubtless, but still the human level of vanity, have we not the emperor's remark the one time that

Sainte-Beuve was presented to him: "I still read you in the *Moniteur*" —a remark made when the critic had been writing for two years in the *Constitutionnel?*

As for his work, I shall say only this, that he wrote *every week* an essay such as, in his day, the great Scotsmen and Englishmen published in the quarterlies and took a quarter year to write; and each of his extenuating productions was so scrupulously documented, so completely informing, so justly weighed, so apt in quotation and finished in expression, that to this day every essay is read with profit; and if one thinks of Matthew Arnold, for example, while looking at the volumes and volumes of *Causeries du lundi* and other essays, one wonders what in heaven's name Arnold did with his time. Perhaps the difference between the two critics is merely the difference between the École Normale and Rugby.

SAINT–ÉVREMOND, Charles de Marguetel de Saint-Denis, Seigneur de, (1610–1703) abandoned law and philosophy to pursue a career of arms in Italy and the Low Countries, and was wounded in the company of the Grand Condé at Dunkirk in August 1646. He read Montaigne, meanwhile, corresponded with the Epicurean philosopher, Gassendi, and wrote a comedy which when produced was very successful. Following the Fronde, he was disgraced in 1661 and withdrew to England, where he became a favourite of Charles II and his successors, declining the opportunity given him to return to France in 1688. A certain number of maxims and essays (an appreciation of Corneille, in particular) have been published and are worth reading.

SAINTIN, Jules Émile, born in 1832, lived in the United States until 1862 and exhibited in Paris a striking canvas depicting New York ragpickers with the title—as *la Grande Encyclopédie* prints it—"Ray Pukers."

SAINT–JUST, Antoine Louis Léon de Richebourg de, (1767–94) lived twenty-seven years and died under the axe, the chief lieutenant of Robespierre, a creature so severe, so inflexible, so coldly eloquent, so proud and handsome, that Desmoulins said of him, "He carries his head like a holy sacrament"—to which the fair and terrible youth retorted, "I will make him carry his like a St Denis"—that is, in his hands. And he did.

[362]

SAINT–SIMON, Louis de Rouvroy, Duke de (1675–1755) was concerned first with his peerage and the rights accompanying it, second with the privileges accorded by Louis XIV to his bastards (whom Saint-Simon hated simply because they were assigned precedence over the peers), and third with, indeed, every littlest thing that went on at court. In his personal affairs Saint-Simon's only good luck was to have married a devoted wife with whom he was happy. Three powerful patrons, each of whom might have placed him in the position to direct great affairs for which he constantly longed, died exasperatingly soon after they came to power. Whatever result another fate might have had for France, the gain is posterity's: of all memorialists, not excepting Tacitus, Saint-Simon is the richest in matter and the most satisfying in style. His curiosity was endless; his industry prodigious; his powers of observation and of assimilation were absolutely unmatched. He was fair without concern for fairness, so absorbed was he in the problem of setting down just what he saw, exactly what he heard, precisely how an event came about and what transpired and what impression he received of the feelings of all the participants in a scene; and he wrote, he wrote, in haste but with genius, in a home-made syntax but with such passion, such verisimilitude, such credibility, such judgment, even, that from beginning to end his memoirs are continually absorbing. And what stories he had to tell! what characters to draw! It is impossible to quote from him except in huge slices, in chunks; and for that I have no space.

SAINT–VICTOR, Paul Bins, Count de (1827–81) dropped his title as inconsistent with his democratic principles when he became drama critic of the *Pays* in 1851 and started on his career as the most ornate journalist of his day. He published books, but they were made up entirely of his articles.

SAND, George, (Aurore Dudevant, née Dupin, 1804–76) the most prolific woman writer in all literature, boasted that she had royal blood in her veins through several generations of illegitimacy, but declared herself at the same time a *fille du peuple*. Unhappily married, she left her husband for Paris, where she sought to earn a living by needlework and painting fans and snuffboxes, exactly as if she were a gentlewoman. As a last resource, she tried writing. Her first few novels (*comme par hasard*) dealt with unhappy marriages and the relation between the sexes, and were filled with a kind of romantic feminism. Somebody called her "a female Manfred", and Dumas complained that she was serving the public *du Lord Byron au kilo.*

The first elective affinity of this high-souled genius was Alfred de Musset ("Alfred was a terrible flirt and George did not behave as a perfect gentleman," was Swinburne's comment). They went off to Venice where Alfred fell ill and George nursed him tenderly while making love to Dr Pagello passionately. (She had said in her novels that love was a divine instinct, and that to love was to be virtuous.) The Chopin affair began wonderfully; but they had a bad time of it in Majorca, where the natives threw stones at them and would not help haul Freddy's piano up the hillside to the house. He left, finally, in a huff. Liszt put it this way: "She catches her butterfly and tames it in her cage by feeding it on flowers and nectar —this is the love period. Then she sticks her pin into it when it struggles—this is the *congé,* and it always comes from her. Afterwards, she vivisects it, mounts it, and adds it to her collection of heroes for novels."

Meanwhile, she was writing, first socialistic novels that captured the ideas in the air about her; later, those little masterpieces of pastoral and bucolic life in which she displayed her true genius and originality. *La Mare au diable, François le Champi, La Petite Fadette,* and even that favourite of Sir Leslie Stephen, *Les Maîtres sonneurs,* are filled with ravishing scenes. To Balzac she wrote, "You are doing the human comedy; it is the human eclogue that I have tried to write."

Exactly as Gautier remarks, she wrote without effort. Buloz, of the *Revue des Deux Mondes,* said of her that she delivered her copy "with the punctuality of a notary."

"SARCEY DE SUTTIÈRES" was one of the pseudonyms used by "Uncle" Francisque Sarcey, (1827–99) the celebrated drama critic of the *Temps,* who seems to have been a masterly judge of acting and direction. He was a Normalien of the "glorious" matriculation of 1848, with Taine, About and Prévost-Paradol. There is a story, also, that he met *une mort glorieuse* in the company of a charming young person in a closed four-wheeler—at the age of seventy-two years!

SCHERER, Edmond Henri Adolphe (1815–89) was ordained a Protestant clergyman in 1843. He advocated the separation of Church and State as well as measures less sweetly reasonable in *L'Anti-Jésuite,* a paper he founded. He wrote in the *Revue des Deux Mondes* on foreign writers (a province peculiarly Protestant in France, with the notable exception of Valéry Larbaud), and then on general literature in *Le Temps.*

SCHOLL, Aurélien, who was born in 1833, was successively editor of *Le Voltaire* and *L'Écho de Paris,* two sprightly sheets in their day, and wrote both plays and novels. His caustic pen and too-ready tongue involved him in a number of duels.

SCRIBE, Augustin Eugène (1791–1861) wrote every sort of manuscript that could be used by a producer of plays, his later output being still regarded (somewhat unrealistically) as models of dramatic construction. Except old men with long memories, who still talk about how much they enjoyed his plays, nobody alive is in Scribe's debt.

SÉNAC DE MEILHAN, Gabriel (1736–1803) was something more than the mere voluptuary one might think him from these diaries. It is said that of his novel, *L'Émigré,* only seven copies are extant; I have never seen it and know about it only that it contains a chapter entitled *"Consolation philosophique sur la perte de sa bibliothèque."* Since the library in question, sold up during the author's flight from the Revolution, contained 12,000 volumes of jurisprudence, history of religion, political science, travel and literature, one is led to believe that the novel must include chapters better calculated to bore the vulgar reader than to excite him. Sénac de Meilhan was, by all accounts, a moralist of the second zone (*not* a second-rate moralist): his *Caractères* and his *Considérations sur l'esprit et les mœurs* have some reputation, and Stendhal was amongst those who pillaged the second of these works.

SÉVIGNÉ, Marie de Rabutin-Chantal, Marquise de (1626–96) possibly could not have written ten readable lines expressly designed for publication, but a selection, at least, of the letters she wrote to her adored daughter, Mme de Grignan, would go into one's private library for a desert island. A Marxian would find her deficient in social sense; but she might point out to him that his finding was unrealistic and ask him to remember that she was a woman living at court in the seventeenth century. She was certainly well bred; she never had a thought that was a foolish one; she saw everything that went on, and saw it fresh, bright, in movement; there was no malice in her, but she could be heartless in exactly the right place, that is, where there was a good story to be told; she had judgment, and she was cultivated without being educated; finally, she wrote the most swiftly paced, the tidiest and most sparkling gossip ever written, in a language of effortless purity. She loved life and wished she could have been assured a hundred years of it, ready thereafter to take her chances about the rest. Her accounts of the death of Turenne, the suicide of Vatel, the projected marriage of Mlle de Montpensier and Lauzun, are famous; but there are a hundred miniature pictures of society, sage remarks, notes on her reading, and sallies of humour no less than wit, equally satisfying to those readers who enjoy spending an hour in the company of a civilized aristocrat.

SMITH, Admiral Sir Sidney, (1764–1840) whom Gavarni saw at the Duchess d'Abrantès', fought with the Swedes against Russia in 1790–92, forced Napoleon to retreat from St Jean d'Acre in 1799, and established the Portuguese royal family in Brazil in 1808. He is said to have been as vain as he was able.

SOULIÉ, Eudore, (1817–76) curator of the Musée de Versailles, editor of various historical papers (*Mémoires* of the Cardinal de Luynes, Dangeau's *Journal*); conducted useful researches into the facts of Molière's life.

STAËL, Germaine Necker de (1766–1817) might have been the daughter of that excessively prudent and bloodless genius, Edward Gibbon, had her mother, Suzanne Curchod, succeeded in bringing to heel the great Englishman she so determinedly pursued. Gibbon escaping her, Mlle Curchod, whose father was an impoverished Swiss clergyman, married the rich banker and one-time finance minister to Louis XVI, Necker, and brought into the world the future Mme de Staël.

Of all bluestockings who ever lived, Mme de Staël was doubtless the bluest and the most influential. With great powers of assimilation, she had a nose for what was in the air, and in her book, *De l'Allemagne* (1813), she introduced into France, and into French-reading Europe generally, the ferment of metaphysical and philological ideas then boiling to the east of the Rhine. Saintsbury said of her that she was "mainly, if not merely, as much of Schlegel as could go clothed in French petticoats, and remember itself to be there." The romantic movement as sentiment and as social thought, as well as the study of comparative literature, in France, owes a great deal both to her writings and to her salon. Her novels were perhaps the first in which was to be found that unbearable creature, the *femme incomprise*. Whether it was thirst for power, or whether it was that she was in love with him, this gifted and ugly woman pursued the first Napoleon with importunities so impolitic that he exiled her from France. When he disappeared, she returned and assumed a very great position indeed.

TAINE, Hippolyte Adolphe (1828–93) is one of the great intellectual drill masters of French youth, the most admirable specimen of severely disciplined, abstract thinker concerned to apply his "method" to life and demonstrate the truth and infallibility of that method. Outside France he is best known—and except to scholars exclusively known—for his history of English literature, a solid and yet readable work in which the great writers of each age are exhibited as the highest and the truly typical products of their epochs. All his works display a deep-seated passion for abstraction and classification, but there is perhaps less of this in the work which France deems his masterpiece, the *Origines de la France contemporaine*. His *Notes sur l'Angleterre*, which I presume exists in English translation, is a most agreeable and absorbing book and deserves to rank with Emerson's English essays. There is a novel, *Thomas Graindorge*, in which he explains himself as well as anyone has ever explained certain phases of his nature. His essay on Art repays reading. Taine devoted his leisure to the piano, with more emotion, I imagine, than is expressed in his well-known encomium on one of the Beethoven piano sonatas (now made everybody's possession by Artur Schnabel): "C'est beau comme un syllogisme."

TALMA, François Joseph, (1763–1806) Napoleon I's favourite tragedian, was taken by the emperor to play before the crowned heads assembled at Erfurt in 1808 and again at Dresden in 1813. The "natural" style of delivery which you hear today in the classics at the Comédie-Française, is due to him who redeemed it from the artificiality of an earlier age.

THÉAULON, Marie Emmanuel Guillaume (1784–1841) returned with the Bourbons from Ghent to Paris in 1815 and wrote everything that a theatre manager might want to produce. It was he who composed in five days not only a failure called *Le Marquis de Brunoy* but also the first version of the famous melodrama, *Kean ou Désordre et Génie,* which was produced as the work of Dumas *père.*

THIERRY, Augustin (1795–1856) wrote a long list of historical works that were based upon the researches of better scholars, if less gifted writers. He had, as he himself said, "a point of view", and if it happened to coincide with good historiography, the reader got history; if not, there was still entertaining narrative in Thierry's pages. When it suited him, he would describe the life of twelfth-century outlaws out of fifteen-century romances.

THIERS, Adolphe (1797–1887) was, like Guizot, both man of politics and historian, but his writings were, in his youth, a response to the spur of ambition and in his middle years the product of enforced retirement from political life. He was not, and made no pretense of being, a scholar.

Born at Marseilles and educated for the law in the university at Aix-en-Provence, this provincial Southerner, five feet four inches tall, bespectacled, ill kempt and unalterably common in manner, with a Provençal accent sounding like a species of garlic in a squeaky, disagreeable voice, incarnated the shifting ideas and sentiments of the French *bourgeoisie* for over half a century. He knew before they did that they were through with the Bourbons, and had Louis Philippe of Orleans ready for the throne when France wanted him in 1830. Like them, he detested Napoleon III but was grateful that socialism was being repressed.

He was, as Pierre de la Gorce says, "less than any man an innovator." His mind worked like lightning to learn what others knew, "and from pupil in the evening he became master the next day." De la Gorce goes on: "Whether on the floor of the House, or in a drawing room, he understood everything, embraced everything, taught everything to everybody, but going brilliantly round and round in a circle, so that it is endlessly amazing to see a mind so ingenious served by an eye so little piercing." Except that he was a Southerner and possessed the vanity and superficiality associated with the Mediterranean Frenchman, one might say of him that he was the Raymond Poincaré of his time, so little sympathetic is his figure, so completely does he stand for all that is most stubbornly unseeing in the French nation. He is still invariably referred to as *Monsieur* Thiers, and seems to have got on better with his mother-in-law than with any other person.

TIPPOO, Sahib, (1753–99) a wasteful and destructive Indian princeling, inferior in military talents to his father, Hyder Ali, made himself sultan of Mysore. His name is known to the French from the circumstance that Louis XVI and he were simultaneously at war against England, and his death coincided with the definitive loss of the French settlements in India. Readers of the spirited *Memoirs of William Hickey* will recall some of the events in that war.

TOURNEMINE, Charles Émile Vacher de, (1824–72) who furnished the Goncourts matter for their *Manette Salomon,* which James Huneker thought the best novel about painting that he knew, was a pupil of Isabey.

TRUBLET, Nicolas Joseph Charles (1697–1770) is better known because of what Voltaire wrote about him than for anything he wrote himself, and there is a certain affectation in the Goncourts' bringing up his name more than once. Out of vanity the little abbé joined an anti-Voltaire group and wrote a paper against the *Henriade,* a solemnly dull poem, it must be agreed. Promptly the old man of Ferney immortalised him:

> L'abbé Trublet avait alors la rage
> D'être à Paris un petit personnage, etc.

Personally, he appears to have been more attractive than all one hears about his unread writings, and after knocking on the door of the French Academy from 1736 to 1761, he was finally admitted. Not even M. Abel Hermant took so long.

TURGENIEFF, Ivan Serguéevich (1818–83) concerns us here only for the fact of his great friendship with that other giant, Flaubert, and his adoration of La Malibran's sister, Pauline Viardot-Garcia, whose faithful lover and intermittent shadow he was from their first meeting in St Petersburg in 1843 until he died with her name on his lips in 1883. George Moore compared his stories to Corot's paintings;

doubtless it is coincidence that Melchior de Vogüé had already made the same comparison.

UCHARD, Mario (1824–93) survived himself by many years. As a young man he wrote plays which were very successful. His wife, the celebrated Mme Brohan, of the Comédie-Française, appeared in some of his plays.

VAILLANT, Jean Baptiste Philibert, (1790–1872) a marshal of the French army, was a professional soldier and professional Bonapartist, serving Napoleon III as grand marshal of the palace, senator, minister of war, and in other capacities, and never drawing less than two men's pay at a time.

VÉRON, Louis Désiré, (1798–1867) the celebrated "Doctor" Véron, began life as the inventor of a pharmaceutical unguent, bought and managed the daily *Constitutionnel* and the *Revue de Paris,* was managing director of the Paris Opéra, paid 200,000 francs to become Rachel's first immensely rich protector, and had the honour of serving as model for that horrible creature, Crevel, in Balzac's *Cousine Bette.* Ponsard summed him up physically as follows: "He is fat, he is ugly, and he has the scrofula." It is not recorded that his moral nature was more prepossessing.

VIARDOT, Pauline, (1821–1910) *née* Garcia, sister of the great Malibran, wife of Louis Viardot who made the translation of *Don Quixote* that Doré illustrated, beloved of Turgenieff and of Berlioz, was one of the most brilliant figures of the mid-nineteenth-century world of music.

VIGNY, Alfred de, (1797–1863) author of two admirable prose works and of poems which are among the most beautiful in French literature (*La Maison du berger, La Mort du loup, La Colère de Samson, La Bouteille à la mer, Le Mont des oliviers*), was a thwarted, tormented and noble genius, as elevated in nature as in art. As poet he was the first in quality of the romantic school, and almost alone in combining intensity of emotion with freedom from blemishes of taste and form. It is related that his father-in-law, an Englishman named Bunbury, once remarked to a Frenchman in London that he had a son-in-law who was a French poet, but he could never remember the fellow's name.

VILLEMAIN, Abel François (1790–1867) as professor in the Sorbonne, was the mentor of a number of gifted members of the romantic generation of 1830, whom he influenced by bringing to their attention the beauties of the literatures of other European countries. He had himself been impressed by Mme de Staël and seems to have got from her a habit of looking beyond the frontiers of France which made him one of the first French students of comparative literature. In his day he enjoyed great distinction as a liberal minister of education under Louis Philippe and as "perpetual" secretary of the "immortals" constituting the French Academy.

VILLEMESSANT, Jean Hippolyte de (1812–79) took his mother's name, his father being apparently identifiable only as "a colonel." He married young, failed as shopkeeper in Blois, and became a publisher in Paris, finally founding *Le Figaro*.

VILLEMOT, Auguste (1811–70) managed the Porte-Saint-Martin Theatre and was for a time editor of the *Figaro*.

VINCENT DE PAUL, St (1576–1660) was captured by Barbary pirates and taken to Tunis, where he was sold in slavery to a renegade Italian whom he converted and with whom he escaped to Europe in 1607. He founded the Congregation of Priests of the Mission, known as the Lazarites, who minister to the poor, the defeated in life, and the miserable, performing one of those noble services which not even the most outrageous psychologists can explain as "compensations" of vanity or inferiority. Louis XIII made him chaplain to the galleys, and he spent much of his life bringing succour to convicts.

VIOLLET–LE–DUC, Eugène Emmanuel (1814–79) compiled dictionaries of architecture and decoration that are still consulted. He was the great *restorer* of mediæval monuments and polished up—among others—Carcassonne as good as new.

VITET, Ludovic (1802–73) has to his credit the fact that he was a student at the École Normale Supérieure de Paris and that he fostered the preservation of historic monuments in France. He wrote on art, both critically and historically, was a protégé of Guizot, and sat as a mediocrity in the legislatures of 1834–48.

WALEWSKI, Alexandre, Count, (1810–68) was the natural son of Napoleon I and that Polish Mme Walewska who is romantically thought to have been the only woman who truly loved the emperor. He was foreign minister to Napoleon III, and while not exactly in the liberal camp was sympathetic with it. Eugénie, the meddlesome empress, detested him, which itself should make him attractive.